Hawaii
The Big Island

Conner Gorry
Julie Jares

LONELY PLANET PUBLICATIONS
Melbourne • Oakland • London • Paris

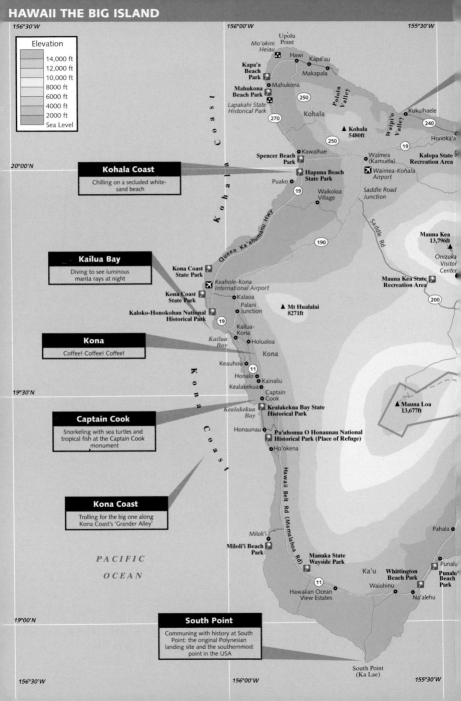

HAWAII THE BIG ISLAND

Elevation
14,000 ft
12,000 ft
10,000 ft
8000 ft
6000 ft
4000 ft
2000 ft
Sea Level

Kohala Coast
Chilling on a secluded white-sand beach

Kailua Bay
Diving to see luminous manta rays at night

Kona
Coffee! Coffee! Coffee!

Captain Cook
Snorkeling with sea turtles and tropical fish at the Captain Cook monument

Kona Coast
Trolling for the big one along Kona Coast's 'Grander Alley'

South Point
Communing with history at South Point: the original Polynesian landing site and the southernmost point in the USA

156°30'W
156°00'W
155°30'W

20°00'N
19°30'N
19°00'N

Upolu Point
Mo'okini Heiau
Hawi
Kapa'au
Kapa'a Beach Park
Makapala
Mahukona
Mahukona Beach Park
Lapakahi State Historical Park
250
Kohala
Pololu Valley
Kukuihaele
270
250
▲ Kohala 5480ft
Waipi'o Valley
240
Honoka'a
19
Kawaihae
Waimea (Kamuela)
Kalopa State Recreation Area
Spencer Beach Park
Hapuna Beach State Park
Waimea-Kohala Airport
Puako
19
Waikoloa Village
Saddle Road Junction
Mauna Kea 13,796ft ▲
Onizuka Visitor Center
190
Saddle Rd
Kona Coast State Park
Keahole-Kona International Airport
Mauna Kea State Recreation Area
Kona Coast State Park
Kalaoa
Palani Junction
▲ Mt Hualalai 8271ft
200
Kaloko-Honokohau National Historical Park
19
Kailua-Kona
Kailua Bay
Holualoa
Kona
Keauhou
Honalo
11
Kainaliu
Kealakekua
Captain Cook
Kealakekua Bay
Kealakekua Bay State Historical Park
Honaunau
Pu'uhonua O Honaunau National Historical Park (Place of Refuge)
Ho'okena
▲ Mauna Loa 13,677ft
Kona Coast
Hawaii Belt Rd (Mamalahoa Rd)
Miloli'i
Pahala
Miloli'i Beach Park
PACIFIC OCEAN
Manuka State Wayside Park
Punalu'u
Whittington Beach Park
Punalu'u Beach Park
Ka'u
11
Hawaiian Ocean View Estates
Waiohinu
Na'alehu
Kohala Coast
Kona Coast
Queen Ka'ahumanu Hwy

South Point (Ka Lae)

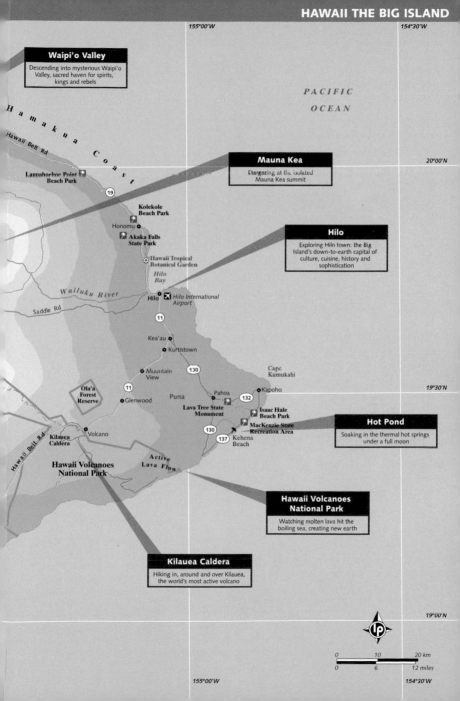

HAWAII THE BIG ISLAND

Waipi'o Valley
Descending into mysterious Waipi'o Valley, sacred haven for spirits, kings and rebels

Mauna Kea
Stargazing at the isolated Mauna Kea summit

Hilo
Exploring Hilo town: the Big Island's down-to-earth capital of culture, cuisine, history and sophistication

Hot Pond
Soaking in the thermal hot springs under a full moon

Hawaii Volcanoes National Park
Watching molten lava hit the boiling sea, creating new earth

Kilauea Caldera
Hiking in, around and over Kilauea, the world's most active volcano

PACIFIC OCEAN

Hamakua Coast

Hawaii Belt Rd

Laupahoehoe Point Beach Park

Kolekole Beach Park

Honomu

Akaka Falls State Park

Hawaii Tropical Botanical Garden

Hilo Bay

Wailuku River

Saddle Rd

Hilo

Hilo International Airport

Kea'au

Kurtistown

Mountain View

Cape Kumukahi

Ola'a Forest Reserve

Glenwood

Puna

Pahoa

Kapoho

Lava Tree State Monument

Isaac Hale Beach Park

MacKenzie State Recreation Area

Kehena Beach

Hawaii Belt Rd

Kilauea Caldera

Volcano

Active Lava Flow

Hawaii Volcanoes National Park

20°00'N

19°30'N

19°00'N

155°00'W

154°30'W

0   10   20 km

0   6   12 miles

Hawaii The Big Island
1st edition – September 2002

Published by
Lonely Planet Publications Pty Ltd ABN 36 005 607 983
90 Maribyrnong St, Footscray, Victoria 3011, Australia

Lonely Planet Offices
Australia Locked Bag 1, Footscray, Victoria 3011
USA 150 Linden St, Oakland, CA 94607
UK 10a Spring Place, London NW5 3BH
France 1 rue du Dahomey, 75011 Paris

Photographs
Many of the images in this guide are available for licensing from
Lonely Planet Images.
W www.lonelyplanetimages.com

Front cover photograph
Ancient Hawaiian grave site (Barbara Havnor/Picturequest)

ISBN 1 74059 345 6

text & maps © Lonely Planet Publications Pty Ltd 2002
photos © photographers as indicated 2002

Printed by The Bookmaker International Ltd
Printed in China

Contents

HAWAII VOLCANOES NATIONAL PARK   208

VOLCANOES: FIREWALK WITH THE GODDESS   229

KA'U   236

SOUTH KONA   246

GLOSSARY   260

ONLINE RESOURCES   263

INDEX   271

MAP LEGEND   280

HAWAII THE BIG ISLAND MAP INDEX

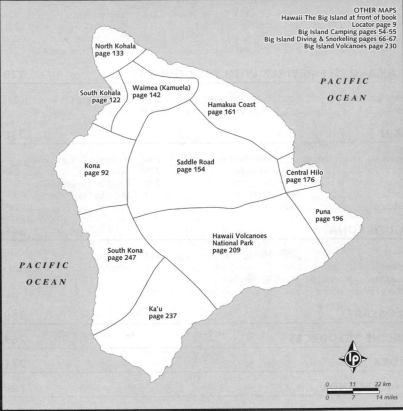

OTHER MAPS
Hawaii The Big Island at front of book
Locator page 9
Big Island Camping pages 54-55
Big Island Diving & Snorkeling pages 66-67
Big Island Volcanoes page 230

North Kohala
page 133

South Kohala
page 122

Waimea (Kamuela)
page 142

Hamakua Coast
page 161

PACIFIC
OCEAN

Kona
page 92

Saddle Road
page 154

Central Hilo
page 176

Puna
page 196

PACIFIC

OCEAN

South Kona
page 247

Hawaii Volcanoes
National Park
page 209

Ka'u
page 237

0   11   22 km
0   7   14 miles

The Authors

Conner Gorry

Conner's first taste of foreign flavors was on a trip to Vieques when she was 8, which partly explains her boundless passion for Caribbean islands that subvert the dominant paradigm. Despite holding a BA in Latin American Studies and an MA in International Policy, real life provides her real education: from a chronic case of aloha contracted in Hawaii to dancing with demigods in Cuba, her horizons have been expanding by leaps and bounds as of late. These days she lives, loves, writes, gains faith and discovers mysteries in New York and Havana. The Big Island was her virgin US voyage for Lonely Planet.

Julie Jares

While her semester studying abroad in Italy fostered Julie's traveler's itch, it could not have prepared her for the two-month adventure that would take her to England and Wales the following summer. In subsequent years she has continued to make use of her BA in English with a variety of food- and travel-writing gigs. Of late, she traded in Stonehenge and scones for Mai Tais and manta rays on her exciting journey to Hawaii's Big Island. Now back to freelancing in San Francisco, she endures the fog while visions of volcanoes dance in her head.

FROM THE AUTHORS

Conner Gorry Like true love, the effect Hawaii bears on the heart, mind and spirit is hard to capture in words. Certainly one of the most powerful places on earth, my Big Island experience was made even more so by the friendship of some extraordinarily special people. Through bad-ass swollen rivers, embarrassingly tacky drag shows, heavenly sunsets and hellish sand storms that nearly wiped off our white (not to mention too many *malasadas!*), Rae Rae Fox was the sistah with the adventurous spirit at my side. Thanks Rae for helping me embrace my inner Corky! Fellow LP scribe Sam Benson was a dreamy roommate and our palace in Puna was made possible by the pure aloha of Mike Haines and Erva Farnsworth. Saintly and inspiring, Jerry and Richard taught me a lot about the power of friendship, love and perseverance. Keep on keepin' on, fellas. Co-author Julie Jares was a terrific collaborator, and Michele Posner – ever the team captain extraordinaire – steered the ship with aplomb. An extra big mahalo to Kanani Kauka, who edited the text with great insight and care. To the entire Oaktown crew, you will be missed; *que vaya bien*.

Of course, I would not be anywhere near where I am today without the unflagging support and love of my family, including that of our newest member. *Recuerdas, compañero mío: 'al final del viaje, estamos tú y yo, intactos'* (Silvio Rodriguez).

Julie Jares From navigating highways with multiple names to mastering the pronunciation of Pu'uhonua O Honaunau, I benefited from the spirit of aloha, both on the Big Island and the mainland. Before I hit the beach running, Ray Woods, Mimi Towle, Sarah Thomas, and Kevin Greenwell were quick to give me invaluable tips. Laura Aquino, Jeannette Vidgen, and Patti Cook provided advice and insights along the way and later fielded my urgent questions, while the friendly folks at Jack's Diving Locker imparted their passion for the incredible world of underwater Hawaii. Generously sharing his good company and crazy driving antics, Csaba Kiss was my energetic partner in crime at the Mauna Kea summit and many hard-to-find beaches.

Big thanks to Michele Posner, both for her guidance on this plum assignment and for years of valued friendship. Mahalo to co-author Conner Gorry, who never skimped on advice or encouragement, and Kanani Kauka, who worked her editorial magic with humor, skill and patience. Thanks also to the rest of the Oakland team for devoting countless hours to this project.

Back home, my fabulous family and friends continue to be constant cheerleaders, making sure I never lack love, support or chatty emails.

This Book

This is the first edition of *Hawaii The Big Island*. Portions of this book were based on material from Lonely Planet's *Hawaii*, which was written by Glenda Bendure and Ned Friary.

FROM THE PUBLISHER

This book is the result of loving collaboration by the many talented people at LP's Oaktown office. The editing was done by *kama'aina* Kanani 'Sorry, I don't do the hula' Kauka, with senior editor Michele 'Kahuna' Posner providing support, guidance and wisdom. Additional assistance was rendered by Valerie Sinzdak, Suki Gear and Maria Donohoe. A big mahalo to proofreaders Michael 'Pakalolo' Johnson, who shared many stories about his years in Hawaii, and Tammy 'Where's my surfboard?' Forlin.

The lead cartographer was Herman 'Halemano' So; Bart Wright served as senior cartographer, the basemap editors were Anneka Imkamp and Narinder Bansal. Cartography manager Alex Guilbert kept an eye on all of them.

Designer Henia Miedzinski expertly laid out the book and colorwraps, and Tracey Croom designed the cover. The new illustrations were created by Justin Marler, with other illustrations courtesy of Mark Butler, Hugh D'Andrade, Hayden Foell, Justin, Rini Keagy, Jim Swanson and Wendy Yanagihara. Ken DellaPenta indexed the book, and art director Susan Rimerman led the design effort.

No Mai Tais were harmed in the making of this book. Puna butter, on the other hand, was spread with a liberal hand.

ACKNOWLEDGMENTS

Special thanks to the Pacific Tsunami Museum, Hilo, for graciously granting permission to reproduce the tsunami photograph in the Hilo chapter.

Foreword

ABOUT LONELY PLANET GUIDEBOOKS

The story begins with a classic travel adventure: Tony and Maureen Wheeler's 1972 journey across Europe and Asia to Australia. There was no useful information about the overland trail then, so Tony and Maureen published the first Lonely Planet guidebook to meet a growing need.

From a kitchen table, Lonely Planet has grown to become the largest independent travel publisher in the world, with offices in Melbourne (Australia), Oakland (USA), London (UK) and Paris (France).

Today Lonely Planet guidebooks cover the globe. There is an ever-growing list of books and information in a variety of media. Some things haven't changed. The main aim is still to make it possible for adventurous travelers to get out there – to explore and better understand the world.

At Lonely Planet we believe travelers can make a positive contribution to the countries they visit – if they respect their host communities and spend their money wisely. Since 1986 a percentage of the income from each book has been donated to aid projects and human rights campaigns, and, more recently, to wildlife conservation.

> Although inclusion in a guidebook usually implies a recommendation, we cannot list every good place. Exclusion does not necessarily imply criticism. In fact, there are a number of reasons why we might exclude a place – sometimes it is simply inappropriate to encourage an influx of travelers.

UPDATES & READER FEEDBACK

Things change – prices go up, schedules change, good places go bad and bad places go bankrupt. Nothing stays the same. So, if you find things better or worse, recently opened or long-since closed, please tell us and help make the next edition even more accurate and useful.

Lonely Planet thoroughly updates each guidebook as often as possible – usually every two years, although for some destinations the gap can be longer. Between editions, up-to-date information is available in our free, quarterly *Planet Talk* newsletter and monthly email bulletin *Comet*. The *Upgrades* section of our website (W www.lonelyplanet.com) is also regularly updated by Lonely Planet authors, and the site's *Scoop* section covers news and current affairs relevant to travelers. Lastly, the *Thorn Tree* bulletin board and *Postcards* section carry unverified, but fascinating, reports from travelers.

Tell us about it! We genuinely value your feedback. A well-traveled team at Lonely Planet reads and acknowledges every email and letter we receive and ensures that every morsel of information finds its way to the relevant authors, editors and cartographers.

Everyone who writes to us will find their name listed in the next edition of the appropriate guidebook and will receive the latest issue of *Comet* or *Planet Talk*. The very best contributions will be rewarded with a free guidebook.

We may edit, reproduce and incorporate your comments in Lonely Planet products such as guidebooks, websites and digital products, so let us know if you don't want your comments reproduced or your name acknowledged.

How to contact Lonely Planet:
Online: e talk2us@lonelyplanet.com.au, W www.lonelyplanet.com
Australia: Locked Bag 1, Footscray, Victoria 3011
UK: 10a Spring Place, London NW5 3BH
USA: 150 Linden St, Oakland, CA 94607

Introduction

A sage *kupuna* (elder) observed today that the Big Island is so beautiful it hurts your eyes; she's right. In this tropical wonder world, azure waves lap at the green-sand beaches and volcanoes flush lava to the sea in a primordial display of fire, boiling water and steam. On this idyll, dolphins and morays, turtles and rays sluice through coves and there's snow for the ski bums, rain forest for the hardy, idyllic beaches for the idle and the world's clearest stargazing.

Like a lover so cherished you conjure pet names in a vain attempt to capture their every essence, so too the Big Island goes by several names: at turns it's Hawaii, the Orchid Isle, and the Volcano Island. It's also the home to Madame Pele, goddess of volcanoes, and Ku, god of war. But above all, it's the superlative island, the singular jewel in the string of Hawaiian beauties making up the archipelago.

What so distinguishes this island is its geography. The Big Island is so big, you could fit all the major Hawaiian Islands within its borders *twice*. The entire mass is five volcanoes fused together, created by eons of magma pulsing from deep within the earth. Stacked layers of lava grew so high that the newly created land eventually emerged from the depths of the sea. The magma is still pumping, new volcanoes are still rising and the Big Island is still growing. Indeed, the newest volcano in the chain is expected to break the surface and unite with the others in as little as 10,000 years – tomorrow in geological terms.

All these tidbits should be sufficient to excite chronic stoics, but you might also

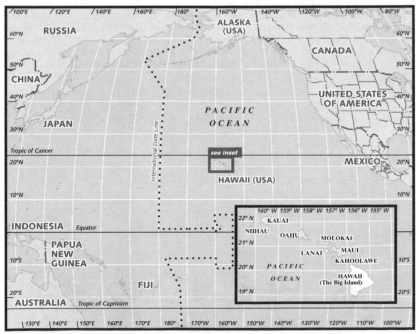

consider that the Big Island is the youngest piece of earth on earth, it's the most isolated piece of rock in the world (2500 miles from the closest landmass) and contains so many microclimates you can realistically go from desert to jungle to permafrost in a day. The diverse flora and fauna here will delight the casual visitor and is a bonanza for birders, orchid lovers and entomologists.

As islanders the world over know, thriving on a piece of land amidst a great sea promotes a certain psychology, philosophy and innate, sometimes subconscious, self-reliance that sets these communities apart. On the Big Island, this unique perspective is intensified by wide open spaces, resulting in the least touristed and most mysterious of all the Hawaiian Islands. Here you'll find mavericks and misfits, astronomers and mystics all dipping into the pools of Big Island *mana* (spiritual power). Much of this power is generated by the gods and goddesses of the land, sea and volcanoes – forces forever worshipped and harnessed by Hawaiians – and you won't have to look long or hard to find ample evidence of this in your travels. Waipiʻo Valley, Halemaʻumaʻu Crater, South Point, Mauna Kea and the Place of Refuge – the list of histori-cally, archaeologically and mythologically significant sites is long and varied and even if that leaves you yawning, each is also a place everyone should set their eyes and heart upon at least once.

Still, there is trouble in Paradise, as struggles amongst man, nature, progress and history threaten to upset Hawaii's state of grace. In a certain sense, Hawaii is stuck between a rock and a hard place, with Mother Nature on the one hand and rapacious developers on the other, forever trying to tame her handiwork into hedonistic oases. Drought on the Kona side and lava and tsunamis on the Hilo side are a constant worry. An economy overly dependent on tourism (which is even more depressed since the events of September 2001) means even higher unemployment in an already anemic job climate, and a heavier reliance on those aforementioned developers.

Nevertheless, nothing defines Hawaii more than the spirit of aloha. Here, this isn't just a cheesy marketing slogan; it translates into genuine friendliness, courtesy and suspension of judgment. Welcome to the Big Island, where you can hike, bike, ski, camp, dive, swim, snorkel, sunbathe, surf and dine finely; this is the place to live your dreams.

Facts about Hawaii the Big Island

HISTORY

It may be the youngest place on Earth, but the Big Island has a rich human heritage. It's where the first Marquesan settlers in Hawaii alit between 500 and 700 AD, where Kamehameha the Great was born and consolidated his power, where Captain Cook was killed and where the first missionaries landed.

Ancient Hawaii

Theories abound as to the precise route taken by the Polynesians that ultimately landed in Hawaii. They may have passed through Southeast Asia and the South Pacific or fanned out from a base in Tonga. What is not in dispute is their incredible seamanship: The journey of some 2400 miles was made on double-hulled voyaging canoes using wayfinding, an ancient system allowing navigators to steer by interpreting natural patterns and phenomena (see 'Art of Wayfinding').

Historians believe the first wave of Tahitians arrived in Hawaii around 1000 AD, whereupon they quickly and violently subjugated and enslaved the Marquesans. Indeed, Hawaiian legends are liberally populated by a tribe of little people called *Menehune*, which may refer to the Marquesans. The Menehune are rumored to still dwell in certain sacred pockets, so keep an eye out for them.

The earliest Hawaiians maintained harmony with the universe through an animistic belief system. Bountiful fishing, smooth journeys and healthy offspring all resulted from being attuned to the spirits of nature and heeding their lessons. Everything in the world from ocean waves to taro had god-like potential and it was imperative to respect and nurture these forces. Offerings to the gods consisted of prayers and a share of the harvest.

Around the 12th century, in a later wave of migration, a powerful Tahitian *kahuna* (priest), Pa'ao, arrived on the Big Island.

Convinced the Hawaiians were too casual in their worship, Pa'ao introduced human sacrifice and built the first *luakini heiau*, a temple where these sacrifices to the gods occurred. This heiau, called Wahaula ('red mouth'), stood for centuries below Kilauea before it was finally buried under lava in 1997. You can see Big Island luakini heiau at Pu'ukohola, Mailekini and Mo'okini Heiau.

Pa'ao, ever the authoritarian, also established the *kapu* system, a practice of taboos that strictly regulated all social interaction. Kapu forbade commoners from eating the same food or even walking the same ground as the *ali'i*, or royalty. A commoner who crossed the shadow of a king could be executed. Kapu prohibited all women from eating coconuts, bananas, pork and certain varieties of fish, leaving little for the *wahine* to nosh on.

Pa'ao also decided that Hawaii's blue blood was too diluted and summoned the chief Pili from Kahiki (Tahiti) to establish a new royal lineage.

King Kamehameha the Great, like all the Big Island chiefs, traced his lineage to Pili. Likewise, Kamehameha's *kahuna nui* (high priest) descended from Pa'ao.

Religion The pantheon of ancient Hawaiian religion revolved around four main gods: Ku, Lono, Kane and Kanaloa.

Ku was the ancestor god for all generations, past, present and future. He presided over all male gods while his wife, *Hina*, reigned over the goddesses. Like yin and yang, they were responsible for heaven and earth.

Ku had many manifestations. His most dastardly was that of *Kukailimoku* (Ku, the snatcher of land), the war god worshipped by Kamehameha the Great. Ku was appeased through sacrifices of food, pigs, chickens and humans.

Lono was god of the elements, peace and agriculture. According to legend, Lono rode a rainbow down from the heavens to

Art of Wayfinding

Have you ever intentionally strayed so far into the ocean that not a spit of land was in sight? Well, imagine being at the mercy of all that powerful, largely unknowable water for 2400 miles, with no charts or compass to guide you. Then, once you've finally stepped on solid ground and offered prayers, thanks and *pupus* to your pantheon for safe passage, turning around and doing it again. This is exactly what historians theorize the first Polynesians accomplished in their colonization of Hawaii.

Successfully navigating the treacherous roundtrip voyage from Hawaii to Tahiti with no instruments whatsoever was again put to the test in 1976, with the launching of *Hokule'a* ('navigational star' in Hawaiian). The Polynesian Voyaging Society (PVS) built this double-hulled canoe according to traditional specifications, with the express purpose of proving the ancient art and science of wayfinding. Through the interpretation of natural signs including wave chop, cloud color, celestial movements and the presence of nearby animals (called expanded landfall), this navigational system allowed the voyagers to cover vast ocean distances.

Like their ancestors more than a millennium before, *Hokule'a*'s sailors were able to sail to Tahiti and back thanks to reliable trade winds. Historians believe this two-way voyaging was integral to the sustainability of the new Hawaiian society.

Hokule'a's successful voyage not only revived the art of wayfinding, it proved a renaissance for Hawaiian culture and united far-flung Pacific Islanders in a common cause. In 1991, a second traditional voyaging canoe called *Hawaiiloa* was successfully built and sailed using only native materials and techniques.

For more on wayfinding and the PVS, see w http://leahi.kcc.hawaii.edu/org/pvs.

Waipi'o Valley, where he fell in love with Kaikilani, a beautiful princess. When Lono discovered another lusting after his maiden, he beat her to death. As she lay dying, she professed her love for Lono alone. Lono traveled about the island challenging every man to a wrestling match. Eventually, broken-hearted Lono sailed away from Hawaii, promising to return. The Hawaiians venerated Lono with a four-month harvest bash called the *makahiki*, with singing, dancing, feasting and interisland sporting competitions similar to the Olympics.

Kane created the first man out of the dust of the earth and breathed life into him (the Hawaiian word for man is *kane*, pronounced **kah**-nay) and it was from Kane that the Hawaiian chiefs were said to have descended.

A powerful triumvirate, together Ku, Lono and Kane created the earth, moon, ocean and stars.

Kanaloa, the fourth major god, was often pitted in struggles against the other three.

When heaven and earth separated, Kanaloa was placed in charge of the earth-dwelling spirits. Forbidden from drinking the intoxicating beverage *kava*, these spirits revolted and along with Kanaloa were driven to the underworld, where Kanaloa became the ruler of the dead.

Below the four main gods, there were 40 lesser gods. *Pele*, goddess of volcanoes, falls into this stratum. Her sister *Laka* was goddess of the hula and fertility, but also had a darker side called *Kapo*, who was the sorcery goddess. Another sister, *Poliahu*, was the goddess of snow.

The spirits of the gods, demi-gods and kings are believed to dwell on the Big Island still. Known as Night Marchers ('*Ka huaka'i o ka po*'), they wander their old stomping grounds at night, reaffirming their commitment and obligation to ancestral lands. Their presence is often heralded by the beating of drums, the fiery glow of torches and chanting. Visitors encountering Night Marchers are advised to strip naked and lie face down on the ground whilst they pass, for interfering with the trekking spirits could prove fatal.

Heiau Ancient Hawaiian temples, called *heiau*, were built in two basic styles, using – what else – lava rock. One was a basic rectangular enclosure of stone walls built on the ground. The other was a more substantial structure built of rocks piled high to form raised, terraced platforms. Many heiau, some amazingly restored, pepper the Big Island.

Inside the heiau were prayer towers, taboo houses and drum houses. These structures were made of native ohia wood, thatched with pili grass and tied with cord from the olona shrub. Carved, wooden god images, called *ki'i*, were stationed around the prayer towers. Impressive, well-endowed ki'i guard the walls and towers at Pu'uhonua O Honaunau (Place of Refuge) on the South Kona coast.

Heiau were built in auspicious sites, often perched on coastal cliffs or in other places with *mana*, or 'spiritual power.' A heiau's significance lay not in the structure itself but in the site's mana. For this reason, Hawaiians often built new temples atop the ruins of old. When a heiau's mana was gone, it was abandoned. The lion's share of Big Island heiau are on the Kona coast, where no fewer than 40 used to line the 'path of the gods,' from Kealakekua to Kailua-Kona.

Captain Cook

The Hawaiian Islands were the last of the Polynesian islands to be 'discovered' by Westerners. Although the English were the first known Europeans to set foot on Hawaiian shores, there is speculation that savvy Spaniards may have stumbled upon Hawaii as early as the 1500s and kept it secret.

British explorer Captain James Cook spent most of a decade exploring and charting the South Pacific before chancing on Hawaii as he searched for a northwest passage to the Atlantic.

On January 18, 1778, Cook spotted the islands of Oahu, Kauai and Ni'ihau. On January 19, the *Discovery* and the *Resolution*, sailed into Kauai's Waimea Bay. Captain Cook named the Hawaiian archipelago the Sandwich Islands, in honor of the Earl of Sandwich.

The Hawaiians sailed out in their canoes to welcome Cook's ships, eager to trade fish and sweet potatoes for nails. The islanders could care less about the baubles Cook had successfully pawned off elsewhere in the Pacific. Metal, which was totally absent from these volcanic islands, was what interested the Hawaiians.

After stocking provisions, Cook's expedition continued its journey north. Failing to find the fabled passage through the Arctic, (or maybe he found it just too damn cold), Cook returned to Hawaii. By coincidence, he arrived on virtually the same date as his first visit the year before.

This time he happened upon the remaining Hawaiian Islands. On January 17, 1779, Cook sailed into Kealakekua Bay on the Big Island, where a thousand canoes sailed to greet him. When Cook went ashore, he was met by the high priest and led to a temple lined with skulls. Everywhere the English captain went, people fell face down on the ground in front of him chanting 'Lono.'

As fate would have it, Cook had landed during the makahiki festival. The tall masts and white sails of Cook's ships – even the way he had sailed clockwise around the island – all fit the legendary descriptions of how the god Lono would reappear.

Of course, Cook and his crew were enamored with the islands and their attendant erotic exoticism. The Westerners were received with classic Hawaiian *ho'okipa*, hospitality that includes sharing food and drink, shelter and, in those days, sex.

On February 4, the English vessels sailed north out of Kealakekua Bay. Off the northwest coast, however, they ran into a storm, and the *Resolution* broke a foremast. Cook

Captain James Cook

opted to come about, returning to Kealakekua to repair the mast.

When Cook and his crew dropped anchor anew at Kealakekua Bay on February 11, the ruling aliʻi considered it a bad portent. Party time was over, the makahiki had ended, and Cook's reappearance carried all the wrong signs: He had come into harbor on a counter-clockwise tack and with a busted mast.

Things turned ugly when a boat was stolen from Cook's flotilla. The Captain blockaded Kealakekua Bay and set off to capture the high chief Kalaniopuʻu. Ever the diplomat, Cook intended to hold him hostage until the cutter was returned. Meanwhile, a Hawaiian canoe attempting to sail out of the bay was fired upon by the Englishmen; the shots killed Noekema, a lower chief. Word reached the village about his death just as Kalaniopuʻu agreed to go with Cook.

Hoping to prevent bloodshed, Cook released Kalaniopuʻu, but bedlam uncorked can't be rebottled. Making for his boat, Cook squeezed off some shots, assuming (as had been the case on other Pacific islands), that once trouble started, he could fire his guns and the natives would rapidly disperse. Hawaiians are a fearless lot, however, and they attacked rather than retreated, responding with a volley of stones. More shots rang out, echoing off the cliffs.

The sailors in the boats fired another round as Cook tottered toward them over slippery rocks. The crowd of Hawaiians pressed in and Cook was struck on the head. Stunned by the blow, he staggered into the shallows, where the Hawaiians clubbed and stabbed him to death.

Cook's men went on a rampage. They burned a village, beheaded two of their victims and rowed across the bay with the heads on poles.

Eventually, Kalaniopuʻu made a truce and returned the parts of Cook's dismembered body he could find. Cook's remains were buried at sea in a military funeral, and the Hawaiians placed a kapu on the bay. A week later, the two English ships set sail, pausing briefly at Oahu, Kauai and Niʻihau

before finally leaving Hawaiian waters on March 15, 1779.

Obviously, Cook and his crew altered the course of Hawaiian history. They introduced advanced weaponry, brought diseases to which the Hawaiians had no immunity and sired the first *hapa* (mixed blood) generation. With tales of a Hawaiian paradise and the charts and drawings to prove it, the crews also opened the way for other explorers and would-be adventurers.

Some of Cook's crew returned to the Pacific, leading their own expeditions. Among them was Captain George Vancouver, who penned another chapter in Big Island history when he imported the first cattle and horses.

Kamehameha the Great

Kamehameha the Great (Kamehameha I), was born on the Big Island in 1758. He was a fearless general and the guardian of Kukailimoku, the war god. In 1782, the ruling chief died and Kamehameha set about taking control of his homeland. First, he killed his cousin Kiwalao, the chief of Kohala, and took over the Kohala region. In 1790 he conquered the island of Maui with the help of John Young and Isaac Davis, two American sailors who distinguished themselves in battle with the Hawaiians and were made chiefs; Molokai soon followed.

In 1795, Kamehameha invaded Oahu and established his reign there as well. But Kauai proved problematic. A prophet directed him to build a heiau to Kukailimoku, upon completion of which, he would rule over all the islands. Kamehameha heeded the advice and constructed Puʻukohola Heiau in Kawaihae, after which he returned his attentions to Kauai.

Kamehameha made two attempts to invade Kauai. In 1796 his canoes were caught in a storm, forcing a retreat before reaching the island. In 1804, Kamehameha's warriors were struck by a deadly feverish disease (probably cholera), and further invasion plans were scrapped. Still, Kamehameha's supremacy was too obvious to ignore, so in 1810 Kauai agreed by treaty to accept Kamehameha's overlordship.

Big Island Beef Power attracts power and by 1792, Kamehameha the Great and George Vancouver (now a Naval captain) had become friends. To show his appreciation, Vancouver gave the king a gift of 20 long-horned cattle. So that the herds could thrive and multiply, a 10-year kapu was put on killing the livestock.

After a decade, the happy animals had largely overtaken the fertile grazing fields of Waimea, becoming a nuisance and a threat. Bounty hunters (unsavory and mysterious penal colonists mostly), were contracted to thin the herds. Later, a wrangler named John Palmer Parker dedicated himself to rustling those herds, which had grown from 20 to 20,000 head in two decades.

From these original cows and a few wild horses known as Mauna Kea mustangs, sprang the prosperous Big Island cattle industry and the Parker empire (see the Waimea chapter for more).

End of the Old Religion

King Kamehameha I died in 1819. Though the crown was passed to his son Liholiho (Kamehameha II), the power really rested with Ka'ahumanu, the favorite of Kamehameha's 21 wives.

Ka'ahumanu was an ambitious and licentious wahine, determined to break down the ancient kapu system that restricted her powers and fun. Barely six months after Kamehameha's death, the widow Ka'ahumanu threw a feast for women of royalty at the Kamakahonu compound. Although one of the most sacred taboos strictly forbade men and women from dining together, Ka'ahumanu persuaded Liholiho to sit beside her and sup.

In that one act, the old religion was cast aside, along with 600 years of restrictive taboos. Hawaiians no longer had to fear being killed for violating the kapu, and a flurry of temple-smashing and idol-burning followed.

The Missionaries

On April 4, 1820, the brig *Thaddeus* sailed into Kailua Bay carrying Hawaii's first Christian missionaries.

It was a timely arrival, as the spiritual and structural vacuum following the revocation of the kapu laws begged to be filled, and the highly spiritual Hawaiians were receptive to the Christians' proselytizing. Led by Hiram Bingham, the 23 Congregationalists aboard the *Thaddeus* believed Hawaii was 'a nation to be enlightened and renovated and added to the civilized world.' Many groups, representing many faiths, (but with similar outlooks), followed in the next three decades.

Until this time, Hawaiian was an oral language. Using the Roman alphabet, the missionaries established a written Hawaiian alphabet that allowed them to translate the Bible. They taught the Hawaiians to read and write and established the first 'American' high school west of the Rocky Mountains. Still, benevolent missionary work was tinged with prejudice, altering Hawaiian society forever: Hula and surfing were banned and a prohibition on alcohol was established. In essence, a new kapu system replaced the old. Over time, western ways, clothing and laws took hold.

The missionaries brought disease, weapons and Puritanism, but also coffee. In 1828, Samuel Ruggles planted the Big Island's first coffee plants. Since 1892, however, Guatemalan varieties have become the Kona bean of choice, (with little change in the hand-picking and sun drying techniques that distinguish Big Island coffee), and this is what visitors sip on visits here.

With power squarely resting with Ka'ahumanu, a floundering Liholiho set sail for England with his favorite wife. He thought he might drop in on King George and chat, one king to another. When Liholiho arrived unannounced in London, misfitted in Western clothing and lacking in royal etiquette, the British press roasted him with racist caricatures. He never met King George. The couple contracted the measles and died in July 1824.

Kamehameha III

The last son of Kamehameha the Great, Kamehameha III ruled for 30 years, from 1825 until his death in 1854. In 1840, he introduced Hawaii's first constitution, established Hawaii's first national legislature and provided for a Supreme Court.

Kamehameha III also extended religious freedoms and universal male suffrage. Educated by missionaries, King Kamehameha III straddled two worlds more than any previous ruler; he was forever in conflict between his ancestral customs and the modern ways of the white men that presaged the future.

And although it was Kamehameha III who uttered the powerful words that remain the state motto: '*Ua mau ke ea o ka aina i ka pono,*' ('the life of the land is perpetuated in righteousness'), he also signed the Great Mahele land act. It was this decree, perhaps more than any other single piece of politicking, that struck at the foundations of Hawaiian society, stripping its people of their rights and sovereignty.

The Great Mahele The Great Mahele of 1848 was introduced through the influence of powerful missionaries (most notoriously Gerritt Parmele Judd), permanently altering Hawaiian concepts of land ownership. For the first time, land became a commodity to be bought and sold.

The Great Mahele dictated that the king, who had previously owned all land, relinquish title to most of it. In turn, chiefs could purchase some of the lands they had previously controlled as fiefdoms. Other lands were divided into 3-acre farm plots called *kuleana*, and were made available to all Hawaiians. In order to retain title, chiefs and commoners had to pay a tax and register the land.

Although the act was promoted as a means to convert Hawaii into a country of small farms, in the end, only a few thousand Hawaiians carried through with the paperwork and received kuleana. For Hawaiians, requiring paperwork for land was like asking permission to give birth.

Whereas few Hawaiians acquired land under the Mahele, the act permitted land purchases by foreigners, who jumped on the opportunity (in fact, some foreign-held deeds pre-dated the act's passage). By the time Hawaiians understood what was hap-

pening, there was little land left worth owning.

Within a few decades, Westerners owned 80% of all privately held lands. Even many of the Hawaiians who had gone through the process of getting their own kuleana eventually ended up selling it to the *haole* (whites) for a fraction of its real value.

Although the missionaries had painted an appealing picture for Kamehameha III (persuading him that most Hawaiians would become small landowners), the Hawaiians were suddenly landless, displaced and drifting into ghettos. Many of the missionaries themselves ended up with sizable estates, with more than a few abandoning the church to become 'gentlemen' farmers.

Sugar Plantations *Ko*, or sugarcane, arrived in Hawaii with the early Polynesian settlers. Here, the cane was sucked for its juices, but never refined into sugar.

In 1835, a young Bostonian, William Hooper, established Hawaii's first sugar plantation. After striking a deal with Kamehameha III and paying a stipend to the royal caretakers so he could hire their laborers, Hooper launched Hawaii's first full scale plantation on Kauai.

The new plantation system, which introduced the concept of growing crops for profit rather than subsistence, marked the advent of capitalism and the introduction of wage labor in Hawaii. By the 1850s, sugar plantations were established on the Big Island.

Sugar was a bittersweet blessing for Hawaii: It formed the backbone of the economy for a hundred years, but nearly broke the backs of the laborers it was built upon. Imported labor changed the racial outlook of the islands and omnipotent plantation owners brought all their power to bear on the Hawaiian political agenda, forever interfering in annexation, labor and land use issues. Indeed, though the last harvest was pulled from Big Island soil in 1993, large landholders descended from powerful sugar interests still flex political muscle.

Hawaii's Immigrants As the sugar industry boomed, Hawaii's native population declined, largely due to foreign diseases. To expand their operations, plantation owners began scouring overseas for labor. In 1852, plantation owners began recruiting Chinese laborers. Workers next were brought from Japan. In the 1870s, Portuguese workers came from Madeira and the Azores. After Hawaii's 1898 annexation to the USA resulted in restrictions on Chinese immigration, plantation owners turned to Puerto Ricans, Koreans and Filipinos. A smattering of Samoans, Scots, Scandinavians, Germans, Galicians, Spaniards and Russians also arrived.

Each group brought its own culture, food and religion. Chinese clothing styles mixed with Japanese kimono and European bonnets. A dozen languages filled the air, and a unique pidgin English developed as a means of intercommunication.

The major immigrant populations – Japanese, Chinese, Filipino and Western European – came to outnumber the native Hawaiians. Together, they created the unique blend of cultures that continues to characterize Hawaii.

Three Kings: 1855-74

The reign of Kamehameha IV (1855-63), was rather confusing, by turns passionate, tragic, humanitarian and homicidal. The tapestry of the king's ancestral Hawaii hung in tatters and this tortured ruler embodied that disarray. While Kamehameha IV established a Hawaiian branch of the Church of England and pioneered the Queen's Hospital, he also murdered his secretary and drowned his young son.

King Kamehameha IV died at the age of 29, depressed and guilt-ridden.

The most significant accomplishment of Kamehameha V, (Lot Kamehameha, 1863-72), was the establishment of a controversial constitution that gave greater power to the king at the expense of elected officials. It also revoked universal male suffrage. During his reign, the specter of US annexation was raised after the treaty purchasing Alaska was signed.

Kamehameha V, a victim of unrequited love, never married and refused to name an heir, becoming the last king in a long royal lineage dating back to the 12th century. His death in December 1872 brought an end to the Kamehameha dynasty. Subsequent kings (and queens) were elected.

King Lunalilo's short reign lasted from 1873 to 1874. His cabinet, made up largely of Americans, paved the way for a treaty of reciprocity with the USA that ensured lower tariffs for Hawaiian sugar (and bigger profits for the territory's sugar barons). In return, the US was ceded Pearl Harbor.

King Kalakaua

King David Kalakaua (1874-91), the 'Merrie Monarch,' saved much of traditional Hawaiian culture from obscurity and fought to protect Hawaii's independence.

King Kalakaua was the greatest Hawaiian revivalist. He brought back the hula, reversing decades of missionary repression against the 'heathen dance,' and penned the lyrics for the national anthem, *Hawaii Pono'i*, now the state song. He also tried to ensure some self-rule for native Hawaiians, who by now were a minority in their own land.

The Merrie Monarch was a world traveler and practiced some shuttle diplomacy during his reign. While in the USA, Kalakaua met with President Ulysses S Grant and persuaded him to accept Lunalilo's reciprocity treaty, which the US Congress had been resisting. Kalakaua also managed to postpone the ceding of Pearl Harbor for eight years.

The king broadened his itinerary, visiting India, Egypt, Europe and finally Southeast Asia in a failed attempt to establish a Polynesian-Pacific empire.

As Kalakaua's debts grew (the construction of the spectacularly regal Iolani Palace in Honolulu at a whopping $360,000 didn't help), his popularity waned, especially among the sugar barons. They formed the Hawaiian League in 1887 and developed their own armies, which stood poised to overthrow Kalakaua. The league presented Kalakaua with a list of demands and forced him to accept a new constitution strictly limiting his powers. The new law of the land also limited suffrage to male property owners, excluding the vast majority of Hawaiians.

On July 30, 1889, a group of about 150 Hawaiians attempted to overthrow the new constitution by occupying Iolani Palace. Called the Wilcox Rebellion after its part-Hawaiian leader, it was a confused and futile attempt, and the rebels were forced to surrender.

Kalakaua died in San Francisco in 1891 and was succeeded by his sister Lili'uokalani.

Queen Lili'uokalani & Annexation

Queen Lili'uokalani (1891-93) was even more determined than Kalakaua to augment the monarchy's power. She charged that the 1887 constitution had been illegally forced upon King Kalakaua and the Hawaii Supreme Court agreed.

In January 1893, as Lili'uokalani was preparing to proclaim a new constitution, a group of armed haole occupied the Supreme Court and declared the monarchy overthrown. The white men announced a provisional government, led by Sanford Dole, son of a pioneer missionary. A contingent of US sailors came ashore, marched on the palace and aimed their guns at the queen's residence. Realizing that it was futile to oppose US forces, Queen Lili'uokalani surrendered.

The provisional government immediately appealed to the USA for annexation, while the queen appealed to the USA for justice. While US President Grover Cleveland initially favored the queen, the provisional government accused him of meddling in 'Hawaiian' affairs and it looked to threaten his standing with the voting public. Cleveland backed off.

The new government, with Dole as (the first and last) president, inaugurated itself as the Republic of Hawaii on July 4, 1894.

In 1895, weary of waiting for outside intervention, a group of Hawaiian royalists mounted a counter-revolution that was easily squashed in a couple of weeks. Lili'uokalani was accused of being a conspirator, placed under arrest, and imprisoned in her own palace.

When she died in November 1917, all of Honolulu came out for the funeral procession. To most islanders, Lili'uokalani was (and still is) their queen.

US expansionist hunger grew following the Spanish-American War of 1898. Along with Pearl Harbor, Hawaii took on a new strategic importance, being midway between the USA and its newest possession, the Philippines. The annexation of Hawaii passed in the US Congress on July 7, 1898 and Hawaii entered the 20th century as a US territory.

In just over a century of Western contact, the native Hawaiian population had been decimated by foreign diseases, including cholera, smallpox, venereal disease and leprosy. By the end of the 19th century, the native population was reduced from an estimated 300,000 to around 30,000; 50 years, later the total was half that again.

Descendants of the early missionaries had taken over first the land and then the government. All in all, annexation was nothing for native Hawaiians to celebrate.

Unionizing Hawaii

Big Island workers were organizing long before the feisty International Longshoremen's and Warehousemen's Union (ILWU) happened on the scene. Indeed, as early as the 1880s, Katsu Goto was lobbying for improved working conditions for fellow cane workers around Honoka'a (see that section of the Hamakua Coast chapter).

In the 1930s, Big Island laborers organized and struck for better working and living conditions, higher wages and the right to collective bargaining. At Hilo port on August 1, 1938, strikers backed by the ILWU and other unions faced off against an Inter-Island Steamship barge operated by strike breakers. The picketers were spattered with water, tear gas, and gunfire. By the end of the 'Hilo Massacre,' fifty were left wounded and solidarity swelled for the Hawaiian union movement.

After WWII, the ILWU further galvanized its support in Hawaii by organizing an intensive campaign against Hawaii's 'Big Five' – C Brewer, Castle & Cooke, Alexander & Baldwin, Theo Davies and Amfac, all sugar manufacturers. These were the territory's largest landholders and the greatest benefactors of the fruits of cane labor.

Following the ILWU's six-month waterfront strike in 1949 and a series of plantation strikes, Hawaii's sugar workers were the world's highest paid.

World War II

On December 7, 1941, at 7:55am, a wave of Japanese bombers attacked Pearl Harbor, on Oahu, forcing the USA into WWII. The attack caught the US fleet by surprise, even though there had been warnings, some far from subtle. Within minutes, the USS *Arizona* sank in a fiery inferno, trapping 1177 men beneath the surface. Twenty other US ships were sunk or damaged, along with 347 aircraft. More than 2500 people died.

Following the attack on Pearl Harbor, some people of Japanese descent in Hawaii were interrogated and interned on the mainland. Properties were seized and families torn apart. Nevertheless, 25,000 Japanese Americans from Hawaii and elsewhere proved themselves in brutal fighting as members of the US Army in Europe. The all-Japanese 442nd Regimental Combat Group was one of the most decorated units of WWII.

Statehood

WWII brought Hawaii into the maelstrom of American politics and that meant revival of the statehood agenda. Three decades had passed since Hawaii's first delegate to the US Congress, Prince Jonah Kuhio Kalanianaole, introduced the original statehood bill in 1919. The bill was received coolly in Washington at that time, and there were mixed feelings in Hawaii as well.

The biggest problem for mainland politicians (especially those from the rigidly segregated South) was that Hawaii was too much of a racial mosaic, too foreign and exotic. Congress was also concerned with the success of Hawaiian labor strikes and the growth of membership in the ILWU.

Statehood was sidelined until the end of the 1950s.

In March 1959 the US Congress finally passed legislation to make Hawaii a state. On June 27, a plebiscite was held in Hawaii, with more than 90% of islanders voting for statehood.

On August 21, 1959, after 61 years of territorial status, Hawaii became the USA's 50th state. Hawaii was scheduled to be the 49th state, but the paperwork got hung up and Alaska slipped in before the deal was sealed.

Hawaiian Sovereignty

In the 1970s, native Hawaiian pride got a shot of adrenaline after Hokule'a's triumphant voyage, sparking a widespread revival of Hawaiian language, arts and self-determination. A push for sovereignty followed. Other rallying points included the Protect Kaho'olawe movement (which successfully halted US Navy bombing practice on that island), growing discontent over the mismanagement of Hawaiian Home Lands (see the boxed text of the same name) and the 1993 centennial anniversary of Queen Lili'uokalani's overthrow.

Today, the sovereignty movement suffers from factionalization. More than 40 groups squabble on a divided agenda and none can rally a majority to its vision for a sovereign Hawaii. Some advocate a nation-within-a-nation model akin to that of mainland Native American groups; others favor 'free association' status (similar to that of Guam); still others fight for the restoration of the Hawaiian monarchy; and some push for secession. While all agree that acquiring and restoring a land base is crucial, beyond that, sovereignty is an emotional and political tinderbox.

Among the largest groups are Ohana O Hawaii and Ka Lahui Hawaii. The former advocates independence, while the latter is pushing for nation-within-a-nation status and has adopted an independent constitution in that vein. Ka Lahui Hawaii wants all Hawaiian Home Lands, plus much of the crown lands taken during annexation, turned over to native Hawaiians.

Hawaiian Home Lands

In 1920, under the sponsorship of Prince Jonah Kuhio Kalanianaole, the Territory of Hawaii's congressional delegate, the US Congress passed the Hawaiian Homes Commission Act. The act set aside almost 200,000 acres of land for homesteading by native Hawaiians. Despite this apparently generous gift, the land was but a small fraction of the crown lands that were taken from the Kingdom of Hawaii when the USA annexed the islands in 1898.

Under the legislation, people of at least 50% Hawaiian ancestry were eligible for 99-year leases at $1 a year. Originally, most of the leases were for 40-acre parcels of agricultural land, although more recently residential lots as small as a quarter of an acre have been allocated under the plan.

Hawaii's prime land, already in the hands of the sugar barons, was excluded from the act. Much of what was designated for homesteading was on far more barren turf.

Still, many Hawaiians were able to make a go of it. Presently, there are about 6500 native Hawaiian families living on about 30,000 acres of homestead lands.

As with many acts established to help native Hawaiians, administration of the Hawaiian Home Lands has been riddled with abuse. The majority of the land has not been allocated to native Hawaiians but has been leased out to big business, ostensibly as a means of creating an income for the administration of the program.

Parker Ranch, for example, has about 30,000 acres of Hawaiian Home Lands under lease at just a few dollars an acre.

In addition, the federal, state and county governments have, with little or no compensation, taken large tracts of Hawaiian Home Lands for their own use.

One sovereignty demand was addressed in 1993, when US president Bill Clinton signed a resolution apologizing 'to Native Hawaiians for the overthrow of the Kingdom of Hawaii on January 17, 1893, with participation of agents and citizens of the United States, and the deprivation of the rights of Native Hawaiians to self-determination.' The apology went on to 'acknowledge the ramifications of the overthrow' and expressed a commitment to 'provide a proper foundation for reconciliation.'

In January 1999, an election organized by Ha Hawaii took place, with voters selecting 85 delegates to form a Hawaiian Convention aimed at charting the sovereignty course. However, many groups boycotted the election, claiming the Ha Hawaii vote was again co-opted by the state. Consequently, fewer than 9000 of the 102,000 eligible voters cast ballots.

In April 2001, Senator Daniel Akaka (D) introduced S 746 into the Senate asking the US government to recognize a process for the possibility of a sovereign Native Hawaiian governing entity. This legislation raised as much ire as all previous attempts to define 'sovereignty,' and created a flurry of revisions, boycotts and Web sites both pro and con. The 'Akaka Bill' was stalled on the Senate floor until the spring of 2002.

Despite all the division, polls show that a significant majority of Hawaii residents support the concept of Hawaiian sovereignty based on a nation-within-a-nation framework. Interestingly, the support doesn't vary greatly along ethnic lines.

Incidentally, the Hawaiian flag flown upside down as a sign of distress is the symbol of the Hawaiian sovereignty movement.

GEOGRAPHY & GEOLOGY

The unique geographical features of the Big Island cannot be overstated, so at the risk of waxing redundant, here are some facts.

First, it's big: All the other major Hawaiian islands could fit within the Big Island's 4038 sq miles twice with little finagling; the Big Island is smaller than Fiji but a bit larger than the US state of Connecticut. Second, the Big Island has the state's – technically the world's – highest mountain and the Earth's most active volcano. Third, Ka Lae is the southernmost point of the USA and way more inspiring than this statistical trivia implies.

The Big Island lies between the equator, some 1400 miles to the south, and the tropic of Cancer nearby to the north. Hawaii is at the same latitude as Havana, Hong Kong and Bombay.

Hawaii's highest mountain is Mauna Kea, which is 13,796 feet above sea level. Purists, read it and weep: According to the *Guinness Book of Records*, it's the world's highest mountain (33,476 feet) when measured from the ocean floor. Mauna Loa is Hawaii's second highest mountain, at 13,677 feet.

The Big Island is the only Hawaiian island with an active volcano, and just to insure its exclusivity, it has two. Geological features specific to volcanic activity include lava molds, lava tubes (both terrestrial and submarine) and black-sand beaches. See the special section for more on Big Island volcanoes.

CLIMATE

As far as climate is concerned, the Big Island has multiple personalities. On the leeward ('kona' in Hawaiian) side, it's hot, dry and drought-prone. The windward side, on the other hand, is exposed to northeasterly trade winds, which bring deluges. Between these two extremes exists almost every climatic condition found in the world.

More than season, elevation accounts for most climatic fluctuations, and the higher you go, the colder and rainier it gets. In Volcano, at about 3500 feet, the average daily temperature in January is 65°F, with some 160 inches of rain falling annually. At sea level in Hilo, the average temperature is 79°F, with 129 inches of rain annually, while in Kona, it's a toasty 81°F, with only 64 inches of rain per year.

November to March is the rainiest time of year, but on the windward side, there's a monthly average of 10 inches of rain, no matter what. Winter brings storms, (some maniacal), when flash floods, high seas and

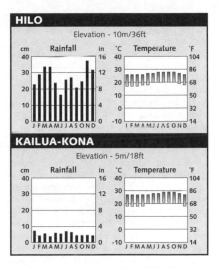

road closures are common. Still, it rarely rains all day here, even in winter.

Kona is well-protected by the mountains from most precipitation, so don't worry, it will likely be sunny there when you arrive. Indeed, according to Hunter S Thompson, 'the Kona coast in December is as close to hell on earth as a half-bright mammal can get.' Fortunately, heavenly Hilo and Volcano are only a couple of hours away.

During *kona* storms, the trade winds shift and blow from the south, bringing hot, humid weather in summer and cold, rainy conditions in winter. The ocean starts acting funky, with calm spots becoming roiled and high surf areas smoothing out. Many drownings occur with this freak weather, so exercise caution in the water.

ECOLOGY & ENVIRONMENT

Like elsewhere in Hawaii, the Big Island's native ecosystems have been greatly stressed by the introduction of non-native flora and fauna. Erosion caused by free-ranging cattle, goats and feral pigs and monocrop sugarcane cultivation has swept topsoil into the sea and choked near-shore reefs.

Tourism-related development has long taken its toll. Large resort hotels and golf courses, which commonly are built on fragile coastal lands, need tons of irrigation. Although grassroots activism has successfully thwarted some mega-resort projects, still others push through. The latest is a professional sports training facility-cum-resort planned for Puna.

Intense volcanic action here carries its own environmental effects. 'Vog' (a portmanteau of 'volcano' and 'smog,' which – for all you wordsmiths – is its own portmanteau of 'smoke' and 'fog'), fouls Big Island air. Kilauea pumps out 275 tons of sulfur dioxide daily. When mixed with water vapor and carbon dioxide, this airborne nasty hangs over the coast. While this sulfur dioxide level exceeds standards set by the US Environmental Protection Agency an average of 22 days a year, studies indicate vog is not dangerous in small doses, though it may be causing respiratory ailments among residents. Due to the trade winds, Kona gets most of the vog.

On the plus side, the Big Island has no polluting heavy industry, roadside billboards are wonderfully kapu and environmental awareness is more advanced than on most of the US mainland.

Greenpeace has logged some Big Island successes over the last decade. In 1992, legal action filed with the Pele Defense Fund, the Sierra Club Legal Defense Fund and other groups ensured the protection of native rain forests near the Puna geothermal plant.

In another challenge, the Sierra Club Legal Defense Fund challenged both the National Rifle Association and the state to force the removal of introduced mouflon game sheep from the slopes of Mauna Kea. The grazing sheep were causing declines in the *palila*, a native honeycreeper, population. A landmark case, it marked the first time that habitat destruction was successfully defined as the 'taking' (meaning killing, harming or harassing) of an endangered species under the US Endangered Species Act.

For terrific coverage of late-breaking developments on Big Island environmental initiatives, refer to Environment Hawaii (**W** www.environment-hawaii.org).

FLORA & FAUNA

From ohia seeds stuck in goose down to a snail suctioned to a piece of driftwood, anything living in Hawaii had to travel 2500 miles on the wind or the waves to do so. As a result, more than 90% of Hawaii's native flora and fauna is endemic.

It's estimated that before human contact, a new species managed to take hold in Hawaii only once every 70,000 years. New arrivals found specialized habitats ranging from desert to rain forest, and elevations climbing from sea level to nearly 14,000 feet. Many species here have adapted to survive in the volcanic environment. Insects, in particular, take to lava easily and quickly, sometimes when the ground is still warm. Consequently, the Big Island sports some of its very own species, including the Hawaiian lava flow cricket.

New species often evolve in volcanic *kipuka*, forested areas spared by uneven lava flows. These oases allow species to adapt and evolve unmolested as the lava forms a natural barrier around their habitat. Scientists theorize that many of the endemic species here, particularly birds, evolved in these forested clumps. Kipuka Pu'u Huluhulu on Saddle Road and Kipuka Pau'ulu in Hawaii Volcanoes National Park are two striking examples.

Non-Native Species

Introducing non-native species into this environment sparks a destructive cycle. Take for example the first Polynesians, who sailed here with many of their staples including pigs, taro and sugar cane, but also some rat stowaways. By the 1880s, rats were overrunning the cane fields, so mongooses were imported to control them. Unfortunately, mongooses are diurnal and rats, as any New Yorker knows, are nocturnal, and rarely did the two meet. The mongooses, meanwhile, fed on small endemic birds and their eggs, and the rat population kept growing. Both pests still run roughshod over the Big Island.

Westerners introduced the bulk of alien species, including goats, cattle and horses. The latest controversy rages over the

Puerto Rican *coqui*, which hitched a flight in 1998 from that tropical idyll. Most Big Islanders consider this frog – near and dear to the Puerto Rican heart – to be a major nuisance. Each of the cacophonous nighttime serenaders croaks at 100 decibels, and is prolific: an acre can support 8100 frogs. All manners of coqui control were being discussed at press time, including dosing them with massive amounts of caffeine. Whether this will kill them or jazz them into making more vociferous love and music is unclear.

Introduced birds are another problem: They spread diseases to which native Hawaiian birds have no immunity and they compete for food with native birds.

Non-native plants are also adversely effecting the environment and Big Island endemics. Among the worst offenders are banana poka, kahili ginger and miconia. Known as the 'purple bubonic plague' for its purple leaves, miconia produce hundreds of thousands of fruits annually, which grow into plants that kill native groundcover. More than 60% of the Big Island has been colonized by miconia.

Today, according to the Bishop Museum, Hawaii is home to more threatened and endangered species per square mile than any other place on the planet. Of approximately 2400 different native plants, half are either threatened or endangered.

Flora

With microclimates from desert to lush tropical rain forests, Hawaii's vegetation runs the gamut.

The most prevalent tree is the *ohia lehua*. It takes early and often to lava flows because its light seeds are spread by any whisper of wind. The ohia survives amid toxic volcanic emissions because its stomata seal shut to keep out poisonous gases. As a result, the ohia is everywhere, recognizable by its red pom-pom flowers. Right with the ohia as an early lava colonizer is the sword fern, which grows in nooks and crannies of lava flows.

There are half a dozen native fern varieties here, and you'll glimpse their coiled heads poised to unfurl at every turn. The false staghorn fern *ulehe* grows with gusto

in the forest understory, the ubiquitous giant tree fern *hapu'u* makes up the middle story and the brilliantly red, fading to green *amau* fern grows around the Halema'uma'u crater among other places.

Koa, endemic to Hawaii, is commonly found at higher elevations. In Hawaii Volcanoes National Park there are many protected stands of old-growth koa, some close to 100 feet high. Koa is threatened by cattle which like to nosh on the young saplings and loggers, who charge a premium for this high-quality hardwood. In ancient Hawaii, canoes and surfboards were fashioned from koa.

The *kukui* tree, which was brought by the early Polynesian settlers, has oily nuts that Hawaiians used for candles – hence its common name, the candlenut tree; it's easily identifiable by its light silver-tinged foliage. Polished, the nuts are prized as good luck lei.

Two useful trees found along the coast are the *hala*, also called pandanus or screw pine, whose spiny leaves are used for thatching and weaving; and the coconut palm, called *niu*, which produces about 75 coconuts a year.

Kiawe, a non-native tree found in dry coastal areas, is a member of the mesquite family that's good for making charcoal but is a pain for beachgoers, as its sharp thorns easily pierce soft sandals and feet.

The Big Island earned its 'Orchid Isle' nickname from the 22,000 varieties grown on the windward side, where you can see everything from wild bamboo orchids to the most wild-looking masdevallias. Other flowers growing here include anthuriums, brilliant orange birds of paradise, splashy bougainvilleas, red, torch and shell ginger, various heliconias with sunburst bracts and more than 5000 hibiscus varieties.

Silverswords are wickedly exotic in their bearing and adaptation: They only survive in the thin air between 5000 and 12,250 feet. What's more, it takes a silversword between nine and 14 years to produce blossoms, whereupon it erupts with flowers, killing itself in the process. Looking upon these beauties on Mauna Kea or Mauna Loa, you'll feel like the Little Prince, transported to B6-12.

Then of course, there's coffee. When the white flowers carpet the leeward upcountry in spring, it's called 'Kona snow.' Then the cherries appear in a burst of waxy green, deepening and maturing to a bruised red color ripe for the picking in the fall.

Fauna

Whales The Big Island boasts a year-round resident population of several types of whales including sperm, false killer, beaked killer, melon-head and pilot whales. No matter when you show up here, you should be able to hop on a whale-watching tour and see one of these varieties.

The really big show however, takes place from January to April when migrating humpbacks come to Hawaiian waters to breed and birth. These giant mammals prefer shallow waters (to about 600 feet), and accustomed eyes can spot them unaided. However, with even cheap binoculars, you can whale watch from your Hilo hotel or Kona condo most late winter and early spring months.

The humpback, with long white flippers and a knobby head, can reach a length of 45 feet and weigh 40 to 45 tons. The toothless humpbacks gulp huge quantities of water, trapping krill and small fish (up to a ton daily) in their filter-like baleen. This is what they do all day, every day in their summer Alaskan feeding grounds as they pad on a thick layer of blubber for the sojourn to Hawaii. Once here, they frolic and mate, returning 10 to 12 months later to give birth.

Humpbacks were once amongst the most abundant of the great whales, but were hunted close to extinction and are now an endangered species. The entire population of North Pacific humpbacks is now thought to be around 8000, and is increasing by about 7% per year. Some 5000 of these winter in Hawaii.

Humpbacks are protected by US federal law under the Marine Mammal Protection Act and the Endangered Species Act. Coming within 100 yards of a humpback (300 yards in cow/calf waters) is prohibited and carries a $25,000 fine. The rules apply to everyone, including swimmers, kayakers, divers and surfers, and they are strictly enforced, whether violators are aware of the law or not.

Dolphins The most common dolphin in Big Island waters is the spinner dolphin (so-called for its graceful mid-air pirouettes, known as 'naia' in Hawaiian). Other varieties include bottlenose, pygmy and spotted dolphins.

Dolphins are nocturnal feeders who often come into calm bays during the day to rest. Early mornings and late afternoons are some of the best times to get a glimpse of these playful creatures. Kehena Beach in Puna and Kealakekua Bay near Captain Cook are popular dolphin spots. Marine Mammal Protection Act guidelines suggest keeping a minimum distance of 50 yards from dolphins in the wild.

Incidentally, the *mahimahi* or 'dolphin' that you'll come across on menus is not the marine mammal but a fish.

Sea Turtles If you're into the order of Chelonia, the Big Island is dreamy. *Honu* (green sea turtles) are visible from cliffs, in coves and right up on the beach. Endangered hawksbills nest here and loggerheads and olive ridleys put in occasional appearances as well.

Turtles paddle about the shallows all over the Big Island and turtle viewing is a near daily event at the Punalu'u black-sand beach in Ka'u district. The Hawaiian green turtle population has grown in recent years, largely due to publicity and conservation efforts (all sea turtles are protected under the Endangered Species Act). Obviously you should not touch or otherwise disturb nesting, basking or swimming turtles.

One of the biggest threats to sea turtles is accidental hooking and netting by fisherman, so be aware if you're casting about in turtle habitat. Honu were powerful figures in Hawaiian legend and recur in petroglyph fields throughout Hawaii.

Birds The Big Island is home to many endangered and threatened bird species. A quick hike through Kipuka Pua'ulu in

Hawaii Volcanoes National park or a drive to the Mauna Kea summit may feature sightings of the native *pueo* (Hawaiian owl), *'io* (Hawaiian hawk), *alala* (Hawaiian crow) or the *palila*, a little yellow fellow that survives only on the slopes of Mauna Kea. Of course, you'll also be courted by the endangered *nene* goose all around the volcanoes.

Very rare species like the Hawaiian hoary bat and the *akiapola'au* (a honeycreeper) can be seen in the remote Hakalau Forest wildlife refuge, which protects no fewer than eight native endangered bird species and six endangered plant species (see the Waimea chapter for details).

Common non-native birds include the Japanese whiteye, cardinal and Kalij pheasant. Flamboyant honeycreepers are seemingly everywhere and they twitter with vigor around dusk all over the island.

Coral Reefs As you might expect, the Big Island has scads of sea fauna. The coral reefs, themselves an animal, are the foundation for many fish varieties. Divers and snorkelers can expect to see finger, brain, snowflake and lobe coral, which support a rainbow cast of fish like tangs, Moorish idols, wrasses, butterfly fish and the fun-to-see-and-say *humuhumunukunukuapua'a* (rectangular triggerfish). Other creatures in and around the reefs include manta rays, sea urchins of many types, 7-11 crabs and moray eels.

National Parks

A national treasure, Hawaii Volcanoes National Park is all volcanoes, all the time. Live lava flows, awesome scenery and several types of terrain await, from beaches to snowy summits and barren lavascapes to tropical rain forests. It's also the main nene habitat, boasts distinct, endemic flora and fauna and protects several endangered birds and plants.

Mauna Loa is often accused of being a 'drive-thru' volcano for its easy access, but that just broadens its appeal, for everyone can enjoy this amazing park. Whether you prefer to cruise along in a climate-controlled Cadillac or trek 18 miles to the summit, you can do it here. For those in the latter camp, the hiking here is incredible and there are a variety of backcountry options. For full details, see the Hawaii Volcanoes National Park chapter.

GOVERNMENT & POLITICS

Hawaii has three levels of government: Federal, state and county. The seat of state government is in Honolulu.

Hawaii has a typical state government with executive power vested in the governor, who is elected to a four-year term. Benjamin Cayetano, the first US governor of Filipino decent, was governor from 1994-2002. The 2002 gubernatorial election promised to be a hot one.

The state's lawmaking body is a bicameral legislature. The Senate includes 25 members elected for four-year terms, and the House of Representatives has 51 members, each elected for a two-year term.

The state of Hawaii also comprises four powerful county governments, each with a mayor and 9-member county council. Hawaii County oversees the Big Island, with its seat in Hilo. The big issue in 2002 was redistricting, which would alter the makeup of the county council.

ECONOMY

Tourism is the Big Island's largest industry, accounting for close to 40% of revenues. As you might expect, the events of September 11, 2001, and their fallout hit the economy hard as leisure travel plummeted.

Immediately after the terrorist attacks, Japanese tourism – the largest revenue earner – fell off by 61%. Projections for 2002 were unencouraging, as authorities estimated a net loss of between $500 million and $1 billion, plus some 12,000 to 28,000 jobs slashed. A scramble to cut state spending, assemble enticing travel promotions and a merger of the two Hawaiian airlines promised to boost the numbers a little, but not much. Industry experts estimated the overall drop in tourism would be around 15% to 20% once all was said and done.

For the Big Island, this was a very dark outlook indeed. Even before the attacks, economic indicators here were bleak. In 2001, Big Islanders had the lowest average income ($23,461), the highest unemployment rate (5.9%) and the most residents living below the poverty level (16.6%) in the entire state. Yet what doesn't kill us makes us stronger, and Hawaii is living proof of that axiom, pushing to diversify in the wake of the attacks.

Nevertheless, the Big Island is already among the most agriculturally diverse of all the Hawaiian islands. It boasts the largest coffee (3 million pounds annually), papaya and anthurium industries in the United States. Cattle is right up there, bringing in almost $21 million annually, and the Big Island is the world's biggest supplier of orchids and macadamia nuts (50 million pounds annually). Honey and aquaculture are gaining economic headway, as are organic vegetables and herbal remedies. Speaking of which, the Big Island is also one of the country's major marijuana producers. Official numbers are unavailable.

Sugar used to be a major economic contributor, but the last cane harvest was in 1993. New crops like eucalyptus and ginger are taking its place.

POPULATION & PEOPLE

The population of the state of Hawaii is an estimated 1,200,000. Of this total, 148,680 live on the Big Island. This is more than double the population of 1970 and it's projected to increase by another 19% by 2010.

Hawaii is a state of minorities, as no ethnic group forms a majority. On the Big Island, 31.5% are Caucasian, followed by 28.4% falling into the 'mixed race' category, 26.7% are Asians, 11.2% are Native Hawaiians and the remaining 1.1% are African American or Native American.

EDUCATION

Hawaii is the only US state to have a public education system run by the state rather than county or town education boards. Education accounts for approximately one-third of the state budget and new school construction is booming on the Big Island; recently facilities have been built in Kea'au, Waikoloa and Kealakekua.

Under Hawaii state law, all children between the ages of six and 18 are expected to attend school. More than 80% of all students are enrolled in Hawaii's public school system, with the remainder in private schools. The Kamehameha Schools are private schools open only to Native Hawaiian students and administered by the Bishop Estate.

ARTS
Hula

Hawaii's most distinctive art form is the hula, a graceful, sacred dance combining facial expressions with hand and body movements to convey stories of historical importance.

Since the Hawaiian language was traditionally only spoken, the drumming, chanting and dancing associated with hula served to pass down legends and mores. With such hefty responsibilities, the hula was necessarily complex, with its artists (men only, until King David Kalakaua's reign), formally trained and widely revered.

Poetic hula chants are called *mele*. They take many different forms and serve various functions. There are prayer, sexual and historical mele. Wooden drums *pahu* provide rhythmic accompaniment and are considered sacred in their own right, for the gods speak through the beat of the drum.

The hula was considered all too sensuous by stoic missionaries who banned its practice, nearly destroying the Hawaiian culture in the process. It was revived during the

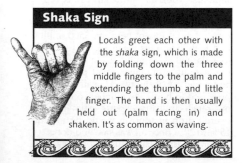

Shaka Sign

Locals greet each other with the *shaka* sign, which is made by folding down the three middle fingers to the palm and extending the thumb and little finger. The hand is then usually held out (palm facing in) and shaken. It's as common as waving.

reign of King David Kalakaua, the 'Merrie Monarch.' Today, the world's most famous hula extravaganza is the week-long Merrie Monarch Festival, which begins on Easter Sunday in Hilo.

Seeing and even learning some hula during your visit is entirely possible. Many hula *halau* (schools) perform in hotels and shopping plazas. Cultural centers such as the Wailoa Center and the East Hawaii Cultural Center, both in Hilo, offer classes.

Music

Hawaiian music is a delicious blend of all the immigrant, native and modern influences that so typify these islands. From 'Hawaiian' or steel guitar (see boxed text) to Puerto Rican *kachi kachi* and Filipino *rondalla*, you'll hear the distinct strains of local music wafting on warm evening winds.

One hot sound right now is 'Jawaiian,' an amalgam of Hawaiian music and Jamaican reggae. Check out Bruddah Waltah, the Ka'au Crater Boys or Hoaikane. These bands occasionally tour the Big Island, so keep an eye peeled.

Other popular contemporary Hawaiian musicians include vocalist-composer Henry Kapono; Hapa, the duo of Keli'i Kaneali'i and Barry Flanagan, who fuse folk, rock and traditional Hawaiian elements; and the Hawaiian Style Band, which merges Hawaiian influences with rock.

The singer and composer Israel Kamakawiwo'ole, ('Bruddah Iz'), was an isle icon and beloved by many; when he died in 1997, this giant of Hawaiian music was laid in state at the Capitol rotunda in Honolulu, attended by 10,000 fans.

For your listening enjoyment, check out the Hawaiian titles in the Smithsonian Folkways catalog, the hula mele put out by the 49th State label and Hula Records' two-volume set *Memories of Hawaii Calls*. Also see the Hawaiian Music Island Web site (**w** www.mele.com) for harder-to-find recordings and a concert calendar.

Literature

The Bamboo Ridge Press publishes a slew of terrific collections by Hawaiian authors;

Hawaiian Guitar Styles

Innovative and unique, Hawaiian guitar sounds are instantly recognizable. Not only did 19th-century Hawaiian musicians develop their own riffs and melodies, they also reinvented several guitar types and tunings.

Mexican cowboys brought the guitar to the islands in the 1830s. Before long, the Hawaiians had adopted it as their own. Most notably, in 1889, Joseph Kekuku designed the steel guitar, one of only two major musical instruments invented in what is now the USA. (The other is the banjo.)

Slack-key is a playing and tuning style developed by Hawaiian guitarists in the mid-1800s. According to one enthusiast, slack-key guitar was 'developed by people who really loved the guitar, but didn't know how to play it' and sometimes it can sound like it, too. 'Slack key' refers to a type of tuning in which certain strings are slackened to produce a soulful harmonic sound. Players use hammering and fingerpicking methods that, when well done, give you 'chicken skin' (goosebumps). Favorite Hawaiian slack-key players include Sonny Chillingworth, Cyril Pahinui, Raymond Kane, Peter Moon, Atta Isaacs Jr, and the late, great Gabby Pahinui.

The ukulele, synonymous with Hawaiian music, was derived from the *braginha*, a Portuguese instrument also introduced to Hawaii in the 19th century. In the Hawaiian language, 'ukulele' means 'jumping flea.' The ukulele is one of the world's easiest instruments to learn and play and the little fellas are busted out at many a luau and BBQ.

Due in part to the 'Hawaii Calls' radio show, which has broadcasted worldwide from Waikiki's Moana Hotel for over 30 years, ukulele and steel guitar music became instantly recognizable as Hawaiian. Present-day ukulele masters include Troy Fernandez and Ledward Ka'apana.

Growing Up Local: An Anthology of Poetry and Prose from Hawaii is a good place to start.

Kiana Davenport's *Shark Dialogues* (Antheneum) is part historical novel, part political tract and part creation myth written in melodic, transfixing prose. It's also a world-class love story.

See the Books section in Facts for the Visitor for more.

Art
Many artists draw inspiration from Hawaii's rich cultural heritage and natural beauty.

The well-known Hawaiian painter Herb Kawainui Kane creates detailed oil paintings focusing on the early Polynesians and King Kamehameha's life. You'll see his work everywhere, along with volcano photographs by G. Brad Lewis.

Some of Hawaii's most impressive crafts are ceramics, bowls made of native woods, and baskets woven of native fibers. The goddess Pele is a source of inspiration for many Big Island artists; you'll see her likeness often. Hawaiian quilting is another uniquely beautiful art form to look for.

A more transitory art form is the *lei* (garland). Although the lei favored by visitors are of the fragrant flower variety (eg, plumeria and tuberose), traditional leis of mokihana berries and maile leaves were more commonly worn in old Hawaii. Both types are still made today and the latter is prized by lovers, for it bestows longevity and fidelity.

SOCIETY & CONDUCT
Contemporary culture in Hawaii resembles contemporary culture in the rest of the USA, but with a distinct tropical twist.

Here, you have the same pop music and TV shows, drug problems and junk food as the rest of the country. But the intriguing thing about Hawaii is that the mainland influences largely stand beside, rather than engulf, the culture of the islands.

The cultural renaissance of the 1970s continues today. Hula and Hawaiian language classes are thriving, and there is a concerted effort to reintroduce Hawaiian words into modern speech. Many Hawaiian artists and craftspeople are returning to tra-

ditional mediums and themes. More esoteric facets of ancient Hawaiian culture also are making a comeback, such as tattoo, wayfinding and 'holua sledding,' in which participants race down steep, grass-lined courses on wooden sleds.

Dos & Don'ts
Hawaii is generally laid-back, but sacred heiau and other historical sites should be respected: climbing on or otherwise disturbing stone structures and temples is seriously bad form, as is running, shouting and disrupting areas around these sites. The influence of Japanese culture in Hawaii is strong and shoes are always doffed upon entering someone's home. Furthermore, rubbing two chopsticks together is considered crass

RELIGION
To say Hawaii's population is religiously diverse is like saying the Bush family is well connected. From Baptists to Taoists, the Big Island is home to all faiths.

Christianity has the largest following, with Catholicism being the predominant denomination. The Mormons have a stronghold and the United Church of Christ (including the Congregationalists who initially converted the islands), also claims many adherents. You can still attend services in Hawaiian on the Big Island.

In addition, Hawaii has Buddhist temples, Shinto shrines, Hindu temples and Krishna gatherings. There are also Tenrikyo, Jewish and Muslim houses of worship.

LANGUAGE
The unifying language of Hawaii is English, but it's liberally spiced with Hawaiian phrases, loaned words from various immigrant languages and pidgin slang. Both English and Hawaiian are official state languages, but pidgin is the language of the people. When locals want to converse privately, they slip into pidgin and it will all be Greek to you.

Closely related to other Polynesian languages, Hawaiian is melodic, phonetically simple and full of vowels and repeated syllables. The Hawaiians had no written language until the 1820s, when Christian missionaries arrived and wrote down the spoken language in roman letters.

Pronunciation

The written Hawaiian language has just 12 letters. Pronunciation is fairly easy, though clusters of diphthongs can be challenging.

Vowel sounds are about the same as in Spanish or Japanese, more or less like this:

a	ah, as in 'father,' or uh, as in 'above'
e	ay, as in 'gay' or eh, as in 'pet'
i	ee, as in 'see'
o	oh, as in 'go'
u	oo, as in 'noon'

Diphthongs are created when two vowels join together to form a single sound; Hawaiian is loaded with them. The stress is on the first vowel, although if you pronounce each vowel separately, you should be understood.

Within each word, the emphasis *usually* is on the penultimate syllable, as it is in Spanish.

The consonant *w* is usually pronounced like a soft English *v* when it follows the letters *i* and *e* and like the English *w* when it follows *u* or *o*. When *w* follows *a*, it can be pronounced either *v* or *w* – thus you will hear both Hawaii and Havaii.

The other consonants – h, k, l, m, n, p – are pronounced about the same as in English.

Glottal Stops & Macrons Written Hawaiian uses both glottal stops and macrons.

The glottal stop (') indicates a break between two vowels, which produces an effect similar to saying 'oh-oh' in English. Written glottal stops also break up words, aiding in pronunciation. A macron, a short straight line over a vowel, stresses the vowel.

Glottal stops and macrons not only affect pronunciation, but can give a word a completely different meaning. For example, *ai* can mean 'sexual intercourse' or 'to eat,' depending on the pronunciation.

Compounds Hawaiian can be confounding at first because many proper names are long and look similar.

When you break each word down into its composite parts, some of which are repeated, it becomes much easier. For example: *Kamehameha* consists of the three compounds Ka-meha-meha. *Humuhumunukunukuapua'a* is broken down into humu-humu-nuku-nuku-a-pu a a.

Some words are doubled to emphasize their meaning. *Wiki* means 'quick,' while *wikiwiki* means 'very quick.'

Common Hawaiian Words

Learn these words first: *aloha* and *mahalo*, which mean hello/goodbye and thank you, respectively; *makai* (toward the sea) and *mauka* (inland), are commonly used in giving directions; you'll see *wahine* (woman) and *kane* (man), on bathroom doors. For many more helpful Hawaiian words, see the glossary at the back of this book.

Pidgin

Hawaii's early immigrants communicated via pidgin, a simplified, broken form of English. It was a language born of necessity, stripped of all but the most needed words and tenses, and spiced with words borrowed freely from other languages.

Modern pidgin is an extensive language, lively and ever-changing. Whole conversations take place in pidgin, or often just a word or two is dropped into a more conventional English sentence.

Visitors rarely win friends by trying to speak pidgin. It's more like an insider's code that you're allowed to use only after you've lived in Hawaii long enough to appreciate the nuances.

Some characteristics of pidgin include a fast staccato rhythm, two-word sentences, dropping the soft 'h' sound from words that start with 'th,' use of loan words from many languages (often Hawaiian) and double meanings that trip up the uninitiated.

For some common pidgin words and expression, see the glossary toward the back of this book.

Facts for the Visitor

HIGHLIGHTS

Hawaii Volcanoes National Park brims with steaming craters and molten lava, while the green and black sand beaches of the southeast make for singular frolicking.

The snorkeling and diving in the sapphire waters of the Kohala and Kona coasts are world renowned, as are the golfing and fishing in those parts. Hidden beaches and elegant resorts are hallmarks of Hawaii's leeward side.

The verdant Hamakua Coast and Waipi'o Valley are ethereal in their near perfection, rivaled only by Mauna Kea and Mauna Loa. Stargazing from the former and simply gazing upon the latter will broaden even the narrowest viewpoints.

All of this is here, plus vivid reminders of an ancient culture: the Place of Refuge, petroglyph fields and canoe moorings at South Point among them.

SUGGESTED ITINERARIES

A week will leave you wanting more. An itinerary might include two days on a Kohala beach, another snorkeling near Captain Cook and the Place of Refuge, one day touring a coffee farm or horseback riding and another day exploring the Hamakua Coast. Save at least two days for Volcanoes National Park, the active lava flow and some stargazing atop Mauna Kea.

Two weeks allows you to uncover some of the Big Island's hidden charms. Follow the one week itinerary, but laze on a beach only accessible by foot or kayak, poke around Puna for a bit, hike the volcanic crater by day and the active lava flow at night, scuba one day and snorkel the next, hike *and* camp in Waipi'o Valley and spend a day exploring the little-known Ka'u district before parking on a beach until the real world calls.

If you're here for a month or more, you undoubtedly have your own agenda. Maybe it involves a Mauna Loa summit attempt or a sacred valley odyssey. A yoga retreat, spa vacation or backcountry camping are other options. Terrific game fishing, diving with manta rays and all the hidden spots no guidebook should divulge await.

PLANNING
When to Go

When deciding when to visit the Big Island, heed the old Hawaiian Consolidated Railway motto: 'Hawaii's Fine Anytime – Come When Convenient.'

While winter sees the greatest number of tourists, summer is another popular time to visit as this is when many families slip away from their daily grind. It's rainier in the winter – the windward side floods once or twice a season – and hotter in the summer, when the Kona side might not see any rain.

Orientation

Navigating the Big Island can be tricky as many places take several names and locals are more likely to say 'veer left at the prayer flags' than give you a proper street address. Lest logistical despair set in, here are some tips:

- Be aware of mile markers: these are used to gauge distance, but more importantly, to give directions to secluded beaches, hidden waterfalls and similar treats.
- When getting directions, break up long words into their components, eg, Lau-pa-hoe-hoe or Holo-holo-kai.
- If a road or town takes several names, go with local usage. In Puna for example, it's known as Red Road, not Hwy 137 or anything else. Also, you'll hear 'Waimea' more often than 'Kamuela.'
- Toward the coast is called *makai*; away from the coast, or inland, is called *mauka*.
- West Hawaii is the leeward side is the Kona side is the sunny side. East Hawaii is the windward side is the Hilo side is the rainy side.
- Getting lost can be the most enlightening part of a trip, so lean into it!
- Last but not least, you'll hear frequent reference to Big Island 'districts,' which are Kona, Kohala, Waimea, Hilo, Puna and Ka'u.

Maps

Big Island maps published by the University of Hawaii Press (UH; $3.95) or Nelles ($5.95) are good, general maps covering roads, beaches, historical sites and hiking trails. Both are widely available.

If you want to beat your own path, the best resource is the *Ready Mapbook* series (Odyssey Publishing). You'll need both the East and West Hawaii editions ($9.95 each) to cover the entire island, but the street-by-street detail and expansive index are invaluable. Basically Books in Hilo carries these maps and many more.

The United States Geological Survey (USGS) publishes topographical maps of Hawaii. Both full-island and detailed sectional maps ($4 per sheet) are available, and there's also an individual USGS map for Hawaii Volcanoes National Park. Order maps directly from the US Geological Survey (☎ 800-435-7627, fax 303-202-4693, hinfoservices@usgs.gov), or buy them at the Middle Earth Bookshoppe in Kailua-Kona, Basically Books in Hilo and the national park.

What to Bring

The key thing to remember when packing for the Big Island is that there are two sides to the coin: the hot, dry leeward side and the chillier, damp windward side.

In Kailua-Kona and around, shorts, sandals and t-shirt are the standard uniform. For visits to Mauna Kea, Hawaii Volcanoes National Park or Hilo, you'll want warm socks, a sweater or jacket and rain gear.

Summit temperatures often dip below freezing, so high elevation campers should bring a four season tent, winter-rated sleeping bag, rain gear and warm clothing. For beach camping, a lightweight cotton bag is all you'll need, but bring a tent too as the mosquitoes are hungry. You can rent camping gear in Hilo or buy it cheap in Kona.

For hiking, footwear with good traction is a must, especially for the lava flows. Hardcore hikers should consider toting their hiking boots.

RESPONSIBLE TOURISM

Obviously, responsible tourism means not disturbing marine life or archaeological treasures, not removing black sand from beaches, treading lightly when hiking, packing out your trash and other common traveler ethos.

What is less obvious is the sometimes strained relationship between tourism and Hawaiian self-determination. Some Hawaiians resent individuals and corporations buying ancient lands for their enrichment. Off the trodden track, you may come across signs that say 'No Trespassing,' 'Keep Out' or '*Kapu.*' Unless you're with a local friend or you receive permission to cross beyond these signs, you should heed them.

TOURIST OFFICES

The Hawaii Visitors and Convention Bureau (HVCB) provides free tourist information. On the US mainland, you can call the HVCB at ☎ 800-464-2924 for general information, or at ☎ 800-648-2441 to order a free Big Island Vacation Planner. You can also order the planner online at w www.gohawaii.com.

Local Tourist Offices

HVCB on the Big Island is called the Big Island Visitors Bureau. The Hilo office (☎ 961-5797) is at 250 Keawe St. The Kailua-Kona office (☎ 886-1655) is at 250 Waikoloa Beach Dr.

Tourist Offices Abroad

The Hawaii Visitors and Convention Bureau frequently changes its overseas agents. The following are the current addresses for HVCB representatives abroad.

Australia
(☎ 02-9955-2619, fax 02-9955-2171, rlane@thesalesteam.com.au)
c/o The Sales Team, suite 2, level 2,
34 Burton St, Milsons Point, NSW 2061

Canada
(☎ 604-669-6691, fax 604-669-6075, compre@intergate.bc.ca)
c/o Comprehensive Travel Industry Services
1260 Hornby St, suite 104,
Vancouver, BC V6Z 1W2

Japan
(☎ 3-3201-0430, fax 3-3201-0433, mukumoto@
hvcb.org)
Kokusai Building, 2nd floor, 1-1
Marunouchi 3-chome, Chiyoda-ku, Tokyo 100

New Zealand
(☎ 9-379-3708, fax 9-309-0725, darragh@
walwor.co.nz)
c/o Walshes World, 11 Shortland Street,
Level 6, Auckland

UK
(☎ 0181-941-4009, fax 0181-941-4001,)
Box 208, Sunbury on Thames,
Middlesex TW16 5RJ

VISAS & DOCUMENTS
Passport & Visas

The requirements for entering Hawaii are
the same as for entering any state in the
USA. Canadians must have proof of Canadian citizenship, such as a citizenship card
with photo ID or a passport. Visitors from
other countries must have a valid passport,
and most visitors also need a US visa.

However, a reciprocal visa-waiver program allows citizens of certain countries to
enter the USA for stays of 90 days or fewer
without first obtaining a visa. Currently
these countries are Andorra, Argentina,
Australia, Austria, Belgium, Brunei, Denmark, Finland, France, Germany, Iceland,
Ireland, Italy, Japan, Liechtenstein, Luxembourg, Monaco, Netherlands, New Zealand,
Norway, Portugal, San Marino, Singapore,
Spain, Sweden, Switzerland, the UK and
Uruguay.

Under this program, you must have a
nonrefundable roundtrip ticket and you
cannot extend your stay beyond the 90 days.
Other travelers need to obtain a visa from a
US consulate or embassy.

Your passport should be valid for at least
six months beyond your intended stay, and
you'll need to submit a recent photo (37 x
37mm) with the application. Documents of
financial stability and/or guarantees from a
US resident are sometimes required, particularly for visitors from the developing
world.

Visa applicants may be required to
'demonstrate binding obligations' that will
ensure their return home. Because of this

requirement, those planning to travel
through other countries before arriving in
the USA are better off applying for their
US visa while still in their home country.

The validity period for US visitor visas
depends on what country you're from. The
length of time you'll be allowed to stay in
the USA is ultimately determined by US
immigration authorities at the port of entry.
Since the events of September 2001, you can
bet the visa process will be protracted, so
plan ahead.

Non-US citizens with the HIV virus
should know that they can be excluded
from entry to the US if they reveal their
HIV status on the immigration question-
naire upon entering the country.

Visa Extensions If you want to stay in the
USA beyond the date stamped on your
passport, you'll need to apply for an extension by contacting the Honolulu office of
the Immigration & Naturalization Service
(☎ 532-3721), 595 Ala Moana Blvd, Honolulu, HI, 96813 before the stamped date.
Extensions can take time so plan ahead.

Travel Insurance

Since health care in the USA is so expensive, it's a good idea to purchase travel insurance, covering medical expenses, luggage
theft or loss, and cancellation or delays in
your travel arrangements. Policies vary, so
get your insurer or travel agent to explain
the details.

Check the small print because some policies exclude 'dangerous activities,' which
can include scuba diving, motorcycling and
even trekking.

While you may find a policy that pays
doctors or hospitals directly, be aware that
many medical providers in Hawaii will
demand payment at the time of service. Be
certain to keep all documentation, in case
you have to make a claim later.

Paying for your ticket with a credit card
often provides travel accident insurance
and may also give you the right to reclaim
your payment if the operator doesn't deliver. Ask your credit card company, or the
issuing bank, for details.

Documents

All US airlines require passengers to present a photo ID as part of the airline check-in procedure. All foreigners (other than Canadians) must bring their passports.

Members of the American Automobile Association (AAA) or other affiliated automobile clubs can get car rental, airfare and some sightseeing admission discounts with their membership cards. Don't forget your driver's license and insurance card.

Divers should bring their certification cards.

Photocopies

All important documents (passport data and visa pages, credit cards, travel insurance policy, air tickets, driver's license etc) should be photocopied before you leave home. Leave one copy with someone at home and keep another with you, separate from the originals.

It's also a good idea to store details of your vital travel documents in Lonely Planet's free online Travel Vault in case you lose the photocopies or can't be bothered with them. Your password-protected Travel Vault is accessible online anywhere in the world – create it at **W** www.ekno.lonely planet.com.

EMBASSIES & CONSULATES
Your Own Embassy

It's important to realize what your own embassy can and can't do to help you if you get into trouble. Generally speaking, it won't be much help in emergencies if the trouble you're in is remotely your own fault. Remember that you are bound by the laws of the country you are in. Your embassy will not be sympathetic if you end up in jail after committing a crime locally, even if such actions are legal in your own country.

In genuine emergencies, you might get some assistance, but only if other channels have been exhausted. If all your money and documents are stolen, your embassy might assist you with getting a new passport, but a loan for onward travel is out of the question – the embassy would expect you to have insurance.

US Embassies Abroad

For more information about US diplomatic representation abroad, see the Web links at **W** www.usembassy.state.gov.

Australia
(☎ 02-6214-5600, **W** usembassy-australia .state.gov/index.html)
21 Moonah Place, Yarralumla, ACT 2600

Canada
(☎ 613-238-5335,
W www.usembassycanada.gov)
490 Sussex Dr, PO Box 866, Station B, Ottawa, Ontario K1P 5T1

France
(☎ 01 43 12 22 22, **W** www.amb-usa.fr)
2 avenue Gabriel, 75382 Paris

Germany
(☎ 30-8305-0, **W** www.usembassy.de)
Neustädtische Kirchstrasse 4-5, 10117 Berlin

Ireland
(☎ 1-668-8777)
42 Elgin Rd, Ballsbridge, Dublin 4

Italy
(☎ 06-4674-1, **W** www.usembassy.it)
Via Vittorio Veneto 119/A, 00187 Roma

Japan
(☎ 03-3224-5000, **W** usembassy.state.gov/tokyo)
10-5 Akasaka 1-chome, Minato-ku, Tokyo

Netherlands
(☎ 70-310-9209, **W** www.usemb.nl)
Lange Voorhout 102, 2514 EJ The Hague

New Zealand
(☎ 4-462-6000, **W** usembassy.state .gov/wellington) 29 Fitzherbert Terrace, PO Box 1190, Thorndon, Wellington

UK
(☎ 020-7499-9000, **W** www.usembassy.org.uk)
24 Grovesnor Square, London W1A 1AE

Foreign Consulates in Hawaii

The following consulates and government liaison offices are hosted in Honolulu:

Australia
Consulate-General of Australia
(☎ 808-524-5050) 1000 Bishop St

Federated States of Micronesia
(☎ 808-836-4775, fax 808-836-6896)
3049 Ualena, suite 908

Germany
Consulate of Germany
(☎ 808-946-3819) 2003 Kalia Rd

Italy
Vice Consulate of Italy
(☎ 808-531-2277) 735 Bishop St, suite 201

Japan
Consulate-General of Japan
(☎ 808-543-3111, fax 808-543-3170
W www.embjapan.org/honolulu/) 1742 Nuuanu Ave

Kiribati
Consulate of Kiribati
(☎ 808-521-7703) 850 Richards St, suite 503

Mariana Islands
Hawaii Liaison Office
(☎ 808-592-0300, fax 808-596-7633)
1221 Kapiolani Blvd, suite 720

Mexico
Consulate of Mexico
(☎ 808-524-4390, fax 808-599-2505)
76 N. King St, suite 208

Netherlands
Consulate of the Netherlands
(☎ 808-531-6897) 745 Fort Street Mall, suite 702

Papua New Guinea
Consulate-General of Papua New Guinea
(☎ 808-524-5414, fax 808-599-5004
W www.diamondhead.net/png.htm)
1154 Fort St Mall, suite 300

Philippines
Consulate-General of the Philippines
(☎ 595-6316) 2433 Pali Hwy, 4231 Papu Circle

Thailand
Royal Thai Consulate-General
(☎ 808-845-7332) 1287 Kalani St, suite 103

Tonga
Tonga Consular Agency (☎ 808-521-5149,
fax 808-521-5264) 220 S King St, suite 1603

CUSTOMS

US Customs allows each visitor to bring one liter of liquor and 200 cigarettes into the country. Before you launch the party, however, remember that you must be 21 to possess the former, and 18 the latter.

Most fresh fruits and plants are restricted from entry into Hawaii and the state is militant about it. Because Hawaii is a rabies-free state, the pet quarantine is Draconian: plan on at least 30 days of isolation for Fido or Felix upon arrival and a $650 price tag for the privilege. For complete quarantine information, and for information about exemptions for guide and service dogs, visit the Hawaiian Department of Agriculture Web site at W www.hawaiiag.org/hdoa/ ai_aqs_info.htm or call ☎ 808-483-7151 in Oahu for a free brochure.

MONEY
Currency

As is true throughout the USA, the US dollar is the only currency used on the Big Island (bartering for buds in Puna doesn't count).

The dollar (commonly called a buck) is divided into 100 cents. Coins come in denominations of one cent (penny), five cents (nickel), 10 cents (dime), 25 cents (quarter) and the rare 50-cent piece (half dollar). Notes come in one-, five-, 10-, 20-, 50- and 100-dollar denominations.

In 2000, the US Treasury redesigned the five-, 10-, 20-, 50-, and 100-dollar bills. Sadly, the designers couldn't produce a sexier color than mold green and the US presidents all have gigantic potato heads on the new bills, which circulate alongside the old. Also legal tender, but only occasionally seen, is the striking but unwieldy Sacagawea one-dollar coin that the government has tried to force into mass circulation. A two-dollar note is so rare people hoard it.

Exchange Rates

At time of press, exchange rates were the following:

country	unit		dollar
Australia	A$1	=	US$0.53
Canada	C$1	=	US$0.63
European Union	€1	=	US$.87
Hong Kong	HK$1	=	US$0.13
Japan	¥100	=	US$0.75
New Zealand	NZ$1	=	US$0.44
UK	UK£1	=	US$1.43

Exchanging Money

Cash & Personal Checks Walking around with a big cash stash is not typical (or necessarily safe) in the US and you'll want to use a mix of credit cards, debit or ATM cards and perhaps some traveler's checks.

If you're carrying foreign currency, it can be exchanged for US dollars at larger banks, including the Bank of Hawaii or First Hawaiian Bank; you can also change a variety of currencies at Honolulu International Airport. Note that banks generally give the best exchange rate; you'll also get a much better rate within the US than outside.

Personal checks not drawn on a Hawaiian bank are generally not accepted.

Traveler's Checks The main benefit of traveler's checks is the theft protection they provide. Large companies such as American Express and Thomas Cook generally offer efficient replacement policies for lost or stolen checks.

Keeping a record of the check numbers and those you've used is vital when replacing checks. You should keep this information separate from the checks themselves. In the event of stolen or lost traveler's checks, call American Express (☎ 800-992-3404) or Thomas Cook (☎ 800-287-7362).

Foreign visitors carrying traveler's checks will find things infinitely easier if the checks are in US dollars. Most mid-range and upscale restaurants, hotels and shops accept US dollar traveler's checks and treat them just like cash, which makes things nice and easy if you're in that budget bracket. If, however, you're camping on hostel lawns and dining on loco moco, you won't be able to do much with a traveler's check but sop up spilled grease.

ATMs Automatic teller machines (ATMs) are great for quick cash influxes and can negate the need for traveler's checks entirely, but watch out for ATM surcharges. Luckily, most banks in Hawaii only charge around US$1.50 per withdrawal.

Major banks such as Bank of Hawaii (W www.boh.com) and First Hawaiian Bank (W www.fhb.com) have plenty of ATMs on the Big Island that give cash advances on major credit cards and allow cash withdrawals with affiliated ATM cards. Most ATM machines accept bank cards from both the Plus and Cirrus systems, the two largest networks in the USA.

Look for ATMs in the Kona airport, outside banks, and in large grocery stores, shopping centers, convenience stores and gas stations.

Credit & Debit Cards Major credit cards are widely accepted throughout Hawaii, including at car rental agencies and most hotels, restaurants, gas stations, grocery stores and tour operators. Many B&Bs and some condominiums – particularly those handled through rental agencies – do not accept credit cards, however. In certain cases, using a credit card may incur a 3% penalty. The most commonly accepted cards in Hawaii are all the usual suspects. A fair number of businesses also accept JCB, Discover and Diners Club cards. Consider prepaying your credit card and taking cash advances against it rather than relying on traveler's checks or ATMs.

International Transfers Wiring money using a transfer service such as Western Union (☎ 800-325-6000, W www.western union.com) is fast and easy. Western Union has over 100,000 agents worldwide, with outlets in Hilo, Kona, Kea'au and Waimea; a $1000 transfer from anywhere in the world to the Big Island costs $75 and takes a snappy 15 minutes.

Transferring funds from your home bank to one in Hawaii is possible, but a hassle. See the Web sites of Bank of Hawaii (W www.boh.com) or First Hawaiian Bank (W www.fhb.com) for details.

Costs

How much money you'll need depends on your traveling style. A Big Island trip can only be so cheap (parsimonious readers should consult the boxed text 'Stretching Your Dollar' immediately), but the sky's the limit where luxury is concerned.

As with all trips, airfare will take a greedy bite of your budget. Fares vary greatly, particularly from the US mainland, so shop around. Interisland flights cost about $60 to $95 one way, depending on how you buy your tickets. To get the cheapest fare, procure an interisland flight coupon (for more information, see the Flight Coupons section in the Getting There & Away chapter).

The Big Island has a limited bus system, but speaking from experience, you can't do

Stretching Your Dollar

Hawaii is like Manhattan in that travelers often think it *has* to be expensive. No doubt both can be among the world's most expensive and lavish destinations, but it doesn't have to be so. Here are some ideas for conserving your budget:

Food
Staying in a place with a kitchen and cooking some of your meals will save bundles. If cooking and cleaning are anathema to your vacation plans, consider picnicking or renting digs with a fridge so you can stock up on beverages and raw foods. When shopping, hit large local food outlets such as CostCo or WalMart for cheap foodstuffs; use coupons (Tuesday is coupon day in the local papers and many stores have individual coupon booklets); and buy fresh ahi roadside (typically $1.50/lb). Local food is cheap and filling. Try a loco moco or plate lunch ($2-4) at a drive-in or a perfectly flame-broiled *hulihuli* (Hawaiian BBQ) chicken ($6.50) from roadside vendors (where there's smoke, there's hulihuli chicken). Sitting through time share pitches can net you free meals; look in the freebie tourist books for these opportunities.

Transportation
No matter how you cut it, getting to and around Hawaii can take a big bite. Check out the possibility of flying to Honolulu and connecting with an interisland flight to save some change (see the Getting There & Away chapter for details). It's usually cheaper to fly to Kona than Hilo, so consider flying to the leeward side and driving to your final destination (it's 2½ hours' driving time between the two farthest points). Again, ask about available discounts when renting a car. Hitchhiking is free (but time consuming) and can be entertaining but LP doesn't endorse it.

Fun Stuff
Tourist brochures like *101 Things to Do* and the *Big Island Beach & Activity Guide* are loaded with coupons for free coffee, discounted tours and reduced admission for museums, gardens and other attractions. In addition, there are tons of free things to do on the Big Island, including stargazing atop Mauna Kea, hiking the Footprints and Mauna Loa Trails in Hawaii Volcanoes National Park, the volcanic steam vents and tide pools in Puna, many of the historic heiau, several waterfalls around Hilo and simply lazing on the beach in Kohala. See Local Tourist Offices, earlier, for contact details.

Hawaii properly without a car, at least for part of your trip. Renting a car usually costs between $150 and $200 a week, but if you aim to visit Mauna Kea or some other hard-to-reach places, you'll want a 4WD; these cost at least $350 a week.

Accommodations on the Big Island range from free campsites to resort digs for $5600 and everything in between. A dorm bed will cost you around $20, and there are many motel-like places in the $40 to $50 range. Stepping up in comfort and location, there are condos, lovely B&Bs or cozy inns starting at around $100. You'll shell out at least $125 for anything on the beach, double that for a similarly located luxury hotel.

If you're staying awhile, there are several ways to cut accommodation costs. Weekly and monthly condo rental rates can beat all but the cheapest hotels. Additionally, most condos are outfitted with everything from towels and beach mats to a fully equipped kitchen. Many hotels and B&Bs also extend discounts for a stay of a week or more.

Since so much of the food here is imported, grocery prices average 25% higher than on the mainland. At the same time, guava, papaya, avocado and other tropical delights are literally falling from the trees, making picnics an attractive, affordable alternative. Food in local neighborhood restaurants is generally good value.

Tipping & Bargaining

Tipping practices are the same as in the rest of the USA. In restaurants, good waiters are tipped at least 15%, while dissatisfied customers make their ire known by leaving 10%. There has to be real cause for not tipping at all. Taxi drivers and hairstylists are typically tipped about 10% and hotel bellhops about $1 per bag.

The Big Island has an extensive network of farmer's and antique markets and you may try dickering over some lilikoi or Hawaiiana. Respectable savings can also be had at hotels during slow periods by flying stand-by on helicopter tours or renting kayaks and other gear by the week.

Taxes

Hawaii has a 4.17% state sales tax that is attached to virtually everything, including meals, groceries, car rentals and accommodations. An additional 7.24% room tax brings the total tax added to accommodation bills to 11.41% (ouch!). Another tax targeted at visitors is a $3-a-day 'road use' tax imposed upon all car rentals.

POST & COMMUNICATIONS

The US postal service (☎ 800-275-8777, w www.usps.gov) is inexpensive and generally reliable. That said, mail delivery to and from the Hawaiian islands usually takes a little longer than similar services on the US mainland.

Post offices are generally open 8am to 4:30pm on weekdays. Main post offices may be open later on weekdays and on Saturday from 9am until noon.

Postal Rates

Postage rates for 1st-class mail within the USA are 34¢ for letters up to 1oz and 21¢ for standard-size postcards. First-class mail between Hawaii and the mainland usually goes by air and takes under a week. For faster delivery, Priority Mail letters cost $3.95 (for up to two pounds) and Express Mail (guaranteed two-day delivery) costs from $12.45.

International airmail rates are 80¢ for a 1oz letter and 70¢ for a postcard to any foreign country, with the exception of Canada and Mexico (60¢ for a 1oz letter and 50¢ for a postcard). International air parcels vary by weight, size and destination, starting at $13 for the first pound.

Receiving Mail

You can have *poste restante* mail sent to you c/o General Delivery at almost any post office in Hawaii. General delivery mail is usually held up to 30 days (only 10 at the Kailua-Kona branch).

Have general delivery mail addressed as follows:

> FAMILY NAME, Your First Name
> c/o General Delivery, Main Post Office
> Anytown, HI 96XXX

Some hotels and condo complexes also hold mail for guests.

Telephone

Public pay phones are everywhere: beaches, gas stations, shopping malls and hotel lobbies. You can pump in coins, use a phone or credit card or make collect calls. Emergency 911 calls and toll-free numbers can be dialed from pay phones without inserting any money.

Pay phone rates are 50¢ for unlimited local minutes. Long-distance calls anywhere within the USA (including inter-island calls) are 25¢ per minute with a $1 minimum. Any calls made with operator assistance will be pricier.

Area Code 808

The entire state of Hawaii takes the ☎ 808 area code. When making calls on the same island, you don't need to dial the area code. When calling to other islands or from outside the state however, you must precede the number with ☎ 808.

All Big Island numbers in this book are given without the area code, but you can understand it as ☎ 808.

Be aware that many hotels add a service charge of 25¢ to $1 for each call (local or toll-free) made from in-room phones, and most impose hefty surcharges on long-distance calls.

International Calls When calling Hawaii from overseas, you must precede the 808 area code with 1, the international country code for the USA.

To make an international call direct from Hawaii, dial ☎ 011 + country code + area code + number. An exception is Canada, where you just have to dial ☎ 1 + area code + number (but beware – international rates still apply!). For international operator assistance dial ☎ 0. However, it's almost always better to use a phone card (see the next section).

Phonecards Lonely Planet's eKno Communication Card is aimed specifically at travelers and provides cheap international calls, a range of messaging services and free email. For local calls, though, you're usually better off with a local card. You can join online at W www.ekno.lonelyplanet.com, or by phone from Hawaii by dialing ☎ 800-527-6786.

There's a wide range of prepaid phone cards that work for local and international calls. Cards sold by major companies like AT&T compete with small upstart companies with catchy card names like Islander or Beautiful Hawaii. The key is to read all of the fine print *before* buying any card. Cards that advertise the cheapest per-minute rates may charge hefty connection fees for each call (especially from pay phones).

Cell Phones The North American GSM1900 cell phone standard is not compatible with the GSM 900/1800 standard used throughout most of Europe, Asia and Africa. If you have a GSM phone from abroad, check with your service provider about using it in Hawaii and beware of calls being routed internationally (making 'local' calls super expensive).

Similarly, visitors from the US mainland and Canada should ask if their service providers add exorbitant long-distance or roaming surcharges on calls made from Hawaii.

The major provider of cell phone products and services in Hawaii is Verizon (W www.verizonwireless.com). Renting a cell phone is very expensive (minimum $15 per day), so you're probably better off using a phonecard.

Fax & Shipping Services

Many business centers provide fax, photocopy and shipping services at competitive rates. Receiving a fax usually costs around 50¢ a page; the cost for sending faxes depends on the destination and length of the document.

Email & Internet Access

If you usually access your email through your office or school network, you'll find it easier to open a free Web-based email account such as Yahoo! (www.yahoo.com) or Hotmail (www.hotmail.com).

If you must bring your notebook or palmtop computer, remember that the power supply voltage in the US may be different. Investing in a universal AC and plug adapter will enable you to plug in anywhere without frying your machine's innards. Also your PC-card modem may not work once you leave your home country – but you won't know for sure until you try. The safest option is to buy a reputable 'global' modem before you leave home. Ensure that you have at least a US RJ-11 telephone adapter that works with your modem. For more technical help, visit W www.igoproducts.com.

Public libraries offer free Internet access with a Hawaii library card (see Libraries, later). Patrons are limited to one 50-minute session per week. You should sign up in advance, as walk-ins are subject to computer availability.

There are also a variety of businesses offering access in Hilo and Kailua-Kona (see those chapters for details).

INTERNET RESOURCES

The World Wide Web is a rich resource for travelers. You can research your trip, hunt down bargain airfares, book hotels, check on weather conditions or chat with locals and other travelers about the best places to visit (or avoid!).

There's no better place to start your Web explorations than the Lonely Planet Web site (**W** www.lonelyplanet.com). Here you'll find succinct summaries on traveling to most places on earth, postcards from other travelers, and the Thorn Tree bulletin board, where you can ask questions before you go or dispense advice when you get back. You can also find travel news and updates to many of our most popular guidebooks, and the subWWWay section links you to the most useful travel resources elsewhere on the Web.

W www.hawaii-nation.org
Hawaii, Independent and Proud, is one of many Hawaiian sovereignty sites. Go here for activism updates and archives.

W www.aloha-hawaii.com
This award-winning Hawaii Webzine has features on Hawaiian culture.

W www.geocities.com/~olelo/hula.html
Nâ 'Ao 'ao Hula (The Hula Pages) allow you to dive into the sacred heart of the dance.

W www.ohanapages.com
Hawaii's Online Community is a fount of knowledge from planning a wedding to table tennis facilities.

In addition, **W** www.hawaii.com, **W** www.planet-hawaii.com and **W** www.alternative-hawaii.com have useful links to a wealth of information, and **W** www.kamuela.com has everything concerning goings-on-about that town. Other Web sites are given throughout this book under specific topics.

BOOKS

There are so many outstanding books about Hawaii, it would be Sisyphian to try and list them all here. Visit your favorite brick-and-mortar or cyber library to get some more ideas. Note that 'UH Press' in this section refers to the University of Hawaii Press in Honolulu.

Most books are published in different editions by different publishers in different countries. As a result, a book that's a hard-cover rarity in one country may be readily available in paperback in another. Fortunately, bookstores and libraries can search by title or author, so your local biblio-outpost is the best place to find out about the following recommendations. The Internet also harbors several efficient search engines, some of which allow you to purchase books online.

Lonely Planet

If you plan on island-hopping, see Lonely Planet's *Hawaii* guide, which covers every island large and small. Those fortunate enough to be heading to the Valley Isle should pick up Lonely Planet's stellar *Maui* guide, which includes information for Molokai and Lanai. If Waikiki or other Oahu spots figure in your itinerary, check out Lonely Planet's *Oahu*.

Activity Guides

Diving & Snorkeling Hawaii by Casey & Astrid Witte Mahaney (Lonely Planet Pisces Books), with site descriptions and a marine life identification glossary, is an excellent guide for underwater explorations. A brilliantly photographed and annotated guide for anything in Poseidon's realm is Ann Fielding and Ed Robinson's *An Underwater Guide to Hawaii* (UH Press). Divers might also check out Dick Dresie's *Let's Go Shore Dive'n*.

Slightly dated but still a great, informed resource is John Clark's *Beaches of the Big Island* (UH Press).

Hawaii Trails, by Wilderness Press, is a comprehensive hiking guide with respectable maps and clear directions. Another favorite is Craig Chisolm's *Hawaii, The Big Island Hiking Trails* (The Fernglen Press).

Anyone up for some single track fun should see John Alford's *Mountain Biking the Hawaiian Islands* (Ohana Publishing). Coverage includes trail descriptions and maps, outfitting and shipping and maintaining your rig.

Readable and engaging, the *Surfer's Guide to Hawaii: Hawaii Gets All the Breaks* by Greg Ambrose (Bess Press) describes five top Big Island surfing spots.

History & Politics

Hawaiian Antiquities by David Malo (Bishop Museum Press), written in 1838, was the first account of Hawaiian culture penned by a Hawaiian.

The perennial favorite *Shoal of Time* by Gavan Daws (UH Press) is a comprehensive and colorful history covering the period from Captain Cook's 'discovery' of the islands to statehood.

Hawaii's Story by Hawaii's Queen by Queen Lili'uokalani (Mutual Publishing), is an autobiographical account of Lili'uokalani's life and the dastardly circumstances surrounding her 1893 overthrow. Another good resource for the period from Polynesian settlement to the overthrow is Michael Dougherty's *To Steal a Kingdom* (Island Press).

The Hawaiian Kingdom by Ralph S Kuykendall (UH Press) is a three-volume set covering Hawaiian history from 1778 to 1893. It's considered the definitive work on the period.

OA Bushnell is one of the best-known contemporary authors writing about Hawaii. UH Press has published many of his titles; try *The Return of Lono*, a historical novel of Captain Cook's final voyage.

With more than 40 groups involved in the movement, Hawaiian sovereignty is a tangled issue. For an overview of this complex cause from a variety of viewpoints, see the anthology *He Alo He Alo (Face to Face): Hawaiian Voices on Sovereignty* (American Friends Service Committee).

Flora & Fauna

The Many-Splendored Fishes of Hawaii by Gar Goodson (Stanford University Press) is a handy, inexpensive book; it has lucid descriptions and 170 color drawings.

Hawaii's Birds (Hawaii Audubon Society) is the best pocket-size guide to the birds of Hawaii. It includes color photos and descriptions of all the native birds and many introduced species.

Mammals in Hawaii by P Quentin Tomich (Bishop Museum Press) is an authoritative book on Hawaii's mammals, including all whale and dolphin species.

Hawaiian Culture

The Kumulipo by Martha Beckwith (UH Press) is a translation of the Hawaiian creation chant. Also see Beckwith's comprehensive *Hawaiian Mythology*.

The Legends and Myths of Hawaii (Mutual Publishing) is a collection of legends as told by King David Kalakaua.

Legacy of the Landscape by Patrick Vinton Kirch (UH Press) is a fascinating and detailed treatment of 50 of the most important Hawaiian archaeological sites, including heiau, fishponds and petroglyphs.

With captivating photos, *Aloha Cowboy* by Virginia Cowan-Smith and Bonnie Domrose Stone (UH Press) is an informative account of 200 years of Hawaiian *paniolo* (cowboy) life.

Pidgin-Language Books What do you call a malahini learning to speak pidgin? Answer: a training brah! If you didn't laugh at that joke, you need to learn some important vernacular with *Pidgin to Da Max Hana Hou* (Peppovision) by Douglas Simonson. Once schooled in the basics, you'll be ready for *Da Word* (Bamboo Ridge Press) by Lee A. Tonouchi, a collection of short stories in pidgin.

Travelogues

Classics worth a read include Isabella Bird's *Six Months in the Sandwich Islands*; *Mark Twain in Hawaii* by that author; and *Stories of Hawaii* by Jack London. An excellent anthology with selections by these writers, plus Captain Cook, Somerset Maugham, David Malo and others is *A Hawaiian Reader*, edited by A Grove Day and Carl Stroven (Mutual Publishing).

In *Volcano: A Memoir*, Garrett Hongo's poetic prose dances off the page as he rediscovers his Big Island birthplace. Lacing the descriptive text are explorations of setting, mind, body and soul – no fluffy beach reading this.

With a Big Island backdrop, the *Curse of Lono* by Hunter S. Thompson and Ralph Steadman is non-stop, aloha-style, drug-addled antics. Even if you're not into his shtick, Thompson's big fish score in Kona, ill-advised bravado and bivouacking in a shoreline shack is pretty hilarious.

FILMS

One of the few movies to insightfully delve into island life is *Picture Bride* (1995). Filmed on the Big Island, it depicts the realities of Hawaiian plantation life for a 19th-century Japanese mail-order bride, albeit with a touch of cinematic license.

Vintage movies filmed on the Big Island include *Song of the Islands* (1942), starring Betty Grable, Victor Mature and Hilo Hattie and *The Old Man and the Sea* (1958), starring Spencer Tracy.

More recently, Kevin Costner's big washout, *Waterworld*, (1995) was filmed in Big Island waters, and the opening sequence of *Planet of the Apes* (2001) was filmed on the lava flows of Puna.

NEWSPAPERS & MAGAZINES

Hilo's *Hawaii Tribune-Herald* is published daily except Saturday and is a good source for local happenings. Kailua-Kona's tabloid-format *West Hawaii Today* has decent international coverage and the daily vog index. Both cost 50¢ on weekdays, $1 on Sundays.

Alternatively, there's the free *Hawaii Island Journal*, a locally-owned, bimonthly paper. It has good general interest stories, entertainment listings and Tom Tomorrow. The *Waimea Gazette* is a handsome monthly published in the upcountry.

Several mainland newspapers are also available (however dated and pricey), including the *Wall Street Journal* and the *Los Angeles Times*. Look for them in fancy hotel lobbies and better bookstores. You can get international newspapers such as the *London Times*, *Sydney Morning Herald*, *O'Globo* and others at Borders, which carries an impressive selection. Magazine choices are what you'd expect in any city of respectable size, including a dizzying array of outdoor sports titles.

Homegrown publications include the infinitely entertaining *Hawaii Fishing News*. In addition to tide information, fishing conditions and the catches of the month (man alive, some of these beasts weigh half a ton!), they have the hilarious Holoholo Style section, where locals write in with their fish tales and pictures as proof.

RADIO & TV

You can find Hawaii National Public Radio (NPR) at 91.1 FM. For Hawaiian music, try local favorite KAPA 100.3 FM in Hilo, 99.1 FM in Kona. Jammin' 107.7 FM plays hip-hop, R&B and old school grooves, while K-Hawaii (92.7 FM in Hilo or 101.5 in Kona) covers 'classic' rock. News, talk and sports fans should tune to KPUA 670 AM.

All the major US networks broadcast on Hawaiian TV channels. Almost anything you can watch on the mainland you can watch here, unfortunate as that may be. Cable channel 9 is Hawaii's Aloha frequency, showing Big Island highlights 24-7.

Most island residents, as well as condos and hotels, have cable or satellite TV. Except for Monday Night Football, few sporting events are tape delayed – nothing like a noon Knicks game!

PHOTOGRAPHY & VIDEO
Film & Equipment

Both print and slide film are readily available here. Disposable underwater cameras costing about $10 are sold everywhere and deliver surprisingly good snaps.

If you're on the Big Island for any length of time, have your film developed here, as the high temperature and humidity greatly accelerate the deterioration of exposed film. Generally, the sooner it's developed, the better. Once developed, get your prints and negatives into plastic fast, to avoid tackiness and curling.

Longs Drugs is one of the cheapest places for developing film and they offer frequent free second-set deals. All the main tourist enclaves have one-hour print shops.

With the implementation of high-powered X-ray at many airports, don't pack film into checked luggage or carry-on bags. Instead carry your film in a baggie to show separately to airport security officials (known as a hand check). Remember to finish off the roll in your camera and take it out, too, or those photos may end up foggy.

Video Systems

Videotapes can be readily purchased throughout Hawaii. North America uses the NTSC system, which is incompatible with the PAL system used in Europe or French SECAM standards.

TIME

Hawaii doesn't observe Daylight Saving Time. When it's noon in Hawaii, it's 2pm in Los Angeles, 5pm in New York and Havana, 10pm in London, 7am the next day in Tokyo and 8am the next day in Melbourne.

The time difference is one hour greater during those months when other countries *are* observing daylight saving time – for example, from the first Sunday in April to the last Sunday in October in North America.

Of course, there's always 'Island Time,' which means that everything happens a tad slower here; it's also a handy excuse for being late.

ELECTRICITY

The USA, like Canada, operates on 110V, 60-cycle electric power. US electronics have a plug with two flat, vertical prongs (the same as in Canada and Mexico) or sometimes a three-pronger with the added ground. Note that gadgets built for higher voltage and cycles (such as 220/240V, 50-cycle appliances from Europe) will function poorly. Visitors from outside North America should bring a universal plug adapter if they wish to use their own small appliances or toys.

WEIGHTS & MEASURES

Hawaii uses the US system of measurement. Distances are measured in feet, yards and miles; weights are tallied in ounces, pounds and tons. The conversion table on the inside back cover of this book is designed to acquaint metric-minded folks with the holdover US system.

LAUNDRY

Many hotels, condominiums and hostels have coin-operated washers and dryers. There are also commercial coin-operated laundries in bigger towns such as Hilo, Pahoa, Kona and Waimea. The average cost is about $1 to wash a load of clothes and another dollar to dry.

HEALTH

Overall, the Big Island is a very healthy place to live and visit. Hawaii ranks first of all the 50 US states in life expectancy, currently about 76 years for men and 81 years for women.

There are few serious health concerns, though the dengue fever outbreak in late 2001 necessitated visits from the Centers for Disease Control (CDC). At the time of writing, no cases were positively identified on the Big Island, but there were more than 80 cases statewide. Visitors should be aware of the possibility of infection via mosquitoes and take precautions against being bitten. Stay tuned to outbreak developments and see the CDC dengue fever Web page for the latest: **w** www.cdc.gov/ncidod/dvbid/dengue/index.htm.

No immunizations are required to enter the USA, including Hawaii, but you should have adequate health insurance before setting out. See Travel Insurance under Visas & Documents earlier in this chapter.

Tap water is not always safe to drink on the windward side, where rain catchments take advantage of crying skies; if you're on a catchment system, make sure there's a good filter system before drinking from the faucet. Most grocery and health food stores have machines dispensing purified water for $0.50 a gallon. Alternatively, there are county water pumps by the side of the road where you can fill up for free.

There are many poisonous plants in Hawaii, and only an idiot would sample a plant they couldn't positively identify as edible.

Medical Problems & Treatment

The Big Island has six hospitals providing acute and outpatient care. Still, for specialized care (including eye problems) and serious illnesses, many islanders have more confidence in Honolulu hospitals than in neighboring island facilities.

Leptospirosis A common danger in Hawaii is leptospirosis, a nasty disease caused by bacteria found in freshwater. Animals such as rats, mongooses and wild pigs are carriers. Humans contract leptospirosis by swimming or wading in water contaminated by animal urine. Leptospires can exist in any freshwater source, including idyllic-looking waterfalls and jungle streams.

The bacteria enter the body through the nose, eyes, mouth or cuts in the skin. Symptoms can occur two to 20 days after exposure and may include fever, chills, sweating, headaches, muscle pains, vomiting and diarrhea. More severe symptoms include blood in the urine and jaundice. Symptoms may last from a few days to several weeks; fatalities are rare.

A few dozen cases statewide are confirmed each year; wetland taro farmers, swimmers and backcountry hikers account for the majority of them.

Some precautions include wearing waterproof *tabis* (reef walkers) when hiking, and avoiding unnecessary freshwater crossings, especially if you have open cuts.

Sunburn Sunburn is always a concern in the tropics, as the closer you get to the equator, the fewer of the sun's rays are blocked by the atmosphere. Don't be lulled into complacency by overcast days – you can get sunburned even through clouds. This is especially true at high altitudes.

Sunscreen with an SPF (sun protection factor) of at least 15 is recommended. If you're headed for the water, use a water-resistant sunscreen. Snorkelers should wear a T-shirt if they plan on a long day in the water.

The fair-skinned among us can get both first- and second-degree burns in the Hawaiian sun, and wearing a hat is advisable. Sensitive lips can be protected with lip balm containing sun block.

Prickly Heat Prickly heat is an itchy rash caused by excessive perspiration trapped under the skin. It usually strikes people who have just arrived in a hot climate and whose pores have not yet opened sufficiently to cope with greater sweating. Keeping cool by bathing often or resorting to air-con may help until you acclimatize.

Heat Exhaustion Dehydration or salt deficiency can cause heat exhaustion. Take time to acclimatize and make sure you drink sufficient liquids. Don't rely on being thirsty as a gauge for when to hit the water bottle: by the time your body registers thirst, you're already about two quarts dehydrated. Not needing to urinate is a danger sign, as is very dark urine.

Salt deficiency is characterized by fatigue, lethargy, headaches, giddiness and muscle cramps, and while salt tablets may help, adding salt to your food is a better preliminary step. Vomiting or diarrhea can deplete your liquid and salt levels, when fluid replacement becomes imperative. Be sure to drink at least the volume of fluids being lost and watch closely for signs of dehydration.

Heat Stroke This serious, sometimes fatal, condition can occur if the body's heat-regulating mechanism breaks down and the body temperature rises to dangerous levels. Long, continuous periods of exposure to high temperatures can leave you vulnerable to heat stroke. Avoid strenuous activity in open sun (such as lengthy hikes across lava fields) when you first arrive.

The symptoms of heat stroke include very little perspiration and a high body temperature (102°F to 106°F). Where sweating has ceased, the skin becomes flushed and red. Severe, throbbing headaches and lack of coordination will also occur, and the sufferer may be confused or aggressive. Eventually the victim may become delirious or convulse. Hospitalization is essential, but in the meantime, you can help by getting sufferers out of the sun, removing their clothing, covering them with a wet sheet or towel and fanning them continuously.

Altitude Sickness People planning on trips to the Mauna Kea or Mauna Loa summits need to be aware of the possibility of Acute Mountain Sickness (AMS), which occurs at altitudes above 8200 feet. The

Onizuka Visitor Center on Mauna Kea is located above 9200 feet, so even here, only part way to the summit, symptoms of AMS may occur and acclimatization is essential.

While AMS can generally be avoided by making slow gains in elevation, Hawaii presents an unusual situation, as most people who visit Mauna Kea do so by car. Many of those visitors drive straight up to nearly 14,000 feet from their hotels on the coast, a mere two-hour ride that offers zero acclimatization time. As a result, AMS is a common problem for summit visitors, even though most cases are fairly tame.

The effects of altitude may be mild or severe and occur because less oxygen reaches the muscles and the brain at high elevations, requiring the heart, lungs and brain to compensate by working harder. Note that children may be more likely to suffer altitude sickness than adults. Pregnant women and individuals with cardiac, pulmonary, high blood pressure or weight problems should consult a physician before hiking at these altitudes.

Mild symptoms of AMS include headache, lethargy, dizziness and shortness of breath. AMS may become more severe without warning and can be fatal. There is no hard-and-fast rule as to what is too high: AMS has been fatal at 9800 feet, although 11,500 to 14,700 feet is the usual danger zone.

Treat mild symptoms by resting at the same altitude until acclimatized – typically a minimum of 30 minutes. Paracetamol or aspirin can be taken for headaches. Other common sense suggestions for tempering mild effects of high altitude include drinking lots of fluids, eating light food that's high in carbohydrates and avoiding alcohol. If symptoms persist or become worse, however, *immediate descent is necessary*; going down even 1500 feet can help. Drug treatments should never be used to avoid descent or to enable further ascent.

For more information, see Dangers & Annoyances in the Saddle Road and Hawaii Volcanoes National Park chapters.

Jet Lag Jet lag is experienced when a person flies across more than three time zones. It occurs because many of the functions of the human body (eg, temperature, pulse rate and emptying of the bladder) are regulated by internal 24-hour cycles. When we travel long distances rapidly, our bodies need time to adjust to the 'new time' of our destination and we may experience fatigue, disorientation, insomnia, anxiety, impaired concentration and appetite loss. These effects usually disappear within three days of arrival. To minimize jet lag:

- Rest for a couple of days prior to departure; try to avoid late night bon voyage bashes.
- Select flight schedules that minimize sleep deprivation; arriving late in the day means you can go to sleep soon after arrival. For very long flights, try to organize a stopover.
- Avoid excessive eating (which bloats the stomach) and alcohol (which causes dehydration) during the flight. Instead, drink plenty of water.
- Try to sleep at the appropriate time for the time zone of your destination.
- Set your watch to the local time of your destination as soon as you're aboard the plane.

HIV & AIDS Infection with the human immunodeficiency virus (HIV) may lead to acquired immune deficiency syndrome (AIDS), which is a fatal disease. Any exposure to blood, blood products or body fluids may put you at risk. The disease is often transmitted through sexual contact or contaminated needles – vaccinations, acupuncture, tattooing and body-piercing can be potentially as dangerous as intravenous drug use.

If you have any questions regarding AIDS while on Hawaii, or if you need referrals, support or general information, contact the AIDS/STD Hotline at ☎ 800-321-1555, the AIDS Hotline for Counseling & Information at ☎ 800-590-2437, the Big Island AIDS Project in Hilo at ☎ 981-2428 or the West Hawaii AIDS Foundation in Kona at ☎ 331-8177.

Sexually Transmitted Diseases Gonorrhea, herpes and syphilis are among these diseases. Sores, blisters or rashes around the genitals, discharges, or pain when urinating are sure signs something is wrong. In some STDs, such as chlamydia and HPV (the virus that causes genital warts), symptoms may be less obvious or not observed at all, especially in women. Syphilis symptoms eventually disappear completely but the disease continues and can cause severe problems in later years.

While abstinence is the only 100% effective prevention (as if!), using condoms can also be effective. Gonorrhea and syphilis are treated with antibiotics. There is no cure for warts, herpes or AIDS.

Pesky Creatures The Big Island is snake-free, but it has its fair share of mosquitoes as well as long, fat centipedes that deliver unpleasant bites. The island also has bees and ground-nesting wasps, which generally pose danger only to those allergic to their stings. (For information on stinging sea creatures, see Ocean Safety under Dangers & Annoyances, later.)

Huge, omnipresent and airborne, Hawaiian cockroaches are like something from a bad Japanese horror flick. Although they don't pose a health problem, they do little for the appetite.

While sightings are not terribly common, there are two dangerous arachnids on the islands: the black widow spider and the scorpion. If you're bitten by either of these, seek immediate help.

Mosquitoes Usually, mosquitoes bites are temporary, itchy messes that can be treated topically with Tiger Balm, lavender or over-the-counter preparations. However, with the 2001 dengue fever outbreak in Hawaii, folks should take steps to limit their exposure to potentially infected skeeters.

Signs and symptoms of dengue include a sudden onset of high fever, intense headache, joint and muscle pains, nausea and vomiting; sometimes a rash of small red spots appears three to four days after the onset of fever. In the early phase, dengue may be mistaken for other diseases, including malaria and influenza. Full recovery from dengue fever may be prolonged, with tiredness lasting for several weeks. If you think you may be infected, seek medical attention quickly, including a blood test. Aspirin should be avoided, as it increases the risk of hemorrhaging. There is neither vaccine nor cure for dengue, so prevention is your best strategy for avoiding infection.

Ciguatera Poisoning Ciguatera is a serious illness caused by eating fish affected by ciguatoxin, which herbivorous fish can pick up from marine algae. Symptoms of food poisoning usually occur three to five hours after eating.

Ciguatoxin is most common among reef fish (which are not typically served in restaurants) and hasn't affected Hawaii's deep-sea fish, such as tuna, marlin and mahimahi. Symptoms can include nausea; stomach cramps; diarrhea; paralysis; tingling and numbness of the face, fingers and toes; and a reversal of temperature sensations, so that hot things feel cold and vice versa. Extreme cases can result in unconsciousness and even death. Vomit until your stomach is empty and get immediate medical help.

Fishermen and foragers should get the free brochure published by the Department of Land and Natural Resources Aquatic Division, listing affected fish and where they're found. For information, call ☎ 974-6201 or visit Ⓦ www.cigua.com for useful links.

WOMEN TRAVELERS

Hawaii presents few unique problems for women travelers and may even be more relaxed and comfortable than many mainland destinations. The one area in which women – especially solo travelers – might feel uneasy is in local bars. In any culture the world over, a scene involving bunches of men knocking back liquor can get dicey, so proceed to local watering holes with a group or with your wits fully about you.

Hitchhiking around the Big Island can be an effective way to move about, but LP does not recommend hitching, especially when alone. Hitching with a buddy can provide peace of mind should you find yourself squeezed in the back seat with a stringy haired dropout at the wheel. If you *do* decide to hitchhike, size up the vehicle's occupants carefully and don't think twice about turning down anyone who makes you feel uncomfortable. Listening to your instincts is one of your best defenses no matter the situation.

If you're camping, opt for popular, well-used camping areas over isolated locales. County parks and campgrounds are notorious for late night beer binges and some (like Isaac Hale south of Pahoa) are known for long-term squatting and may be unpleasant for solo travelers. Beach parties can foster malevolent rowdiness, so women walking alone on beaches after dark will be well served to be alert to any nefarious, drunken vibes floating their way.

GAY & LESBIAN TRAVELERS

The Big Island is not a gay destination per se; in terms of queer nightlife, there is none (the single gay bar here was for sale at the time of writing). Everyday queer life, though, is rich, with picnics, potlucks and organized outdoor adventures creating a sense of community and family. Indeed, the Big Island has a particularly tight lesbian community and interested sisters should consult the rainbow wireless: ask around and you'll find friends. Also keep an eye open for the Wyld Womyn's Weekend, an extravaganza of live entertainment, workshops and beachfront camping that moves from island to island each year.

Kalani Honua in Puna (see that chapter for details) hosts many retreats geared to the gay community.

Pacific Ocean Holidays (☎ 923-2400, 800-735-6600, fax 923-2499), PO Box 88245, Honolulu, HI 96830, arranges vacation packages for gay men and women. The company also produces a booklet called *Pocket Guide to Hawaii*, which is geared to the gay community and costs $5 by mail.

For links to a variety of gay and lesbian sites covering travel, entertainment, politics and more, browse W www.gayhawaii.com. Purple Roofs (W www.purpleroofs.com) has a fantastic on-line directory of queer-friendly accommodations.

Although Hawaii was enticingly close to legalizing gay marriages in 1996, the legislation was ultimately defeated, though a progressive (for the US) domestic partner law was enacted in 1997.

DISABLED TRAVELERS

Overall, the Big Island is a relatively accommodating destination, with many accessible activities and places to stay. The Kona side is easier to navigate than the Hilo side, which simply doesn't have comparable tourist traffic or infrastructure. However, at the Kona airport, passengers disembark directly onto the tarmac via stairs, so call ahead to make specific arrangements if this poses a problem.

Most large hotels and resorts have elevators, TTD-capable phones, wheelchair-accessible rooms, and other features to smooth the way. The Hele-On bus system (☎ 961-8744) extends large monthly discounts (up to 33%) to disabled travelers.

Seeing eye and guide dogs are not subject to the same quarantine as run-of-the-mill pets, provided they meet the Department of Agriculture's minimum requirements; see W www.hawaiiag.org/hdoa/ai_aqs_info.htm for the complete story.

The Commission on Persons with Disabilities (☎ 808-586-8121 in Honolulu), 919 Ala Moana Blvd, Rm 101, Honolulu, HI, 96814 distributes the three part Aloha Guide to Accessibility. Part I contains general information and is obtainable free by mail. Parts II and III ($15) detail beach, park, shopping center and visitor attraction accessibility and list hotels with wheelchair access or specially adapted facilities.

Accessible Vans of Hawaii (☎ 800-303-3750, W www.accessiblevanshawaii.com,), 296 Alamaha St, Ste C, Kalahui, Maui, 96732, is a well-regarded organization that books accommodations and personal assistants, rents accessible vans and arranges various activities for disabled travelers.

Travelers should also pack their disabled parking placard or apply for a new one upon arrival. Placards are available, with a doctor's note, from the Mayor's office in Hilo (☎ 961-8223), 25 Aupuni St, Rm 217. For a list of services available to disabled passengers by airline, go to W www.every body.co.uk/airindex.htm.

SENIOR TRAVELERS

Kupuna (elders) are accorded much respect, and the average life expectancy for Hawaii's residents is four years longer than anywhere on the mainland.

Generally, visitors over the age of 65 can qualify for big discounts on transportation and entry to attractions, historic sites, museums and cinemas. Some hotels and motels may also offer reductions – it's worth inquiring. The National Park sells a $10 lifetime pass for visitors 62 years and older.

Elderhostel (☎ 978-323-4141, 877-426-8056, W www.elderhostel.org), 11 Avenue de Lafayette, Boston, MA 02111-1746, is a nonprofit organization offering study vacations for those 55 or older. It runs programs investigating everything from Hawaiian culture to the environment. Trips start at $1400 for two weeks, including accommodations, meals and classes (but not airfare). For more information, see W www.bishop museum.org/vac/elderbigisl.html

For those over 50, the American Association of Retired Persons (AARP; ☎ 800-424-3410), PO Box 199, Long Beach, CA 90801, offers travel information and substantial savings on auto and medical travel insurance. The annual membership costs $10, but the Web site (W www.aarp.org) resources are free. AARP has an office on the Big Island (☎ 334-1212), PO Box 2078, Kailua-Kona, HI 96745. Members of the Canadian Association of Retired Persons (CARP; ☎ 800-363-9736, W www.50plus.com) can also qualify for discounts.

The YMCA offers some superb water classes and the myriad steam baths and hot ponds around the national park are a few ways to soothe tired bones.

TRAVEL WITH CHILDREN

Hawaii is a superlative family destination as it offers adventurous activities galore, accessible cross-cultural opportunities, plus all the necessary amenities to stave off crankiness: food for the finicky, video arcades and loads of bugs to mess around with.

Be aware that some B&Bs and historic inns prohibit kiddies *(keiki)*, so it's important to inquire about their policies before making reservations. On the flipside, many boutique inns provide futons for kids, so don't reject these out of hand.

For those vacationing with children, Lonely Planet's *Travel with Children* by Cathy Lanigan has lots of valuable tips and interesting anecdotes written by mom-and-pop travelers from all over the world.

If you're traveling with infants and come up short, Baby's Away (☎ 800-996-9030, on the Big Island, W www.babysaway.com) rents cribs, strollers, playpens, high chairs, gates and more. Pacific Rent-All in Hilo (☎ 935-2974), 1080 Kilauea St, rents children's car seats for $7/21/35 and cribs for $9/18/36 for a day/week/month.

Look for activities specifically for kids like Snuba Doo, a program for kids ages four and up, offered by Kona Snuba outfits. Hawaii Volcanoes National Park also has a junior ranger program. See those chapters for details.

USEFUL ORGANIZATIONS

The American Automobile Association (AAA; ☎ 808-593-2221 on Oahu, 800-736-2886, W www.aaa-hawaii.com), 1270 Ala Moana Blvd in Honolulu, provides members with Hawaii information and maps and extends roadside assistance (☎ 800-222-4357). AAA members are also entitled to car, hotel and other discounts. A first-time annual membership starts at $75.

Entertainment (☎ 800-374-4464) travel club publishes an annual membership book good for 50% discounts at participating hotels and coupons for sightseeing activities and two-for-one meals. Entertainment books are sold by mail-order or at various outlets in Hawaii, including Borders bookstore. The coupons are good for one calendar year starting 1 November.

Another travel club, Encore (☎ 800-638-0930) offers 50% off accommodations at member hotels and resorts. An annual membership costs $70 to $100 and is valid for 12 months from the date of enrollment. However, many business refuse to honor travel club discounts during peak season and some hotels may not accept reservations more than 30 days in advance, so you'll have to be flexible.

LIBRARIES

Hawaii has a fabulous statewide system of public libraries, with nearly 50 branches. Visitors can check out books with a Hawaii library card; a non-renewable visitor's card valid for three months costs $10. A non-resident library card ($25) is valid for five years and is renewable. Not only is the same library card good at all branches, but you can borrow a book at one branch and return it at another – even on another island.

The Big Island has branches in Hilo, Laupahoehoe, Honoka'a, Waimea, Kapa'au, Kailua-Kona, Holualoa, Kealakekua, Na'alehu, Pahala, Pahoa, Mountain View and Kea'au. Most have excellent Hawaiiana sections and subscribe to Hawaii and mainland newspapers and magazines. For information on library Internet access, see Internet Resources earlier.

DANGERS & ANNOYANCES
Theft & Violence

For the most part, Hawaii is a relatively safe place. Crime is lower here than in most of the US mainland. That said, break-ins and car theft are quite common and rental cars are big-time targets. Don't leave anything of value in your car (or lock it in the trunk before you set out). Many locals leave their car doors unlocked to avoid paying for busted windows.

Ocean Safety

Drowning is the leading cause of accidental death in Hawaii, with an average of 60 people (visitors and residents) drowning annually.

It's best not to swim alone in any unknown place. If you're not familiar with local water conditions, ask someone who is. This can't be overstated. Lifeguards, surfers and beach regulars are helpful – they'd rather apprise you of conditions than pull you out later.

Dangerous Surf Shorebreaks – waves that break close to or directly on shore – form when ocean swells pass abruptly from deep to shallow waters. If only a couple of feet high, they're generally fine for novice bodysurfers, but leave more gnarly ones to the experts. Large shorebreaks can result in broken bones, neck injuries, dislocated shoulders and loss of wind.

Rip currents are fast-flowing ocean currents and are most common in conditions of high surf, but can occur almost anytime. Rips form when waves are coming in faster than they can flow out, so the water runs along the shoreline until it finds an escape route out to sea. Swimmers caught in a rip can be swept out before they even realize it. Anyone caught in one should either go with the flow until it loses power, (usually necessitating going farther out to sea), or swim parallel to the shore to slip out of it. Trying to swim directly against a rip current toward shore can exhaust (and then drown) even the strongest swimmers. Usually you can see a rip from shore as it collides with other normal or rip currents.

Undertows are common along steeply sloped beaches when large waves backwash directly into incoming surf. The outflowing water picks up speed as it flows down the slopes. When it hits an incoming wave it pulls under it, creating an undertow. Swimmers caught in an undertow can be pulled beneath the surface. The most important thing is not to panic. Go with the current until you get beyond the wave.

STRONG CURRENT   MAN-OF-WAR   SHARP CORAL

HIGH SURF   DANGEROUS SHOREBREAK   WAVES ON LEDGE

Never turn your back on the ocean. Waves don't all come in with equal height or strength. An abnormally high 'rogue wave' can sweep over shoreline ledges or tear up onto beaches. You need to be particularly cautious during high tide and in stormy weather or high surf.

Coral Cuts Most coral cuts occur when swimmers are pushed onto a reef by rough waves or surges. Wearing diving gloves when snorkeling over shallow reefs can mitigate this. Avoid walking on coral, which can cut your feet and damage the coral.

Because living animal matter gets left behind in coral cuts, they can take a painfully long time to heal. If you do get cut, wash the wound thoroughly with soap and water, then a half-water solution of hydrogen peroxide. Follow with an anti-bacterial topical gel and cover the wound with a dry, non-adhesive dressing. Repeat cleaning and dressing twice daily until healed.

Jellyfish Peek before you plunge, as these gelatinous creatures, with saclike bodies and stinging tentacles, are fairly common here. They're most apt to be seen eight to 10 days after the full moon, when they come into shallow waters starting in the morning.

The pain from a sting varies from mild to severe, depending on the variety of jellyfish. Unless you have an allergic reaction to their venom, though, the stings are not dangerous. The generally accepted treatment for stings is rinsing the affected area with water and applying ice for pain. Seek medical attention for serious reactions.

Portuguese Man-of-War The body of a Portuguese man-of-war consists of a translucent, bluish, bladder-like float, which in Hawaii generally grows to four or five inches long. Known locally as 'bluebottles,' they're most often found on the windward coasts, particularly after storms.

The sting of a Portuguese man-of-war is very painful and you're likely to get multiple stings, as they have clusters of long tentacles. Each tentacle contains hundreds of stinging cells that can be up to 75% as toxic

as cobra venom. Even touching a bluebottle a few hours after it's washed up onshore can result in burning stings.

If you do get stung, quickly remove the tentacles, *using a stick or gloved hand,* and thoroughly wash the area with seawater or fresh water (do not use vinegar, urine or alcohol).

Man-of-war

Do not rub the area. Apply ice for pain. For serious reactions, including chest pains or difficulty in breathing, seek medical attention immediately.

Sharks Unpleasant encounters with sharks are unlikely. About 40 varieties of sharks are endemic to Hawaiian waters, including the nonaggressive whale shark, which can reach lengths of 50 feet. Nevertheless, in recent years, increasing numbers of shark attacks have been reported in Hawaii, with serious attacks now occurring on average two or three times a year.

The most dangerous specimens here are the tiger and Galapagos sharks. The tiger shark, which averages 12 to 18 feet in length, is identified by its blunt nose and vertical bars along its side. The Galapagos shark is harder to identify, but in shallow water, any large grey shark over six feet long probably qualifies. Scalloped hammerhead sharks are also known to be agressive.

Should you encounter a shark, the best thing to do is move casually and quietly away. Don't panic, as sharks are attracted by thrashing.

Thumping or kicking an attacking shark on the nose or sticking your fingers into its eyes may confuse it long enough to give you time to escape. Indeed, some divers who dive in shark waters carry a billy club or bang stick.

Other Sea Creatures Encounters with venomous sea creatures in Hawaiian waters are rather rare. You should, however, learn to recognize scorpionfish and lionfish, two related species that can inject venom through their dorsal spines if touched. Both are sometimes found in quite shallow water.

The Hawaiian lionfish, which grows up to 10 inches long, is striking, with vertical orange and white stripes and feathery appendages that contain poisonous spines. It likes to drift along reefs, particularly at night. The scorpionfish has shorter and less obvious spines, is about six inches in length, and tends to sit immobile on the ocean bottom or on ledges.

The sting from either can cause a sharp burning pain, followed by numbness around the area, nausea and headaches. Immediately stick the affected area in water that is as hot as bearable and go for medical treatment.

The *wana*, or spiny sea urchin, has long brittle spines that can puncture the skin and break off, causing burning, numbness and infection. The spines sometimes inflict a toxin and can cause extreme muscle spasms, difficulty in breathing and even collapse. You can try to remove the spines with tweezers or by soaking them in hot water, but more serious cases may require surgical removal.

Cone shells should be left alone. There's no safe way of picking up a live cone shell, as the animal inside has a long harpoonlike tail that can dart out and reach anywhere on its shell to deliver a painful or even fatally venomous sting. The wound should be soaked in hot water and medical attention sought immediately.

The *puhi*, or moray eel, is often spotted by snorkelers around reefs and coral heads. Eels don't attack, but will protect themselves by clamping down with razor-sharp teeth and refusing to let go if someone sticks a hand in their door while poking around reef crevices or holes.

Tsunamis

Hawaii has had a tsunami every 10 years or so over the last century, and they've killed more people statewide than all other natural disasters combined. When they hit, they usually hit hard, prompting evacuation and causing severe damage. That said, it's pretty unlikely you'll experience one.

Earthquakes, typhoons or volcanic eruptions can cause tsunamis (Japanese for 'harbor wave'). Tsunamis are *not* tidal waves, which are caused by the gravitational pull of the sun and moon on the sea. The largest tsunami to ever hit Hawaii made landfall north of Hilo on April 1, 1946. The result of a 7.4 earthquake in the Aleutian Islands, the waves reached a height of 55.8 feet, swept away entire villages and killed 159 people. Hawaii promptly installed a modern tsunami warning system, which is aired through speakers around the islands. They're tested on the first business day of each month at 11:45am.

Tsunamis can also be caused by nearby earthquakes or volcanic eruptions. For these there may be scant warning. Any earthquake strong enough to have you reaching to steady yourself is a natural tsunami warning. If you're in a low-lying coastal area when one occurs, head for higher ground immediately. Surfers are warned against yielding to their big wave dreams, which will quickly turn to a nightmare in the face of these giants.

EMERGENCIES

Dial ☎ 911 for police, ambulance and fire emergencies. The inside front cover of island phone books lists vital service agencies, such as poison control, Coast Guard rescue and various crisis lines. The 24-hour sexual assault hotline can be reached by dialing ☎ 935-0677.

If you lose your passport, contact your consulate in Honolulu; a complete list of consulate phone numbers can be found in the telephone book yellow pages.

For refunds on lost or stolen American Express traveler's checks, call ☎ 800-221-7282; for MasterCard traveler's checks, dial ☎ 800-223-9920. For other types of theft, if you plan to file an insurance claim, contact the nearest police station immediately for an incident report.

LEGAL MATTERS

Anyone arrested on the Big Island is (theoretically) innocent until proven guilty and has the right to a lawyer, from their arrest to their trial. The Hawaii State Bar Association (☎ 888-808-4722, toll free) makes referrals; foreign visitors may want to call their consulate for advice.

In Hawaii, anyone driving with a blood alcohol level of .08% or higher is guilty of driving 'under the influence,' which carries severe penalties. Driving while on any substance, be it beer, buds or barbiturates, is a decidedly bad idea. As with most places, the possession of marijuana and narcotics is illegal in Hawaii.

Hawaii's Department of Commerce & Consumer Affairs offers a handy recorded information line for consumer issues. Dial ☎ 808-587-1234 for information on your rights regarding refunds and exchanges, time-share contracts, car rentals and similar topics.

According to the letter of the law, hitchhiking is illegal statewide.

BUSINESS HOURS

Typical office hours in Hawaii are 8:30am to 4:30pm Monday to Friday. Some gas stations, pharmacies, grocery and convenience stores are open 24 hours, but liquor may legally be sold only between 6am and 11pm.

Banks are usually open 8:30am to 4pm Monday to Thursday, staying open until around 6pm on Friday. Most ATMs are 24-hours.

PUBLIC HOLIDAYS & SPECIAL EVENTS

On national public holidays, all banks, schools and government offices (including post offices) are closed.

As dates for many events change from year to year, check local newspapers, the Internet or tourist offices for exact schedules. There are many more events than space here allows.

January

New Year's Eve/Day
New Year's Eve means massive fireworks, of both the neighborhood and extravagant resort variety; many businesses are closed on New Year's Day.

International Festival of the Pacific
This culinary event in mid-January is capped by A Taste of Hilo, a gourmet feast.

Chinese New Year
Festivities begin at the second new moon after the winter solstice (mid-January to mid-February) with lion dances and miles of firecrackers.

Martin Luther King Jr Day
This national holiday is observed on the third Monday of the month.

Senior Skins Game
This senior PGA tour golf tournament takes place in late January at Mauna Lani Resort.

February

Presidents' Day
This national holiday is observed on the third Monday of the month.

March

Kona Brewer's Festival
This festival in early March features 50 beers and a wide variety of food.

Prince Kuhio Day
On March 26, this state holiday honors Jonah Kuhio Kalanianaole, Hawaii's first delegate to the US Congress.

Kona Stampede Rodeo
Held in mid-March in Honaunau, this has all the usual rodeo events, done with unique island flare.

Merrie Monarch Festival
Named after King David Kalakaua, this is Hawaii's biggest hula competition and Hawaiiana festival. Hosted in Hilo, it lasts a week starting on Easter.

April

Easter
This Christian holiday falls in March or April. Many business offices are closed on Good Friday (the Friday before Easter Sunday).

May

May Day
Known as Lei Day in Hawaii, the first day of May finds everyone with their lei on.

Keauhou-Kona Triathlon
Starting at the Big Island's Keauhou Bay, this grueling half-Ironman competition is held on the last Sunday in May.

Memorial Day
The last Monday in May is a national holiday honoring fallen soldiers.

Na Mea Hawaii Hula Kahiko
This popular event held in May and June features hula performances in Hawaii Volcanoes National Park.

June

King Kamehameha Day
This state holiday is celebrated on June 11 or the nearest weekend. In the king's hometown of Kapa'au, the Kamehameha statue is draped thick with leis.

July

Pu'uhonua O Honaunau Cultural Festival
Held at the Place of Refuge, this festival includes a 'royal court,' hula and traditional craft displays. It takes place on the weekend closest to July 1.

Independence Day
Fireworks and festivities mark this national holiday on July 4.

Parker Ranch Rodeo
A Hawaiian-style rodeo and horse race, sponsored by Hawaii's largest cattle ranch, takes place on July 4.

Annual Slack Key Festival
Held each year in Hilo in July, this guitar fest features some of Hawaii's greatest slack key players.

Kilauea Volcano Wilderness Runs
These contests, held at Hawaii Volcanoes National Park, include a 10-mile run around the rim of Kilauea, a 5.5-mile race into Kilauea Iki Crater and a marathon through the Ka'u Desert. The event happens at the end of July.

August

Hawaiian International Billfish Tournament
The world's number-one marlin tournament takes place in Kailua-Kona. It lasts two weeks, usually beginning in early August.

Admission Day
This state holiday, on the third Friday of August, observes the anniversary of Hawaiian statehood.

September

Labor Day
This national holiday is observed on the first Monday of the month.

Queen Lili'uokalani Outrigger Canoe Race
Held over Labor Day weekend, this is the world's biggest long-distance canoe race, traversing 18 miles from Kailua-Kona to Honaunau.

Aloha Week
This Hawaiiana celebration includes parades, cultural events, canoe races, music and an international food shindig. Festivities are staggered from mid-September to early October.

October

Columbus Day/Día de la Raza
This national holiday is observed on the second Monday of the month.

Ironman Triathlon
Considered by many to be the ultimate endurance race, this is the triathlon that started it all. The 2.4-mile swim, 112-mile bike race and 26.2-mile run begins and ends at the Kailua Pier on the Saturday in October closest to the full moon.

November

Kona Coffee Cultural Festival
The Big Island's oldest food festival is held in the first week in November; a must for java junkies.

Election Day
The second Tuesday of the month is a state holiday during election years.

Veterans Day
November 11th is a national holiday honoring veterans of the armed services.

Hawaii International Film Festival
Some 150 films from all over the world are screened in theaters in Kona, Hilo and Honoka'a during this festival in mid-November.

Ka Hula Lea Festival
This statewide hula festival takes place in mid-November in Waikoloa.

Thanksgiving
This national holiday is celebrated on the fourth Thursday of the month.

December

Christmas
December 25 is a national holiday.

WORK

US citizens can pursue work in Hawaii as they would in any other state – the problem is finding a decent job. Foreign visitors who are in the USA on tourist visas are not legally allowed to take up employment.

The Big Island has the highest unemployment rate in the state; work is not easy to drum up. Many of the available jobs are likely to pay minimum wage. Waiting tables at restaurants or cafés is about the best you can hope for.

Still, teachers and nurses are in chronically short supply and other professional jobs do crop up occasionally. Cruise the online classifieds of Hilo's *Hawaii Tribune-Herald* (W www.hilohawaiitribune.com) or Kailua-Kona's *West Hawaii Today* (W www.westhawaiitoday.com) to get an idea of employment opportunities.

For a list of government jobs available throughout the state, contact the State Workforce Development Division (☎ 974-4126) at 180 Kinoole St, Ste 205 in Hilo or in Kona (☎ 327-4770), at 74 5565 Luhia St, Bldg 3.

VOLUNTEER WORK

The National Park Service has volunteer programs at Hawaii Volcanoes National Park. Duties may include staffing information desks, leading hikes, tagging turtles or controlling invasive plants.

Competition is stiff; out of hundreds of applications, only about 25 volunteers are selected each year. Candidates with a natural sciences background and a knowledge of practicalities like first aid are preferred. A three- to six-month (40 hours a week) commitment is required. Volunteers receive no salary or help with airfare, though barracks-style housing and a stipend of about $10 a day to offset food costs are provided. For information, write to Volunteers in Parks, Hawaii Volcanoes National Park, PO Box 52, Hawaii National Park, HI 96718 or visit W www.ifa.hawaii.edu/info/vis/volunteers.html.

Another option is volunteering at the Mauna Kea Visitor Information Station. Among several positions available are visitor center guides, trail maintenance crew, summit guides and stargazing volunteers. For more information, call or write Mauna Kea Observatories Support Services (☎ 808-961-2180, 177 Makaala St, Hilo, HI 96720) or see their Web site at W www.ifa.hawaii.edu/info/vis/volunteers.html.

Interesting and varied volunteer opportunities exist with the Ironman Triathlon, held each October in Kona. Some 7000 volunteers are enlisted to pull off this world renowned competition. While certain positions require experience (eg, medical staff and massage therapists), others, such as clean up, are open to everyone. Visit W www.ironmanlive.com/vnews/volunteer for an application (deadline September 1).

The Hawaii chapter of the Sierra Club (W www.hi.sierraclub.org) coordinates backcountry trail work, fence building and plant control trips. Tours of duty usually last one week, with groups of up to 20 people. Participants pay $100 to cover administrative costs. For information, call ☎ 808-538-6616 on Oahu or write to: Hawaii Service Trip Program, PO Box 2577, Honolulu, HI 96803.

A few Big Island retreats also offer volunteer opportunities. The Kalani Honua Oceanside Eco-Retreat (W www.kalani.com) in Puna has an established volunteer and residency program; see the Puna chapter for details.

ACCOMMODATIONS

The Big Island has a wide range of accommodations, from camping to condominiums and everything in between. Don't overlook state park cabins as an option: these are quite inexpensive and lovely if you prefer scenery to amenities. Consider moving around and exploring from a couple of different bases to maximize your time here.

Except where noted, the rates given in this book are the same for singles or doubles. Rates do not include the whopping tax of 11.41%, which is added to the price of all accommodations.

A word about geckos, which are small green and tan lizards that run across ceilings and appear even in Hawaii's finest hotels: don't hurt them. They won't bite you and they eat bugs, particularly flying termites. Some people in Hawaii consider it good luck to have a resident gecko, and bad luck to harm one.

Camping

Cheap, picturesque and fun, camping is an excellent way to experience Hawaii. There are about two dozen established camping facilities island-wide. In many cases, private

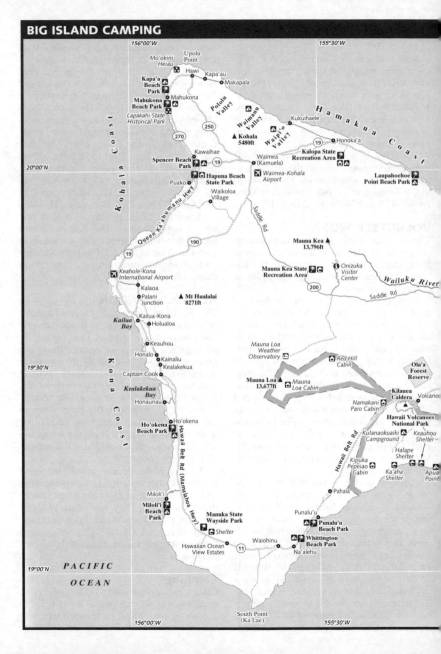

BIG ISLAND CAMPING

156°00'W   155°30'W

Mo'okini
Heiau
Upolu
Point
Kapa'a
Beach
Park
Hawi   Kapa'au
Makapala
Mahukona
Beach Park   Mahukona
Lapakahi State
Historical Park   (270)   (250)
Pololu
Valley
Waimanu
Valley   Kukuihaele
Kohala
5480ft   Waipi'o
Valley   (19)   Honoka'a
Kohala Coast
20°00'N   Kawaihae   Waimea
(Kamuela)   Kalopa State
Recreation Area
Spencer Beach
Park   (19)   Laupahoehoe
Point Beach Park
Hapuna Beach
State Park   Waimea-Kohala
Airport
Puako   Waikoloa
Village   Saddle Rd
Queen Ka'ahumanu Hwy
(190)
(19)
Mauna Kea
13,796ft
Keahole-Kona
International Airport   Mauna Kea State
Recreation Area   Onizuka
Visitor
Center   Wailuku River
Kalaoa   (200)   Saddle Rd
Palani
Junction   Mt Hualalai
8271ft
Kailua-Kona   Kailua-Kona
Bay   Holualoa
Keauhou
Honalo   Mauna Loa
Weather
Observatory
Kainaliu   Red Hill
Cabin   Ola'a
Forest
Reserve
Kealakekua
19°30'N   Captain Cook
Kealakekua
Bay   Mauna Loa
13,677ft   Mauna
Loa Cabin   Kilauea
Caldera   Volcano
Honaunau   Namakani
Paio Cabin   Hawaii Volcanoes
National Park
Ho'okena
Beach Park   Ho'okena   Kulanaokuaiki
Campground   Keauhou
Shelter
Halape
Shelter
Kipuka
Pepeiao
Cabin   Ka'aha
Shelter   Apua
Point
Miloli'i   Hawaii Belt Rd (Mamalahoa Hwy)
Miloli'i
Beach
Park   Pahala
Manuka State
Wayside Park   Punalu'u   Punalu'u
Beach Park
Shelter   Whittington
Beach Park
Hawaiian Ocean
View Estates   (11)   Waiohinu   Na'alehu
19°00'N   PACIFIC

OCEAN

Hamakua Coast

Kona Coast

156°00'W   South Point
(Ka Lae)   155°30'W

individuals and hostels also extend patches of grass to pitch camp.

Some of the nation's best camping is in Hawaii Volcanoes National Park. Administered separately from the state and county sites, the options range from cabins with beds to backcountry lean-tos. Waipi'o Valley camping (privately administered) is another superlative camping option.

For details on amenities and services, see the regional chapters.

State Parks Tent camping is permitted at both the Kalopa and MacKenzie State Recreation Areas (on the Hamakua and Puna coasts, respectively). The latter has no water and a forsaken legacy: Hawaiians believe powerful spirits dwell amongst the MacKenzie bluffs and a camper was murdered here in 1980. Camping sites cost $5 for up to four people. Primitive shelters (no water) are also available at Manuka State Wayside Park in Ka'u.

Additionally, there are A-frame cabins at Hapuna Beach on the Kohala coast ($20 for four people) and self-contained housekeeping cabins with hot showers and kitchens at Kalopa State Recreation Areas ($55 up to eight people). Unfortunately, the cabins at Mauna Kea State Recreation Area are closed until further notice. Officials say the cabins should re-open in late 2002, but that's what they said in 2001.

Reservations are required and can be made by phone, mail or in person; a picture ID must be presented. Priority is given to walk-ins, then mail requests, then phone. The maximum allowable stay is five nights per month. The Big Island office (☎ 974-6200, W www.hawaii.gov/dlnr/dsp/hawaii.html) is at 75 Aupuni St or write to PO Box 936, Hilo, HI 96721.

County Beach Parks The county allows camping at 10 parks: Kolekole and Laupahoehoe, north of Hilo; Isaac Hale in Puna; Spencer, Kapa'a, Mahukona, Ho'okena and Miloli'i, all on the leeward side; and Whittington and Punalu'u, both in Ka'u.

With the exception of Spencer, which is patrolled by a security guard, most county parks can be rough and noisy areas, as they're popular with late-night drinkers. Isaac Hale could be the worst in this regard and is not recommended for solo female campers. Elsewhere, midweek tends to be quieter and the remote Ka'u sites don't get much traffic.

Camping permits are required and are obtainable online (W www.ehawaiigov.org/cgi-bin/bi-camp/camp_welcome.cgi), by mail or in person from the Department of Parks & Recreation (☎ 961-8311), 25 Aupuni St, Room 210 Hilo, HI 96720. Office hours are 8:30am to 4pm Monday to Friday, but before 3pm is recommended. Checks (payable to the County Director of Finance) are accepted up to two weeks before your reservation, otherwise it's cash only. Prices are $5/2/1 for adults/teens/children.

The maximum allowable stay in any one campground is one week in summer, two weeks the remainder of the year. In the office is an informative binder (with photos) describing all the campgrounds.

You can also make reservations by phone through the Hilo office and then pick up the permit at Park & Recreation satellite offices in Kailua-Kona, Captain Cook, Pahala, Na'alehu and Waimea.

Only Laupahoehoe and Spencer have drinking water. Some of the others have treatable catchment water.

Hawaii Volcanoes National Park The Hawaii Volcanoes National Park chapter has details on the park's two drive-up campgrounds, trail shelters, cabins and backcountry tent sites.

Backcountry folks have to register at the visitor's center. All sites are free, available on a first-come, first-served basis and rarely filled.

Waipi'o Valley Waipi'o Valley lands are owned and administered by the Bishop Estate. Camping permits are required for the four primitive sites within the valley. They're free and issued on a first-come, first-served basis. The maximum allowable stay is four days and you must reserve two weeks in advance. For information call ☎ 322-5300

from 7:30am to 4:30pm, Monday through Friday.

Once approved, permits can be mailed, faxed or picked up at the Kamehameha Schools office in the Keauhou Shopping Center just south of Kailua-Kona.

Camping in Waimanu Valley is handled by the Division of Forestry & Wildlife in Hilo (see the Hamakua Coast chapter for details).

Camping Supplies There are a few places to rent or buy gear if you don't feel like lugging it along.

Pacific Rent-All (☎ 935-2974, 1080 Kilauea Ave, Hilo, HI 96720) Rentals per day/week; 3-person tent $23/46, lightweight sleeping bag $8/24. This store also rents stoves, lanterns, water jugs and other supplies. The limited selection is generally geared towards drive-up camping, not backcountry use.

Hilo Surplus Store (☎ 935-6398, 148 Mamo St) This store sells camping supplies including rain gear, stoves, sleeping bags, tents and backpacks. You can also try one of the discount department stores, such as Kmart or Wal-Mart in Kailua-Kona or Hilo.

Hostels

The only Big Island hostel associated with Hostelling International is the sweet Holo Holo Inn near Hawaii Volcanoes National Park. Otherwise, there are a handful of private hostel-style places offering inexpensive digs and/or camping space. Look for them in Kailua-Kona, Hilo, Captain Cook and Kurtistown en route to the national park. Puna has its share of cheap places that fall somewhere between hostel and crash pad. Rates for dorm beds range from about $14 to $17.

B&Bs

For a little more money, you'll get way more comfort and character in a B&B. Some are modest bedrooms in family households, while others are romantic hideaways. B&Bs generally begin around $50, although the average is closer to $75 and the most exclusive go up to $150. Continental breakfast is often included in the price. Many require a minimum stay of two or three days, and some give discounts if you stay a week or more.

Keep in mind that Hawaiian B&Bs are small scale – most have only a few guest rooms. Out of consideration for their neighbors and guests, B&B hosts discourage unannounced drop-ins. Because of this, most B&Bs do not appear on maps in the destination chapters.

Many of the B&Bs recommended herein you can book directly. Others hand off their booking duties to reservation services. Some of these agencies book whole houses, condos and studio cottages as well. All require at least part of the payment in advance and have cancellation penalties. The following are reputable services that don't charge booking fees:

All Islands Bed & Breakfast
(☎ 808-263-2342, 800-542-3044, fax 808-263-0308, ⓦ home.hawaii.rr.com/allislands) 463 Iliwahi Loop, Kailua, HI 96734

Bed & Breakfast Hawaii
(☎ 822-7771, 800-733-1632, fax 822-2723, ⓦ www.bandb-hawaii.com) PO Box 449, Kapa'a, HI 96746

Hawaii's Best B&Bs (☎ 808-885-4550, 800-262-9912, fax 808-885-0559, ⓦ www.bestbnb.com) PO Box 563, Kamuela, HI 96743

In addition to these organizations, also see the plethora of B&Bs collected at the Ohana Network (ⓦ www.ohananet.com/travel/bednbrkfst.html) or those belonging to the Hawaii Island B&B Association (ⓦ www.stayhawaii.com/index.html).

Condos

Condominiums are fully furnished, individually owned apartments. Condos are spacious, user-friendly (with everything from linens to cutlery) and many also have washer-dryers, sofa beds and a *lanai* (veranda).

Although some condo complexes operate similarly to hotels, with a front desk, most condos are booked through rental agents. Unlike hotels, most don't have daily maid service.

If you're staying awhile or are traveling with several people, condos almost always work out cheaper than hotels. However, most condo units booked through rental agents have a three- to seven-day minimum stay, require deposits and carry hefty cancellation penalties.

Condos often offer weekly and monthly rates. The general rule is that the weekly rate is six times the daily rate and the monthly is three times the weekly.

There are far fewer condo properties on the Hilo side than the Kona side.

Hotels

Before booking any hotel, it's worth asking if any specials are available – some places actually have room/car packages for less than the 'standard' room rate! While a good travel agent at home may know about some of these discounts, many of the best deals are advertised only in Hawaii. To learn of deals, pick up a Honolulu newspaper; the travel section of the Sunday *Honolulu Advertiser* is best.

The Hawaii Visitors Bureau (see Tourist Offices, earlier) mails out a free annual accommodations guide listing member hotels with addresses and prices. It includes virtually all of Hawaii's resort hotels and most of those in the moderate price range.

The Waikoloa area, north of Kailua-Kona, has the island's most expensive beach resorts. All of Hilo's high-rise hotel-resorts are located near downtown on Banyan Drive.

FOOD

Food in Hawaii epitomizes multicultural harmony. Here you'll find the taro of Polynesian settlers mingling with the staples of the various Diaspora: Portuguese sausage, Japanese sushi and pad Thai. Meanwhile, the heart of Hawaiian soul food beats through poi, poke and laulau. Last, but certainly not least, there's local food, a cornucopia of foodstuffs endemic to these islands. Such gems as SPAM musubi, loco moco and saimin should be tried – if but once!

Many renowned chefs have made their reputation here through 'Hawaii Regional' cuisine, which incorporates fresh local ingredients and borrows liberally from the islands' various ethnic groups. It's marked by exotic combinations such as grilled freshwater shrimp with taro chips, wok-charred *ahi* (yellowfin tuna) with island greens, and Peking duck in ginger-*lilikoi* (passion fruit) sauce. Some of the best restaurants are at the ritzy hotels and mega-resorts, although a number of famed chefs have opened their own places.

Fruit

The Big Island bursts with fruit, including avocado, banana, breadfruit, star fruit, coconut, guava, lychee, mango and pineapple. A whopping 95% of the state's papayas are grown in windward side orchards, so like them or not, papaya will likely figure in some relish, smoothie or continental breakfast during your stay. Sweet Ka'u oranges are grown in the south.

Wild fruits grow with abandon along trails, roads and even the Belt Highway. Look for strawberry guava, the ubiquitous common guava, thimbleberries, mountain apples, ohelo berries and avocado. Only pick what you can personally consume and never violate someone's private patch.

Hawaiian Food

The traditional Hawaiian celebratory feast is the *luau*. These days, local luau are still hosted for special events such as a baby's first birthday. These are far more authentic than any of the commercial luau, but they're family affairs and short-stay visitors would be lucky indeed to get invited to one. Church luau may provide just such an opportunity, so ask around.

The centerpiece of any luau is *kalua* pig, which is roasted in a pit-like earthen oven known as an *imu*. The imu is readied by building a fire and heating rocks in the pit. When the rocks glow red, layers of damp banana trunks and ti leaves are placed over the stones. A pig is split open, stuffed with some of the hot rocks and laid atop the bed. Other foods wrapped in ti and banana leaves are placed around it. It's all covered with more ti leaves and a layer of mats and topped with dirt to seal in the heat, which then bakes and steams the food. Anything cooked in this style is called *kalua*.

The process takes four to eight hours, depending on the size of the swine. A few of the hotel luau still bake the pig in this traditional manner and you can often go in the morning and watch them prepare and bury the pig.

Wetland taro is used to make *poi*, a paste pounded from cooked taro corms. Water is added to make it pudding-like, and its consistency is measured as one-, two- or three-finger poi – depending on how many fingers you'll need to transport it from bowl to mouth. Poi is highly nutritious and easily digestible, but it's an acquired taste. It is sometimes fermented for a few days to give it more zing.

Laulau is fish, pork and taro wrapped in a ti leaf bundle and steamed. *Lomi* salmon (sometimes called *lomilomi* salmon) is made by massaging and marinating thin slices of raw salmon with diced tomatoes and green onions.

Other Hawaiian foods include baked *ulu* (breadfruit), *opihi* (yummy, tiny limpet shells picked off the reef at low tide) and *pipikaula* (beef jerky). *Haupia*, the standard dessert, is a stiff pudding made of coconut cream thickened traditionally with arrowroot but more commonly with cornstarch nowadays. Spices particular to Hawaiian cooking and available everywhere include *alaea* (an iron-rich, red salt), *limu* (the generic term for a variety of edible seaweeds) and chili pepper water.

In Hawaiian food preparation, ti leaves are indispensable: food is wrapped in them, cooked in them, and served upon them,.

There are several outstanding Hawaiian eateries on the Big Island and you should seek them out to appreciate the dynamic palate of traditional cooking.

Local Food

The distinct style of food called 'local' refers to all the food endemic to Hawaii. Among these delights are *saimin*, a noodle soup with infinite variation; loco moco, a Hilo invention featuring a bed of rice topped with

Fish Talk

Eating fresh fish is bound to be a pricey experience, so you should know what you're ordering, right? Some names of the most popular locally caught fish and other seafood are as follows (a few are better known by their Japanese names than traditional Hawaiian terms):

ahi	yellowfin tuna; a mild-tasting fish, often served as sashimi or poke
aku	bonito or skipjack tuna (katsuo in Japanese); a fish with firm, red flesh
akule	big-eyed mackerel
au	any species of marlin (mostly Pacific Blue in Hawaii); a lean and extremely tender fish
mahimahi	a fish called 'dolphin' (not the mammal) with white, almost tasteless flesh
mano	shark
onaga	red snapper (called *ulaula* in Hawaiian); a tender, moist fish that is especially popular for sushi
ono	wahoo; a fish similar to mackerel, with white flaky, delicate flesh
opah	moonfish; a versatile, fatty fish
opakapaka	Hawaiian pink snapper; similar to onaga, the flesh is firmest and fattiest in winter, when it's used for sashimi
opelu	mackerel scad; best eaten dried or broiled with poi
tako	Japanese for octopus (he'e in Hawaiian); often eaten as poke or sushi
uku	gray snapper; delicate, moist pink meat and a pronounced fishy taste
ula	Hawaiian lobster (clawless); ula are smaller than mainland lobsters
wana	sea urchin; the gonads are eaten as *haute* sushi

a fried egg, hamburger patty and rivulets of oozing brown gravy; and plate lunch. A typical plate lunch averages 1400 calories and consists of 'two scoop rice,' (the plural form is not used in pidgin), a scoop of macaroni salad and a serving of beef stew, mahimahi or teriyaki chicken.

Plate lunch is available everywhere, especially at drive-ins and *kaukau* wagons (kitchens on wheels).

Snacks

Pupu is the word for all kinds of appetizers. Boiled peanuts (a popular, but soggy, bar snack), soy-flavored rice crackers called *kaki mochi* and sashimi are among the more common pupus.

Poke A local favorite is *poke*, (pronounced **po**-kay or **po**-key), which is cubed, raw fish marinated in salt, soy sauce, chili peppers, and seaweed traditionally, though the possibilities are endless. Technically, poke refers to the process of cutting anything into cubes, be it tofu, escargot or oysters.

Crack Seed Crack seed is a Chinese snack food that can be sweet, sour, salty or some combination of the three. It's often made from dried fruits, such as plums and apricots. More exotic ones include sweet-and-sour baby cherry seeds, pickled mangoes, lemon strips and any of the above seasoned à la *li hing mui* – a preserving process that spikes the fruit with salt, sugar and licorice. This treat is an 'oldie but goodie,' although it's an assault on uninitiated taste buds.

Shave Ice Shave ice is similar in concept to snow cones. In practice, however, shave ice is to snow cones what pâté is to head cheese. Here, the ice is shaved as fine as powdered snow, packed into a paper cone and drenched with delicious (and sweet) fruit-flavored syrups in psychedelic hues. Typical choices include lilikoi, coconut or banana, strawberry, green tea or li hing mui if you dare. Get wild and request sweet adzuki beans in the bottom.

DRINKS
Nonalcoholic Drinks

Most tap water is safe to drink, unless your supply is from a rain catchment system lacking proper filters. County tap water is safe to drink; look for county pumps along the road for free water. All water from freshwater streams should be boiled or otherwise treated.

The variety of fruit drinks on the Big Island is truly sybaritic. Coconut water straight from the nut, guava nectar, fresh papaya juice or addictive smoothies with choice ingredients including lilikoi, banana and papaya are some of the delights you'll find here.

Tea drinkers will rejoice here, with maté, herbals, blacks and greens, both loose and bagged, readily available. Of course, the Big Island grows the best-known coffee in the United States. Kona coffee, though not robust enough for some, is world-renowned.

The Big Island is also one of the main kava *(awa* in Hawaiian) growing regions in the United States. This root has a long history in Polynesia and when steeped with water and extracted through a fine cloth, makes a pleasing, mildly narcotic drink.

Alcoholic Drinks

The drinking age in Hawaii is a pretty strict 21, and baby-faces will be asked to produce photo ID when buying booze. All grocery stores sell liquor, as do most smaller food marts.

There are two microbreweries on the Big Island: Kona Brewing Company (**W** www .konabrewing.com) and Mehana Brewing in Hilo. They sell in restaurants, groceries, health food stores and online. You're encouraged to support your local brewmeisters!

Of course, all of Hawaii is synonymous with those rum-defiling cocktails dolled up with paper umbrellas and who knows what all. Three popular varieties are: piña colada, with rum, pineapple juice and cream of coconut; mai tai, a mix of rum, grenadine and lemon and pineapple juices; and lava

---

Smoothing the Edges with Awa

Called *awa* in Hawaiian, kava *Piper methysticum* is a traditional medicinal and sacramental root plant from Polynesia. The Hawaiians hold the gods Kane (ruler of the forests and sunlight) and Kanaloa (ruler of the oceans and healing) responsible for cultivating awa throughout Hawaii.

Like most sacraments, this stuff tastes bad but might work wonders. The lactones (active ingredients) in kava relieve anxiety, fatigue and insomnia, while fostering restful sleep and vivid dreams. No wonder savvy Polynesians considered it a staple, using it to commune with their deities. There's also burgeoning proof that kava promotes a healthy urinary tract, relieves arthritis pain and generally lowers stress levels. However, it may also cause liver damage.

Typically, the root of the plant is chewed or pulverized and mixed with water to produce a milky concoction that numbs the mouth and tastes sharp and earthy. The effect from an 8oz glass is mildly narcotic, but not mind altering, and smoothes out sharp edges without making you dopey. Custom dictates you clap twice as thanks before drinking your kava.

You can sample this 100% legal stuff at many places on the Big Island, including the Kava Bar at the Pahoa farmer's market, The Landing in Hawi and the Kanaka Kava bar in Kailua-Kona (see relevant regional chapters). You can also purchase tea, elixirs and the root powder (8oz costs $16 to $30, depending on the grower) in health food stores.

Kava is not recommended for daily use as it can tax the kidneys, and pregnant women are advised against partaking of this potent potable.

To learn more, visit **W** www.punakava.com or **W** www.konakavafarm.com.

flow, which is everything but the kitchen sink and a bit of rum for the buzz. For natural flavor and subtlety, nothing beats a coconut fresh from the palm. The top is whacked off and the water inside is spiked with rum.

The Volcano Winery makes fruit, honey and grape wines, which are a bit of a stretch for diehard oenephiles. Wine, of course, is more expensive here than on the mainland and if you've a taste for the grape, you'll either sacrifice quality or your budget to slake that thirst.

ENTERTAINMENT

Make no mistake, the Big Island hurts for nightlife and it's among visitors' loudest complaints. To be fair, Hilo has a surprisingly sophisticated theater and cinema community, as does Honoka'a on the Hamakua Coast (see those chapters for more). If recent gigs by Blues Traveler and the Roy Brown Trio are any indication, big-time mainland performers draw big, energized crowds.

With so little action, locals often make their own fun. This mostly means raucous raves and full moon parties, a lively DJ scene and decent Mardi Gras and Halloween celebrations. Oftentimes these are spontaneous and with no fixed address, so ask around.

There's plenty of Hawaiian entertainment as well, including contemporary Hawaiian music, slack-key guitar performances and hula shows. For detailed information, see the Entertainment sections in the regional chapters.

SPECTATOR SPORTS

Since Hawaii has no major sports teams, there's a lively college athletic scene and games are accessible and affordable to the public.

The University of Hawaii at Hilo is a Division II school with phenomenally talented volleyball teams (men and women's). Though hardly headed to the pros, the basketball and baseball squads are fun to watch too. Basketball and volleyball games are held at the Hilo Civic (also called Afook

Chinen Civic) and baseball is played in the adjacent Victor Baseball Complex. Tickets start at $4; see the Vulcan's Web site for details at **W** http://vulcans.uhh.hawaii.edu.

Still, some of the most popular spectator sports in Hawaii aren't mainland imports. Cock fights (called chicken fights here) are wild, woolly and with big purses. Though technically illegal, the fights are tolerated by officials and are best visited with local friends. Big Island rodeos pre-date their mainland counterparts and there are several here throughout the year. Check **W** www.rodeohawaii.com for details.

For information on specific sporting events, see the Public Holidays & Special Events section earlier in this chapter.

SHOPPING

There is so much great stuff to buy here, from the highest quality coffee and macadamia nuts to board shorts and vintage aloha wear, you'll want to set aside a bit of your budget for souvenirs.

Handicrafts

Woodworkers here use beautifully grained native Hawaiian hardwoods, such as *koa*, to create bowls of unsurpassed sublimity. The thinner and lighter the bowl, the finer the artistic skill and the greater the value. Although woodwork is found all over the Big Island, the Volcano Art Center in the national park and Dan De Luz Woods in Kurtistown are particularly noteworthy.

Ceramics is another art form in which island craftspeople excel. Many potters are influenced by Japanese styles and aesthetics. Good *raku* work in particular can be found at reasonable prices; hit one of the many galleries in Holualoa. Also look for the amagama (tunnel kiln) style of pottery.

Lauhala, the leaves of the pandanus tree, were woven into sleeping mats and any manner of household items by ancient Hawaiians. Today, master weavers make them into purses, placemats, hats and baskets. The work of the Kimura family in Holualoa is considered among the best.

Hawaiian quilts are dazzling works of art. With the loving care that goes into crafting them, they aren't cheap (quality, full-size quilts start at around $1000), but will last a lifetime. Drums, nose flutes, gourd rattles and other traditional hula instruments are sold in music shops and make interesting gifts.

Flora & Food

The Big Island is known as the Orchid Island and the anthurium capital of the world; both plants make remarkable, splashy gifts for folks back home. You can choose, buy and ship these and other flowers straight from the growers. Orchids start at $25 for a double-spiked *oncidium* shipped directly to the mainland.

Kona coffee at $18 a pound direct from the farm (around $22 with shipping), macadamia nuts (plain or chocolate covered), and tropical fruit butters such as mango, guava and lilikoi are some good perishable choices.

Fans of Japanese food should look for dried seaweed, *mochi* and *ume* plums at their favorite supermarket.

Clothing

For first timers, it's a little surprising that everyone over here actually wears tropical prints. Some of the best aloha wear is vintage: look for those of silk or rayon, with wood or coconut buttons and an uninterrupted pattern flow, especially along the pocket. There are some fantastic thrift stores in Hilo and Honoka'a with treasures galore. Crazy Shirts, with outlets in Kailua-Kona, sells quality T-shirts with homegrown Hawaiian designs.

Activities

The Big Island is singular for so many reasons and this is doubly true when it comes to outdoor and adventure activities. Granted, it doesn't have the wild swells of Oahu's North Shore, or the billowy winds of Maui's Ho'okipa Beach. But of all the Hawaiian Islands, only one boasts snowboarding in winter, the Ironman Triathlon in fall, the world's clearest stargazing almost every night and live lava flows every day.

From hiking to scuba, and horseback riding to surfing, you can do it here. Maybe you've dreamt of pursuing these activities and never made it a reality. Well, now's your opportunity to *carpe diem,* because instruction in these and other activities is available and affordable on the Big Island. What's more, you don't have to arrange anything before you touch down: just get here, figure out what you itch to do, rent the equipment, take the lessons and go for it.

Of course, you can also golf, loll on the beach, jog, swim, snorkel, kayak and cycle here. It engenders envy that you're headed to Hawaii!

More detailed information on all activities – including shops, tour providers, prices and phone numbers – is given in the appropriate regional chapters. For books on specific pursuits, see Activities in the Book section of the Facts for the Visitor chapter.

DIVING

There's terrific year-round diving on the Big Island. The Kona side has the best overall conditions, with a panoply of sites ranging from shallow beginner dives to challenging nighttime and lava tube dives. Though summer generally offers calmer waters and better visibility, the diving is rewarding any time of year. Some of the best leeward sites include Place of Refuge and the Old Airport in Kona and Puako in South Kohala.

Hilo dive shops offer windward-side trips, but this is hardly the preferred diving region, as the shores are usually buffeted by trade winds.

Hawaiian waters have excellent visibility (usually to 100 feet), with water temperatures ranging from 72°F to 82°F (22°C to 27°C), though the deeper you go, the chillier it gets; most divers don a 5mm wetsuit.

The marine life here is nothing short of phenomenal and since the Big Island is such a baby – geologically speaking – most of the reefs are of the fringe variety, close to and accessible from the shore. Almost 700 fish species live in Hawaiian waters, and nearly one-third of them are endemic.

Among the underwater treats you can expect to see are spinner dolphins, green sea turtles, manta rays and moray eels. Although it's rare for divers to see humpback whales underwater, you may get lucky and hear them singing. Whales of all types churn Big Island waters year-round, but the best time to see humpback, false killer, pilot and sperm whales is from January to April. Coral spawning events are another opportunity available to divers here.

There are dive shops on both the Kona and Hilo sides where complete gear can be rented or purchased. Prices start at $55 for a one tank boat dive or $75 for two tanks. A few outfits in Kona also offer live-aboard, kayak dive and night diving options. See the individual regional chapters for complete information.

Getting Certified

Hawaii is perfect for virgin divers: the waters are shallow, calm, clear and teeming with life, and a variety of lesson and certification programs are available.

If you just want to test the waters, so to speak, go for a beginner's 'try scuba' or 'resort' course (also see the Snuba section, later). These usually include three hours of instruction, followed by a shallow beach or boat dive. The cost ranges from $75 to $100, depending upon the outfit and whether it's a shore or boat dive. Oftentimes, completing this course allows you to dive for the balance of your vacation with a certified

Considerations for Responsible Diving

The popularity of diving places immense pressure on many sites. Please consider the following tips when diving and help preserve the ecology and beauty of reefs.

- Do not use anchors on the reef, and take care not to ground boats on coral. Encourage dive operators and regulatory bodies to establish permanent moorings at popular dive sites.

- Avoid touching living marine organisms or dragging equipment across the reef. Polyps can be damaged by even the gentlest contact. Never stand on coral, even if they look solid and robust. If you must hold on to the reef, only touch exposed rock or dead coral.

- Be conscious of your fins. Even without contact, the surge from heavy fin strokes near the reef can damage delicate organisms. When treading water in shallow reef areas, take care not to kick up clouds of sand. Settling sand can easily smother delicate reef organisms.

- Practice and maintain proper buoyancy control. Make sure you are correctly weighted and that your weight belt is positioned so you stay horizontal. If you haven't dived for a while, have a practice dive in a pool before taking to the reef. Be aware that buoyancy can change over the period of an extended trip: Initially you may breathe harder and need more weight; a few days later you may breathe more easily and need less.

- Take great care in underwater caves. Spend as little time within them as possible, as your air bubbles may be caught within the roof, thereby leaving previously submerged organisms high and dry. Taking turns to inspect the interior of a small cave will lessen the chances of damage.

- Resist the temptation to collect or buy coral or shells. Aside from the ecological damage, taking home marine souvenirs depletes the beauty of a site and spoils the enjoyment of others.

- Ensure that you take home all your rubbish and any litter you may find as well. Plastics in particular are a serious threat to marine life.

- Resist the temptation to feed fish. You may disturb their normal eating habits, encourage aggressive behavior or feed them food that is detrimental to their health.

- Minimize your disturbance of marine animals. In particular, do not ride on the backs of turtles, as this causes them great anxiety.

instructor. This is a good introduction for kids (ages 12 and up) and people intrigued by scuba but not yet hooked on the idea.

Visitors can obtain full open-water PADI or NAUI certification (both are internationally recognized and more or less comparable). Courses for residents or long term visitors typically convene over four days, (two days of class and two days of diving), and cost as little as $125 (though expect to pay closer to $200 on the Kona side). If your time is short and you can't be constrained by class schedules, you can contract one-on-one instruction at your convenience; expect to pay between $400 and $600 for the full course.

A third option is the Open Water referral program whereby you do the classroom work at home and the actual dives in Hawaii. There are restrictions to this program, so research the details beforehand. Certified divers can also obtain advance credentials on the Big Island.

There are several organizations involved in diving certification and safety.

Professional Association of Diving Instructors *(PADI;* ☎ *800-729-7234,* ⓦ *www .padi.com)* This worldwide association certifies scuba divers; they have a searchable Web site.

National Association of Underwater Instructors *(NAUI;* ⓦ *www.naui.org)* This is the other worldwide association certifying divers.

Divers Alert Network (DAN; ☎ 919 684-8111/4326, both lines are 24-hour emergency hotlines, dial ☎ 800-446-2671 to join, W www.diversalertnetwork.org) DAN advises on diving emergencies, and offers supplemental insurance for evacuation, decompression services, illness and injury.

Snuba

Snuba is a happy medium for those who want to slip beneath the surface but aren't keen on taking a dive course. Somewhere between snorkeling and diving, snuba allows divers to breathe through a long hose attached to an air tank, which is floating on a raft at the surface. With a mask and a weight belt, you can dive down as far as the air hose allows (usually between 20 and 40 feet).

Snuba programs include elementary dive techniques including clearing your face mask and equalizing ear pressure. An instructor is in the water with you during the entire dive. Generally, the best snuba experiences are those from boats, because you can reach better dive sites, but snuba from the beach is also available. A beach dive generally lasts an hour and costs $60; boat dives are three-hour affairs and cost $90/115 for one/two dives. Most outfits offer morning and afternoon dives: the former has more sun.

Snuba makes for a quick and easy introduction to the underwater world, especially for kids, who will surface squealing with delight. Children eight and older can do snuba. A special program for kids aged four to 7 years (where they float on the surface and breathe through a tube) is an option for the younger set.

Note that snuba is available only on the leeward coast; see the Kona chapter for details.

SNORKELING

By donning a mask and snorkel, you can turn the ocean into an underwater aquarium. Several of Hawaii's top snorkeling sites are on the Big Island, where you can swim with sea turtles and dolphins, sidle up to Technicolor reef fish or feast your eyes on exuberant coral gardens.

Hawaii's near-shore waters harbor some 20 different kinds of butterfly fish, large rainbow-colored parrotfish, numerous varieties of wrasses, lemon yellow tangs, graceful Moorish idols and ballooning puffers, just to list a few.

Some travelers cart along their own mask, snorkel and fins, but gear can be rented easily enough from dive shops for around $6/24 a day/week or from huts on some of the busier beaches, though rates tend to be higher there. If snorkeling is your bag, you can purchase a good snorkel set for around $30.

Among the Big Island's sweetest spots to snorkel are Kahalu'u Beach, a bit south of Kailua-Kona; Two Step, just north of the Place of Refuge; Kealakekua Bay; and the Kapoho tide pools in Puna. These last offer a terrific opportunity for hydrophobes to sample snorkeling, as many of the shallow pools don't require you to get in the water: you can just don a mask and dip your head into the underwater wonder world.

SWIMMING

With more than 300 miles of shoreline, coming to Hawaii means going to the beach. The Kohala Coast north of Kona has scores of picture-perfect beaches, some only accessible by 4WD and/or foot. Tucked away in coves and fringed by palm trees, these are the white sandy stretches of tropical fantasies. The entire leeward side is strung with beaches of varying accessibility and popularity. Here you'll find some of the best swimming conditions on the island. The coast around Waikoloa and Hapuna, Anaeho'omalu and Spencer beaches are easy to get to and great for families.

The windward side of the island is too often dismissed as not having notable beaches. Granted, East Hawaii beaches are not your typical tropical idylls – those of the calm, turquoise waters and powdery sand. Windward gems are, however, mysterious and unique to the Big Island: the olivine green-sand beaches, ephemeral black-sand

BIG ISLAND DIVING & SNORKELING

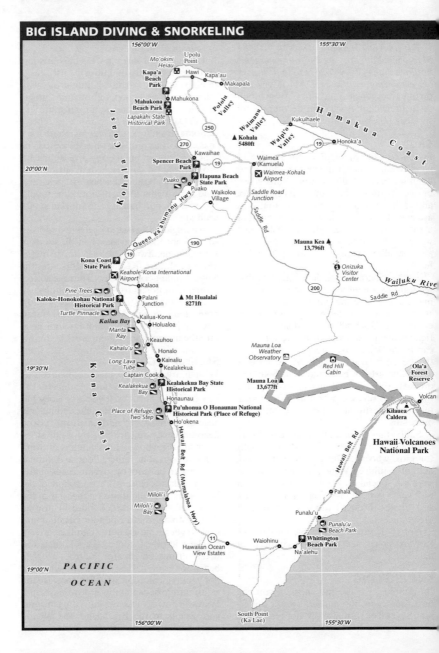

beaches where you can swim with dolphins or sea turtles, entire bays pocked with teeming tide pools and secret hideaways that this book won't disclose. Some are clothing optional.

When you're looking to kick it at a Big Island beach, you should know that in Hawaii all coastal access is public access: if you can see the shore, you're *technically* allowed access to it, regardless of how many no trespassing or *kapu* signs have been posted to the contrary.

Additionally, the Big Island has green crater lakes, waterfalls galore, and indoor pools, all of which offer terrific swimming opportunities. For a list of indoor pools maintained by the county, call the County Aquatics Division at ☎ 961-8694 or see W www.hawaii-county.com/parks/aquatics _program_guide.htm. Many folks also like to stroke the 2.4-mile swimming portion of the Ironman Triathlon; see that section below and regional chapters for details.

SURFING & BOOGIE BOARDING
Let's not beat around the bush: Big Island swells will leave adrenaline junkies jonesing. The waves just never get that big here (tsunamis don't count) and rocky, reef-encrusted shorebreaks are real hazards. On balance, surfing conditions are better on the leeward side and winter brings in bigger sets than summer. Boogie boarders and surfers often compete amicably for the same diminutive swells.

Nevertheless, there are some jamming spots good for beginners, boogie boarders and surfers with low expectations. On the windward side, check out Pohiki Bay in Isaac Hale Beach Park, Honoli'i Cove north of Hilo, Kolekole Beach Park a bit further north (which is very popular with cute, supremely experienced boogie boarders showing off – you go, guys!), and the Waipi'o River mouth at the northern terminus of Hwy 19.

On the Kona coast, there are good breaks at Kahalu'u Beach south of Kailua-Kona, Banyan's on Ali'i Drive, nearby Lyman's and Pine Trees. Locals may exhibit proprietary dispositions at some leeward swells.

Lessons and rentals are available at shops on both sides of the island. A three hour group lesson typically costs $85. Private and multiple lessons can also be arranged. The daily Big Island surf report is at w www.hawaiisurfnews.com.

KAYAKING

Big Island kayaking gains fans daily as rental outfits, tours and enthusiasts spread the gospel of paddling fun.

On the leeward side, you can paddle all the way from Mahukona Beach Park in North Kohala to the Manuka State Wayside Park in Ka'u, but your arms would be really tired! (Hardcore enthusiasts could split this stretch into a multi-week trip of a lifetime). Perhaps the most popular launch site is from Napo'opo'o County Park at Keala-kekua Bay, a haven for dolphins, a splendid snorkel locale and the spot where Captain Cook met his maker. Kona Coast State Park and Kailua Bay are other popular Kona side kayaking grounds.

Up north, there's spectacular summer kayaking from Upolu Point to the Waipi'o Valley. These waters are rough other times of the year. Down Hilo way, kayakers usually put in at the Hilo Bayfront Beach Park or at Richardson Ocean Park.

Kayak rentals are available in Hilo, Honala (just inland from Kailua-Kona) and in Kailua-Kona proper. Serious paddlers will want to refer to Audrey Sutherland's *Paddling Hawai'i* (UH Press).

A super popular kayak tour called Flumin' Da Ditch launches from Hawi; see the North Kohala chapter for details.

WINDSURFING

If you're a serious windsurfer, this is the wrong island and you need to pull a U-turn to Maui. However, if you want to just trim your sail for an afternoon, the Big Island has a few decent spots.

The hands-down favorite is Anaeho'-omalu Bay (known as 'A' Bay among locals), where you can rent equipment and take lessons. This is a good spot for beginners and experienced short-boarders aiming to perfect their form. In December and

January when the Kona winds are blowing, there's plenty of thrilling chop-hopping (winds typically reach 18 to 35 knots when these freak storms blow through). Blustery trade winds in spring also make for exciting sailing, but novices are warned off at this time, and rental places may be shuttered.

See the Waikoloa Beach Resort section of the South Kohala chapter for details.

FISHING

People come from the four corners to score the big one in the waters off the Kona coast. At the time of writing, more than 56 'grander' marlin (over 1000 lb), had been caught on this stretch of Big Island coast (which also holds the most marlin world records). Head to Kona, hop on a charter and you're in for the best game-fishing of your life.

June to August typically sees the biggest hauls for blue marlin, while January to June is the best for striped marlin. Still, thousand-pounders have been caught in Kona waters in every month of the year save October and November, so you can count on superb fishing year-round. The waters here are also rich with tuna (yellowfin and skipjack), swordfish, spearfish and mahimahi. The world-famous International Billfish Tournament is held here each August.

There are literally hundreds of charter companies, and while deep-sea fishing is something even first-timers can enjoy, you should ask a few questions of yourself and the charter operator before signing on and paying up, including:

- How big is the boat and how many clients does it accommodate?
- What happens to the fish if and when I catch it?
- Can I catch and release or tag and release?
- Is there a discount if I don't catch anything?
- Am I one to get seasick?

Shared, half-day (four-hour) charters start at $60 per person, with a maximum of six people. If your honey fishes but you don't, you can do a 'ride along' for $37. Half-day private charters range from $200 to $425, depending on the boat. A full-day private charter ranges from $495 to $750. You should bring your own food, drinks and camera (for all those action shots!). Information on many charters are listed in the informative *Fishing* freebie available at tourist offices and airports.

Voyeurs can ogle the day's catch as it's weighed on the Honokohau Marina scales at 11am and 3pm. Boats flying white flags have scored ahi, blue flags mean marlin and inverted flags signify the return of a catch-and-release excursion.

While there are too many high-quality charters to list here, a handful of clearing houses books recommended boats:

Charter Services Hawaii
    (☎ 334-1881, 800-567-2650)
Fins & Fairways
    (☎ 325-6171, fax 325-6378, W www.fishkona.com)
Kona Charter Skippers Association
    (☎ 329-3600, 800-762-7546)
The Charter Desk
    (☎ 329-5735, 888-566-2486)

In addition to ocean fishing, there's a state-maintained public freshwater fishing area at Waiakea in Hilo Bay. Stocked fish include rainbow trout, largemouth and smallmouth bass, channel catfish, tilapia and carp.

No licenses are required for fresh or saltwater fishing, but there are seasons, size limits and other regulations.

The booklets *Hawaii Fishing Regulations* and *Freshwater Fishing in Hawaii* will tell you everything you need to know. You can obtain them free from the Division of Aquatic Resources (☎ 974-6201), at 75 Apuni St, Rm 204, Hilo or in Kona (☎ 327-6226) at the Honokohau Harbor fuel dock. They'll also pop these guidelines in the mail upon request.

Reef fish, specifically mullet, papio and ulua, are subject to ciguatera poisoning. Reef fishermen should seek local advice and check out the web site of Oceanit Test Systems, W www.cigua.com. Also see Health in the Facts for the Visitor chapter.

HIKING

The hiking in Hawaii is top-notch, and there's enough diverse terrain to sate even the shortest attention spans. Hikes range from brief, laid-back nature strolls perfect for kids and seniors to multi-day backcountry treks that will set anyone's calves quaking.

With over 140 miles of beautiful, well maintained trails, Hawaii Volcanoes National Park offers unparalleled trekking. Here you can take a cool jaunt through a mystical ohia forest into a steaming crater, hike at sunset to the world's most active lava flow or trek to the fiery home of Pele. Hardcore hikers won't want to miss the 18-mile hike to the summit of Mauna Loa, the world's most massive mountain.

There are few superlatives that accurately capture the majesty of hiking to, through and beyond the ancient Waipi'o Valley. This is the fabled Valley of the Kings and even cynics can't deny the mana that imbues the place. Multi-day treks and camping are highly recommended.

Hiking to secluded beaches on the Puna or Kohala coasts and to hidden waterfalls and bays on the Hamakua coast will re-awaken your explorer's spirit. Many of these hikes are fairly quick descents to the sea or hot, but fairly easy, hikes across lava. That such a fresh sense of discovery is still attainable in Hawaii will surprise everyone except those already familiar with the ways of the Big Island. There are also trails through nature preserves, botanical gardens and less frequented parks where you can observe native plants and birds and enjoy lots of solitude.

There are a number of organizations offering guided hikes throughout the Big Island.

Hawaii Forest & Trail (☎ 331-8505, fax 331-8704, W www.hawaii-forest.com, 74-5035B Queen Ka'ahumanu Hwy, Kailua-Kona, Hi 96740) These folks offer a variety of high end and exclusive tours (full- and half-day) with expert interpreters. The Hakalau Forest and Pu'u O'o Ranch will interest birders.

Na Ala Hele Hawaii Trails And Access System (NAH; ☎ 974-4217, W www.hawaii trails.org, 19 East Kawili St, Hilo 96720) NAH maintains over a dozen trails island-wide and acts as a clearing house for guides offering hikes on their trails.

Sierra Club *(☎ 965-9695,* **w** *www.hi.sierra club.org/Hawaii/mokuloa.html, PO Box 1137, Hilo, HI 96721)* The local club offers day hikes on different trails each week.

Safety

Hiking in and around volcanoes presents a variety of dangers. Hydrochloric acid and sulfur fumes in volcanic steam can lead to respiratory problems; benches on the edge of lava flows can unexpectedly collapse; crevasses in the earth like to wrench ankles; and thin crusts over lava tubes sometimes give way without warning. Heed all posted warning signs and hike with a buddy.

Flash floods are a real danger in many of the steep, narrow valleys that require stream crossings. This is especially true in the winter when it can rain daily on the windward side. If the water begins to rise, get to higher ground immediately and wait until the water level drops (this can sometimes take days!). Other warning signs of a flash flood include a distant rumbling, the smell of fresh earth and a sudden increase in the river's current.

Falling rocks are another hiking hazard here. Be aware when swimming under high waterfalls, as rocks can dislodge from the top, and be extra careful on the edge of steep cliffs; cliffside rock can be crumbly.

Darkness falls fast once the sun sets and ridge-top trails are no place to be caught unprepared in the dark. Carry a flashlight when you're hiking, just in case. Long pants offer welcome protection from overgrown parts of the trail, and sturdy footwear with good traction is a must, especially on lava.

A walking stick is good for bracing yourself on slippery approaches, gaining leverage and testing the depth of rivers and streams. It's also an effective cockroach-squashing tool.

Hawaii has no snakes, no poison ivy, no poison oak and few wild animals that will fuss with hikers. On secluded trails, there's a slim possibility of meeting up with a wild boar; err on the side of caution with these beasts.

Other general hiking advice includes packing two liters of water per person for a day hike, carrying a whistle and something bright to alert rescue workers should the need arise, wearing sunscreen, toting a first aid kit and starting out early.

TENNIS

From coast to coast, municipal tennis courts dot the Big Island. These aren't sun-cracked concrete and saggy net affairs: most county courts are well maintained, with fresh nets and night lighting. There are even some indoor courts. You can call the County Parks and Recreation office (☎ 961-8311 in Hilo) for the long list of tennis courts under their auspices.

Obviously, most resorts have tennis facilities for their guests, but several also allow regular folks like us to rally on their courts. Racket rentals range from $3 to $8 per day, depending on their condition, and court fees range from $5 to $10 per person, per day.

In Kailua-Kona, for example, the ***Royal Kona Resort*** *(☎ 329-3111 ext 7188)* and ***Kings Sport & Racquet Club*** *(☎ 329-2911, in the King Kam Kona Beach Hotel)* allow non-guests to use their courts.

In South Kohala resortland, the ***Outrigger Waikoloa Beach Hotel Tennis Center*** *(☎ 886-6789)*, the ***Mauna Kea Beach Hotel*** *(☎ 882-7222)* and the ***Orchid at Mauna Lani*** *(☎ 885-2000)* extend court privileges to non-guests. There are few private courts open to the public in Hilo, but try the ***Waikea Racquet Club*** *(☎ 961-5499)*.

In addition, most resorts offer private and group lessons and affordable round-robin practice sessions. Rates vary, but expect to drop at least $55 an hour for a private lesson.

GOLF

The links are a major Big Island draw; there are more than a dozen golf courses, some world-class. The Mauna Kea Golf Course, Francis Ii Brown Course (at the Mauna Lani Resort) and the two courses at the Waikoloa Beach Resort, to name but a few, are tops and beautifully situated on the leeward coast. Environmentalists will cringe at these irrigated oases in the sere lava landscape, but hey, you can't win them all.

Lest you think that golf is an elitist sport, there are some good deals for Big Island golfers. The municipal course in downtown Hilo charges just $25 for 18 holes and cart, and the Volcano Golf and Country Club, sitting beneath the majestic peaks of Mauna Kea and Mauna Loa, charges a reasonable $62.50. Many courses offer deep *kama'aina* (local) discounts and greens fees are usually slashed by 50% if you take an afternoon tee time; definitely ask about discounts. Super thrifty golf hounds should consider packing a driver and putter and renting the rest at the links of their choice.

SKIING & SNOWBOARDING

Yes, it snows on the Big Island. Not as much as it used to, according to old timers, but you can still schuss in some semblance of the white stuff here. Whereas snowfall used to be common from November to March, these days snow bunnies are limited to January, February and March on the Mauna Kea slopes. When there's base enough for skiing and snowboarding, Tahoe and Colorado transplants flock to the flanks so you'll have to share runs.

Akin to skiing the world's highest downhill (patchy) run at Chacaltaya, Bolivia, skiing the Big Island is basically a notch on your novelty belt: there are no lifts and no trails, though there are some vertical drops of 5000 feet. Exposed lava rock and ice sheets are potential hazards. You get to the top via 4WD (yours or with a guide) and point yourself down. You'll pay between $250 and $450 for the thrill (including gear, guide, lunch and transport). You can also rent gear only for $50.

Would-be skiers should be very careful about ascending Mauna Kea from sea level without proper acclimatization (see Altitude Sickness in the Health section of the Facts for the Visitor chapter). Scuba divers should be especially conscious of this potentially fatal hazard; skiing or ascending the summit can cause the bends and should not be attempted until 24 hours (at least) after diving.

For a basic run map, Mauna Kea weather conditions and summit cam, see **W** www.ski hawaii.com.

WHALE WATCHING

Approximately 5000 North Pacific humpbacks winter in Hawaiian waters, providing visitors with unparalleled whale-watching opportunities

The best time to view humpbacks is from January to April, when the ocean jumps with the breaching giants. They start arriving in November and some stick around as late as May (even for them it's hard to leave), so you're not limited to the late winter and early spring for sightings. They often can be spotted right from shore, though binoculars help. They cruise all about the island and you can see them in Kailua-Kona, the Hamakua Coast and Hilo, to name a few spots.

Whale watching is not only limited to humpbacks here. Sperm, false killer, dolphin and melon-headed whales can also be observed, especially from May to December. The Kona coast offers the best viewing opportunities, and there are several outfits of-

---

Whale Songs

Humpbacks are remarkable not only for their acrobatic breaching but also for their operatic singing.

Each member of the pod sings the same set of songs, in the same order. Whale songs last anywhere from six to 30 minutes and evolve as the season goes on, with new phrases added and old ones dropped, so that the songs the whales sing when they arrive in Hawaii become different songs by the time they leave.

Marine biologists believe that humpbacks fall mute in their Alaskan feeding grounds. When they return to Hawaii six months later, however, they recall the songs from the last season and begin where they left off. The humpback's complex songs include the full range of frequencies audible to the human ear.

fering cruises (some guarantee sightings). Tours typically cost $55/35 for adults/children, but expect to pay more for more esoteric submarine or glass-bottomed boat tours. Tour clients should be aware that it's against the law to approach humpbacks within 100 yards by any means (including boat, plane or swimming stroke).

See the Kailua-Kona chapter for tour details, and also Whales under Flora & Fauna in the Facts about the Big Island chapter. For everything you want to know about humpbacks, visit the National Marine Sanctuary Web site at ⓦ www.hihwnms .nos.noaa.gov.

HELICOPTER TOURS

These are a popular way to get a big picture view of the Big Island. Helicopter tours are also a good (though expensive) option for seniors, kids or folks with physical challenges who can't hike to the volcanoes or valleys. Of course, the lazy like them too.

There are two basic tour options: buzzing around the valleys and waterfalls of the Kohala and Hamakua coasts, or touring the Kilauea Caldera and live lava flows of the East Rift Zone (both options are 45 minutes and $119-$160). A third option combines the first two into an all-in-one longer tour (one to two hours, $149-$350).

Do a bit of research before booking a tour. You should be assured of 180° views or at the very least, a window or front-facing seat. Pilot narration, exterior-mounted cameras, noise canceling headsets and seat configuration are other questions you may pose. Of course, the more amenities you have, the more the tour costs. Prices also vary depending on your departure point: volcano tours out of Hilo are the cheapest, followed by Kona and finally Waikoloa.

These tours are canceled during inclement weather, but may fly when it's overcast, which limits visibility. Wait for a sparkling clear day if you can and remember that even if it's sunny in Kona, it may be soupy over Volcano. Also ask specifically about flying over the Pu'u O'o vent, since this is where the action is and what you want to see.

Look for coupons in the freebie tourist booklets and ask about flying stand-by to save some money. Here are some of the Big Island operators:

Blue Hawaiian Helicopters (☎ 961-5600, 800-786-2583, ⓦ www.bluehawaiian.com)

Island Hoppers (☎ 969-2000, 800-538-7590, ⓦ www.fly-hawaii.com/above)

Safari Helicopters (☎ 969-1259, 800-326-3356, ⓦ www.safariair.com)

Sunshine Helicopters (☎ 882-1223 in Kona, 969-7501 in Hilo, 800-621-3144, ⓦ www.sunshine helicopters.com)

Tropical Helicopters (☎ 961-6810, ⓦ www.tropical helicopters.com)

Another exciting airborne option are the remarkable sunrise **hot air balloon** tours offered by **Paradise Balloons** (☎ 887-6455, ⓦ www.paradiseballoons.com). Soar over Mauna Kea, Waimea and the beautiful escarpments of the Kohala Coast for $240/190 for adults/children.

CYCLING

Big on space, long on single track and short on tourists, mountain biking is fast becoming the hip adventure sport here. The biking community is organized, hosts group rides, builds new trails and promotes responsible and safe cycling. Many shops also offer rentals, repairs, sales and tours.

The county is also jumping into the mix, designating several cycle-specific areas and funding a mountain-biking trail map. While the trail descriptions are reliable, you may want to procure another map source, as the details are a tad sketchy. Among the 10 routes described are the 45-mile Mana Rd loop circumnavigating Mauna Kea and the 6½-mile beach trail to Pine Trees on the Kona Coast.

Aside from established trails, there are also miles of 4WD roads to scream through and scratchy trails leading to little secret beaches that will surely catch the passing fancy of a cyclist or two.

Several local organizations actively maintain and designate trails, and host weekly rides. Look to these terrific resources for the latest on cycling the Big Island:

Big Island Mountain Bike Association(BIMBA; ☎ 961-4452, Ⓦ *www.interpac.net/~mtbike/,* PO Box 6819, Hilo, HI 96720)

People's Advocacy for Trails Hawaii (PATH; ☎ 326-9495, fax 327-9429, Ⓦ *www.hialoha.com/ path/,* 74-5565 Luhia, Ste CA1, Kailua-Kona, HI 96740)

Hawaii Cycling Club (no ☎, Ⓦ *www.hawaiicycling club.com,* PO Box 3246, Kailua-Kona, HI 96745)

Kona Coast Cycling Tours (☎ 877-392-2453, Ⓦ *www.cyclekona.com/tours.htm)* publishes a do-it-yourself cycling package including a detailed map, trip log (including elevation gains and ride distances) and a bibliography for $18.50.

For all manner of annual races including biking, running, swimming and outrigger canoeing, see the listings in the Big Island Race & Training Schedule (Ⓦ www.bigisland raceschedule.com).

RUNNING

If you think Black Sabbath when someone says 'Ironman,' skip this section. If, however, it means running, swimming and peddling to personal (and, if you're really good, public) triumph, read on.

Each October, Kona hosts the world-renowned Ironman Triathlon (see the boxed text, below), which combines a 2.4-mile ocean swim, 112-mile bike race and a full marathon (26.2 miles) into one exhaustive endurance race. Some 1500 men and women from 50 countries compete each year.

The competition usually takes place on the Saturday nearest the full moon, so late finishers won't have to run along the pitch-black highway. It begins and ends near Kailua Pier. Top competitors finish in a mere eight hours, while stragglers might take double that to stumble across the finish line (but kudos to everyone for seeing it through!).

The Keauhou-Kona Triathlon is a half-Ironman, held in Keauhou Bay each May.

You would be hard pressed to find a more beautiful running circuit than the craters and calderas of Hawaii Volcanoes National Park. Local running enthusiasts agree, and

Ironman Triathlon

The Ironman, the first and foremost of all triathlons, takes place each October on the sunny Kona Coast, starting and ending in Kailua-Kona. It's a grueling, 2.4-mile swim, 112-mile bike race and marathon-run combo that draws the world's top triathletes. The total prize purse is $325,000, with the first place male and female finishers receiving $70,000 each.

The Ironman began in 1978 with just 15 participants. The following year, the event was covered by *Sports Illustrated,* which labeled it 'lunatic.' By 1980, the Ironman was covered by ABC's Wide World of Sports, and since that time its popularity has grown by leaps and bounds.

These days, some 50,000 triathletes compete in worldwide qualifiers in hopes of earning one of the 1500 berths in the Ironman event. Every US state and Canadian province and some 50 other countries are represented in the race's ranks. The youngest competitor is 18, the oldest is pushing 80. The current men's record, set by Luc Van Lierde (Belgium) in 1996, is 8 hours and 4 minutes, while the women's record, set by Paula Newby-Fraser (USA) in 1992, is 8 hours and 55 minutes.

Harsh Kona conditions make the event the ultimate endurance test, even by triathlon standards. Heat reflected off the lavascape race route commonly exceeds 100°F, making dehydration and heat exhaustion major concerns, and headwinds are another challenge. Many contenders arrive weeks before the race to acclimatize. On race day, nearly 7000 volunteers line up along the 140-mile course to proffer 100,000 gallons of fluids (soda, water and soup) to passing racers. In addition, a whopping 600 bottles of sunscreen are squeezed onto rippling, sweaty bodies.

To learn more about the race, including qualifying requirements and volunteer opportunities, contact the Ironman Triathlon World Championship (☎ 329-0063, fax 326-2131, Ⓦ www.iron manlive.com), 75-5722 Kuakini Hwy, suite 101, Kailua-Kona, HI 96740.

each July the park is the site of the Kilauea Volcano Wilderness Runs.

There are four separate events: a 10-mile run around the Kilauea Caldera rim; a 5-mile run and a 5-mile walk that go down into Kilauea Iki Crater; and a marathon through the Ka'u Desert. For information, contact the *Volcano Art Center* (☎ *967-7565,* W *www .volcanoartcenter.org, PO Box 104, Hawaii Volcanoes National Park, HI 96718).*

The *Hawaii Race* (☎ 808-538-0330, W www .hawaiirace.com), 9 N Pauahi, No 200, Honolulu, HI 96817, includes statewide running, swimming and cycling race schedules, qualification details and entry forms.

HORSEBACK RIDING

Ranches, rodeos, cattle and cowboys are an integral part of Big Island history and culture and it lives on around Parker Ranch and Waimea town. There are some fantastic trail rides in this area, around the Kohala Mountains and beyond into the Waipi'o Valley.

Two-hour trail rides typically start at around $75. All the terrain here is drop-dead gorgeous and trotting along on the back of a Big Island steed will be memorable. Custom rides, cattle drives and tours appropriate for kids and beginners are all possible; see the relevant regional chapters.

Getting There & Away

AIR
Late in the writing of this book, a merger was announced between Aloha and Hawaiian Airlines, so the following information will likely change. While higher prices are threatened, more competition from other carriers entering the market may result in more flights and ultimately, better fares.

Most visitors fly into Honolulu and connect with an interisland flight to either Kona or Hilo on the Big Island. Kona is the main airport and a handful of direct flights from the mainland, London and Tokyo land here. Aloha Airlines (in partnership with United) serves Hilo from Los Angeles, San Francisco and Tokyo. If your heart's set on Hilo, it will probably be cheaper to fly to Honolulu and hop an interisland flight or fly to Kona and travel overland.

Airport security has been tightened since the September 11th terrorist attacks on the USA. Only ticketed passengers are allowed

beyond the airline check-in counters and all baggage is subject to random search. Even seemingly innocuous items, such as staplers or matches, are being confiscated from carry-on baggage; if possible, check all of your luggage at the front counter. Be sure to arrive at the airport 2½ hours before international departures and 90 minutes early for interisland flights.

All taxes for US airports are normally included in the price of tickets when you buy them, whether they're purchased in the USA or abroad. There are no additional departure taxes to pay when leaving Hawaii.

There are no foreign exchange services at either Big Island airport. There are, however, several Thomas Cook counters at the Honolulu airport. There are ATMs at the Honolulu and Kona airport, but not Hilo.

Due to heightened security precautions (sound familiar?), there are no baggage storage facilities at any Hawaiian airports. This could change in the future, though it's not likely.

Keahole-Kona Airport
The first taste of the Big Island for most visitors is the Keahole-Kona Airport. Located on Hwy 19, about 7 miles north of Kailua-Kona, it's 12 miles from the resorts at Waikoloa and the secluded beaches strung along the Kohala coast. This can be a long, slow drive in afternoon traffic.

For a relatively busy airport, it's surprisingly casual, and all open-air, imparting an immediate tropical feel. Additionally, there are no jetways and you deplane via stairs directly on to the tarmac.

It has all the usual amenities: an ATM, visitor information booth, lei stand, restaurant, taxi queue, car rental booths and a newsstand selling good Big Island maps and major mainland newspapers.

Hilo Airport
The Hilo Airport is off Hwy 11, a little under a mile south of the Hwy 11 and Hwy 19

intersection. It has a visitor information booth, car rental counters and a taxi stand. As the last interisland flight arrives before 8 pm, things shut down early. Public parking costs $1 for the first 30 minutes, $1 for each hour (or fraction thereof), with a maximum of $7 for 24 hours.

Flying from Hilo provides unsurpassed vistas of Mauna Kea, the amphitheater valleys of the Kohala coast and more; sit on the left.

Airlines

The following airlines serve Honolulu International Airport on Oahu; United and Aloha also serve Kona from the US mainland. Those that begin with 800 or 888 are toll-free numbers.

Air Canada	☎ 888-247-2262
Air New Zealand	☎ 800-262-1234
All Nippon Airways	☎ 800-235-9262
Aloha Airlines	☎ 800-367-5250
America West Airlines	☎ 800-235-9292
American Airlines	☎ 800-433-7300
China Airlines	☎ 800-227-5118
Continental Airlines	☎ 800-523-3273
Delta Air Lines	☎ 800-221-1212
Garuda Indonesia	☎ 800-342-7832
Hawaiian Airlines	☎ 800-367-5320
Japan Airlines	☎ 800-525-3663
Korean Air	☎ 800-438-5000
Northwest Airlines	☎ 800-225-2525
Philippine Airlines	☎ 800-435-9725
Qantas Airways	☎ 800-227-4500
Singapore Airlines	☎ 800-742-3333
United Airlines	☎ 800-241-6522

Buying Tickets

Numerous airlines fly to Hawaii, though certain fares and flights are more attractive than others. As airfares are constantly in flux, do some research and shop around to take advantage of lurking bargains. Usually the cheapest fares are for midweek during low season with restricted tickets. These tickets may have advance purchase requirements and be nonrefundable or nonchangeable.

Nothing determines fares more than demand, and when things are slow, regardless of the season, airlines slash fares to fill seats. The longer you intend to stay in Hawaii, the more expensive your ticket will be. With few exceptions, one-way tickets to the islands are just as expensive as return fares. However, Round-the-World or Circle Pacific fares can reap substantial savings and interesting stopover destinations (see the 'Round-the-World Tickets' section later).

Ways to lower your fare include maintaining flexibility (providing alternate departure and return dates especially); departing from a secondary, smaller airport; and accepting stopovers.

Doing your own research can pay off: travel sites like Travelocity (W www.travelocity .com) and Expedia (W www.expedia .com) are useful for giving you ballpark estimates and many airlines offer Internet-only special fares if you book on-line. On-line travel discounters who handle Hawaii flights can also net substantial savings. Try W www.smarterliving.com or W www.air fare.com. Another option for Web users are ticket auction sites including Priceline (W www.priceline.com) and Orbitz (W www .orbitz.com). Ticket consolidators who advertise in the travel sections of major newspapers and free alternative weeklies also offer cut-rate tickets, as do student and youth specialist travel agencies.

If you hope to redeem your frequent flyer miles for a ticket to Hawaii, think again. Hundreds of other people try to do exactly the same thing every year. Unfortunately, frequent flyer award seats are tough to come by, though you might get lucky.

For routes besides California-Kona or (occasionally) London-Kona, it is much cheaper to fly to Honolulu and connect with an interisland flight to the Big Island. For this reason, many flights listed here are to Honolulu; for the scoop on interisland flights and coupons, see the Within Hawaii section.

Round-the-World Tickets Round-the-World (RTW) tickets allow you to circumnavigate the globe by flying on the combined routes of two or more airlines. These tickets are typically valid for 12 months and require you travel in one general direction without backtracking. This means you can't fly in and out of the same airport twice, effectively putting half the world out of reach. Also note that a few heavily traveled routes (eg, Honolulu-Tokyo) are sometimes blacked out.

Fares fluctuate depending on which countries and airlines you select, as well as when you start traveling; with the utmost flexibility and an advance purchase, you can net a UK£600, A$2200 or US$1300 fare. As a general rule, travel solely in the Northern Hemisphere is cheaper than itineraries that include Southern Hemisphere destinations. Whereas RTW tickets used to include unlimited stopovers, recently airlines have been capping the number of free stopovers (added stops cost extra). Some airlines prohibit any rerouting after you purchase the ticket, while others allow you to change dates without incurring penalties or add or delete stops for $25 to $75, depending on the carrier.

Major international airlines and partnerships, such as the Star Alliance and OneWorld, all offer RTW tickets through code-sharing flights on different routes and continents. It may be more time- and cost-efficient to price all the variations of your trip with a RTW specialist agent, rather than calling the airlines directly. US-based Air Treks (☎ 800-350-0612, 415-912-5600, **w** www.airtreks.com) and Air Brokers (☎ 800-883-3273, 415-397-1383, **w** www.airbrokers.com) have Web sites with helpful itinerary builders to get you started.

Circle Pacific Tickets If you're only interested in visiting Hawaii, Polynesia and the Pacific Rim, a Circle Pacific fare might be just the ticket. Rather than simply flying between Point A and Point B, Circle Pacific options allow you to swing through eastern Asia and the Pacific, taking in many destinations. As with RTW tickets, you have to travel in the same circular direction and stick with the same partner airlines.

Airline Merger

As this book went to press, Hawaiian Airlines and Aloha Airlines announced that they would merge operations starting in 2002. Airline representatives say that fares for interisland flights will not change for the next two years, after which fares will jump based on inflation. In the long run, the merger will mean higher prices and route cutbacks across the board, including fewer flights from Hawaii to the mainland and around the Islands. Even the airline names themselves are subject to change. Contact Hawaiian or Aloha directly for updates on the merger situation when making your travel plans.

The routes and airline combinations are numerous, and your itinerary can be built from scores of saucy destinations. For example, a Qantas-American-Cathay Pacific One World ticket could take you from Los Angeles to Honolulu, on to Tokyo, over to Bangkok, followed by Sydney and returning to Los Angeles.

Circle Pacific routes are essentially the same price regardless of your origin point. At the time of research, the standard fare for the above route was $2656. This permits four free stopovers with the option of additional stops at $50 each. There's typically a seven-day advance purchase requirement and a maximum stay of six months.

A titillating variation to the Circle Pacific ticket is Air New Zealand's Pacific Escapade fare. In conjunction with Singapore Airlines, this fare costs a maximum of $2600 and allows unlimited stops as long as you don't travel more than 22,000 miles. With itinerary and dates in hand, you can lower the price; call Air New Zealand for details.

Air New Zealand also offers a Coral Explorer fare that allows travel from Los Angeles to New Zealand, Australia and a number of South Pacific islands with a return via Honolulu. Fares start at $1178 for a maximum three-month stay and one stopover (three more stops can be added at

$150 each) and top out at $2218 with a year's maximum stay and four stopovers.

Discount Fares from Hawaii Honolulu is a good place to get discount fares to virtually any place around the Pacific or North American mainland.

Often you can find a roundtrip ticket to Los Angeles, San Francisco or Vancouver for around $300; to Tokyo for $400; to Toronto for $450; to Hong Kong or Seoul for $500; to Bangkok or Singapore for $550; to Sydney for $625; and to Bali for $700. Check the travel pages of the Sunday *Honolulu Advertiser* for current advertised fares and discount travel agencies.

Two reliable Honolulu-based travel agents are: Cheap Tickets (☎ 800-652-4327, 888-922-8849, **w** www.cheaptickets.com) and King's Travel (☎ 930-8888 on the Big Island, 808-593-4481 on Oahu, 800-801-4481, **w** www.kingstravel.com) Imperial Plaza Bldg, Ste C-103, 725 Kapiolani Blvd.

Travelers with Special Needs

If you have special needs of any sort – you're a vegan, traveling with a surfboard or have a medical condition – you should let the airline know as soon as possible so they can make arrangements for your traveling comfort. Remind them when you reconfirm your booking and again when you check in at the airport. It may also be worth calling around the airlines before buying a ticket to find out how each of them can handle your specific needs; if they are recalcitrant with your request, try another carrier.

Most international airports, including Honolulu International Airport, will provide an escorted cart or wheelchair from check-in desk to plane when needed, and have ramps, lifts and accessible toilets and phones. Aircraft toilets, on the other hand, are likely to present a problem for some passengers; travelers should discuss this with the airline at an early stage and, if necessary, with their doctor. Interisland flights may be on smaller aircraft and involve deplaning via stairs onto the tarmac. Also note that all flights into Kona deplane via stairs onto the tarmac.

As a general rule, children under two travel for 10% of the standard fare (or free on some airlines) as long as they don't occupy a seat. They don't get a baggage allowance either. 'Skycots,' baby food and diapers should be provided by the airline if requested in advance. Children between two and 12 can sometimes occupy a seat for half to two-thirds of the full fare, and they do get a baggage allowance.

US Mainland & Canada

Only a few international airlines and charter companies fly directly to the Big Island, and at any given time any one of them could be offering the cheapest fares.

Competition is higher among airlines flying to Honolulu, from where you can easily hop on an interisland flight to Kona or Hilo (see Within Hawaii later), thereby saving some money. Also, package tour companies sometimes offer juicy airfare deals, and you aren't always required to buy the whole 'package' (see Organized Tours later).

Typically, the lowest roundtrip fares from the US mainland to Honolulu are $300 to $450 from the West Coast, $600 to $850 from the East Coast. For those flying from other parts of the US, it may be cheaper to buy two separate tickets – one to the West Coast and then another ticket to Hawaii. A few charter airlines, such as American Trans Air (ATA; ☎ 800-435-9282, **w** www.ata .com), fly direct from the West Coast to Honolulu. Their fares are competitive, but they only schedule a few flights per week.

Hawaiian and Aloha Airlines/Island Air announced a merger in December 2001. The most heavily affected routes were slated to be direct flights from the mainland to the Big Island. Still, nonstop flights to Honolulu are surely to continue, albeit with price hikes.

At the time of writing, one or the other of the Hawaiian carriers flew from Honolulu to San Francisco, Oakland, San Diego, Portland, Seattle, Las Vegas, Washington, DC, and Juneau, Alaska.

At $119 one way, Air Tech's Space-Available FlightPass is surely the cheapest way to fly between the US mainland and the Big Island. Air Tech (☎ 212-219-7000, W www .airtech.com) sells standby seats: you pro vide them with a two- to four-day travel window and they'll get you a seat at the nice price. They currently offer service between San Francisco and Kailua-Kona; locals swear by Air Tech.

From Canada, the cheapest round trip Air Canada (☎ 888-247-2262) fares to Hon olulu are C$585 from Vancouver, C$665 from Calgary, C$700 from Toronto and C$1000 from Montreal. Many of these low fares are only available at W www.air canada.com. Canadian charter flight compa nies and ticket consolidators offer competi tive deals, and discounts for flights from Montreal are especially attractive. Unfortu nately, direct flights to the Big Island will cost around twice as much as these fares to Honolulu.

Travel agencies specializing in student and under-26 youth discount airfares like Council Travel (☎ 800-226-8624, W www .counciltravel.com) and STA Travel (☎ 800-781-4040, W www.statravel.com) have offices in all major US cities. In Canada, try Travel CUTS/Voyages Campus (☎ 866-246-9762, W www.travelcuts.com).

Cut-rate travel agents (also known as ticket consolidators) often advertise discount fares in major newspapers and weeklies. In New York, try the *New York Times, Village Voice* and the *NY Press*. In California, look for the *Bay Guardian, San Francisco Chronicle* and *LA Times*. In Canada, there's *The Globe & Mail,* Toronto's *Now* and Van couver's *Georgia Straight*.

Latin America

Most flights to Hawaii from Central and South America go via a US gateway city: New York, Houston or Los Angeles, usually, but also occasionally through Atlanta, San Francisco or Miami.

United Airlines offers flights from cities in Mexico and Central America, including Mexico City, Guadalajara and Cancún and Guatemala City. United's lowest roundtrip fare from Mexico City to Honolulu is $792 and allows a maximum stay of 30 days.

UK & Continental Europe

From Europe, most travelers to Hawaii fly west via New York, Chicago or Los Angeles. From the last you can fly directly to Kailua-Kona. If you're interested in heading east with stops in Asia, it may be cheaper to get a Round-the-World ticket instead of return ing the same way.

At the time of writing, United offered a roundtrip fare from London to Kailua-Kona for £612. The lowest roundtrip fare from Frankfurt to Kona via LA was €1029 for a stay of up to 21 days; from Paris to Kailua-Kona via London and LA the fare was €1052. For the last it would probably be cheaper and faster to fly directly to Hon olulu and connect with an interisland flight, or get to London and fly from there.

You can usually beat the published airline fares at 'bucket shops' and other travel agencies specializing in discount tickets. London is arguably the world's headquarters for bucket shops, and they are well-advertised. Good, reliable agents for cheap tickets in the UK include Trailfinders (☎ 0171-938-3939, W www.trailfinders.com), 194 Kensington High St, London and STA Travel (☎ 0171-465-0484, W www.statravel .com.uk), 117 Euston Rd, London. STA also has offices in Germany, Switzerland and Scandinavia.

The travel sections of the *Evening Stan dard, Time Out* or *TNT* can give you an idea of current fare deals.

Australia & New Zealand

Qantas flies to Kailua-Kona via Honolulu from Sydney or Melbourne (via Sydney), with roundtrip fares of A$1780. These tickets have a maximum stay of 60 days. North American mainland carriers serving this route include American, Air Canada and United.

Unfortunately, no airline offers attractive fares between Auckland and the Big Island or even Auckland and Honolulu for that matter; at the time of research, the cheapest roundtrip fare for Auckland to Honolulu was NZ$2573. At this price, you'd be much better off with a Circle Pacific fare (see that section, earlier).

These fares are only the airlines' official fares. You will find the best deals by shopping around, checking the travel sections of the *Sydney Morning Herald* or Melbourne's *The Age* and over the Internet. In Australia, Flight Centre and STA travel agencies in Melbourne and Sydney have competitively priced tickets. STA also operates an office in Auckland, New Zealand.

South Pacific Islands & Micronesia

Air Pacific offers a roundtrip fare from Fiji to Honolulu for F$1520.

Polynesian Airlines flies to Honolulu from Tahiti and American Samoa. From Pago Pago in American Samoa, the fare is $732 roundtrip and good for 12 months. From Tahiti to Honolulu the standard roundtrip fare is a steep $1442, but you may be able to corral a special fare off the Internet.

Air New Zealand flies to Honolulu from Tonga, the Cook Islands and Western Samoa. The lowest roundtrip fare from Tonga to Honolulu costs T$1246.

From Rarotonga on the Cook Islands, Air New Zealand's cheapest roundtrip fare to Honolulu is NZ$1549, has a seven-day advance purchase and allows a stay of up to six months.

From Apia in Western Samoa, Polynesian Airlines roundtrip fare to Honolulu costs WS$2807 with no advance purchase requirement and a 90-day maximum stay.

Island addicts should look into Continental's Circle Micronesia Fare, which takes in several of the Federated Sates of Micronesia. You must originate in the United States, (either the mainland or Honolulu), and have two route options: Guam-Yap-Palau or Guam-Truk-Pohnpei-Majuro. Departing from Los Angeles or San Francisco, the first option costs $1230, while the second is $1650. Leaving from Honolulu, the Guam-Yap-Palau route costs $920 and the Guam-Truk-Pohnpei-Majuro option is $1250. These fares permit unlimited stops, as long as you continue traveling in the same circular direction.

Asia

Many flights from Asia to the US mainland allow a stopover in Honolulu at little or no extra charge. Not only that, these tickets are only slightly more expensive than typical round trip fares to Hawaii only. From Honolulu to the Big Island, you can easily catch an inexpensive interisland flight (see Within Hawaii).

Hawaii is a top destination for Japanese tourists. Japan Airlines (JAL; ☎ 0120-25-5971, W www.jal.com) flies direct to Honolulu from Tokyo, Osaka, Fukuoka and Sapporo. Excursion fares vary with the departing city and the season, but they can dip as low as ¥75,000. Discount fares to Honolulu with All Nippon Airways (ANA; ☎ 0120-029-006 in Osaka, W www.ana.co.jp) are sometimes as low as ¥44,500.

Remember that during Japanese holiday periods, particularly New Year's, Golden Week in May and Obon in August, these fares instantly triple or even quadruple. A few discount travel agencies (mainly in Tokyo, Osaka and Kyoto) offer unbeatable multi-stop USA tickets for less than ¥100,000 roundtrip.

For elsewhere around Asia, the major international carriers are Northwest Airlines, Singapore Air, Korean Air, China Airlines and Thai Airways. Although seasonal variations exist, the lowest published roundtrip fares to Honolulu average B31,000 from Bangkok; W1,155,000 from Seoul; HK$7800 from Hong Kong; S$1850 from Singapore, and about P57,500 from Manila. Again, add the equivalent of at least US$100 for flights to the Big Island.

Many discount travel agencies in Bangkok, Hong Kong and Singapore sell cut-rate tickets for less than half the major airline fares. For example, a one-way ticket from Bangkok to Hawaii may go for as little as B6400. A few such discount agencies are of the hit-and-run variety, so ask around before you buy. In Singapore, try STA Travel (☎ 65-737 7188, W www.statravel .com.sg), 33A Cuppage Road or the agencies at Chinatown Point shopping center, New Bridge Rd.

Bangkok and Hong Kong each have a number of excellent, reliable travel agencies, and some not-so-reliable ones. Both types are found along Bangkok's Khao San Rd, or in Hong Kong on Nathan Rd in Tsimshatsui. A good way to check on a travel agent is to look it up in the phone book.

Within Hawaii

Hawaiian Airlines (☎ 808-838-1555 on Oahu, 800-882-8811 Neighbor Islands, 800-367-5320 US mainland & Canada, W www .hawaiianair.com) and Aloha/Island Air (☎ 935-5771 in Hilo or Kona, 808-484-1111 on Oahu, 800-367-5250 US mainland & Canada, W www.alohaairlines.com) announced a merger in late 2001, but the new airline promised to hold interisland fares steady until 2004.

Once the two combine, other changes will include a younger fleet, fewer direct flights from the mainland to the Big Island and an abbreviated schedule between Neighbor Islands.

There are frequent flights in full-bodied jets between the major island airports, but usually with stops or transfers in Honolulu.

Interisland flights often have empty seats, so if your original flight arrives in Honolulu early or you have a lengthy layover, ask at the gate if you can fly stand-by on the next flight to the Big Island. Chances are you'll get a seat. The flip side of this phenomenon, however, is that a few interisland flights each day are canceled, so remain flexible.

The highest standard one-way fare for any interisland flight is $104. Round trips cost exactly twice the one-way fare. However, only fools and descendants of Croesus pay the standard fare. When you call to make a reservation, ask what promotions are being offered. AAA and frequent flyer members can count on a 10% discount on standard coach seats. Also, check the airline's Web site for steep interisland discounts.

Teeny Paragon Air (☎ 800-428-1231 Neighbor Islands & US mainland, W www .paragon-air.com) has some of the cheapest promotional flights around for the Kahului, Maui-Kona route at $110 roundtrip. These flights are on small prop planes and offer good views.

Because interisland flights can work out to be so inexpensive, travelers might save hundreds of dollars by booking their flight from home only as far as Honolulu and then making an interisland flight reservation for the final leg of their trip to the Big Island. The only trick is to secure a great interisland fare directly from the airline or plan to pick up a discount flight coupon in Honolulu (see Flight Coupons).

Pacific Wings (☎ 888-575-4546 toll free) is a commuter airline flying every day but Tuesday from Waimea-Kahului, Maui and Waimea-Honolulu for $61.50 one way.

Flight Coupons Unless you already have a super promo fare directly from the airline, you'll save heaps by buying discount flight coupons. Usually these cost $60-70, depending on where you buy them. One of the many advantages of using flight coupons is that there are no penalties for changing the date and time of your flight reservation, as long as seats are still available.

Using interisland flight coupons is totally straightforward. Just make your flight reservations as you normally would and let the representative know you'll be paying with a coupon. You can make your booking before buying the coupon and since there are no advance purchase requirements, you could theoretically put off buying the coupon until the very last minute.

Coupons are sold at discount travel agencies, Cut Rate Ticket outlets and KTA supermarkets in Hilo and Kona (see those chapters). At the time of writing, coupons were also sold for $65.25 per ticket from Bank of Hawaii ATMs, one of which can be found in the interisland terminal at Honolulu Airport. You need to use your PIN number along with your credit card (Visa or MasterCard). To check on the going rate for interisland coupons, visit W www.cutrate tickets.com.

Coupon booklets containing six interisland flight tickets are available at airport ticket counters in Hawaii. Usually these can be used by any number of people on any flight without restrictions. At the time of writing, a coupon booklet cost $390.

SEA

Due to pernicious seas, there is no boat transport to the Big Island, except with cruise ships (see Cruises in the Organized Tours section later) and private sailing vessels. There's always *some* scheme floating about to introduce interisland ferry service, but nothing has materialized on this front.

Yacht

Most private yachts weighing anchor in Hawaii do so in Honolulu, though each year a handful of boats head west from the Big Island to the South Pacific. Your best bet for landing with a skipper is to start poking around the dry dock at the Kawaihae port north of Kailua-Kona in early spring. Experienced crew looking to sail between Hawaii and the US mainland or the US and the South Pacific via Hawaii should try one of the following Web sites that connects skippers and crews:

w www.boatcrew.net
This well organized site has a database of boats leaving from various mainland ports; requires membership (free at the time of writing).

w www.sfsailing.com
This site lists skippers sailing from the San Francisco Bay Area; a few are long distance ocean cruisers.

w www.latitude 38.com
This has skippers looking for crew to many exotic destinations and lists preferred crew skills (eg, 'have more desire than experience' and 'be willing to bust butt preparing the boat').

ORGANIZED TOURS

For those with limited time, package tours can be the cheapest way to go. The basic ones cover airfare and accommodation (or airfare only), while deluxe packages include car rental, island hopping and all sorts of activities. If you're interested, travel agents can help you sort through the various options.

Costs vary, but one-week tours with airfare and generic hotel accommodations start as low as $500 from the US West Coast, or $800 from the US East Coast, based on double occupancy. Special sales may include car rental for the same rates.

Sun Trips (☎ 800-786-8747, w www.sun trips.com) offers airfare-only and other packages from SFO or LAX airports. Airfare only specials to Kona can dip as low as $259 round-trip, but departures are limited to a few flights per week.

Pleasant Hawaiian Holidays (☎ 800-742-9244, w www.2hawaii.com) has departures from the US West Coast, Midwest and East Coast.

Cruises

A handful of cruise ships offer tours that include Oahu, Maui, Kauai and the Big Island. Because US federal law bans foreign-flagged ships from cruising solely between US ports, a foreign port must be included on all trips (typically Kiribati).

The best way to land a decent deal is to go through a cruise specialist travel agent. Most of these cruises last 10 to 12 days, although some last up to a month. Fares start at around $150 a day per person, based on double occupancy, but discounts and promotions can easily drop that price to under $100 a day.

If you've never been on a cruise before, you'll want to ask certain questions before hopping aboard, including: How much time is spent off-ship? What is the crew-to-passenger ratio? How big is the ship, what is the size of my room and where is it located? What kind of extra activities and perks, such as free babysitting, are available?

Princess Cruises (☎ 800-774-6237, w www .princesscruises.com) offer the longest Hawaii cruising season and the most varied trips. Shorter cruises lasting 10 to 15 days depart from Vancouver or Los Angeles. Tahiti cruises stop over at Bora Bora and Easter Island, while the 25-day sailing between Tokyo and San Francisco includes Midway Island, the Marianas and Marshall Islands.

Royal Caribbean Cruise Line (☎ 800-307-8413, w www.rccl.com) typically has Hawaii cruises departing from Ensenada, Mexico or Vancouver, Canada.

Norwegian Cruise Lines (☎ 800-327-7030, ⓦ www.ncl.com) travel between Honolulu and Kiribati. Others depart from Vancouver or Ensenada, Mexico.

Holland America (☎ 877-932-4259, ⓦ www.hollandamerica.com) departs from San Diego, Vancouver or Ensenada, Mexico.

Norwegian Cruise Lines is the only company offering cruises between the Hawaiian islands. Launched in December 2001, the 7-day inter-island cruise stops in Kiribati, Maui, Kauai and Kona. Longer 10-day itineraries (slated to include the Hilo side) are also on the drawing board. Staterooms for the 7-day route start at $900 and top out at $25,000 for an on-board villa.

Cycling Tours
Big Island cycling tours are all the rage and there are some well-organized outfits filling the demand. Among the more popular alternatives are:

Backroads (☎ 800-462-2848, ⓦ www.backroads .com). This well-regarded company offers 6-day bike tours circling the island and a multisport option incorporating cycling, kayaking and hiking. Prices start at $2300, excluding airfare.

Bicycle Adventures (☎ 800-443-6060, ⓦ www .bicycleadventures.com). This outfit has been around for years and offers frequent 8-day multi-sport bicycling, hiking and snorkeling tours with full support. Prices start at $2350, excluding airfare.

Odyssey World Cycling Tours (☎ 800-433-0528, ⓦ www.odyssey2000.com). This outfit offers a 7-day 'Wheeling Hawaii' tour that circumnavigates the island beginning in Kona. Riders average 50 miles per day and camp and stay in hotels en route. Prices start at $900, excluding airfare. These tours are separate from the (in)famous Odyssey 2000 trips.

Getting Around

AIR

For a big island, there isn't much local air traffic. In fact, the one daily flight that used to connect Hilo and Kona was recently discontinued.

TO/FROM THE AIRPORT

From the Keahole-Kona airport, you have the choice of a rental car, taxi ($20/40 to Kailua-Kona/Waikoloa) or the Speedi Shuttle bus (☎ 329-5433, ⓦ www.speedi shuttle.com). The last has door-to-door service from 7am to 9pm and costs $17.50 to Kailua-Kona and $30 to the Waikoloa resorts.

There is no public bus service from the Hilo airport, so your choices are limited to a rental car or taxi. A taxi to downtown costs around $15. Guests of Arnott's Lodge (see Places to Stay in the Hilo chapter) should avail themselves of the hostel's free shuttle; the last one is at 8pm.

BUS

The Hele-On bus (☎ 961-8744) circumnavigates the island and can be useful for moving between Kona and Hilo ($5.25, three hours), Hilo and Hawaii Volcanoes National Park ($2.25, one hour), or to other towns of interest, such as Waimea, Honoka'a, Pahoa and Na'alehu.

Service is but once daily on weekdays, so a Big Island bus odyssey isn't practical. Still, with a little planning, you can get yourself between major towns and attractions. There are also a few intra-Hilo and intra-Kona buses that are helpful for getting about those hubs. See Getting Around in the regional chapters for schedules.

Fares are reasonable and if you purchase a sheet of ten tickets, you save 10% off the regular fare. Monthly passes for student, disabled and senior passengers are 33% cheaper. Backpacks and luggage carry a $1 surcharge.

CAR & MOTORCYCLE

The minimum age for driving in Hawaii is 18 years, though car rental companies usually have higher age restrictions. Readers younger than 25 should call the rental agencies in advance to check their policies regarding restrictions.

With very few exceptions, no matter where you're from, you can legally drive a car, scooter or moped in Hawaii as long as you have a valid driver's license issued by your home country. If your license is not in English, you may be required to show an international driver's license as well.

Gasoline in Hawaii costs more than anywhere else in the US, with the price for regular unleaded averaging around $2 a gallon. Gas costs about $0.20 less on the Hilo side than the Kona side. Aloha and Tesoro usually have the cheapest gas in town.

Driving Times

It takes about five hours to drive all the way around the Big Island, but that's at a hellbent pace with nary a 'look at that sunset!' photo op stop. And you will want to pull over for views, repeatedly. There are so many special pockets, you might break the drive in whatever cool place strikes a chord.

Road Rules

As with the rest of the USA, driving is – mostly – on the right-hand side of the road (folks tend to drift while checking out passing shore breaks and the glorious Mauna Kea).

Drivers at a red light can turn right after coming to a full stop and yielding to oncoming traffic, unless there's a sign at the intersection prohibiting the turn.

Hawaii requires the use of seat belts for drivers and front-seat passengers. Heed this, as the ticket is stiff. State law also strictly requires the use of child-safety seats for children aged three and under, while four-year-olds must either be in a safety seat or secured by a seat belt. Most car rental companies lease child-safety seats for around $5 a day, but they don't always have them on hand; reserve one in advance if you can. You can also rent car seats at Baby's Away and Pacific Rent-All (see Travel with Children in the Facts for the Visitor chapter for details).

Speed limits are posted and enforced, if not always respected. If you're stopped for speeding, expect a ticket, as the police rarely just give warnings. Cruising unmarked police cars come in hot makes and models on the Big Island, so they're not always easy to spy: look for the blue dome light on the roof.

Road courtesy is contagious here and you can join in by slowing to let people pass, ceding space so cars can exit driveways and yielding to other drivers whenever it's safe to do so. Cool moves likes this are acknowledged by waving the shaka sign. Popular bumper stickers include: 'Slow Down. This Ain't Da Mainland' and 'Drive with Aloha.' Horn honking is considered rude unless required for safety. Unless otherwise posted, downhill traffic must yield to uphill traffic on one-lane bridges and roads.

Unfortunately, drivers under the influence can be a hazard – no matter if it's 9am or pm, or marijuana, beer or ice the vice. Big-ass frogs like baseballs plopped in the middle of lonely roads and darting cats are other hazards to watch for.

Car Rental

Rental cars are available at the Hilo and Kona airports. Rates vary by company depending on season, time of booking and current promotions. Be sure to ask the agent for the cheapest rate, as the first quote given is rarely the lowest. If you belong to a travel or automobile club or frequent-flier program, you'll likely be eligible for some sort of discount. You'll often need to get that discount code from your own organization before booking a car. Internet specials

Road Distances and Times

From Hilo

Destination	Mileage	Time
Hawi	86	2¼ hours
Honoka'a	40	1 hour
Kailua-Kona	92	2½ hours
Na'alehu	64	1¾ hours
Pahoa	16	25 minutes
Volcanoes NP	28	45 minutes
Waikoloa	80	2¼ hours
Waimea	54	1½ hours
Waipi'o Lookout	50	1¼ hours

From Kailua-Kona

Destination	Mileage	Time
Hawi	51	1¼ hours
Hilo	92	2½ hours
Honoka'a	61	1½ hours
Na'alehu	60	1½ hours
Pahoa	108	3 hours
Volcanoes NP	98	2½ hours
Waikoloa	18	45 minutes
Waimea	43	1 hour
Waipi'o Lookout	70	1¾ hours

are definitely worth checking out, as on-line bookings often beat all other discounts.

Walking up to the rental counter without a reservation is never a good idea: it will subject you to usurious rates, and may strand you without a ride as it's not uncommon for cars to be sold out altogether during weekends and busy periods. Daily rates are usually for a 24-hour block, so you could get two days' use by renting at midday and driving around all afternoon, then heading out to explore somewhere else the next morning before the car is due back.

For a small car, the daily rate ranges from $25 to $45, while typical weekly rates are $150 to $200. Unfortunately, there's no real discount for monthly rentals. When requesting price quotes, make sure they include all surcharges and taxes. In Hawaii rental cars usually enjoy unlimited mileage, but there's a $3-a-day state road tax, an airport concession tax and sales tax.

Having a major credit card greatly simplifies the rental process. Without one, some agents simply won't rent vehicles, while others will require prepayment by cash or traveler's checks, as well as a hefty deposit of a few hundred dollars. Be aware that many car rental companies are loathe to rent to people who list a campground as their address on the island, and a few specifically add 'No Camping Permitted' to their rental contracts.

All rental agencies (except Harper's) prohibit driving their vehicles on the Saddle Road. Once you've driven it you'll think, 'Gee, that was tame. I wonder why you're not supposed to drive the Saddle Road in a rental?' Well, there's no problem until you break down and the agency has to send someone hundreds of miles up the road to tow your ass. That's why it's prohibited.

The approaches to Waipi'o Valley, Green Sands Beach, the Kalapana lava flow and all other dirt or lava roads are technically off-limits to rental cars, including 4WDs, but let's face it: some of the best of the Big Island hides down treacherous lava roads and people are going for it. You can too, but at your own risk and with the knowledge that if you screw up the car on one of these 'roads', you'll be liable.

If you plan on camping or tend to say 'aw hell, it's a rental' a lot, make sure to have it thoroughly washed and/or detailed before returning it to the agency or they'll work it over with a fine-toothed comb and charge you accordingly.

Insurance Rental companies in Hawaii have liability insurance, which covers injury to people that you might hit with their vehicles, but not property damage to either rental vehicle or anything else that got in your way. For this, a collision damage waiver (CDW) is available from car rental agencies, typically for an additional $9 to $15 a day.

The CDW is not insurance per se, but rather a guarantee that the rental company won't hold you liable for any damages to their car (though even here there are exceptions). If you decline the CDW, you are usually held liable for any damage up to the full value of the car. Remember that the littlest ding – someone bumping you in a parking lot for instance – can cost hundreds of dollars to fix.

If you have collision coverage on your vehicle at home, it might cover damages to vacation car rentals. Some credit cards, including most 'gold cards' issued by Visa and MasterCard, offer reimbursement coverage for collision damages if you rent the car with that credit card and decline the CDW. Check before you travel.

If damages do occur and you find yourself in a dispute with the rental company, call the state Department of Commerce & Consumer Affairs at ☎ 808-587-1234 for recorded information on your legal rights. Photograph any alleged damage before surrendering the vehicle and keep copies of any incident reports.

Car Rental Agencies The following international companies operate in the Kona and Hilo airports; these companies have worldwide offices and their cars can be booked on the Internet. The first number given is for Hilo, the second for Kona. The toll-free numbers are valid from the US mainland.

Alamo (☎ 961-3343, 329-8896, 800-327-9633, **w** www.alamo.com)

Avis (☎ 935-1290, 327-3000, 800-321-3712, **w** www.avis.com)

Budget (☎ 877-283-2468 in Hilo or Kona, 800-527-0700, **w** https://rent.drivebudget.com.)

Dollar (☎ 961-6059, 329-2744, 800-800-4000, **w** www.dollar.com)

Hertz (☎ 935-2896, 329-3566, 800-654-3131, **w** www.hertz.com)

National (☎ 935-0891, 329-1674, 800-227-7368, **w** www.nationalcar.com)

Thrifty (☎ 961-6698, 329-1339, 800-367-5238, **w** www.thrifty.com)

The only local rental agency on the Big Island is Harper Car & Truck Rental (☎ 969-1478, 800-852-9993, **w** www.harpershawaii.com). This is the only rental agency which allows its vehicles on the Saddle Road and Mauna Kea.

Motorcycle & Moped

The minimum age for renting a scooter or moped (the former can go highway speeds while the latter is only for around town) is 16 years.

Would-be bikers can rent motorcycles on both sides of the Big Island. The minimum age to rent a bike at most places is 21 and you'll need to show a valid motorcycle license. There are no helmet laws in the state of Hawaii and even the most cautious riders will likely seize the opportunity to be bathed in tropical breezes as they lean into turns down the Kohala or Puna coasts. Please be careful and remember that rental agencies often provide free helmets.

Riding on the windward side requires hardcore foul weather gear, as it rains early and often. Snug cuffs and waterproof seams are essential, and a stash of double-sided Velcro and seam sealer will work wonders for your disposition. Some rental agencies also supply rain gear. Ask.

Motorcycle Rental Agencies Several
places rent motorcycles on the Big Island. All but one are on the Kona side. While some places only rent motorcycles (Harleys, mostly), a few also rent mopeds and scooters. Count on spending at least $125 a day for a motorcycle, $50 a day for a moped or scooter. Note that a day rental usually means you have the vehicle from 7am to 6pm, not a 24-hour period. For that you pay extra. Liability insurance also costs extra, with rates varying by agency.

DJ's Rentals (☎ 329-1700, 800-993-4647, **w** http://harleys.com), 75-5663 Palani Rd, Kailua-Kona

Hilo Harley Davidson (☎/fax 934-9090), 200 Kanoelehua Ave, Hilo

Xtreme Rentals (☎ 327-9840), 76-5785 Kuakini Hwy, Kailua-Kona

Big Island Harley Davidson (☎ 326-9887, fax 329-5588, **w** www.konaharleydavidson.com), 74-5615 Luhia St, Ste E, Kailua-Kona

Buying a Vehicle

If you're thinking of staying a couple of months, it might behoove you and your wallet to buy a used car. If you're lucky and it holds up well enough, you can resell it later. Start by perusing the classified ads in *West Hawaii Today* and the *Hilo Tribune-Herald* and bulletin boards at coffee shops, grocery stores and shopping centers. You may find OK deals at used car dealerships in Kona or Hilo, too. Oftentimes, used cars for sale will be grouped along the highway or in municipal parking lots (eg, on Kamehameha Ave fronting Hilo Bay), and there can be real steals here. Common problems encountered with used cars here include: rust, busted undercarriages, crappy steering and squishy brakes.

All vehicles in Hawaii must have a safety inspection sticker (available at most gas stations) and carry no-fault insurance. If you're buying from a used car lot, the car should already be 'legal,' ie safety-checked. After you purchase the vehicle, you then have 10 days to change the title and 30 days to register the car with the Department of Motor Vehicles.

Shipping a Vehicle

Shipping a vehicle from home is also an option for longer term visitors. Note, however, that prices from the west coast are much more palatable than from the east (did someone say road trip?!). If your ride isn't a total junker, you'll probably be able to sell it when you leave. Toyotas, Fords, pick-ups and 4WDs provide the most attractive resale value.

Matson Navigation (☎ 800-462-8766, **w** www.matson.com), ships passenger vehicles to Hilo and Kawaihae (Kailua-Kona's nearest port), from Oakland, Los Angeles and Seattle for $880. It usually takes one to three weeks for cars to arrive and their service is speedy and reliable. To get all the details, call the toll free number or see their website.

From New York, you can expect to pay around $1900 for shipping your vehicle to the Big Island. It takes three to four weeks. Two outfits providing solid service include All America Auto Transport (☎ 800-227-7447, w/eb www.carmoving.com/aaat/) and Transcar Auto Shippers (☎ 800-264-8167, **w** www.transcar.org).

Shipping a motorcycle from Oakland to the Big Island costs $1235 with Berklay Cargo Worldwide (☎ 718-656-6066 ⓦ www .motorcycleshipping.com). This includes pickup, a custom crate and container shipping to Hilo or Kawaihae. The same service from New York to the Big Island costs $2125. For an exhaustive list of worldwide auto and motorcycle shippers, see Move-Cars.com (ⓦ www.movecars.com).

TAXI

Taxis are metered on the Big Island and cost $2 a mile. The cabs are often of the station wagon or mini-van variety, and so are good for groups (a valuable tip if you're out partying without a designated driver). Disabled clients should request an accessible van or vehicle. You can't generally hail a taxi, but hey, if the hacks are driving with aloha, they just might pick you up.

In Hilo, we like Marshall's Taxi (☎ 936-2654) and Percy's Taxi (☎ 969-7060); in Kona try Paradise Taxi & Tours (☎ 329-1234) or Elsa Taxi (☎ 887-6446).

BICYCLE

It's possible to cycle around the Big Island, but it's not without its challenges. First, the terrain is up and down, with quick, steep elevation gains that will stretch even stalwart peddlers. Second, there are many winding roads and few bicycle lanes. Lastly, the windward side is, well, windy and wet and the leeward side seesaws between hot and hellishly hot. Both sides and their extremes can present problems for cyclists. On the upside, there are some great rides, including lots of secluded single track and gorgeous coastal routes.

There are places to rent bicycles in Kona and Hilo. Daily costs run about $10 for an around-town model or $15 for a mountain bike. Shops renting bicycles also rent safety equipment and car racks, and handle repairs and sales. As with most things here, shops are concentrated in Kailua-Kona and Hilo.

If you bring your own bike to Hawaii, you can transport it on interisland flights for $25, double that for mainland flights. The bicycle can be checked at the counter, the same as any baggage, but you'll need to prepare the bike first by breaking it down to a manageable size and shape (ie, securing the handlebars and removing the pedals, panniers and seat).

For more on cycling the Big Island, see the Activities section.

HITCHHIKING

Hitchhiking, though technically illegal statewide, is common and practical although Lonely Planet does not recommend it. It can be an efficient, cheap way to get around, but is not without risks, obviously. Hitchhikers should size up each situation carefully before getting into cars, and women should be especially wary hitching alone (for more, see Women Travelers in the Facts for the Visitor chapter).

Hitchhiking is never entirely safe anywhere in the world. Travelers who decide to hitchhike should understand that they are taking a serious risk. People who do choose to hitchhike will be safer if they travel in pairs and let someone know where they are planning to go.

ORGANIZED TOURS

All of these sightseeing tours can be booked after arrival in Hawaii. The only times you might need to book ahead are in December or July and August. Other tours geared toward activities such as whale-watching, snorkel trips and cycling are found in the Activities chapter.

Bus & Van Tours

If you're without a car and your time is limited, there are a number of companies that operate half-day and full-day sightseeing bus tours. One option is the 12-hour run around like mad circling the island tour. Starting in Kona, these usually take in the Place of Refuge, Punalu'u Black Sand Beach, Hawaii Volcanoes National Park, Rainbow Falls, the Hamakua Coast, Parker Ranch and Waimea. Whew!

Another possibility is an 8-hour volcano tour, which leaves from Hilo and focuses on the national park and the edge of the flow at Kalapana.

Thumbing It

Let's get it out of the way straight away: hitchhiking can be risky and LP does not endorse it, especially for solo women travelers. But as a solo woman traveler, I also realize it's sometimes necessary: middle-of-nowhere Guatemala and the entirety of Cuba immediately leap to mind. Hitchhiking can also lead to some of the best travel experiences: being welcomed in for tea; having locals lead you to a rain forest waterfall; or becoming stranded miles from your intended destination and discovering the hidden beauty therein

Hawaii differs from the mainland in so many ways, and while I haven't hitched a ride in the continental US in 20 years (yes, Mom took us around by thumb every so often in the old days), it's standard operating practice on the Big Island. Nowadays, I'm the one taking Mom around with our thumbs and here are some rules of the road we learned in our Big Island travels:

- Set out early, as it's wicked difficult catching a nighttime ride.
- Location, location, location: make sure there's a shoulder where potential lifts can pull over; road junctions offer more passing traffic and possible rides; and park yourself under a street lamp after dark.
- Heavily touristed routes (eg, Hwy 11 between Volcano and Hilo or the county road out to the live lava flow) can be very difficult places to land rides indeed and you may need to beg.
- Conversely, it's also possible to get rides in the most unlikely spots; the miles of road snaking through the Waikoloa resorts serve as one recent example (who knew those resorts were so spread out?!)
- Making regular deposits into your karmic account by picking up others when you can will greatly help you out when the shoe is on the other foot
- Remember the local axiom: 'Ass, gas or grass. No free rides!'

– Conner Gorry

Roberts Hawaii (☎ *800-831-5411,* W *www.roberts-hawaii.com*) This giant among Hawaiian tour companies offers the Grand Circle Island Tour for $55/$48 for adults/children and the volcano tour for $42/$36. They also have a Mauna Kea stargazing and summit tour starting at $135 per person.

Polynesian Adventures (☎ *329-8008, 800-622-3011, fax 329-0985,* W *www.polyad.com*) Polynesian prices for the Grand Circle tour start at $58/45 for adults/children, the volcano tour costs $46/38. You may find discounts for on-line bookings.

Arnott's Adventure Tours (☎ *969-7097, fax 961-9638,* W *www.arnottslodge.com*) Arnott's runs popular tours for the backpacking and budget traveler set. Prices are $48/96 for guests/non-guests and include options such as Mauna Kea, Volcanoes National Park, Waipi'o Valley and more.

Jack's Tours (☎ *961-6666 in Hilo, 329-2555 in Kona*) This outfit offers a variety of tours in Japanese, including Big Island Circle ($125) and Stargazing ($99) options.

Neighbor Islands

If you want to visit another island while you're in Hawaii and only have a day or two to spare, it might be worth looking into 'overnighters,' which are mini-package tours to the Neighbor Islands.

Rates usually include roundtrip airfare, car rental and hotel accommodations, with a one-night package at a no-frills hotel starting around $150 per person, based on double occupancy. Prices rise for better-quality accommodations, and extra days usually cost about $75 to $100 per person. Last-minute specials may be cheaper. These companies also sell room/car packages (ie, without the airfare), but their prices don't always beat those packages offered by some hotels or car rental agencies.

Two of the biggest agents for Neighbor Island package tours are **Roberts Hawaii** (☎ 966-5483 in Hilo, 800-899-9323, fax 808-522-7870, W www.robertsovernighters.com), which has an Oahu overnight option for $195, and **Pleasant Island Holidays** (☎ 808-922-1515 on Oahu, 800-654-4386, W www.gtesupersite.com/pih). Pleasant Island Holidays offers discounts to seniors, military personnel and Hawaii residents.

Kona

Kona literally means 'leeward.' The Kona Coast refers to the dry, sunny west coast of the Big Island. However, to make matters a little more confusing, the name Kona is also used to refer to Kailua, the largest town on the Kona Coast. The town's name is compounded as Kailua-Kona by the post office and other officialdom to avoid confusion with Kailua on Oahu.

The weather here gives tourists few headaches. It's so consistent on this side of the island that the local paper commonly alternates two forecasts: 'Sunny morning. Afternoon clouds with upslope showers' or 'Sunny morning. Cloudy afternoon with showers over the slopes.' Because of the wonderfully predictable sunshine, Kona is a solid vacation destination throughout the year.

KAILUA-KONA

In the 19th century, Kailua-Kona (population 9,870) was a favorite vacation retreat for Hawaiian royalty. These days, it's the largest vacation destination on the Big Island.

Marvelous weather, reasonably priced lodgings and a central location for exploring the entire Kona Coast are the big draws here. While the setting on the leeward side of Mt Hualalai is pretty, and a number of ancient Hawaiian and missionary-era historic sites are scattered in and around town, the endless trinket shops and mini-malls detract from the town's historic flavor. That said, Kailua-Kona is a lively place to hang out, and also boasts activities ranging from snorkeling cruises to world-class deep-sea fishing (see the Activities chapter for more information) .

Most of Kailua-Kona's condos are lined up along Ali'i Drive, the 5-mile coastal road that runs from the town center at Kailua Bay south to Keauhou. This strip sees a lot of power-walkers and joggers, particularly in the early morning hours, but the hottest activity occurs in October when the road serves as the finish line of the world-famous Ironman Triathlon.

Kailua-Kona's biggest disappointment is the lack of fabulous beaches. There are a few swimming, snorkeling and surfing spots, but the island's best beaches are up the coast to the north.

Highlights

- Watching fire dancers at a traditional Polynesian luau
- Diving in the Pacific at night to see luminous manta rays
- Trekking across lava flow to reach a spectacular white-sand beach
- Seeing green sea turtles on Ali'i Drive's Kahalu'u Beach
- Sampling locally-produced microbrews and Hawaiian chocolate
- Attempting the swimming portion of the Ironman Triathlon

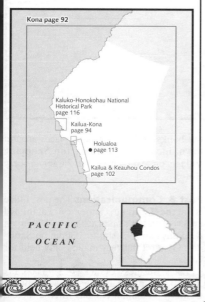

Kona page 92

Kaluko-Honokohau National Historical Park page 116

Kailua-Kona page 94

Holualoa
● page 113

Kailua & Keauhou Condos page 102

PACIFIC
OCEAN

KONA

PACIFIC
OCEAN

Anaeho'omalu Bay

To South Kohala

Waikoloa Rd

King's Hwy Trail

19

Kiholo Bay

Luahinewai Pond

Wainanalii Pond

Lookout

Queen Ka'ahumanu Hwy

4WD

190

Kahuwai Bay

Ka'upulehu

Kona Village Resort

Kukio Bay

Four Seasons Resort Hualalai

Kua Bay

19°48'N   19°48'N

Puu Kuili ▲ 342ft

Donkey Crossing

Hawaii Belt Rd

Mahaiula Bay

Kona Coast State Park

Makolea Point

Lava Tubes

Keahole-Kona International Airport

Keahole Point

Kaiminani Dr

Kaloko Dr

Kalaoa

Wawaloli (OTEC) Beach

Pine Trees

19

Hina Lani St

Honokohau

Palani Junction

▲ Mt Hualalai 8271ft

Pohakuloa Military Training Area

Kaloko-Honokohau National Historical Park

Honokohau Bay

Honokohau

Hawaii Belt Rd

Palani Rd

180

19°38'N   19°38'N

Old Kona Airport Beach Park

Kailua-Kona

Kailua Bay *Oneo Bay*

Holualoa

Holualoa Bay

11

Kahalu'u Bay   White Sands Beach

He'eia Bay   Keauhou

Keauhou Bay

0   3   6 km
0   2   4 miles

To South Kona

Kainaliu

156°00'W   155°50'W

Information

Tourist Offices The Big Island Visitors Bureau (☎ 886-1655) has inconveniently moved to Waikoloa. While numerous 'tourist information' booths dot Ali'i Drive, they primarily house aggressive salespeople who try to lure visitors into listening to timeshare pitches. For useful tourist information, head to concierge and activities desks at the larger hotels in Kailua-Kona.

Money Bank of Hawaii and First Hawaiian Bank both have branches at Lanihau Center on Palani Rd. You'll find ATMs at

the banks and at numerous places around town, including the Kona Inn Shopping Village on Ali'i Drive and larger grocery stores.

Post & Communications The post office is in the Lanihau Center on Palani Rd (☎ 331-8307). It's open 8:30am to 4:30pm on weekdays and 9:30am to 1:30pm on Saturday. General delivery mail is only held for 10 days.

Zac's Business Center (☎ 329-0006, fax 329-1021), at the North Kona Shopping Center on Kuakini Rd, has Internet access for $8 an hour, or $2.75 for 15 minutes. You can also receive faxes for 50¢ a page and send faxes at varying rates. It's open 8am to 7pm Monday to Friday, 9am to 6pm Saturday and 10am to 4pm Sunday. You'll pay $4 per 20 minutes to hop online at Big Island Photo (☎ 329-4221) in Kona Square across from the pier.

Travel Agencies Cut Rate Tickets (☎ 326-2300), in the Kona Coast Shopping Center on Palani Rd, sells discounted tickets for interisland travel. This is a consistently better deal than calling the airlines directly. It's open 7am to 7pm weekdays, 9am to 5pm Saturday and 9am to 2pm Sunday.

Bookstores Middle Earth Bookshoppe (☎ 329-2123), in the Kona Plaza on Ali'i Drive, is a well-stocked central bookstore with Hawaiiana and general travel sections. It's open 9am-9pm Monday to Saturday and 9:30am to 6pm Sunday. Borders, on Hwy 19, is the area's largest bookstore and also carries a wide selection of US and foreign newspapers, including the *London Times* and *Le Monde*. They're open 9am-9pm Sunday through Thursday, 9am-10pm on Friday and Saturday. Bargain Books (☎ 326-7790), tucked away in the North Kona Shopping Center, buys, sells and trades new and used books.

Libraries Kona's modern public library, on Hualalai Rd (☎ 327-4327), subscribes to both Neighbor Island and mainland newspapers, including the *Los Angeles Times* and *USA Today*. It also sells used paperback books for just 25¢. It's open 10am to 8pm on Tuesday, 9am to 6pm on Wednesday and Thursday, 11am to 5pm on Friday and 9am to 5pm on Saturday. Folks with a library card have free Internet access, but since there's only one computer, advance sign-up is required.

Photography Longs Drugs, in the Lanihau Center on Palani Rd, sells cameras and film and handles processing by major developers, including Kodak and Fuji. Longs also offers same-day print processing ($6 for 24 prints). However, if you can wait a day, the send-out service is slightly cheaper.

Laundry Hele Mai Laundromat (☎ 329-3494) in the North Kona Shopping Center on Kuakini Rd and the Kona Wash Tub in the industrial area (☎ 326-4776, 74-5589 Alapa St) are both coin laundries. In addition, most condos have washers and dryers in the units, or a laundry room on-site.

Kamakahonu & Ahuena Heiau

Kamakahonu, the beach at the north end of Kailua Bay, was the site of the royal residence of Kamehameha the Great. Shortly after his death here in 1819, Kamehameha's successors came to Kamakahonu and ended the traditional kapu system, sounding a death knell for the old religion.

The ancient sites are now part of the grounds of King Kamehameha's Kona Beach Hotel. A few thatched structures along with carved wooden *ki'i* (images) of gods have been reconstructed above the old stone temple.

Ahuena Heiau, which was once a place of human sacrifice, juts out into the cove and acts as a breakwater, offering protection to swimmers. The waters at Kamakahonu, which means 'Eye of the Turtle,' are the calmest in Kailua Bay.

The little beach in front of the hotel is the only downtown swimming spot. The hotel beach hut rents snorkels, kayaks, beach chairs and umbrellas.

King Kamehameha's Kona Beach Hotel

Be sure to take a stroll through the sprawling lobby of this hotel, which is full of displays on various aspects of Hawaiian culture, including traditional foods, fishing methods, music, dress and more.

One display features Hawaiian musical instruments, including a nose flute, coconut-shell knee drum, shell trumpet, bamboo rattles and hula sticks. Others contain feather capes and leis, *kapa* (bark cloth) beaters, quilts, war clubs, calabashes and gourd containers. The displays have brief interpretive plaques, but you'll find free brochures at he

KONA

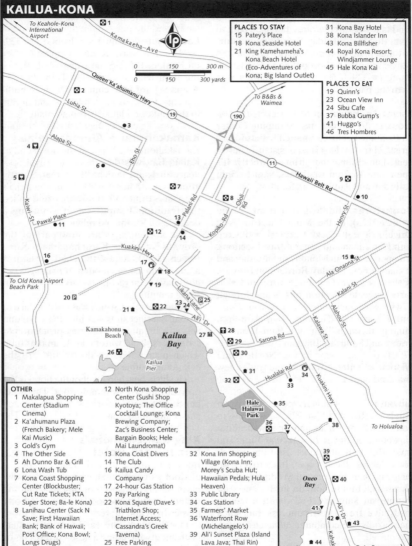

KAILUA-KONA

To Keahole-Kona
International
Airport

Kamakaeha Ave

Queen Ka'ahumanu Hwy

Luhia St

Alapa St

Eho St

Kaiwi St

Pawai Place

Hawaii Belt Rd

Henry St

Palani Rd

Kopiko Rd

Ololi Rd

Kuakini Hwy

To Old Kona Airport
Beach Park

Likana Lane

Ali'i Dr

Kamakahonu
Beach

Kailua
Bay

Kailua
Pier

Ala Onaona St

Kalani St

Kalaoa St

Sarona Rd

Hualalai Rd

Kuakini Hwy

To Holualoa

Hale
Halawai
Park

Oneo
Bay

Ali'i Dr

Kahakai Rd

To La Bourgogne
& Honalo

To Saltwater Pool
& Kailua &
Keahou Condos

Wailia Rd

To La Bourgogne
& Honalo

To B&Bs &
Waimea

PLACES TO STAY
15 Patey's Place
18 Kona Seaside Hotel
21 King Kamehameha's
   Kona Beach Hotel
   (Eco-Adventures of
   Kona; Big Island Outlet)
31 Kona Bay Hotel
38 Kona Islander Inn
43 Kona Billfisher
44 Royal Kona Resort;
   Windjammer Lounge
45 Hale Kona Kai

PLACES TO EAT
19 Quinn's
23 Ocean View Inn
24 Sibu Cafe
37 Bubba Gump's
41 Huggo's
46 Tres Hombres

OTHER
1 Makalapua Shopping
  Center (Stadium
  Cinema)
2 Ka'ahumanu Plaza
  (French Bakery; Mele
  Kai Music)
3 Gold's Gym
4 The Other Side
5 Ah Dunno Bar & Grill
6 Lona Wash Tub
7 Kona Coast Shopping
  Center (Blockbuster;
  Cut Rate Tickets; KTA
  Super Store; Ba-le Kona)
8 Lanihau Center (Sack N
  Save; First Hawaiian
  Bank; Bank of Hawaii;
  Post Office; Kona Bowl;
  Longs Drugs)
9 Crossroads Shopping
  Center (Kona Natural
  Foods; Oodles of
  Noodles; Manna's;
  Safeway)
10 Borders
11 Kona Aggressor

12 North Kona Shopping
   Center (Sushi Shop
   Kyotoya; The Office
   Cocktail Lounge; Kona
   Brewing Company;
   Zac's Business Center;
   Bargain Books; Hele
   Mai Laundromat)
13 Kona Coast Divers
14 The Club
16 Kailua Candy
   Company
17 24-hour Gas Station
20 Pay Parking
22 Kona Square (Dave's
   Triathlon Shop;
   Internet Access;
   Cassandra's Greek
   Taverna)
25 Free Parking
26 Ahuena Heiau
27 Hulihee Palace
28 Mokuaikaua Church
29 Kona Plaza (Middle
   Earth Bookshoppe)
30 Kona Marketplace
   (Sam's Hideaway)

32 Kona Inn Shopping
   Village (Kona Inn;
   Morey's Scuba Hut;
   Hawaiian Pedals; Hula
   Heaven)
33 Public Library
34 Gas Station
35 Farmers' Market
36 Waterfront Row
   (Michelangelo's)
39 Ali'i Sunset Plaza (Island
   Lava Java; Thai Rin)
40 Coconut Grove
   Marketplace (Jack's
   Diving Locker; Hard
   Rock Café; Lulu's;
   Jake's; Kanaka Kave;
   Giggles)
42 Snorkel Bob's

activity desk in the lobby that describe them in greater depth.

The hotel offers free, guided historical tours that visit the indoor displays and take in the hotel's historic grounds. Check at the activity desk for the latest schedule.

Kailua Pier

Kailua Pier was long the center of sports fishing on Hawaii, but it simply got too crowded to handle all the action. These days, Kona's charter fishing boats use the larger Honokohau Harbor north of town, and Kailua Pier is mainly used by dive boats and cruise ship tenders, though its hoist and scales are still put to use for weigh-ins during billfish tournaments.

Kailua Bay was once a major cattle shipping area. Cattle driven down from hillside ranches were stampeded into the water and forced to swim out to waiting steamers, where they were hoisted aboard by sling and shipped to Honolulu slaughterhouses. Kailua Pier was built in 1915, and cattle pens were still in place until the 1960s.

The tiny patch of sandy beach on the east side of Kailua Pier is known as **Kaiakeakua**, 'Sea of the Gods.' It once served as Kamehameha's canoe landing.

Moku'aikaua Church

On April 4, 1820, Hawaii's first Christian missionaries landed at Kailua Bay, stepping out onto a rock that is now one of the footings for the Kailua Pier. When the missionaries landed, they were unaware that Hawaii's old religion had been abolished on this same spot just a few months before. Their timing couldn't have been more auspicious. Given a favorable reception from Kamehameha's successors, the missionaries established Hawaii's first Christian church on Kailua Bay, a few minutes' walk from Kamehameha's ancient heiau and house site.

The temporary church the missionaries erected was replaced in 1836 by the current Moku'aikaua Church (☎ 329-0655), a handsome building with walls of lava rock held together by a mortar of sand and coral lime. The posts and beams, hewn with stone adzes

and smoothed down with chunks of coral, are made from strong termite-resistant *ohia* wood, and the pews and pulpit are made of *koa*, a native hardwood. The steeple tops out at 112 feet, making the church still the tallest structure in Kailua.

From 9am to 4pm Monday to Saturday, an interpreter is often on site to talk about the church's history. An 8-foot model of the brig *Thaddeus*, the ship that brought those first Congregational missionaries to Hawaii, is also on display.

Hulihe'e Palace

Governor 'John Adams' Kuakini built Hulihe'e Palace, a modest two-story house, in 1838 as his private residence (☎ 329-1877, 75-5718 Ali'i Dr; adult/child under 12 years $5/1; open 9am-4pm Mon-Fri, 10am-4pm Sat & Sun). The Kona Historical Society, based in Kealakekua, also gives **tours** of historic Kailua Village (☎ 323-3222, admission $15). The 75-minute tours, offered at 9:30am and 1:30pm every Tuesday and Friday, include admission to the palace.

Kuakini was also the contractor for the Moku'aikaua Church, and both buildings shared the same lava-rock construction. The palace got its current look in 1885, when it was plastered over inside and out by King Kalakaua, who had taken to a more polished style after his travels abroad.

The palace belonged to a succession of royal owners until the early 1900s, when it was abandoned and fell into disrepair. The Daughters of Hawaii, a group founded in 1903 by daughters of missionaries, took it over and now operate the property as a museum.

Like many Hawaiian royals, Princess Ruth Keelikolani, who owned the palace in the mid-19th century, was a lady of some presence who reportedly weighed more than 400 pounds. She was an earthy woman, preferring to live in a big grass hut on the palace grounds rather than being confined within the palace. After her death, the wooden posts that had supported her grass hut were carved with designs of taro, leis and pineapples and used as posts in one of the beds upstairs.

The palace is furnished with antiques, many picked up on royal jaunts to Europe. Some of the more Hawaiian pieces include a table inlaid with 25 kinds of native Hawaiian woods, some of which are now extinct, and a number of Kamehameha the Great's personal war spears.

Admission includes a 40-minute tour, which provides interesting anecdotes about the former royal occupants. Alternatively, take a free peek in the gift shop (☎ 329-6558) or at the **fishpond** behind the palace. Though no longer stocked, the pond holds a few colorful tropical fish. It also once served as a Queen's Bath and a canoe landing.

Kona Brewing Company

The Kona Brewing Company (☎ 334-2739), in a warehouse adjacent to the North Kona Shopping Center, is the Big Island's first microbrewery. Started in 1994 by a father and son from Oregon, this little family-run operation now ships its brew to the Neighbor Islands. The brewery's mainstay, Pacific Golden Ale, blends pale and honey malts to produce a traditional ale. If you prefer a little island flavor, try the Lilikoi Wheat, which has a light, passion-fruit bouquet. These handcrafted ales can be sampled at the conclusion of the free brewery tours, offered at 10:30am and 3:00pm Monday to Saturday. They're also served at the brewery's outdoor cafe.

Old Kona Airport Beach Park

The old Kona Airport, which was replaced by the current Kona Airport in 1970, has been turned into a state recreation area and beach park. It's easy to overlook, but worth visiting. The beach is much larger than Kailua-Kona beaches and far more peaceful, offering soothing ocean sounds rather than urban traffic noise. It's about a mile north of downtown Kailua-Kona, at the end of Kuakini Hwy.

The old runway skirts a long sandy beach, but lava rocks run the length of the beach between the sand and the ocean, and smaller rocks shift around with the waves. Although this makes for poor swimming conditions, it's ideal for fishing and exploring tide pools. At low tide, the rocks reveal an intriguing system of little aquarium-like pockets holding tiny sea urchins, crabs and bits of coral.

A couple of breaks in the lava, including one in front of the first picnic area, allow entry into the water.

Garden Eel Cove, a little cove that can be reached by a short walk from the north end of the beach, is a good area for scuba divers and confident snorkelers. The reef fish are large and plentiful, and a steep coral wall in deeper waters harbors big moray eels and a wide variety of other sea creatures, such as lionfish and cowries.

When the surf's up, local surfers favor the offshore break. In high surf, though, it's too rough for other water activities.

Despite its popularity, this local park is much too big to ever feel crowded. Facilities include rest rooms, showers and covered picnic tables on a lawn dotted with beach heliotrope and short coconut palms.

The Kailua-Kona end of the park contains a gym, soccer and softball fields, a pool and four outdoor lighted tennis courts. Pueo horseshoe pit, right behind the tennis courts, is free and open to the public. Next to the old runway is a mile-long loop that locals use as a track.

North of Old Kona Airport Park is **Pawai Bay**, a great area for spotting marvelous marine life. A visit demands either a 20-25 minute walk over treacherous cracked lava coastline, or arrival by boat. Companies like Jack's Diving Locker (see Scuba Diving, later) take groups here because the diving and snorkeling is so incredible – it's like swimming in an aquarium. Keep in mind that the land behind Pawai Bay is inaccessible to tourists, as it's part of the Queen Lili'uokalani Trust and dedicated to the children of Hawaii.

White Sands Beach Park

Though it's known as White Sands, Magic Sands and Disappearing Sands, it's all the same beach, midway between Kailua-Kona and Keauhou, to the south. In winter when the surf is high, the sand can disappear literally overnight, leaving only rocks on the

Beautiful Keauhou Bay, Kona

Mural at Patey's Place hostel, Kona

Yellow frog fish

Kahiko hula

St Peter's church, Kahulu'u Bay

Sunset over 'A' Bay, Waikoloa

Pu'ukohola heiau, South Kohala

Looking over the 17th hole at the Mauna Lani Resort, Kohala

shore. But then it returns just as magically, creating a fine white-sand beach once again.

This is a very popular bodysurfing beach when the rocks aren't exposed, and the sand is often crowded with local kids. The facilities include rest rooms, showers, a few picnic tables, a large parking lot and a volleyball court. Palm trees offer some shade and a lifeguard on duty offers protection. I like Kahalu'u and many other Kona beaches, this spot is right next to busy Ali'i Drive.

Scuba Diving

With marvelous marine life at its shores, Kona is the logical home to numerous dive operations. In addition, the Kona Reefers Dive Club (☎ 323-9529) meets on the third Friday of the month and holds shore dives (and sometimes boat dives) open to the public on weekends once a month. Look for announcements in *West Hawaii Today*, or inquire at any dive shop.

A few outfits also offer live-aboard, kayak and night diving options. Most companies offer multi-day discounts, so inquire when making reservations. The *Kona Aggressor* (☎ 329-8182, 74-5588 Pawai Place, Building F, W www.konaaggressor.com) is an 85-foot live-aboard dive boat that accommodates up to 10 guests. All-inclusive one-week trips cost $1895 and start each Saturday.

The more established dive operations include the following:

Jack's Diving Locker (☎ 329-7585, 75-5819 Ali'i Drive, Kailua-Kona, W www.jacksdivinglocker.com) Located at the Coconut Grove Marketplace, Jack's is one of the best outfits for introductory dives ($135 with equipment), plus they have a fantastic night dive to see the lovely manta rays. Rated five stars by PADI. Two-tank dives are $90-115.

Dive Makai (☎/fax 329-2025, W www.divemakai.com) A personable dive charter operation run by husband-and-wife team Tom Shockley and Lisa Choquette, the duo is conservation oriented and has a good word-of-mouth reputation. A two-tank dive is $95 if you have your own equipment, $119 if you don't.

Eco-Adventures of Kona (☎ 329-7116, 75-5660 Palani Road, W www.eco-adventure.com) This well-regarded, five-star PADI operation is based at King Kamehameha's Kona Beach Hotel. Day and night dives are available for the same rates: $102 plus $5 extra for each piece of equipment.

Kona Coast Divers (☎ 329-8802, 75-5614 Palani Road, W www.konacoastdivers.com) A five-star PADI outfit that's one of the largest on the Big Island. One- and two-tank dives are $64.50-99; $5 extra for each piece of equipment.

Sea Paradise Scuba (☎ 322-2500, Keauhou Bay Pier, Building 2) Based in Keauhou Bay, this operation tends to head south, often to Red Hill or Kealakekua Bay. Rates are $90 for a two-tank dive; $105 for folks who need to rent equipment.

Snorkeling

Kahalu'u Beach in Keauhou (see that section later) is the area's most popular easy-access snorkeling haunt and a good place for beginners to try out the sport. Cruises to Kealakekua Bay are listed below, but see the Beaches and Snorkeling sections in the South Kona chapter at the end of the book for additional information.

Cruises The most popular snorkeling cruise is to Kealakekua Bay. Try to book a trip in the morning, when the sea is calmer and the waters clearer. Prices for the following tours include snorkeling gear, beverages and food.

Fairwind (☎ 322-2788, 800-677-9461, W www.fair-wind.com) makes trips to Kealakekua Bay aboard a 60-foot catamaran. The trips leave from Keauhou Bay, which allows for more snorkeling time than other boats. You can choose either a 4½-hour morning tour that costs $85/48 for adults/children ages six to 17, or a 3½-hour afternoon tour that costs $50/32 for adults/children.

Captain Zodiac (☎ 329-3199, W www.captainzodiac.com) offers four-hour tours aboard bouncy rubber rafts, which depart from Honokohau Harbor at 8am and 1pm daily, with pick-up possible at the Kailua-Kona and Keauhou piers. The cost of $76/62 for adults/children ages four to 12 includes about an hour of snorkeling time at Kealakekua Bay followed by visits to sea caves.

Kamanu Sail and Snorkel (☎ 329-2021) takes a 36-foot catamaran out of Honokohau Harbor for snorkeling at Pawai Bay, just north of the Old Kona Airport. The boat, which motors down and sails back, takes a maximum of 24 people. It departs daily at 9am and 1:30pm. Cost, which includes sandwiches, fruit and beverages, is $55/35 for adults/children under 12 years.

Snorkelers can often tag along with divers on dive tours if space is available, but remember that ideal dive conditions don't always make good snorkeling conditions. The cost typically ranges from $45 to $65.

Gear Rentals A couple of places in Kailua-Kona rent snorkel sets for around $8 a day, $15 a week. Try **Morey's Scuba Hut** at the south end of the Kona Inn Shopping Village or the beach hut at King Kamehameha's Kona Beach Hotel.

Snorkel Bob's (☎ 329-0770) has a branch off Ali'i Drive by the Royal Kona Resort. You can get low-grade snorkel gear as cheaply as $9 per week. Rates go up to $36/week for top-notch equipment.

Many of the dive shops also rent snorkel gear, though prices tend to be higher.

Snuba
A cross between snorkeling and scuba diving (see the Activities chapter for details), this exciting sport is only offered on the island's leeward side, and **Big Island Water Sports** (☎ 324-1650, W www.bigislandwatersports.com) owns the market.

All dives have a two-person minimum, and the prices listed do not include tax. Beach dives cost $69 per person. Boat dives are $100 for a single dive and $125 for two dives. The company is also a concession on Fairwind boat cruises (see above). In addition to the cost of the cruise, snuba divers pay an extra $50.

Fishing
Not surprisingly, fishing is popular on the Kona coast. A number of shops rent or sell fishing gear; for more information on charter cruises, see the Activities chapter.

In the industrial area, **Kona Fishing Tackle** (☎ 326-2934, 74-5583 Luhia Street, No B-8) sells throw nets, fishing tackle, deep-sea fishing and shoreline casting equipment. In Honokohau Harbor **Reel Action Tackle**

(☎ 325-6811) is a charter service, offering bottom fishing, fly fishing, casting and trolling tours on their boat *Reel Action*.

Kayaking
Kealakekua Bay is the most common kayaking destination on the Big Island, but if you just want to paddle around Kailua Bay, the beach hut at King Kamehameha's Kona Beach Hotel rents kayaks for $15 for the first hour, $5 for each additional hour.

Swimming
The public pool at the Old Airport Park in the Kona Community Aquatic Center is free and open to the public. The hours for the two lap pools are weekdays 6:15am to 7:30pm and weekends 8:15am to 5:30pm. Holiday hours are the same as weekend hours.

The Club in Kona (see above) has a pool, and the gym offers daily and weekly rates.

Many folks also like to stroke the 2.4-mile ocean swim portion of the Ironman Triathlon, which starts at the Kailua Pier. You can jump off the pier or waltz right into the water.

Cycling
Hawaiian Pedals (☎ 329-2294, *Kona Inn Shopping Village*) rents mountain and hybrid bikes for $20/day. At **HP Bike Works** (☎ 326-2453; 74-5599 Luhia St), higher-end bikes mean slightly higher rental prices of $25/day for front-suspension and road bikes. Inquire about challenging monthly group rides.

Dave's Triathlon Shop (☎ 329-4522, *Kona Square*) rents road bikes for around $25/75 a day/week and bike racks that hold up to three bikes for $5/15. Mountain bikes and hybrids are a reasonable $15/60 a day/week. The shop also sells and repairs high-caliber equipment.

For those interested in going on group rides led by a guide, **Kona Coast Cycling Tours** (☎ 327-1133, W www.cyclekona.com, 74-5588 Pawai Place) offers half-day ($95, including lunch) and full-day excursions ($145) for cyclists of varying ages and abilities. Kids are half-price.

Surfing

Two places in town offer surfing lessons, and both have solid instructors. **Hawaii Lifeguards Surf Instructors** (☎ 324-0442) gives lessons at Kahalu'u Beach Park and charge $70/hour; $115/two hours. However, they don't rent the boards.

For rentals, head to **Kahalu'u Bay Beach Rentals** (☎ 322-4338), right across the street from the waves. Shortboards/longboards rent for $20/25 per day. You'll find some cheaper rates at **Pacific Vibrations** (☎ 329-4140, 75-5702 Likano Lane, off Ali'i Drive), which rents boards for $10-20 per day.

Ocean Eco Tours (☎ 324-7873, W www .oceanecotours.com, Honokohau Harbor), a friendly mom-and-pop outfit, teaches the surfing moves and includes rental gear; a 2-3 hour group lesson is $85; private lessons are $125.

Whale Watching

Marine mammal biologist Dan McSweeney of **Whale Watch** (☎ 322-0028) leads three-hour whale-watching cruises leaving from Honokohau Harbor daily. Hydrophones allow passengers to hear whale songs. The cost is $54.50/34.50 for adults/children 11 and under. The tours have a 24-hour non-refundable cancellation policy.

A couple of the snorkeling tour boats and fishing boats also do whale watches during humpback season, so check listings in the tourist magazines.

Fitness Centers

Centrally located, **The Club** (☎ 326-2582), 75-5699 Kopiko Rd, has cardio equipment, weight machines and a pool. The daily/weekly rate is $12.50/35. It's open 5am-10pm Monday to Friday, 7am-7pm Saturday and Sunday. **Gold's Gym** (☎ 334-1977), 74-5583 Luhia St, charges $15 daily and $35 weekly. They also have cardio machines and weights, along with Pilates, yoga and step aerobics classes. Guests of certain Kona hotels and condos qualify for a special rate, so inquire about discounts. It's open 5am-10pm Monday to Friday, 7am-7pm Saturday and Sunday.

Special Events

With its glorious sunshine and bustling atmosphere, Kailua-Kona is the perfect place for festivals and special events year-round.

The world watches Kona every October as hundreds of fit athletes and thousands of spectators descend on the town for the elite Ironman Triathlon, an endurance event with participants from all over the globe. The big event – a 2.4-mile swim, 112-mile bike ride and 26.2-mile run – is preceded by a week of festivities (for more information, see the Ironman Triathlon aside in the Activities chapter). Other athletic events during the year include the Keauhou Kona Triathlon (half an Ironman) in May, and the Kona Marathon every June.

The **Hawaiian International Billfish Tournament** (☎ 329-6155, e billfish@lava.net), the granddaddy of all such tournies, is held here in early August and accompanied by a week of entertaining activities.

Both morning and evening brews provide more fodder for celebrations. The annual **Kona Brewers Festival** (☎ 334-1133) in early March features more than 50 types of beer, while the **Kona Coffee Cultural Festival** (☎ 326-7820, W www.konacoffeefest.com)

'And for our next number...'

fetes Kona's important industry and the coffee connoisseurs who keep it thriving. Dozens of events from tastings to farm tours to heated contests occur during the course of a week in early November.

Places to Stay

Hostels & B&Bs Though they lack the ocean views, Kona's hostels and B&Bs are a consideration for travelers who enjoy meeting friendly hosts and other visitors.

Patey's Place (☎ 326-7018, fax 326-7640, e patey@mail.gte.net, 75-195 Ala-Ona Ona St) Dorm bed $19.50, semiprivate rooms $27.50 per person, singles/doubles $35/46, all rates include tax. Office open 8am-noon, 4pm-10pm. The cheapest lodging in town is Patey's Place. This hostel-style accommodation, painted with aquatic murals, is in a residential neighborhood a 10-minute walk from the town center. Clean but run-down dorm rooms sleep four to six. There are also semiprivate rooms with two bunk beds and simple private rooms. All rooms have ceiling fans, shared baths and access to a shared kitchen. Other amenities include Internet access ($2 for 20 minutes), bike rentals and laundry facilities. There's an airport shuttle for $10 each way.

Kiwi Gardens (☎ 326-1559, fax 329-6618, w www.kiwigardens.com, 74-4920 Kiwi St) Single/double with shared bath $70, master suite $75. Former San Franciscans Ron and Shirlee Freitas rent out three rooms in their contemporary home, located 3 miles northeast of Kailua-Kona center. One room has a queen bed with a lanai and a sunset view, another room has a twin and a double bed. Both these rooms share a bath. The third room is a master suite with a king brass bed, private bath and lanai. There's a shared guest phone and a large common area with '50s decor, complete with vintage soda fountain and jukebox. Each room has a fridge. Breakfast includes seasonal fruits from the 80+ trees in the yard, where guests may spot doves and quail.

Nancy's Hideaway (☎/fax 325-3132, 866-325-3132, w www.nancyshideaway.com, 73-1530 Uanani Pl) Studio cottage $95, 1-bedroom cottage $125. Located in Kona's

upcountry 6 miles from town, Nancy recently opened her B&B on 3 acres of property. The immaculate cottages are separate entities on the grounds with private lanais, phones, TV/VCRs and wet bars. A breakfast of pastries and beverages is stocked in the units. While this set-up is a less intimate guest/owner situation than most B&Bs, Nancy happily provides insider advice. She preserves the serenity by discouraging children under 13.

Hotels Hotel options in Kona are more convenient than charming, with all price ranges represented.

Kona Tiki Hotel (☎ 329-1425, fax 327-9402, 75-5968 Ali'i Drive) Doubles $59-65, $70 with kitchenette, plus $8 each extra person. Squeezed on a narrow jut of land between the ocean and the road, this older three-story complex is the area's best hotel deal. Most of the 15 pleasant rooms have a queen and a twin bed, and all have a fridge and a breezy oceanfront lanai (the heavenly sound of the surf drowns out traffic noise). Along with personable service, amenities include a small seaside pool, a barbecue grill and complimentary coffee, juice and breakfast pastries. The hotel is popular with return visitors and books up early during high season. Credit cards are not accepted.

Kona Bay Hotel (☎ 329-1393, 800-367-5102, fax 935-7903, e unclebillys@aloha.net, 75-5739 Ali'i Drive) Rooms $89-99. For those who want to be right in the center of town, there's Uncle Billy's. The older cinder-block buildings lack charm, but the place is relatively cheap and the rooms have TV, air-con, refrigerators and phones. There's a pool.

Kona Seaside Hotel (☎ 329-2455, 800-367-7000, fax 922-0052, w www.sand-seaside .com, 75-5646 Palani Rd) Rooms in older/modern section $98/110-140. Kona Seaside Hotel's 242 rooms, which attract an older clientele, are in two wings. One's a modern six-story building with private lanais. The older rear poolside wing is simpler and has walls that carry sound, making the rate for those rooms lesser value. Try booking within Hawaii for a cheaper local rate: a package with a free Budget rental car and two nights' stay is perpetually advertised in the Sunday Honolulu paper. To get the best deal, call the Honolulu booking desk (☎ 808-737-5800) directly. You don't have to be a Hawaii resident to qualify for the cheaper rates.

King Kamehameha's Kona Beach Hotel (☎ 329-2911, 800-367-6060, fax 329-4602, W www.konabeachhotel.com, 75-5660 Palani Rd) Rooms $130-195. This 460-room hotel at Kailua Bay is on the only beach in town. Located at the site of King Kamehameha's former residence, it has a sprawling koa-wood lobby (with blasting AC!) full of interesting Hawaiiana displays. Each comfortable room has two double beds, a lanai, air-con, room safe, refrigerator, TV and phone. Bathrooms are fairly small. Other amenities include a pool, a sauna, lighted tennis courts, a shopping complex and free guest parking.

Royal Kona Resort (☎ 329-3111, 800-774-5662, fax 329-7230, W www.royalkona .com, 75-5852 Ali'i Drive) Rooms $160-260. This former Hilton has an oceanfront location on the edge of town. Spread across three buildings, the 452 rooms were recently upgraded with new furniture and carpeting. Amenities include lanais, TVs, refrigerators and room safes. Non-smokers should request a room in the main building. Discount deals are available, including a room and car package for $125 daily. There's no sandy beach, but there is a conventional swimming pool as well as a natural saltwater pool that's deep enough for swimming, plus tennis courts and a waterfront restaurant (the views are far better than the food).

Condos In Kona, condos outnumber hotels many times over. Condos tend to be cheaper than hotels if you're staying awhile, although if you make advance reservations, which are recommended in the high season, you'll often have deposits and stiff cancellation penalties.

Many of Kona's condominiums can be booked through more than one rental agency, and most units are handled by at least one of the following agencies. Each

will send its latest listings and rates upon request. It's worth comparing the listings before booking.

Hawaii Resort Management (☎ 329-9393, 800-622-5348, fax 326-4137, W www.konahawaii.com, 75-5776 Kuakini Hwy, suite 105C)

Knutson & Associates (☎ 329-6311, 800-800-6202, fax 326-2178, e knutson@aloha.net, W www.kona hawaiirentals.com, 75-6082 Ali'i Drive, suite 8)

SunQuest Vacations (☎ 329-6488, 800-367-5168 from the USA, 800-800-5662 from Canada, fax 329-5480, e sqvac@sunquest-hawaii.com, W www .sunquest-hawaii.com, 77-6435 Kuakini Hwy)

Triad Management (☎ 329-6402, 800-345-2823, fax 326-2401, 75-5995 Pottery Terrace, Kuakini Hwy, suite 221, Orchid Building)

Most of Kona's condos have complete kitchens and are fully furnished with everything from linen to cooking utensils. The general rule is that the weekly rate is six times the daily rate and the monthly rate is three times the weekly. However, in the high season, if business is brisk, many places offer only the daily rate, while in the off-season months of April, May and September you might be able to negotiate an even better deal.

Most rental agents typically require a three-day minimum stay, but Triad Management requires a five-day minimum stay in the low season and a seven-day minimum in the high season.

If you wait until you arrive in Kona to look for a place, you can sometimes find a good deal under 'Vacation Rentals' in the classified ads of West Hawaii Today. However, this is risky during the high season, when many of the better-value places book up well in advance.

All condos listed here have swimming pools, unless otherwise noted.

Budget Inexpensive condos are plentiful in Kona, and some even have soothing ocean views.

Kona Islander Inn (☎ 329-3333, 800-622-5348, e kona@konahawaii.com, 75-5776 Kuakini Hwy) Low/high season rates daily $35-59/$69-79. Hawaii Resort Management handles most of the 144 units in this older

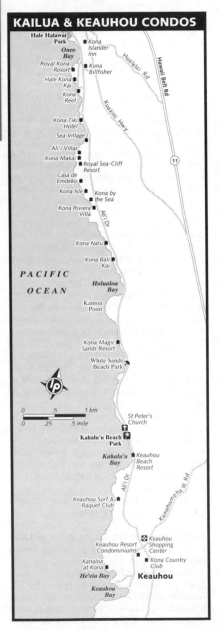

KAILUA & KEAUHOU CONDOS

Hale Halawai
Park
Oneo
Bay
Kona
Islander
Inn
Royal Kona
Resort
Kona
Billfisher
Hale Kona
Kai
Kona
Reef
Kona Tiki
Hotel
Sea Village
Ali'i Villas
Kona Makai
Royal Sea-Cliff
Resort
Casa de
Emdeko
Kona Isle
Kona by
the Sea
Kona Riviera
Villa
Kona Nalu
Kona Bali
Kai
PACIFIC
OCEAN
Holualoa
Bay
Kamoa
Point
Kona Magic
Sands Resort
White Sands
Beach Park
St Peter's
Church
Kahalu'u Beach
Park
Kahalu'u
Bay
Keauhou
Beach
Resort
Keauhou Surf &
Raquet Club
Keauhou Resort
Condominiums
Keauhou
Shopping
Center
Kanaloa
at Kona
Kona Country
Club
He'eia Bay
Keauhou
Keauhou
Bay

Hualalai Rd
Hawaii Belt Rd
Kuakini Hwy
Ali'i Dr
11
Ali'i Dr
Kamehameha III Rd

0   .5   1 km
0   .25   .5 mile

development in the town center, and their office is conveniently located at the side of the lobby. Some ground-floor units have a musty air, but others are fixed up nicely. Furnishings vary, but rooms have TV, air-con, kitchenettes and phones with free local calls. Some units have VCRs. Guests often gather around the pool to cook dinner on the BBQ, and the complex tends to draw a young, lively crowd. Cheap rates make it easier to cope with the severely inadequate parking.

Kona Billfisher (☎ 329-9277, ℮ bilfish@ gte.net, 75-5841 Ali'i Drive) Hawaii Resort Management low/high season rates; 1-bedroom units $70/85, 2-bedroom units $90/115. Kona Billfisher tends to have more consistent decor and better upkeep than other moderately priced complexes. The 65 well-outfitted units boast lanais, queen sofa beds, king beds in the bedrooms, new carpeting, recently renovated kitchens and bathrooms, and both ceiling fans and air-con. Amenities include laundry facilities, BBQ and ping-pong. Telephone service is $5 extra. Guests can borrow a VCR. All units are closed for maintenance on the 13th and 14th of each month. It's good value for this price range and within walking distance of town.

Ali'i Villas (75-6016 Ali'i Drive) Knutson & Associates low/high season rates; 1-bedroom units $70/85. Restful Ali'i Villas, about half a mile out of town, has 126 units, an oceanfront pool and an unobstructed view of the sunset. A fair number of seniors enjoy the large and comfortable units at this quiet place, though the beige building looks a bit weathered. Each unit has a private lanai, cable TV and washer/dryer, and most have a phone and sofa bed. You must book through Knutson & Associates or SunQuest Vacations.

Kona Isle (75-6100 Ali'i Drive) Knutson & Associates one week minimum $490-665. If the Kona Islander is like the party dorm in college, this complex is comparable to the studious dorm, a reputation that gives the place plenty of repeat business. Amenities include picnic tables, barbecue grills and chaise lounges overlooking the ocean. Units have both air-con and microwaves. ATR Properties (329-6020, 888-311-6020, e atr@ ilhawaii.net) rents more than a dozen units.

Kona Riviera Villa (☎ 329-1996, 75-6124 Ali'i Drive) Knutson & Associates low/high season rates; garden-view units $75/85, ocean-view units $80/100, oceanfront units $100/110. This charming little complex right on the ocean has brick walkways and a fountain that spouts from a dolphin statue. There are just 14 homey, comfortable units, each with a full kitchen, a living room, a separate bedroom with a king or queen bed, ceiling fans and a vanity with a sink. Most have a sofa bed in the living room. The complex has coin laundry.

Casa de Emdeko (☎ 329-2160, 75-6082 Ali'i Drive) Knutson & Associates low/high season rates for 1-bedroom units $80/105. Casa de Emdeko is a pleasant white building with rather standard one-bedroom units. The units can feel a bit cramped because of the low ceilings, but they do have lanais and full kitchens. The convenience store and swimsuit shop in the complex are nice perks. There are both freshwater and saltwater pools.

Mid-Range Condos in this price range tend to have better amenities than the budget choices, but since units can vary tremendously, ask plenty of questions when booking reservations.

Kona Makai (☎ 329-6488, 75-6026 Ali'i Drive) SunQuest Vacations rates; 1-bedroom units start at $90. Kona Makai, on the seaward side of Ali'i Drive next to Ali'i Villas, has air-con one-bedroom units that are fully equipped with everything down to a washer/dryer. The complex has an exercise room and tennis courts. Knutson & Associates rents some 2-bedroom units.

Sea Village (☎ 329-6488, 75-6002 Ali'i Drive) Knutson & Associates low/high season rates; 1-bedroom units garden view $85/100, oceanview $105/120. Located 2 miles from town, the clean and cheerful grounds of this 131-unit complex include a tennis court, oceanside pool and Jacuzzi. Spacious condos have full kitchens. SunQuest Vacations also handles units here.

Kona Nalu (☎ 329-6488, 800-367-5168, 76-6212 Ali'i Drive) Low/high season rates; 2-bedroom units $165/225. Property Management Hawaii handles several of the 15 units here. All the condos in this quiet, older three-story building have lanais overlooking the ocean. Furnishings and amenities differ greatly in each unit. The property also has a teeny pool and easy access to the beach.

Kona Magic Sands Resort (☎ 329-3333, 800-622-5348, e kona@konahawaii.com, 77-6452 Ali'i Drive) Hawaii Resort Management low/high season rates; studio units $95/115. This is a small, cheerful complex perched at the side of White Sands Beach. Hawaii Resort Management handles 14 of the 36 units. These are compact studio units, but they have full kitchens, TVs, phones, rattan furnishings and oceanfront lanais. Although it's an older building, the bright, white units have recently been upgraded, and it's a good value for being on the water.

Hale Kona Kai (☎/fax 329-2155, 800-421-3696, 75-5870 Kahakai Rd) Rates for two people; 1-bedroom units $125, corner units $135, plus $10 each extra person. If you enjoy the sound of the surf, Hale Kona Kai is a pleasant find on the ocean just beyond the Royal Kona Resort. The 22 one-bedroom units for rent aren't brand new, but they're comfortable and have the usual amenities like full kitchens and cable TV. All units have waterfront lanais with great ocean views. The corner units boast a lovely wraparound lanai. Each floor has laundry. There's a three-day minimum on most units, a $150 security deposit and no holiday check-in.

Kona Reef (☎ 329-2959, 800-367-5004, fax 329-2762, w www.castleresorts.com, 75-5888 Ali'i Drive) 1-bedroom units rates; Castle Resorts & Hotels $170-230, Sun-Quest Vacations $100, Hawaii Resort Management $85-185. This is a 130-unit condo complex run like a hotel by Castle Resorts & Hotels. The tasteful units have the usual amenities, including full kitchens, VCRs, stereos, washer/dryers and private lanais. Rates are for up to four people in a one-bedroom unit, which also has a sofa bed in the living room. It's cheaper, however, to book through SunQuest Vacations or Hawaii Resort Management.

Top End Spacious units and upscale amenities accompany these higher prices.

Kona by the Sea (☎ 327-2300, 800-922-7866, W www.aston-hotels.com, 75-6106 Ali'i Drive) Low/high season rates; 1-bedroom units $245-275/$290-325, 2-bedroom units $300-320/$360-380. The last Aston property left in Kona, this complex boasts its own stretch of sand and a saltwater swimming pool next to the ocean. Roomy units come with all the amenities including TV, full kitchen, washer/dryer and private lanai. While the furnishings here are tasteful, they are hardly stylish. If you're willing to spend this kind of money, the grounds and units at the Royal Sea-Cliff are far more elegant. Inquire about AAA discounts and 'fourth night free' deals.

Royal Sea-Cliff Resort (☎ 329-8021, 800-688-7444, fax 326-1887, 75-6040 Ali'i Drive) Low/high season rates; studios $180/220, 1-bedroom units $210-240/250-280, 2-bedroom units $240-275/280-325. Outrigger's modern 154-unit complex has some of Kona's nicest, roomiest condo units, complete with large balcony, stylish furnishings, thermostatic air-con, modern kitchen and washer/dryer. There are tennis courts, freshwater and saltwater pools, a sauna, outdoor lounge areas and covered parking. The Outrigger chain runs the place like a hotel with a front desk. There's no minimum stay. Call for information about the various discount schemes that are available, including 50% off for Entertainment and Encore travel club members.

Places to Eat

Budget Budget dining in Kailua-Kona means filling fare that spans all types of cuisines.

French Bakery (☎ 326-2688, Ka'ahumanu Plaza) Open 5:30am-3pm Mon-Fri, 5:30am-2pm Sat. For a cheap meal on the run, try this bakery in the industrial area's Ka'ahumanu Plaza. It makes sticky buns, large muffins and a delicious apple coffee cake ($1.50). The Tongan bread ($5), filled with cheese and spinach, makes a good lunch for two and can be heated on request. Order it one day in advance.

Ocean View Inn (☎ 329-9998, 75-5683 Ali'i Dr) The complete breakfast $3-6. Lunch/dinner $5-11. Open for breakfast-lunch 6:30am-2:25pm, dinner 5:15pm-9pm Tues-Sun. This unassuming eatery in the town center is the best place for cheap local food. Counter seating lends it a diner atmosphere. They serve complete breakfasts with coffee and inexpensive sandwiches with French fries ($3-6). You can get budget Chinese, American and Hawaiian dishes, and it's a good place to try *lomi* salmon or a side dish of *poi*, the Hawaiian taro paste.

Ba-le Kona (☎ 327-1212, Kona Coast Shopping Center) Open 10am-9pm Mon-Sat, 11am-7pm Sun. French sandwiches and baked goods are served alongside Vietnamese fare at this brightly lit, fast-food style gem. A frequent special is Vietnamese happy pancakes, crepes made with rice flour, which are then wrapped with lettuce, mint and cilantro and dipped in sauce. Ba-le also has unusual sandwiches like pate and steam pork ($3.75-4.25) and hot egg noodle dishes ($6.50-6.75).

Island Lava Java (☎ 327-2161, Ali'i Sunset Plaza) Sandwiches $3.75-6.75. Open 6am-10pm. The outdoor tables at this popular café are always crowded with locals and tourists alike. Return visitors vouch for the espresso, sandwiches and good selection of homemade cinnamon rolls, muffins and pies.

Thai Rin (☎ 329-2929, Ali'i Sunset Plaza) Lunch dishes $7-8, dinner dishes $7-13.

Open lunch 11am-2:30pm Mon-Sat, dinner 5pm-9pm daily. Another worthwhile option at Ali'i Sunset Plaza is Thai Rin, which has curries, pad Thai and stir-fry dishes at lunch. The same dishes cost a bit more at dinner.

Manna's (☎ 334-0880, Crossroads Shopping Center) Dishes $5.50-8. Open 10am-8:30pm Mon-Sat. A Korean BBQ fast-food style restaurant packs 'em in, despite the lack of ambience. Manna plates come with four 'veggies' and two scoops of rice. Entrees include chicken katsu, deep-fried fillets in a panko batter, charbroiled marinated short ribs, and pan-fried butter fish with Korean sauce ($8). No credit cards are accepted.

Sushi Shop Kyotoya (☎ 987-8490, North Kona Shopping Center) Open 9am-6pm Mon-Fri; 9am to 5pm Sat. Filling, inexpensive sushi without any fuss is the point at this take-out window. Patrons dash off with the food or dine at one of several outdoor tables. Try a 12-piece tekka maki (ahi) roll ($4) or select your own 6-piece nigiri ($6).

Mid-Range These restaurants offer better atmosphere and higher quality than their budget counterparts.

Bianelli's (☎ 326-4800, Nani Kailua Rd, Pines Plaza) Open 11am-10pm Mon-Fri, 5pm-10pm Sat & Sun. Because it's a bit off the beaten path on the road towards Holualoa, this bustling Italian trattoria attracts its share of locals. It's not fancy, with plastic checked tablecloths and water glasses, but it's friendly. Filling fare includes all-you-can-eat pasta dinners where you select the pasta and the sauce ($9.45), calzones ($9) and traditional pizzas ($9 and up). Brews from around the world appear on the extensive beer list ($2.75-6).

Hard Rock Cafe (☎ 329-8866, Coconut Grove Marketplace) Dishes $9-16. Open 11:30am-11pm Sun-Thur, 11:30am-11:30pm Fri & Sat. Rock music plays continuously and music memorabilia covers the walls at Kona's Hard Rock Cafe at the south end of town in the Coconut Grove Marketplace. The menu features the chain's standard salads, sandwiches and burger platters. The splendid 2nd-floor ocean view may well be the best Hard Rock Cafe vista anywhere in the world.

Bubba Gump's (☎ 331-8442, 75-5776 Ali'i Drive) Dishes $8-18. Open 11am-10pm Sun-Thur, 11am-11pm Fri & Sat. This chain, with its heavy-handed *Forrest Gump* concept, has locations on Maui, Oahu and the mainland. While the 1994 film seems like a passe theme, the owners have a winning formula: a family-oriented place serving large portions of good food like Lt Dan's shrimp in bourbon sauce ($17) or Jenny's peace 'n' love veggie plate ($10). The waiters fire Forrest trivia questions at patrons. Request an oceanside lanai table and a mute waiter.

Kona Brewing Company (☎ 329-2739, North Kona Shopping Center) Open 11am-10pm Mon-Thur, 11am-midnight Fri & Sat, 1pm-9pm Sun. Kona Brewing Company, at the back of the North Kona Shopping Center, has a lively outdoor cafe with good Greek, spinach and Caesar salads ($4-8) and creative pizzas ($10-19). Wash it all down with one of the fresh brews made on site, or opt for the beer sampler: four 6oz glasses for $6.50.

Sibu Cafe (☎ 329-1112, Banyan Court) Lunch special Mon-Fri $6-7. Open lunch 11:30am-3pm, dinner 5pm-9pm. Sibu Cafe serves good Indonesian food in a casual café setting. There's a hearty gado gado salad ($11.50), and combination plates that offer three dishes (with choices like Balinese chicken, spicy Indian curry and shrimp satay) with brown rice at dinner ($13). Credit cards are not accepted.

Tres Hombres (☎ 329-2173, Walua Rd off Ali'i Drive) Open 11:30am-9pm daily. Better than Pancho & Lefty's, the busier Mexican joint on Ali'i Drive, Tres Hombres serves a fine margarita and fresh chips. Menu items include steak fajitas ($15), chile relleno ($9) and fish tacos ($14). Service is attentive, but the restaurant isn't scenic: The main room has a view of Ali'i Drive rather than the ocean, and the outdoor patio isn't much better.

Quinn's (☎ 329-3822, Palani Rd) Open 11am-midnight. This bar, on Palani Rd opposite King Kamehameha's Kona Beach Hotel, serves meals in its rear courtyard.

The crowd is mostly longtime local residents who come for the consistently good fish and steak dinners. For the setting, prices aren't cheap – $9 for fish and chips or the famous fresh fish sandwich, $22 for an ahi dinner – but the portions are large. Burgers, soups and salads are also available.

Top End High-end restaurants can disappoint in Kona, but the spots below are among the best.

Oodles of Noodles (☎ 329-9222 Crossroads Shopping Center) Dishes $10-20. Open 11am-9pm Mon-Thur, 11am-10pm Fri & Sat, 11am to 7pm Sun. Former executive chef at one of the Kohala Coast resorts Amy Ferguson-Ota runs the trendiest place in town. Her restaurant features noodles in all variations – from Vietnamese pho soup, pad Thai and Peking duck to grilled chicken fettuccine and a delicious wok-seared ahi noodle casserole. The menu also includes creative salads, soups and appetizers.

Kona Inn (☎ 329-4455) Entrees $15-25. Open 11:30am-10:30pm. Kona Inn, in the center of town, opened in 1929 as the Big Island's first hotel. It's now a shopping center with a large water-view restaurant of the same name. There are steak and seafood dinners and light meals like calamari sandwiches ($9), chicken Caesar salad ($10) and steak sandwiches ($12).

Huggo's (☎ 329-1493, 75-5828 Kahakai Rd) Dinner dishes $18-30. Open lunch 11:30am-2:30pm Mon-Fri, dinner 5:30pm-10pm daily. Huggo's, near the Royal Kona Resort, is a popular open-air restaurant right on the water's edge – a nice spot for a sunset drink. It attracts the biggest crowd at lunchtime on Tuesday and Thursday, when it features barbecued beef ribs served with baked beans and French bread ($9.50). Rather pricey steak and fish dishes punctuate the dinner menu.

Cassandra's Greek Taverna (☎ 334-1066, Kona Square) Appetizers $5-8, entrees $15-30. Open daily lunch 11am-4pm, dinner 4pm-10pm. For authentic Greek food, try Cassandra's. For around $15 you can get souvlaki, moussaka or a gyros plate, all served with rice. Appetizers ($5-9) include Greek salad, hummus, calamari and pickled octopus.

La Bourgogne (☎ 329-6711, Kuakini Plaza, Hwy 11 at Lako) Open 6pm-10pm Mon-Sat. Dishes $24-32. Despite its location in a mini-mall sans ocean view 3 miles south of Kailua-Kona, this intimate French restaurant has no trouble filling its dozen or so tables. Consider the roast duck with raspberries and pinenuts ($24) or the sweetbreads of veal ($28). The staff can help you navigate the extensive wine list.

Groceries Kona has everything from supermarkets to farmers' markets to organic foods.

Safeway (☎ 329-2207, Crossroads Shopping Center), a 24-hour supermarket, is Kona's biggest and has a good bakery, deli and reasonably priced wines. The Lanihau Center on Palani Rd has a *Sack N Save* supermarket (☎ 326-2729; open 5am-midnight daily), where patrons sacrifice higher quality and baggers for lower prices. *KTA Super Store* (☎ 329-1677, Kona Coast Shopping Center) isn't gourmet, but it has a better selection.

Kona Natural Foods (☎ 329-2296, Crossroads Shopping Center) Open 9am-9pm Mon-Sat, 9am-7pm Sun. Come here for organic wines and produce, along with a good variety of dairy and bulk food products and vitamins. The excellent café, which closes about an hour earlier than the store, serves veggie sandwiches and generous takeout salads ($5-7). The servers can get testy when closing time looms.

Fresh island fruits, vegetables and flowers are available direct from the growers at the *farmers' market* that sets up opposite Waterfront Row from 8am to 3pm on Wednesday, Friday, Saturday and Sunday. The Sunday market is scaled back a bit.

Entertainment

Bars & Clubs With many restaurants and bars lined up along Ali'i Drive, Kona has no shortage of sunset views and happy hours.

Huggo's (☎ 329-1493, see Places to Eat, Top End) Huggo's, right on the water near the Royal Kona Resort, has dancing to Top

40, reggae or Hawaiian music from 9pm to at least midnight nightly.

Sam's Hideaway (Kona Marketplace) is a loud spot with nightly karaoke entertainment. Someone will inevitably stick a mike in your face, so don't come if you're not willing to belt one out.

LuLu's (☎ 331-2633, Coconut Grove Marketplace) Next door to the Hard Rock Cafe, LuLu's boasts 13 TV monitors that plug into sports programs.

Jakes (☎ 329-7366, Coconut Grove Marketplace) In the same building as LuLu's, Jakes offers dancing to live music on most nights and cheap local draft beers during happy hour. Wednesday night is Hawaiian music and hula dancing. Belly dancing happens on Saturday night.

Windjammer Lounge (☎ 329-3111, Royal Kona Resort) Patrons stop by the hotel's oceanside bar for the pleasant sunset hula show Tuesday through Sunday at 6pm. They stay for pupus and cocktails at the oceanside bar.

Kanaka Kava (☎ 327-1660, Coconut Grove Marketplace) The newest craze to hit Hawaii, kava is a legal relaxant that's said to 'induce aloha.' The kava bar, which also serves pupus, is open till 10pm daily.

If you escape the hubbub of Ali'i Drive, you'll sacrifice an ocean view in favor of bars with more locals than tourists.

Ah Dunno Bar & Grill (☎ 326-2337, Kaiwi St) Pro football is the special du jour on Mondays at this industrial area bar, while Wednesday through Sunday features live tunes, typically rock and blues. Come play pool during happy hour (3pm-6pm weekdays), when drafts are $1.50.

Down the street from Ah Dunno is *The Other Side (☎ 329-7226, 74-5484 Kaiwi St)* The spacious, high-ceilinged bar is split in two: 'The Edge' has more disco, while the 'Other Side' concentrates on rock. It's mostly a local crowd that comes for darts, Foosball, pool and televised sports. During happy hour (noon to 6 pm daily) domestic beers are $2.25.

The Office Cocktail Lounge (☎ 329-2525, North Kona Shopping Center) This is a tiny,

intimate watering hole located in a shopping mall; it's perfect for a mellow drink with a friend, but don't expect an energetic atmosphere.

Kona Bowl (325-2695, Lanihau Center) Don't waste the daylight hours in a bowling alley, but consider renting a lane in the evening.

Cinemas Makalapua Shopping Center is home to the *Stadium Cinemas (☎ 327-0444)*, which show current popular films on 10 different screens. Bargain matinees are before 6pm.

Movie rentals are a viable option, as many condos and B&Bs have VCRs. The ubiquitous *Blockbuster (☎ 326-7694, Kona Coast Shopping Center)* is open till 11pm Monday through Thursday; midnight Friday through Sunday. Longs Drugs in the Lanihau Center has cheaper movie rentals, though the selection is inferior.

Luaus Kailua-Kona's two big hotels offer lively, albeit hokey, evening luaus.

King Kamehameha's Kona Beach Hotel (☎ 326-4969, see Places to Stay) Adult/child 6-12 years $55/21, child 5 years & under free. Luau 5:30pm-9pm Tues-Thur & Sun. This hotel offers a popular luau on its beach in front of Ahuena Heiau. The luau begins with a shell-lei greeting, followed by torch lighting, a buffet dinner and a Polynesian dance show. There's also limited seating at 7pm, minus the dinner (adult/child $30/14.50). If you stop by around 10am on luau days, you can watch staff members bury the pig in the *imu* (underground oven) – they'll explain it all to you.

The Royal Kona Resort (☎ 329-3111, see Places to Stay) Adult/child 6-12 years $55/23. The other luau in town is also right on the water. Guests sit at long tables and enjoy the same traditional activities mentioned above, with a buffet of shredded pork, steamed sticky rice, fish poke, poi and more. Post-dinner entertainment features a fashion show of lava-lava styles, Polynesian music, dancing, singing and fire-dancing. One caveat: Cocktails like Mai Tai punch are weak, and the 'all night' open bar only lasts until 7:30pm.

Limited seating at 7pm, excluding dinner (adult/child 6-12 years old $28/18).

Shopping

The center of Kailua-Kona is thick with small shops selling trinkets, clothing, crafts and other tourist-related goods. Of course, you'll never be far from one of the ubiquitous *ABC discount marts*, which can be a good place to pick up vacation necessities such as cheap beach mats, sunblock, killer coffee and sundry goods.

King Kamehameha's Kona Beach Hotel (☎ 329-2911) has a *Big Island Outlet* store that features a wide variety of island crafts, T-shirts and oddities like potted fuku bonsai trees. *Giggles (☎ 329-7763)* in the Coconut Grove Marketplace has fun items for kids, including thongs, sunglasses, clothes and toys.

Kona Inn Shopping Village's *Hula Heaven (☎ 329-7885)* warrants a closer look for its more authentic and original merchandise. The store sells vintage aloha shirts and clothing, prints, note cards and old maps. Consequently, the prices are higher. You'll find good selections of Hawaiian music at *Mele Kai Music (☎ 329-1454, Ka'ahumanu Plaza)*.

Kailua Candy Company (☎ 329-2522, 74-5563 Kaiwi St) Open 8am-6pm Mon-Sat, 8am-4pm Sun. This store in the industrial area makes delicious homemade chocolates using island fruits and nuts. The candies aren't cheap, but they'll please those chocoholics in your life. At the gift shop you can get free samples, a brief chocolate overview and a peek at the company's operations.

Ali'i Gardens Marketplace (☎ 334-1381, Ali'i Drive 1½ miles south of town) Open 8am to 5pm Wed and Fri-Sun. Several dozen vendors sell varied items at this outdoor market, including sarongs, kids' clothes, tropical flowers, jewelry, pottery and gecko key chains.

Getting Around

The Ali'i Shuttle (☎ 775-7121) between Kailua-Kona and Keauhou (45 minutes, 8 times northbound; 7 times southbound) Monday through Saturday. The bus leaves every 90 minutes from the Kona Surf Resort in Keauhou from 8:30am to 7pm. Stops include Keauhou Shopping Center, Keauhou Beach Resort, Royal Kona Resort, Kona Inn Shopping Village, King Kamehameha's Kona Beach Hotel and the Lanihau Center. In the southbound direction, buses leave the Lanihau Center every 90 minutes from 9:20am to 6:20pm. Among other things, the shuttle makes a good option for getting to Kahalu'u Beach Park (next to the Keauhou Beach Resort). The fare anywhere along the route is $2 each way, or you can get a day/week/month pass for $5/20/40.

Kona Coast Express (☎ 331-1582) has an 80-minute loop running from 7:40am until 8:20pm. The southbound route begins at the King Kamehameha Hotel and stops at Kona Inn Shopping Village, Coconut Grove Marketplace, Royal Sea Cliff, Casa de Emdeko, Kona by the Sea, Ali'i Gardens Marketplace, Kona Bali Kai, Keauhou Beach Hotel, Keauhou Shopping Center, Kona Surf Hotel and Keauhou Pier. The northbound route makes the same stops. An all-day pass costs $5.

Hitching in and around Kailua-Kona is also standard practice. As always, use common sense when accepting rides from or giving rides to strangers.

For details on rental cars and taxis at the airport, see the Getting Around chapter.

Parking The center of Kailua-Kona gets congested, but free and cheap parking is there for the taking.

Free public parking is available in the lot behind Kona Seaside Hotel, between Likana Lane and the Kuakini Hwy. The Kona Inn Shopping Village provides complimentary parking for patrons in the lot behind the Kona Bay Hotel. Patrons of Kona Marketplace can park free at the rear of that center. The Coconut Grove Marketplace and Ali'i Sunset Plaza share an enormous free parking lot behind their complexes.

At the north end of Ali'i Drive, the big parking lot behind King Kamehameha's Kona Beach Hotel offers free parking for

KONA

the first 15 minutes; it costs $1 per half hour after that. If you purchase something in one of the hotel shops or restaurants, you can get a voucher for free parking.

KEAUHOU
Keauhou is the coastal area immediately south of Kailua-Kona. It starts at Kahalu'u Bay and runs south beyond Keauhou Bay and the Kona Surf Resort.

Keauhou contains a planned community of three hotels, nine condo complexes, a shopping center and a 27-hole golf course, all neatly spaced out with a country club atmosphere. Bishop Estate, Hawaii's biggest private landholder, owns the land.

The area was once the site of a major Hawaiian settlement. Several historical sites can still be explored, although they now share their grounds with the hotels and condos.

Information
Inside the KTA Super Store (☎ 322-2311, Keauhou Shopping Center, on the corner of Ali'i Drive and Kamehameha III Rd) is a branch of the Bank of Hawaii, open 10am to 7pm on weekdays and 10am to 3pm on weekends. KTA also has a Bank of Hawaii ATM where you can get cash and interisland coupons.

The local post office is at the Keauhou Shopping Center. It's open 9am to 4pm on weekdays and 10am to 3pm on Saturday.

Keauhou Shopping Center contains a Longs Drugs, and KTA has a small pharmacy.

St Peter's Church
The precious little blue and white church on the north side of Kahalu'u Bay is a Catholic church dating back to 1880, although it was moved from White Sands Beach to this site in 1912. Several tidal waves and hurricanes have unsuccessfully attempted to relocate it.

St Peter's is Hawaii's most photographed 'quaint church' and is still used for weekend services and weddings.

Christians were not the first to deem the site a suitable place to worship the gods. At the north side of the church, you'll find the remains of **Kuemanu Heiau**, a surfing temple. Hawaiian royalty, who surfed the waters at the north end of Kahalu'u Bay, paid their respects at this temple before hitting the waves.

Locals keep up the surfing tradition here, although high surf usually generates dangerous northward rip currents.

Kahalu'u Beach
Kahalu'u, which means the 'Diving Place' in Hawaiian, is the island's best easy-access snorkeling spot. The bay is like a big natural aquarium, loaded with colorful marine life. If you haven't tried snorkeling, this is a great place to learn. The main drawback is the beach's proximity to Ali'i Drive and the jarring traffic noise.

Green Sea Turtles

Green sea turtles (*honu*) are the most abundant of the three native species of sea turtles found in Hawaiian waters. Because green sea turtles feed on algae that grows in the shallow waters of coastal reefs, they often share beach space with snorkelers. Weighing upward of 200 pounds at maturity, these turtles are a thrill to behold in the water.

The green sea turtle population in Hawaii has been on the increase in recent years, with frequent sightings at places like Kahalu'u Beach. The turtles are not permanent residents of the main Hawaiian Islands. About once every four years, they return to their ancestral nesting grounds in the remote French Frigate Shoals, 700 miles east of the Big Island, where they mate and nest.

Hawaii's other two native sea turtles are the hawksbill, which is about the same size as the green sea turtle but far rarer, and the leatherback, which weighs up to a ton and is found in deep offshore waters.

Large rainbow parrotfish, schools of silver needlefish, brilliant yellow tangs, butterfly fish and colorful wrasses are among the numerous tropicals easily seen here.

The fish are tame enough to eat out of your hand; bring along fish food and frenzied swarms will engulf you. There are lots of fish in the shallows, but generally deeper water means better coral and larger fish. At high tide, green sea turtles often swim into the bay to feed.

An ancient breakwater, said to have been built by the *Menehune* (legendary 'little people'), is on the reef and protects the bay. Still, when the surf is high, Kahalu'u can have strong currents that pull in the direction of the rocks near St Peter's Church, and it's easy to drift away without realizing it. Check your bearings occasionally to make sure you're not being pulled. Before jumping in, take a look at the water conditions posted on the weathered display board by the picnic pavilion.

A lifeguard is on duty daily, and a snack van sells burgers, sodas and ice cream. Another van rents body boards and silicone snorkel sets (per 2 hours/day $6/8). It also sells fish food for $3 and disposable underwater cameras for $14.

The park has a salt-and-pepper beach composed of black lava and white coral sand with palm trees. Facilities include showers, rest rooms, changing rooms, picnic tables, plentiful parking and grills. This small stretch of beach is a popular place and often draws a crowd, so it's best to hit the sand early. Beach hours are 7am to 11pm.

Keauhou Beach Resort

The grounds of the Keauhou Beach Resort, immediately south of Kahalu'u Beach, contain a number of easily explored historical sites. Ask at the front desk for a brochure and site map.

The ruins of Kapuanoni, a **fishing temple**, are on the north side of the hotel. The reconstructed summer **beach house of King Kalakaua** is inland, beside a spring-fed pond once used as a royal bath. You can peek into the simple three-room cottage and see a portrait of the king in his

European-style royal dress, a Hawaiian quilt on the bed and *lauhala* (pandanus-leaf) mats on the floor.

Other heiau sites are on the south side of the hotel. The remains of the seaside **Keeku Heiau**, just beyond the footbridge that leads to the now defunct Kona Lagoon Hotel, is thought to have been a luakini heiau.

The shelf of *pahoehoe* (smooth, ropelike lava) at the south side of the Keauhou Beach Resort holds interesting **tide pools**, best explored at low tide. The pools contain numerous sea urchins, including spiny and slate pencil types, and small tropical fish.

When the tide is at its very lowest, you can walk out onto a flat lava tongue carved with numerous **petroglyphs**. The site is directly in front of the northern end of the Kona Lagoon Hotel, with most of the petroglyphs about 25 feet from shore. Unless it's low tide, the petroglyphs are submerged and hidden from view.

Keauhou Bay

Keauhou Bay, which has a launch ramp and space for two dozen small boats, is one of the most protected bays on the west coast.

If you come by on weekdays in the late afternoon, you can watch the local outrigger canoe club practicing in the bay. There are rest rooms and showers.

In a small clearing just south of the harborside dive shacks, a stone marks the site where Kamehameha III was born in 1814. The young prince was said to have been stillborn and brought back to life by a visiting *kahuna* (priest/spiritual healer).

To get to the bay, turn *makai* (toward the ocean) off Ali'i Drive onto Kamehameha III Rd. Or, alternatively, drive down Kaleopapa Rd toward Kona Surf Resort, but continue to the end of the road instead of turning into the resort.

Hawaiian Chocolate Factory

The only chocolate grown on US soil comes from this tiny factory on Mt. Hualalai. Owners Bob and Pam Cooper came to Hawaii in 1997 knowing nothing about chocolate. Now Bob offers an informative tour of the orchids and factory, located near the Keauhou Shopping Center (☎ 322-2626, 78-6772 Makenawai St; tours are free and by appointment only; call for directions).

It's hard to believe that the sinful 4oz bars of milk and dark chocolate produced here come from chocolate beans that smell like stinky socks. The pods, however, are beautiful shades of yellow, gold and fuchsia, and they're harvested every two weeks year-round. Removing the beans from the pods is done by hand. The drying process takes three to four weeks.

This is a mom-and-pop operation, and Cooper offers self-deprecating anecdotes about some of his makeshift equipment while his wife hand-wraps the bars in a climate-controlled room.

Places to Stay

Keauhou Resort Condominiums (☎ 322-9122, 800-367-5286, fax 322-9410, 78-7039 Kamehameha III Rd) Low/high season rates for 1-bedroom units; garden-view $70/97, ocean-view $80/107. This place has 48 units with full kitchens and washer/dryers. Although the units are about 30 years old, most are well maintained, and the property is the cheapest in Keauhou. Add about $25 more to the above rates for a two-bedroom unit for up to four people. The minimum stay is five days. It's near the golf course and has a pool.

Keauhou Surf & Racquet Club (☎ 329-3333, 800-622-5348, 78-6800 Ali'i Drive) Low/high season rates for 2-bedroom units; golf-course view $115/150, ocean-view $125/175. The large, modern complex conveniently located near the Keauhou shopping center has three tennis courts, a grass volleyball court and a pool. Not all units have views, but each is spacious and comes equipped with lanai, full kitchen, washer/dryer and TV/VCR. One drawback here: The pool doesn't overlook the ocean. Hawaii Resort Management handles some rentals; Knutson & Associates rates are a bit higher.

Keauhou Beach Resort (☎ 322-7987, 800-462-6262, fax 322-3117, ⓦ www.ohanaho tels.com, 78-6740 Ali'i Drive) Garden-view/oceanfront rooms $165-185/205-225. This 314-room hotel adjoins Kahalu'u Beach Park and has interesting grounds that include historical sites and tide pools. The hotel reopened in the spring of 1999 after a lengthy renovation and is now a member of the Outrigger chain. The spacious, tastefully furnished rooms have mini-refrigerators, TVs, lanais, and air-con. Outrigger offers a number of discounts ranging from 25% off for AAA auto club members to fifth-night-free deals.

Kanaloa at Kona (☎ 322-9625, 800-688-7444, ⓔ reservations@outrigger.com, 78-261 Manukai St) Golf-course view 1-bedroom apartments $205, ocean-view 2-bedroom units $290. At the other end of the spectrum from Keauhou Resort Condominiums is this establishment with 100 condo units. All units have lanais with wet bars as well as the standard amenities. The oceanfront units also have spas. There are three pools and two lighted tennis courts. The condo is a member of the Outrigger chain.

Other Keauhou condos are priced between the two and are largely booked through vacation rental agents. **SunQuest Vacations** (☎ 329-6488, 800-367-5168, 77-6435 Kuakini Hwy) handles units in most of them.

Places to Eat

Royal Thai Café (☎ 322-8424, Keauhou Shopping Center) Open 11am-10pm. Asian statues and a large aquarium dominate this restaurant, but the food holds its own. Light and refreshing basil rolls ($6) are filled with shrimp, lettuce and herbs. A tasty variety of curry dishes come in red, green, yellow or pineapple ($9-10), while pad Thai, Thailand's most famous culinary export, is a reliable favorite ($9).

Drysdale's Two (☎ 322-0070, Keauhou Shopping Center) Dishes $6-8. Open 11am-midnight. Specializing in sandwiches and burgers, this spot is the happening place to watch sports on TV.

The Vista Restaurant & Lounge (☎ 322-3700, Ali'i Drive in the Kona Country Club) Dishes $6-12. Open 11am-2pm Mon-Fri; 8am-2pm Sat & Sun. Calming views of the ocean and the golf course accompany the

Manta Rays

Pacific manta rays are gorgeous, gentle creatures with a wingspan that can measure an impressive 12-14 feet across. While spotlights off the Kona Surf Hotel used to shine down on the ocean and create a fantastic dinner show of mantas – light attracts plankton and plankton, in turn, attracts mantas – the hotel has long been shuttered.

But don't despair. Several dive outfits offer night dives to see these luminous creatures (see the Scuba section, earlier). Even if you're not a certified diver, you can snorkel at the surface and view the mantas from above. As they cruise around in the surf with their white underbellies flashing against the dark waters, it's hypnotic to watch, and an unforgettable Hawaiian adventure.

Remember that mantas make their best showings when there's no moon.

basic fare like omelets ($9) and burgers and chicken sandwiches ($10); several TVs are tuned into sports action.

Edward's at Kanaloa (☎ *322-1434, Kanaloa at Kona*) Open 11am-8:30pm Mon-Fri; 8am-8:30pm Sat & Sun. Oddly situated in a condo complex, the truly spectacular sunset view and knowledgeable service at this restaurant draws locals here when they have reason to celebrate. Make early reservations and sip a Kanaloa sunset cocktail ($6.50) with dark rum, amaretto, grenadine and pineapple juice. Try beef tenderloin with creamy port wine and Gorgonzola sauce, or Moroccan spiced chicken on a bed of couscous ($17.25).

Entertainment

Verandah Lounge (*Keahou Beach Resort*) The hotel bar features contemporary jazz on Tuesday nights and mellow Hawaiian music Wednesday through Saturday. Drink prices are reasonable, considering the oceanfront location, and the crowd skews a bit older. The lounge is open till 10pm nightly.

Keauhou Cinema (*Keauhou Shopping Center*) This multiscreen theater shows first-run movies.

Getting Around

Keauhou has a free on-call shuttle service (☎ 322-3500) that runs around the Keauhou Beach Resort and environs between 8am and 4:30pm every day.

HOLUALOA

Holualoa is a sleepy village perched in the hills, 1400 feet above Kailua-Kona. The slopes catch afternoon showers, so it's lusher and cooler than on the coast below.

Holualoa is an artists' community with craft shops, galleries and a community art center, all of which makes it a fun place to poke around.

This is pretty much a one-road village, with everything lined up along Hwy 180. There's a general store, a Japanese cemetery, an elementary school, a couple of churches and a library that's open a few days a week.

From Kailua-Kona, it's a scenic 4 miles up Hualalai Rd to Holualoa. The landscape is bright with poinsettia flowers, coffee bushes and fruit trees of all kinds.

While Holualoa remains off the beaten path, Kona's relentless development is (understandably) creeping up this way. It's an enviable location, with a fine view of Kailua Bay's sparkling turquoise waters below.

Kona Blue Sky Coffee

More than 400 coffee belt acres on Mt. Hualalai's slopes belong to the Twigg-Smith Estate's Kona Blue Sky farm (☎ *322-1700, 76-973A Hualalai Rd*), headquartered just down the road from Holualoa's gallery row. Visitors are first welcomed with a short video before their tour of the grounds. Then they can see the roasting and packaging that takes place on the premises.

The tasting room has requisite coffee samples and freebies of chocolate-covered beans. Other coffee gift items include coffee-flavored jellies and coffee-scented candles. Free visitor tours are 8:30am-4pm Mon-Fri.

Kimura's Lauhala Shop

Kimura's Lauhala Shop (☎ 324-0053, intersection Hualalai Rd & Hwy 180) Open 9am-5pm Mon-Sat. This shop sells items woven from lauhala, the lau (leaf) of the *hala* (pandanus) plant.

This was once an old plantation store that sold salt and codfish. During the 1930s, Mrs Kimura started weaving lauhala hats and coffee baskets and selling them at the plantations. Three generations of Kimuras still weave lauhala here. Their work is supplemented by the wives of local coffee farmers, who do piecework at home when it's not coffee season.

The most common items are placemats, open baskets and hats of a finer weave.

Kona Arts Center

The soul of Holualoa is the Kona Arts Center (*no* ☎, *open 10am-3pm Tues-Sat*), set in a ramshackle former coffee mill with a tin roof and hot-pink doors on Hwy 180. Carol Rogers, who's been here since 1965, directs this nonprofit organization and teaches crafts, nurturing the spirit as much as the art.

This is a community scene and everyone's welcome to join. For a nominal monthly fee, you can participate in the workshops, which include pottery, batik, tie-dye, basketry, weaving and painting.

Visitors are free to drop in and look around. There's also a small display area with items for sale, including paintings, pottery and baskets made of natural fibers.

Galleries

Gallery hopping is the main activity in Holualoa. They're typically open 10am to 4pm Tuesday to Saturday.

Studio 7 Gallery (☎ 324-1335)is a Holualoa highlight. The gallery showcases the artwork of owner Hiroki Morinoue, who

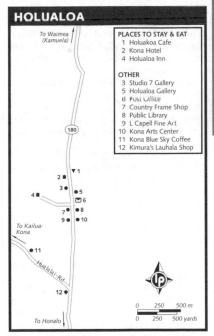

HOLUALOA

To Waimea (Kamuela)

To Kailua-Kona

To Honalo

180

Hualalai Rd

PLACES TO STAY & EAT
1 Holuakoa Cafe
2 Kona Hotel
4 Holualoa Inn

OTHER
3 Studio 7 Gallery
5 Holualoa Gallery
6 Post Office
7 Country Frame Shop
8 Public Library
9 L Capell Fine Art
10 Kona Arts Center
11 Kona Blue Sky Coffee
12 Kimura's Lauhala Shop

0   250   500 m
0   250   500 yards

works in watercolors, oils, woodblock and sculpture. His wife, Setsuko, is a potter and the gallery's director. The gallery's Zen-like setting blends both Hawaiian and Japanese influences, with wooden walkways over lava stones.

Holualoa Gallery (☎ 322-8484) sells paintings with a Hawaiiana theme, including a few works by the noted Big Island artist Herb Kawainui Kane, and some creative raku pottery by gallery owner Matt Lovein.

Country Frame Shop (☎ 324-1590) features watercolors and other paintings by artist Darrell Hill. He also stocks a small collection of more affordable souvenirs.

L Capell Fine Art (☎ 937-8893), opposite the Kona Arts Center, was once the old Holualoa post office building. Now that she's settled into her new gallery, the owner/ artist is shifting her focus from representational to more abstract artwork.

Places to Stay & Eat

Kona Hotel (☎ 324-1155, Hwy 180, Holualoa, HI 96725) Singles/doubles with shared bath $20/26. This old, bright pink wooden building in Holualoa center retains the small-town character (and room rates!) of a bygone era. This old local hostelry has high ceilings and some nice views. Rooms are basic with just a bed and dresser, but they're clean. Bathrooms are shared and down the hall. With only 11 rooms, the place is often full.

Holualoa Inn (☎ 324-1121, 800-392-1812, fax 322-2472, **e** inn@aloha.net, **w** www .konaweb.com/hinn, 76-5932 Mamalahoa Hwy) Doubles $150-195, plus $30 each extra person. Run by Michael Twigg-Smith, this gorgeous upscale B&B is perched atop 40 acres of sloping meadows with grand views of the Kona Coast. The contemporary house was built as a getaway by Michael's uncle, chairman of the *Honolulu Advertiser*. The exterior is all western red cedar, and the interior floors are red eucalyptus from Maui. The 6000-sq-foot house has six charming guest rooms, each with private bath. If you're traveling with more than two people, go for the Bali suite; it has a bedroom with a king bed, a separate sitting room with a queen sofa bed, and absolutely unbeatable views. Amenities include a black-bottom tile swimming pool, Jacuzzi, billiard table, rooftop gazebo, TV lounge and facilities for preparing light meals. Rates include a continental breakfast.

Holuakoa Cafe (☎ 322-2233) Open 6:30am-3pm Mon-Sat. Holuakoa Cafe has good pastries, sandwiches, salads, espresso and herbal teas, plus daily specials listed on the chalkboard. Patrons can stretch out in the pleasant courtyard or dine in the inviting interior with hardwood floors.

North Kona

Hot, arid country lies along Hwy 19 (Queen Ka'ahumanu Hwy), which runs north 33 miles from Kailua-Kona up the Kona Coast to Kawaihae in the South Kohala district. Along the route you'll notice the Big Island's sanitized version of graffiti – sweet messages spelled out in stones of white coral against the black lava background. From much of this coast, you can look inland and see Mauna Kea, and to the south of it Mauna Loa, both of which are often snowcapped in winter.

Heading north out of Kailua-Kona, you'll first pass Honokohau Harbor and the Kaloko-Honokohau National Historical Park, just a couple miles from town. A big open lava tube lies on the inland side of Hwy 19, north of the 91-mile marker and just before a speed limit sign. It's apt to seem rather tame if you've been to Hawaii Volcanoes National Park but interesting if you haven't. The tube and the expansive lava flow surrounding the airport are both from the last eruption of Mt Hualalai, in 1801.

Farther north is Kona Coast State Park, which provides vehicle access to a nice undeveloped section of the coast. Many more beautiful secluded beaches and coves lie along this sparsely populated coastline, but they're hidden from the road and accessible only by foot. Once you hike in, you'll find white-sand beaches tucked between a sea of hardened lava and a turquoise ocean.

Continuing up the highway, you'll pass the 87-mile marker and the turnoff to the Kona Village Resort, built on the site of a former fishing village. The shoreline between Kailua-Kona and Waikoloa was once dotted with tiny fishing villages, but most were wiped out by the tsunami of 1946.

The flat, straight highway is part of the Ironman Triathlon route and has wide, smooth bike lanes bordering both sides of the road. Cyclists take heed: When the air temperature is above 85°F, reflected heat from asphalt and lava can edge the actual temperature above 100°F, and no drinking water or services are available along the road.

HONOKOHAU HARBOR

Honokohau Harbor was built in 1970 to take some of the burden off Kailua Pier. Charter fishing boats occupy most of the harbor's 155 slips, and these days almost all of Kona's catch comes in here. The harbor is about 2 miles north of Kailua-Kona on Hwy 19, between the 98- and 97-mile markers.

If you want to see the charter fishing boats pull up and weigh their catches of marlin and yellowfin tuna, drive straight in, park near the gas station and walk to the dock at the rear of the adjacent building. The best times to see the weigh-ins are generally around 11:30am and 3:30pm.

Harbor House Restaurant in the harbor complex serves frosted mugs of beer ($2 during happy hour), shrimp and chips ($7.50) and chicken, turkey and beef burgers ($5.75-7). They're open 11am-7pm Monday to Saturday; 11am-5:30pm Sunday. There's also a fish market that sells fresh fish and smoked marlin by the piece.

KALOKO-HONOKOHAU NATIONAL HISTORICAL PARK

Despite its 1978 designation as a national historic park, Kaloko-Honokohau *(☎ 329-6881; entrance on Hwy 19 between the 97 and 96-mile marker; park gates open 8am-3:30pm daily)* remains in the development stages. The park encompasses 1160 acres, including Aimakapa and Kaloko Fishponds, burial caves, petroglyphs, a *holua* (sled course), a Queen's Bath, the entire oceanfront between Kaloko and Honokohau Harbor, and a restored 1-mile segment of the ancient stone footpath known as the **King's Trail**, or Ala Mamalahoa Trail.

There's speculation that the bones of Kamehameha the Great were buried in secret near Kaloko. This, combined with the fact that Aimakapa Fishpond is a habitat for endangered waterbirds, was enough to help squeeze the national park designation through Congress.

On the coast near the north end of the park is **Kaloko Fishpond**, acquired in 1986 from Huehue Ranch. Before the park took over the land, red mangrove had invaded the fishpond and spread rapidly, causing native birds to abandon the habitat. The park service eradicated the mangrove in a labor-intensive process that involved cutting and torching the trees, then tearing the new shoots up one by one and burning

the roots. Native birds have now returned to Kaloko.

Aimakapa Fishpond, at the south side of the park just inland from Honokohau Beach, is the largest pond on the Kona Coast and an important bird habitat. Like Kaloko, a mangrove invasion required intensive eradication efforts. If you visit this brackish pond, you're likely to see two endangered waterbirds: the *aeo* (Hawaiian black-necked stilt) and *alae-keokeo* (Hawaiian coot). Found nowhere else, they've made a significant return since the pond was cleared.

While much of the focus within the park is natural restoration (the 700-year-old Kaloko fishpond wall, for example, is undergoing a long-overdue repair job), trails are slowly being developed, and plans call for establishing a visitor center that will feature displays on Hawaiian culture and natural history.

In the meantime, free brochures at the site explain the cultural and archeological significance of the area, and a ranger is often on site to answer questions. The 3/4 mile-long access road is unpaved, but navigable without a 4WD. There's also access to the park from the harbor (see Honokohau Beach).

If you're interested in birds, wetlands and archaeological sites, you'll enjoy wandering around here for a couple of hours. But keep in mind that amenities are scarce in the vast park, aside from a few portable bathrooms. Come equipped with water, sunscreen and anything else you might need.

Honokohau Beach

Just north of the harbor, Honokohau Beach is part of the Kaloko-Honokohau National Historical Park. For many years, nude sunbathers came in droves, but park rangers now patrol the area and swimsuits are de rigueur.

The beach is composed of large-grained sand – a mix of black lava, white coral and rounded shell fragments. It's not a bad spot for swimming and snorkeling if you happen to be in the area, but the bottom is a bit rocky. Kua Bay and Kona Coast State Park

KONA

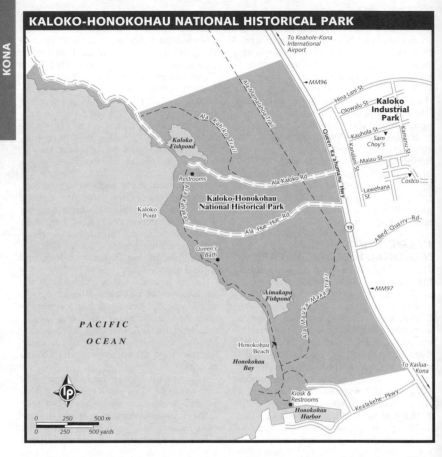

KALOKO-HONOKOHAU NATIONAL HISTORICAL PARK

To Keahole-Kona
International
Airport

MM96

Hina Lani St

Olowalu St   **Kaloko**
Industrial
Park

Kauhola St

Sam
Choy's

Kamanu St

Kalahuli St

Maiau St

Costco

Lawehana
St

Ala Mauna loa Trail

Queen Kaʻahumanu Hwy

Ala Kaloko Rd

Kaloko-Honokohau
National Historical Park

Ala Hue-Hue Rd

19

Allied Quarry Rd

Kaloko
Fishpond

Ala Kahiko Trail

Restrooms

Ala Kahakai

Kaloko
Point

Queen's
Bath

Aimakapa
Fishpond

Ala Mauka-Makai Trail

MM97

PACIFIC

OCEAN

Honokohau
Beach

Honokohau
Bay

To Kailua-
Kona

Kiosk &
Restrooms

Kealakehe Pkwy

Honokohau
Harbor

0   250   500 m

0   250   500 yards

(see those sections later) have far superior, though less accessible, beaches.

To get there, turn onto the Honokohau Harbor road from Hwy 19, then turn right in front of the marina complex and follow the road a quarter mile. Pull off to the right after the dry dock boatyard. The trail begins at a break in the lava wall on the right, near the end of the road. It's a five-minute walk along a well-beaten path to the beach.

The only facilities are some pit toilets at the end of the trail. Consider packing some good insect repellent in case the gnats are feasting.

Though only accessible by boat off the coast of Honokohau Harbor, **Turtle Pinna-cle** is a premier dive site in the area for spotting turtles, which congregate here to clean their shells (small fish feed off the algae and parasites on the turtles' shells). The turtles are accustomed to divers, so they don't shy away from photo ops. Other frequent sightings in the water include frogfish, octopuses and pipefish.

Places to Eat
Costco (☎ 334-0770, 73-5600 Maiau St, Koloko Industrial Park) Open 11am-8:30pm

weekdays; 9:30am-6pm Sat; 10am-6pm Sun. Membership costs $45. Members can stock up on bulk groceries and drygoods and get some grub at the inexpensive food court (☎ 331-4834).

Sam Choy's (☎ 326-1545, 73-5576 Kauhola St) Open 6am-2pm Mon-Sat; 7am-2pm Sun. A mix of locals and tourists come to feast on the famous cuisine of Big Island native Sam Choy, who has a string of popular restaurants around Hawaii. The setting in Kaloko Light Industrial Park is casual, with Formica tables and the chef's photos and awards adorning the walls. Try the fried poke omelet ($8.50) or a heaping wok rice bowl with meat or veggies ($7.50) and discover what the fuss is about.

KEAHOLE POINT & WAWALOLI (OTEC) BEACH

Keahole Point has ideal conditions for something called ocean thermal energy conversion (OTEC). The seafloor drops steeply just offshore, providing a continuous supply of both cold water from 600-meter depths and warm water from near the surface. The OTEC system operates like a steam turbine, with the difference in temperature between the cold and warm waters providing the energy source. Scientists at the site have successfully generated electricity, and research continues on ways to make this an economically viable energy source. Curious parties can learn more at one of the Natural Energy Laboratory of Hawaii's (NELH) Thursday morning **lectures** (☎ 329-7341; $3 per person; 10am-noon).

The turnoff leading to OTEC Beach and NELH, a state hydroenergy research facility, is 1 mile south of the Kona Airport between the 94- and 95-mile markers.

From the highway, it's about a mile in to Wawaloli (OTEC) Beach, where there are rest rooms and showers. This windswept lava coastline is rocky and not very good for swimming, although a large, naturally enclosed pool 200 yards south of the rest rooms is deep enough to wade in and great for kids. The major downside here is listening to six or more planes per hour swooping overhead.

The rough dirt road that continues south from the beach leads half a mile to **Pine Trees**, one of the best surfing breaks in the Kona area. Look left as you drive in to OTEC and you'll see the cluster of trees and stretch of sand. Spare your rental car unless you have a 4WD.

ONIZUKA SPACE CENTER

The Astronaut Ellison S Onizuka Space Center, (☎ 329-3441; adult/child $3/1; open 8:30am-4:30pm daily), opposite the car rental booths at the Kona Airport, pays tribute to the Big Island native who perished in the 1986 Challenger space shuttle disaster.

The little museum features exhibits and educational films about space and astronauts. Items on display include a moon rock, a NASA space suit and scale models of spacecraft. There's also a small space-themed gift shop.

KONA COAST STATE PARK

The attractive sandy **beach** at Mahaiula Bay is open to the public as part of the Kona Coast State Park (open Thur-Tues). The park has shaded picnic tables, barbecue grills and portable toilets but is otherwise completely undeveloped. The facilities are at the south side of the beach, but the park's loveliest section is at the north end, about a five-minute walk away.

The inshore waters are shallow, and the bottom is gently sloping. Snorkeling and swimming are usually good, but during periods of high surf, which are not infrequent in winter, surfing is the sport of choice. It's best on the north side of the bay.

The road into the park, which begins 2½ miles north of the airport off Hwy 19, is nearly as interesting as the beach. It runs for 1¾ miles across a seemingly endless lava flow that's totally devoid of trees and greenery, before depositing you at this little oasis. The road is passable in a regular car, but take it slooow.

If you want to explore further, take the trail leading north from Kona Coast State Park about 1¼ miles to **Makalawena**, an even more beautiful stretch of beach. Part of the trail goes through an expanse of lava fields, and the sun reflecting on the black rock will get your blood pumping en route. But the payoff is immediate: Makalawena is backed by sand dunes and contains some fine coves with good swimming and snorkeling. Walking barefoot on the sand is like walking through soft, beige flour, in sharp contrast to the lava rocks that decorate the coastline and create inlets. On weekdays you're likely to see some nude sunbathers here. There are no facilities.

South of Kona Coast State Park is another hidden treasure called **Makolea Beach**, a small, quiet black-sand beach where you probably won't encounter another soul. The most interesting way to get here is on the easy-to-navigate 'path' along the lava fields; follow the coastline and you can't lose your way (it's actually an easier walk than the rocky path to Makalawena). Not only does this beach lack shade, but the lava fields and black sand add to the heat, so remember to bring plenty of water. Again, there are no facilities.

On Wednesday, Kona Coast State Park is closed and the entrance gate is locked.

KUA BAY

Kua Bay, also known as Maniniowali, has a secluded beach with turquoise waters and gleaming, fine white sands.

The beach has a gentle slope, and the waters are inviting for swimmers most of the year and for boogie boarders and bodysurfers in winter. Conditions are generally calm, but winter storms can generate currents in the bay and can also temporarily clear the beach of its sand. Alas, there are no trees or awnings to provide shade, very little vegetation and no facilities.

The turnoff to the beach is just north of both the 88-mile marker and the grassy 342-foot Pu'u Kuili, the highest cinder cone on the seaward side of the highway. Look for the stop sign and gate at the head of the road.

The road is rough and over loose lava stones. Some people do drive down it about half a mile and then park near the roadside,

but if you park near the highway it only takes about 15-20 minutes to walk in.

At the end of the road, a path crosses the rocks to the south end of the beach. There are no facilities.

KA'UPULEHU

In ancient times, Ka'upulehu was the site of a large fishing village, and a few Big Island fishers still lived along this shoreline until the tsunami of 1946 swept their homes away. The area, accessible only by boat, was then abandoned until the early 1960s, when a wealthy yachter who had anchored off Ka'upulehu concluded this would be the perfect place for a hideaway hotel. The Kona Village Resort opened in 1965. It was so isolated it had to build its own airstrip to shuttle in guests – the highway that now parallels the Kona Coast wasn't built for another decade.

The Kona Village Resort is a unique, albeit costly, Hawaiian getaway with thatched Polynesian-style *hale* (houses) on stilts. The hales are spaced around a spring-fed lagoon and along the white sands of Kahuwai Bay. The resort limits nonguest access, but guided tours are offered (see below).

In 1996, a second upscale hotel, the Four Seasons Resort, opened at Ka'upulehu Beach, about a 10-minute walk south of Kona Village Resort. Originally begun as a multistory resort, the developers got so much resistance from island environmentalists that they dismantled the buildings halfway through the project and replaced them with low-rise, low-impact bungalows.

Four Seasons also opened up the shoreline, making the white-sand beach at **Kukio Bay** and a string of pristine little coves to the south of it easily accessible to the public for the first time. Kukio Bay now has public beach access, showers, rest rooms, drinking water and visitor parking. A mile-long coastal footpath through the lava connects the Kukio Bay beach with the Four Seasons resort. Along the historic path is Waiulu, an area of reddish lava with brackish water where turtles frequently enjoy their own R&R.

KONA

Places to Stay & Eat

Four Seasons Resort Hualalai (☎ *325-8000, 800-332-3442, fax 325-8100,* **w** *www .fourseasons.com*) Rooms $475-675. Possibly the most elegant, understated hotel on the island, the Four Seasons offers the pampering luxury of a posh country club on its 33 acres. The 243 rooms, which are spread around three dozen low-rise buildings, are spacious, with large lanais, concealed TVs, fax lines, stereos and other upscale amenities. Ground-level rooms have outdoor showers. The resort has an 18-hole golf course (and a second golf course in the works is one of many torn-up construction sites), eight tennis courts, five pools and displays on Hawaiian art and culture. For spenders or dreamers, rates top out at $5600 for the three-bedroom presidential suite.

Kona Village Resort (☎ *325-5555, 800-367-5290, fax 325-5124,* **w** *www.konavillage.com*) One-room standard/two-room garden view $480/785. The 125 freestanding cottages here look like rustic thatched huts on the outside but are modern and comfortable inside, with high ceilings, rattan furnishings and ceiling fans. In keeping with the getaway concept, the units do not have phones, radios or TVs. Daily rates include meals and recreational activities. If you can't get over the obvious irony of paying this kind of money to 'go native,' be a voyeur and avoid the steep price tag: There's a tour of the property and its historic petroglyphs every Tuesday and Saturday.

Resorts cater to your needs, including your need for food.

Pahuia (☎ *325-8000, Four Seasons Resort Hualalai*) Entrees $25-48. Open 5:30pm-10pm daily. This elegant oceanfront dinner restaurant features reliably good Hawaii Regional cuisine, emphasizing local fish in a variety of preparations.

Kona Village Resort (☎ *325-8555*) Lunch buffet $30, 12:30pm-2pm daily. Kona Village Resort is open for meals to non-guests, with advance reservations, except when the resort is at 100% occupancy. There is a daily outdoor lunch buffet; dinner is served at Hale Samoa, where full meals start at $60.

Donkey Crossing

In the evenings, donkeys come down from the hills to drink at spring-fed watering holes and to eat seed pods from the kiawe (mesquite-like) trees along the coast between Kua and Kiholo Bays. The donkeys are descendants of the pack animals that were used on coffee farms until the 1950s, when jeeps replaced them.

Growers, who had become fond of these 'Kona nightingales,' as the braying donkeys were nicknamed, released many of the creatures into the wild rather than turning them into glue. The donkeys were largely forgotten until Hwy 19 went through in 1974.

Keep an eye out for the donkeys at night: They need to cross the road for their evening feedings, and they often ignore the 'Donkey Crossing' signs on the highway!

Entertainment

Beach Tree Bar & Grill (☎ *325-8000*) Ranking at the top of the list for sunset-watching destinations, this oceanside bar even allows the hoi polloi to pop in for a cocktail. Come for live music Tuesday through Saturday. They also serve lunch daily till 4pm.

Kona Village Resort (☎ *325-5555*) Kona's best and most expensive luau happens here every Friday night. Wine is included in the $74 per person price tag, but all other alcohol is extra. The elegant setting and post-buffet show are what set this event apart: It feels more authentic and less tacky, and the fire-eaters, dancers and singers earn their pay. Arrive early for a short tour of the remarkable grounds.

KIHOLO BAY

Halfway up the coast, just south of the 82-mile marker, you'll come to a lookout that commands a great view of Kiholo Bay. With its intense blue waters and line of coconut trees, the bay appears like a little oasis in the midst of the lava.

An inconspicuous trail down to the bay starts about 100 yards south of the 81-mile marker. Walk straight from the highway, then veer to the left and follow a 4WD road, the beginning of which has been blocked off by boulders to keep vehicles out. As you near the end of the trail, look for a smaller footpath heading to the ocean; at the time we wrote this, it was marked with a beach access sign. The hike down takes about 20-25 minutes.

Kiholo Bay is almost 2 miles wide, and the south end of the bay has a lovely, large spring-fed pond called **Luahinewai**. It's refreshingly cold and fronted by a wide black-sand beach. There's also good ocean swimming when it's calm.

As you walk south to the freshwater pond, don't overlook the **Queen's Bath**, a freshwater swimming hole that seems small but extends back into the rock for about 40 feet. Look for the opening in the trees on the inland side of the path after you pass the gargantuan yellow estate and tennis courts.

Cattle were shipped from here in the 1890s, and there was once a small hotel. Now the bay is ringed with a few private homes, including an unusual circular structure formerly owned by country singer Loretta Lynn.

South Kohala

Considered the Gold Coast of the Big Island, this stretch of Hwy 19 is home to Hawaii's swankiest resorts and fanciest golf courses.

At Waikoloa Beach Resort you'll enter the South Kohala district. South Kohala was an important area in Hawaiian history, and today's visitors will find ancient trails, heiau, fishponds, and petroglyph sites to explore. The resorts have wonderful drive-up beaches, as do the nearby Anaeho'omalu and Hapuna Beach Parks.

Waikoloa village, about 6 miles inland from the beach at the 75-mile marker, is a modern residential development and bedroom community for workers in the nearby resorts. Although it offers little of interest for visitors, the village does have a gas station and a shopping center with a grocery store and a pharmacy. The 12-mile Waikoloa Rd connecting Hwys 190 and 19 runs through the village.

The tiny harbor town of Kawaihae lies on Hwy 270, which is the coastal continuation of Hwy 19. With just a few shops and restaurants, it's not a destination but rather a pit stop for North Kohala-bound travelers.

Highlights

- Sipping a frozen rum concoction at a swanky resort's oceanside bar
- Exploring the Disneyland-esque grounds of the Hilton Waikoloa by boat
- Discovering ancient petroglyphs carved by dedicated Hawaiians
- Learning how to windsurf from a weathered pro at 'A' Bay
- Finding out what all the fuss is about at Mauna Kea Beach
- Putting at Mauna Kea's famously scenic third hole

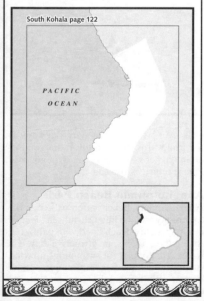

South Kohala page 122

PACIFIC OCEAN

WAIKOLOA BEACH RESORT

Just after crossing into the South Kohala district, a single turnoff leads to the Outrigger Waikoloa Beach and Hilton Waikoloa Village hotels and to Anaeho'omalu Beach Park. Waikoloa Beach Drive is just south of the 76-mile marker.

The Kings' Shops complex houses the Kohala branch of the Big Island Visitors Center (☎ 886-1655, 800-648-2441, e big island@havb.org), at 250 Waikoloa Beach Drive, suite B15; it's open weekdays 8am to 4:30pm. Visitors can call or email the office to request a Hawaii planner.

Waikoloa Petroglyph Preserve

As you travel west down Waikoloa Beach Dr, a lava field etched with petroglyphs is off to the right, immediately before the Kings' Shops complex. If you park at the shopping complex, it's about a five-minute walk along a signposted path to the first of the etchings.

Many of the petroglyphs date back to the 16th century, and most were made with a

SOUTH KOHALA

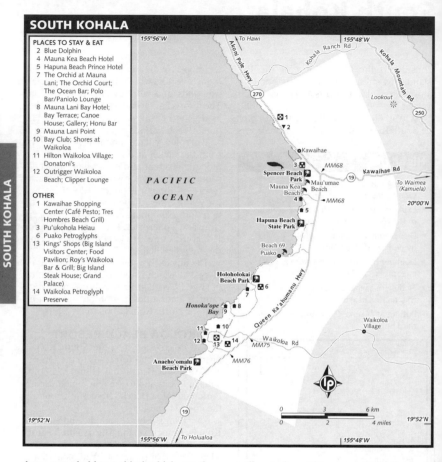

SOUTH KOHALA

PLACES TO STAY & EAT
2 Blue Dolphin
4 Mauna Kea Beach Hotel
5 Hapuna Beach Prince Hotel
7 The Orchid at Mauna
   Lani; The Orchid Court;
   The Ocean Bar; Polo
   Bar/Paniolo Lounge
8 Mauna Lani Bay Hotel;
   Bay Terrace; Canoe
   House; Gallery; Honu Bar
9 Mauna Lani Point
10 Bay Club; Shores at
   Waikoloa
11 Hilton Waikoloa Village;
   Donatoni's
12 Outrigger Waikoloa
   Beach; Clipper Lounge

OTHER
1 Kawaihae Shopping
   Center (Café Pesto; Tres
   Hombres Beach Grill)
3 Pu'ukohola Heiau
6 Puako Petroglyphs
13 Kings' Shops (Big Island
   Visitors Center; Food
   Pavilion; Roy's Waikoloa
   Bar & Grill; Big Island
   Steak House; Grand
   Palace)
14 Waikoloa Petroglyph
   Preserve

sharp stone held as a chisel, which was then struck with a hammer stone. Some carvings are graphic (humans, birds, canoes), others cryptic (dots and lines). Western influences show up in the form of horses and English initials.

Although the footpath that leads through the petroglyphs is called the King's Trail, this section was actually a horse and cattle trail built in the late 19th century. The trail once connected Kailua-Kona with Kawaihae. It's possible to continue on to a historical preserve at the Mauna Lani Resort, about 2 miles away, but it's a hot unshaded

walk over lava, plus a modern-day kapu on the trail warns, 'Beyond this point you may be in danger of being struck by a golf ball. Please return as you came.'

Anaeho'omalu Beach Park

Anaeho'omalu Beach, often called A Bay for brevity and the linguistically challenged, is a long, sandy beach lined with palm trees that curves along an attractive bay. The waters are popular for swimming and windsurfing and have a gently sloping sandy bottom. Winter weather can produce rip currents, but the water is usually quite calm.

This is a fine beach for an outing if you're staying in Kona, though beaches like Hapuna to the north have more glorious sand. The south end of the beach has public facilities, with showers, toilets, changing areas, drinking water and parking. The north end of the beach, which fronts the Outrigger Hotel, has a little fitness area and a volleyball net. Trash cans placed every 20 feet help keep the beach immaculate.

Both ends of the bay are composed of prehistoric lava flows from Mauna Kea, with a'a (rough, jagged lava) to the north and smooth pahoehoe to the south.

Anaeho'omalu was once the site of royal fishponds, and archaeologists from the Bishop Museum have found evidence here of human habitation dating back more than a thousand years.

Two large **fishponds** lie just beyond the line of coconut trees on the beach. A short footpath starts near the showers and winds by the fishponds, caves, ancient house platforms and a shrine. Interpretive plaques along the way explain the area's history.

The folks at the beach hut (☎ 886-6666, ext 1) in front of the hotel can give you the latest on water conditions. They rent **windsurfing** and snorkel equipment and offer windsurfing lessons, beginning scuba lessons, boat dives, catamaran cruises and glass-bottom-boat rides. Windsurfing costs $25 per hour ($45 for two people); a lesson and gear is $50.

There's a good spot for snorkeling at the north end of the beach, directly in front of the sluice gate. Here you'll find coral formations, a fair variety of tropical fish and, with a little luck, sea turtles. If you're not a snorkeler, you can still sometimes see the turtles by simply walking out onto the rock wall that encloses the sluice gate and looking down into the surrounding waters.

Hilton Waikoloa Village

Islanders nicknamed the 62-acre Hilton Waikoloa Village 'Disneyland' because it has the air of an over-the-top theme park. You won't find serenity at this extravagant resort development, but there's abundant eye candy.

The hotel had no beach, so it built its own, along with a 4-acre saltwater lagoon stocked with tropical fish, a dolphin pool with at least a dozen of those friendly creatures, a 'river' with a current for rafting, and sprawling swimming pools with cascading waterfalls (one pool is crossed via suspension bridge).

Guests navigate the grounds in Disney-engineered canopied boats that cruise artificial canals and on a modernistic tram that looks like something straight out of downtown Tokyo. Because the complex is so large, the boats and the trams actually do function as public transport, and the novelty of using and waiting for them wears off quickly.

When it opened in 1988 at a cost of $360 million, the hotel billed itself as the world's most expensive resort. But despite all the excess, it's surprisingly casual, and guests and nonguests alike are welcome to explore the grounds on the free boats and tram.

You can browse a multimillion-dollar **art collection** along a mile-long walkway that runs in both directions from the front lobby. The museum-quality pieces include extensive collections from Melanesia, Polynesia and Asia. It's particularly big on Papua New Guinea, with war clubs and spears, carved fighting shields and a partial replica of a ceremonial house.

You can park free at the hotel or walk over from the Outrigger, a quiet 15-minute stroll away along the lava coast.

Places to Stay

Outrigger Waikoloa Beach (☎ 886-6789, 800-688-7444, fax 800-622-4852, e *reservations@outrigger.com, 69-275 Waikoloa Beach Drive*) Garden-view rooms start at $315. This 545-room hotel, now part of the Outrigger chain, has comfortable rooms and a beachside location that's far superior to the Hilton's. Each room has either two double beds or one king bed, cable TV, phone, air-con and private lanai. The grounds include trails, a pool and a watersports hut. And the Kings' Shops are within walking distance, so you're not captive to resort prices for all your meals. Outrigger offers numerous discounts that can save you hundreds of dollars; inquire when you call.

Hilton Waikoloa Village *(☎ 886-1234, 800-445-8667, fax 885-2900,* **w** *www.hilton waikoloavillage.com, 1 Waikoloa Beach Resort)* Garden- and mountain-view/oceanview rooms $190-450/$230-540. This is a megahotel with 1241 rooms and all the usual Hilton amenities, plus two 18-hole golf courses. Rates vary dramatically depending on the season, the occupancy and the views. Costs top out at $5500 for the lavish presidential suite.

There are two upscale, fully equipped condominium complexes in the area. Each has a pool, but they're both about a 15-minute walk from the beach.

The Bay Club *(☎ 886-7979, 877-229-2582, fax 886-4538, 5525 Waikoloa Beach Drive)* 1-bedroom units $300, 2-bedroom units $350. Shuttle service to the beach and shopping center is provided.

The Shores at Waikoloa *(☎ 885-5001, 800-922-7866, 5460 Waikoloa Beach Drive)* Low/high season rates; 1-bedroom apartments $275-285/$335-345, 2-bedroom apartments $320-330/$390-400. AAA members receive a 25% discount, as do seniors; inquire about fourth-night-free deals at this Aston-managed property.

Places to Eat

The **Kings' Shops**, an outdoor shopping mall with Bulgari and other high-end stores, also has an enclosed food pavilion, a couple of sit-down restaurants and a small sundries store. The food court is open 9:30am-9:30 pm daily and contains a Mexican stand and a pizza and plate-lunch eatery, among others. Walk through the pavilion to reach the fish 'n' chips outpost overlooking the manmade lake.

Roy's Waikoloa Bar & Grill *(☎ 886-4321, Kings' Shops)* Lunch dishes $9-13, dinner salads & appetizers $7-10, dinner mains $22-25. Lunch 11:30am-2pm, dinner 5:30pm-9:30pm. This is a branch of the popular Roy's on Oahu. It has excellent Hawaii Regional cuisine and a changing menu of creative dishes. At dinner, main courses include rack of lamb in a *lilikoi*

(passion fruit) cabernet sauce or blackened ahi with pickled ginger.

Big Island Steak House *(☎ 886-8805, Kings' Shops)* Entrees $16-23. Open 5pm-10pm. The popular, bustling restaurant has a noisy atmosphere, making it a welcoming choice for families who want to escape stuffier resort dining. Sweet macadamia nut bread arrives soon after you're seated, but save room for sautéed mahi mahi served with pineapple salsa (market price) or a 12-oz cut of top sirloin ($19).

Grand Palace *(☎ 886-6668, Kings' Shops)* Dishes $8.50-19. Open 11am-9:30pm. Another alternative to hotel restaurants, this reasonably priced Chinese eatery has an extensive selection of favorites such as kung pao chicken ($9.50) and mu shu pork ($10), which share space with more unusual concoctions like shark's fin soup ($15 per person).

Donatoni's *(☎ 885-1234, Hilton Waikoloa Village)* Entrees $24-37. Open 6pm-9:30pm Tues-Sat. The most highly regarded of the Hilton's fine-dining dinner restaurants features authentic Italian food. Look for starters like carpaccio, followed by pasta dishes and seafood or steak courses.

Entertainment

Outrigger Waikoloa Beach *(☎ 886-6789)* Adult/child 6-12 years $64/32. Luau 6pm Wed & Sun. The Outrigger's poolside luau with a traditional Hawaiian buffet includes dinner, an open bar and a Polynesian show of singing and dancing. The hotel's **Clipper Lounge** serves tropical drinks and pupus until 11pm nightly.

Hilton Waikoloa Village *(☎ 886-1234)* Adult/child 5-12 years $58/25. Performance 6:30pm Fri. At the Hilton's 'Legends of the Pacific' dance show every Friday, the cost includes a dinner buffet and one cocktail. Also at the Hilton, a guitarist strums from 6pm to 10pm in the Kamuela Provision Company lounge.

Getting There & Away

Hele-On bus leaves daily at 4:15 pm from Hilton Waikoloa and heads up the coast before cutting into Hawi ($2.25, 65 minutes).

While hitchhiking is common in Kailua-Kona and other parts of the island, you won't see many hitchers in the chichi Kohala area, so don't rely on thumbing a ride.

MAUNA LANI RESORT

After a brief encounter with coconut palms and bright bougainvillea at the highway entrance, visitors turning down Mauna Lani Drive head through a long stretch of lava with virtually no vegetation. Halfway along there's a strikingly green golf course sculpted into the black lava. Mauna Lani Bay Hotel is at the end of the road. The Orchid at Mauna Lani hotel and Holoholokai Beach Park are to the north.

The area is currently undergoing a lot of development, including the soon-to-be-built Shops at Mauni Lani. Details are few, but the complex is certain to be upscale.

Mauna Lani Bay Hotel

This ritzy but low-key hotel is a modern open-air structure centered around a breezy atrium that holds waterways, orchid sprays and full-grown coconut trees. A saltwater stream that runs through the hotel and out into the sun is home to small black-tipped sharks, stingrays and a variety of colorful reef fish. The atrium hosts **live Hawaiian music** and **hula dancing** nightly from 5:30pm-8:30pm.

The hotel has solid beaches and interesting historical sights, all open to the public. Snag a free trail map from the concierge desk.

Beaches The beach in front of the Mauna Lani Bay Hotel is protected, but the water is rather shallow. Snorkelers might want to explore a coral reef beyond the inlet.

A less-frequented cove is down by the Beach Club restaurant, a 15-minute walk to the south.

An old coastal foot trail leads about a mile farther south to **Honoka'ope Bay**. It passes by a few historical sites, including a fishers' house site and other village remains. The southern end of Honoka'ope Bay is protected and good for swimming and snorkeling when the seas are calm.

Fishponds The ancient **Kalahuipua'a Fishponds** are along the beach just south of the hotel in a shady grove of coconut palms and *milo* (native shade trees).

The ponds are stocked, as they were in ancient times, with *awa* (Hawaiian milkfish). Water circulates from the ocean through traditional *makaha* (sluice gates), which allow small fish to enter but keep the fattened ones from leaving. You might notice fish sporadically jumping into the air and slapping down on the water, an exercise that knocks off parasites.

The Kalahuipua'a ponds are among the few continuously working fishponds in Hawaii; the awa raised here have provided stock for commercial fisheries.

Historic Trail The Kalahuipua'a Trail begins on the inland side of the Mauna Lani Bay Hotel, at a marked parking lot opposite the resort's little grocery store.

The trail, which is particularly pleasant in early-morning or late-afternoon light, merges historic sites and scenic views. It's also a fabulous walk for spotting quail, northern and red-crested cardinals, saffron finches and Japanese white-eyes.

The first part of the trail meanders through a former Hawaiian settlement that dates from the 16th century, passing lava tubes once used as cave shelters and a few other archaeological and geological sites marked by interpretive plaques.

The trail then skirts fishponds lined with coconut palms and continues out to the beach, where you'll find a thatched shelter with an outrigger canoe and a historic cottage with a few Hawaiiana items on display. If you continue southwest past the cottage, you can loop around the fishpond and back to your starting point – a roundtrip of about 1½ miles. Take a break en route at the attractive cove at the southern tip of the fishpond, where the swimming is good and a lunchtime restaurant offers simple fare.

Puako Petroglyphs

With more than 3000 petroglyphs, the Puako petroglyph preserve at Holoholokai beach Park has one of the largest collections of ancient lava carvings in Hawaii.

Holoholokai Beach Park

North of The Orchid at Mauna Lani, the park *(open 7am-6:30pm)* has a rocky shoreline composed of coral chunks and lava. It's not a great bathing beach, but snorkeling is reasonably good when the waters are calm, and winter can bring good surf. To get there, take Mauna Lani Drive and turn right at the rotary, then right again on the beach road immediately before the grounds of The Orchid.

From the inland end of the beach parking lot, a well-marked trail leads three-quarters of a mile to the petroglyphs, which are more interesting than the petroglyphs near the Kings' Shops in Waikoloa.

The human figures drawn in simple linear forms are some of Hawaii's oldest. Those with triangular shapes and curved forms are more recent. Like all petroglyphs in Hawaii, their meaning remains enigmatic.

The aging petroglyphs are fragile, as the ancient lava flow is brittle and cracking. Stepping on the petroglyphs can damage them, so be respectful. If you want to make rubbings, use the authentically reproduced petroglyphs that have been created for that purpose; they're just a minute's walk down the trail from the parking lot. Bring rice paper and charcoal and you can make your own souvenirs of 'old Hawaii.'

Because of the sharp thorns along the trail, wearing flip-flops is unwise – the thorns can easily pierce their soft soles and your tender feet. The path has some shade, but wear sunscreen.

The park has showers, drinking water, rest rooms, picnic tables and grills.

Places to Stay

Mauna Lani Bay Hotel (☎ 885-6622, 800-367-2323, w www.maunalani.com, 68-1400 Mauna Lani Drive) Mountain-/ocean-view rooms $355/$500, villas $550-910. This is widely regarded as one of the finest resort hotels in the islands. All 350 rooms have TVs, phones, room safes, private lanais and bathrobes. From May through September rates drop about 10%, and a fifth-night-free deal is offered year-round. In addition to the rooms, the resort has villas with full kitchens; rates depend upon the number of bedrooms.

The Orchid at Mauna Lani (☎ 885-2000, 800-845-9905, fax 885-5778, w www.orchidmaunalani.com, 1 N Kaniku Drive) Garden-/ocean-view rooms $425-495/595-695. The Orchid, on Pauoa Bay just north of the Mauna Lani Bay Hotel, is a rather subdued place, with 539 rooms and elegant hallways; rooms have marble bathrooms, lanais and other upscale amenities. Originally part of the Ritz chain, the property is now affiliated with Sheraton. Inquire about deals available for families.

Mauna Lani Point (☎ 667-1666, 800-642-6284, fax 661-1025, w www.classicresorts.com, 50 Nohea Kai Drive) Low/high season rates; 1-bedroom garden view $290/305, ocean view $340/395, 2-bedroom garden view $380/405, ocean view $430/505. The luxurious Mauna Lani Point, a condo complex at the south side of the Mauna Lani Resort, is booked through Classic Resorts. See the condos online at their Web site.

Places to Eat

Bay Terrace (☎ 885-6622, Mauna Lani Bay Hotel) Breakfast buffet $14.50 (continental) & $24 à la carte breakfast $8-20, dinner entrees $12-32 Breakfast 6:30am-11:30am, dinner 5:30pm-9pm. The open-air Bay Terrace offers a simple but delicious breakfast buffet daily. À la carte items like brioche French toast ($9) and omelets ($12.25) are also available. Hours vary with the season.

Canoe House (☎ 885-6622) Salads & appetizers $9-19, mains $27-50. Open 5:30pm-9pm. Fronting the beach beside the Mauna Lani Bay Hotel, this romantic, open-air restaurant makes a superb splurge night out. The menu blends Far East and Hawaiian influences, with an emphasis on seafood. There are dishes such as grilled lemon-pepper scallops or pancetta-wrapped mahi mahi with coconut spinach risotto. The opening hours vary with the season.

Gallery (☎ 885-7777, Mauna Lani Bay Hotel) Lunch 11am-3pm daily, dinner

5:30pm-9pm Tues-Sat. Lunch dishes $8-14.50, dinner entrees $25-30. Situated in the resort's golf clubhouse, the Gallery serves continental and Pacific Rim dishes. The fresh fish is a specialty; it changes every day, but the *onaga* (red snapper) with a macadamia crust appears frequently. As everything is strictly à la carte, expect dinner for two to edge up to $100.

The Orchid Court (☎ 885-2000, *The Orchid at Mauna Lani*) Breakfast dishes $8.50-18, dinner entrees $10-28. Open breakfast 6:30am-11:30am, dinner 6pm-10pm. One of the hotel's more reasonable options, this lovely outdoor restaurant serves an excellent buffet breakfast ($24) in the morning, and in the evening they prepare island cuisine like pan-seared opakapaka ($20) and Asian-style grilled chicken pizza ($16).

Beach Club (☎ 885-5910, *Kaniku Drive*) Lunch dishes $6-10. Open 11am-4pm daily. A bit easier on the lunch wallet than Gallery is this casual restaurant at the south end of Kaniku Drive overlooking a swimming cove. The menu includes an organic chicken salad ($9.50), hot dogs ($6.75) and a turkey and avocado sandwich ($9).

Entertainment

The Ocean Bar (☎ 885-2000, *The Orchid at Mauna Lani*) This seaside bar is one of the best places around to watch the sunset. The view from the bar stools is obscured by trees, but walk yourself and your $8-mai tai over to a chaise lounge and the problem is blissfully solved.

Polo Bar/Paniolo Lounge (☎ 885-2000, *The Orchid at Mauna Lani*) An upscale hotel hangout, this cigar bar (you can buy 'em and smoke 'em here) has leather chairs and hardwood floors. Entertainment includes pool, elegant checkerboards and shelves stocked with leather-bound books. The bar is open 6pm to 11:30pm; pupus are available.

Honu Bar (☎ 885-6622, *Mauna Lani Bay Hotel*) The resort bar stays open till midnight and features billiards, appetizers, and cigars from the Dominican Republic and Honduras. Call about live entertainment.

PUAKO

Puako is a quiet one-road coastal village where everyone either lives on the beach or across the street from it. You can reach Puako via the marked turnoff from Hwy 19 or a bumpy side road from Hapuna Beach State Park.

The town is lined with giant **tide pools**, set in the swirls and dips of the pahoehoe lava that forms the coastline. Some of the pools are deep enough to shelter live coral and other marine life. Snorkeling can be excellent off Puako, although the surf is usually too rough in winter. A narrow beach of pulverized coral and lava lines much of the shore.

Hoku Loa Church, which dates back to 1858, is about half a mile beyond the Puako Bay boat ramp. A plain plastered building with a few simple wooden pews, it's still used for Sunday services, but at other times it's usually locked up tight. The town also has a general store.

Beaches

About half a dozen shoreline access signs to **Puako Beach** line the main road, but the easiest beach access is at the south end of the village, just 150 yards before the road dead-ends. Here, a short dirt drive leads to the water. You won't find a proper beach but rather a small cove with a good entry point for snorkeling and shore diving (sightings may include reef fish, manta rays and sea turtles). The undertow can be strong at Puako, so be aware of the conditions. A couple of minutes' walk north along the beach will bring you to a few petroglyphs, a konane game board chinked into the lava and tide pools deep enough to cool off in.

Easy access and generally gentle waves make **Beach 69** a worthwhile destination. There's plenty of shade, and trees help segment the sedate beach, making it feel like each group of sunbathers has a private little plot. The beach lacks facilities, and it's a mix of lava rock and sand. Neil Young supposedly owns a home near Beach 69.

Turn down Puako Road, located between the 70- and 71-mile markers. Make the first right turn, and the road quickly becomes

SOUTH KOHALA

one lane. Look for telephone pole No 71 on the left-hand side and park. A 4WD can get you a bit closer, but it's a short walk; follow the 'road' to its end and then tramp along the footpath that runs parallel to a wooden fence. PS to those with overactive imaginations: once upon a time, telephone pole No 71 was numbered 69, which gave the beach its nickname.

HAPUNA BEACH STATE PARK

The long beautiful stretch of white sand along Hapuna Bay is the Big Island's most popular beach.

When it's calm, the beach has good swimming, snorkeling and diving. In the winter, it's a hot bodysurfing and boogie-boarding destination. The high winter surf can produce strong currents close to the shore and a pounding shorebreak. Waves over 3 feet should be left for the experts. Hapuna has had numerous drownings and many of the victims have been tourists unfamiliar with the water conditions.

A tiny cove with a small sandy beach lies about five minutes' walk north of the park. The water is a bit calmer there and in winter, less sand is kicked up by the waves.

The 61-acre state park includes the beach, A-frame cabins for overnight stays and a landscaped area with picnic facilities, showers, rest rooms, drinking water and pay phones. Lifeguards are on duty daily.

A snack bar called *3 Frogs Café (open 10am-4pm)* sells burgers ($6.25), jumbo sodas ($2.50) and shave ice. A window at the side rents boogie boards or snorkel sets (half day rental $5).

This lovely beach is marred by only one thing: disgusting bathrooms with toilets that don't flush and stalls without doors.

Places to Stay

The state maintains six A-frame *camping cabins* ($20) just up and inland from the beach. These $20 digs with million dollar views are the best deal in Kohala. Each cabin accommodates four people on two plywood sleeping platforms (you sleep head to head). They're surprisingly bug-free, plus they have lights and electricity. Other amenities include clean, shared bathrooms, showers and a cooking pavilion with stove and fridge. The ocean view from cabins Nos 5 and 6 is phenomenal, and this is a terrific place to check out frequent meteor showers. For information on state camping permits, see the Camping section of the Facts for the Visitor chapter.

Hapuna Beach Prince Hotel (☎ 880-1111, 800-882-6060, fax 880-3112, 62-110 Kaunaoa Drive) Garden-view rooms $350, oceanfront rooms $575. This 350-room behemoth opened in 1994 at the northern end of Hapuna Beach. Part of the Prince Resorts chain along with the neighboring Mauna Kea Resort, it largely gears its services to Japanese tourists and even has a bilingual concierge desk. The elegant, sprawling hotel has manicured lawns, a golf course and restaurants, but it has neither the charm of the Mauna Kea nor the energy of the Waikoloa resorts. Since 1995, however, the hotel has hosted the annual Sam Choy Poke Festival. Among other festivities, finalists compete for titles like best cooked poke, best traditional poke and best poke recipe using tofu.

MAUNA KEA RESORT

In the early 1960s, Laurance Rockefeller obtained a 99-year lease on the land around Kaunaoa Bay from his friend Richard Smart, owner of Parker Ranch. Five years later Rockefeller opened Mauna Kea Beach Hotel, the first luxury hotel on the Neighbor Islands, at the north side of this bay just north of the 68-mile marker.

The resort hosts a recommended **luau** every Tuesday night (☎ 882-7222; adult/child $72/36), and a lively Saturday night beachfront **clambake** (☎ 880-5801; adult/child $72/36), with oysters on the half shell, sashimi, Keahole lobster and, of course, steamed Manila clams. If you're spending an evening here, don't miss the luminous **manta rays** at Manta Ray Lookout Point; the best viewing is from 7pm-10pm.

Mauna Kea Beach

Kaunaoa Bay is a gorgeous crescent bay with a white-sand beach that has since come

Looking toward Mauna Kea from Waimea

Mist over Akaka Falls, Hamakua Coast

Falling water on the lush Hamakua Coast

SIMON FOALE

The Wailuku River above Rainbow Falls

LEE FOSTER

Nani Mau Gardens, Hilo

LEE FOSTER

Port of Hilo

to be known as Mauna Kea Beach. It has a gradual slope and fine swimming conditions most of the year. There's good snorkeling on the north side when it's calm. The beach is open to the public, and 30 parking spaces are set aside for beach visitors. If you're having a drink or lunch at the hotel, you can bypass the issue of obtaining a parking pass (latecomers may miss out on the 30 spots).

Mau'umae Beach

Just north of Mauna Kea Beach is this delightful gem with soft white sand, and the best part is that unlike some of Kona's top beaches, access here doesn't entail a 25-minute walk across hot lava fields. The area is fairly protected, so the waves aren't too rough, and numerous trees provide shade. Despite clear water, fish don't swim in abundance; snorkelers migrate to the south end of the small beach.

To get here, enter the Mauna Kea resort, turn right on Kamahoi and cross two wooden bridges. Look for pole No 22 on the left and park on the side of the road. Walk down the trail to Ala Kahakai post, then turn left. It takes less than five minutes.

The resort issues 10 parking passes daily. Beachgoers can also park at nearby Spencer Beach (see that section later) and access Mau'umae on foot via the Ala Kahakai Trail. The walk takes about 10 pleasant minutes along a shady coastal path.

Places to Stay

Mauna Kea Beach Hotel (☎ 882-7222, 800-882-6060, fax 882-5700, ⓦ www.maunakea beachhotel.com, 62-100 Mauna Kea Beach Drive) Mountain-/ocean-view rooms $350/545. Kohala's grand dame is charming, but it's showing signs of age despite a major renovation in 1995. The hotel lobby and grounds have displays of Asian and Pacific artwork, including bronze statues, temple toys and Hawaiian quilts. The north garden holds the most prized possession, a 7th-century pink granite Buddha taken from a temple in southern India.

The hotel has all of the expected resort amenities, including a fitness center, tennis courts and an 18-hole golf course. Rooms,

Decadent Sunday Brunch

Everyone should enjoy a leisurely all-you-can-eat buffet brunch at the Mauna Kea Beach Hotel at least once. Served in a covered outdoor area overlooking the stellar beach, the buffet is an ostentatious spread including sushi, dim sum, prime rib, lobster bisque, domestic and imported cheeses and a Belgian waffle station, plus the usual array of bacon, eggs, made-to-order omelets and fresh fruit. Over at the dessert table, you'll think Al Capone just robbed a bakery *and* the local ice cream shop.

A Hawaiian band performs relaxing music during the meal. The fare should render you full for the remainder of the day. Reservations are essential (☎ 882-7222; adults/children $36/$18). Brunch served every Sunday from 11am-2pm.

like the hotel itself, are simple yet elegant. That said, if you're forking over this kind of money, you may be a bit disappointed.

SPENCER BEACH PARK

At Spencer Beach Park, off Hwy 270 just south of Kawaihae, you'll share space with sand castles and plastic shovels; the shallow sandy beach is protected by a reef and by the jetty to the north, making this a perfect family destination. Plentiful shade provides a respite from the strong sun, but the area may be too protected: the water tends to get silty.

The rocky south end of the beach past the pavilion is better for snorkeling, although entry is not as easy. Kayaking is not permitted anywhere on this beach. Beachgoers can also park here to access Mau'umae (see above) via the Ala Kahakai footpath; the trailhead is at the south side of the beach, so park accordingly.

Beach amenities include a lifeguard station, picnic tables, barbecue grills, rest rooms, toasty warm showers, drinking water and rather dilapidated basketball and volleyball courts. *Camping* is allowed with a permit from the county. Despite the fact that sites are exposed and a bit cramped, this is a pleasant place to sleep under the stars. For information on obtaining a camping permit, see Camping in the Accommodations section of the Facts for the Visitor chapter.

PU'UKOHOLA HEIAU

The Pu'ukohola Heiau National Historic Site (☎ 882-7218; admission free; visitor center open 7:30am-4pm daily), which is off the side of the road that leads down to Spencer Beach, contains the last major temple built in Hawaii.

In 1790, after his attempt at a sweeping conquest of the islands was thwarted, King Kamehameha sought the advice of Kapoukahi, a soothsayer from Kauai. He told Kamehameha that if he built a temple to his war god here above Kawaihae Bay, then all of Hawaii would fall to him in battle and he would rule the islands. Of course, Kamehameha began construction of Pu'ukohola Heiau right away and actually labored with his workers.

Completing the temple in 1791, Kamehameha then held a dedication ceremony and invited his last rival on the Big Island, Keoua, the chief of Kau. When Keoua came ashore, he was killed and brought up to the temple as the first offering to the gods (in fact, this was a luakini heiau, meaning that human sacrifice was required). With Keoua's death, Kamehameha took sole control of the Big Island and then went on to fulfill the soothsayer's prophecy.

Pu'ukohola Heiau, terraced in three steps, was covered with wooden idols and thatched structures, including an oracle tower, an altar, a drum house and a shelter for the high priest.

After Kamehameha's death in 1819, his son Liholiho and powerful widow Ka'ahumanu destroyed the heiau's wooden images and the temple was abandoned. These days, only the basic rock foundation remains, but it's still an impressive site.

Pu'ukohola means 'Hill of the Whales.' Migrating humpbacks can often be seen offshore during winter.

The visitor center has a few simple displays and someone on duty to provide a brief introduction to the park. A free brochure describes the historic sites spread over the park's 77 acres.

A trail to the heiau starts at the visitor center and takes only two minutes to walk. If you arrive after hours, you can park at Spencer Beach Park and walk up to the heiau via an old entrance road that's now closed to vehicle traffic.

Just beyond Pu'ukohola Heiau are the ruins of **Mailekini Heiau**, which predates Puukohola and was later turned into a fort by Kamehameha. **Hale o Kapuni Heiau**, a third temple dedicated to shark gods, lies submerged just offshore; nearby on land you can see the stone leaning post where the high chief watched sharks bolt down the offerings he made.

The path continues down by the creek to **Pelekane**, the former site of the royal court. Warbling silverbills, doves and mosquitoes frequent the kiawe woods, but there's not much else to see. Those wondering why the fabulous beach is surprisingly empty should be warned that visitors are asked not to swim here because of frequent shark sightings over the centuries.

The trail then leads across the highway to the site of **John Young's homestead**. Young, a shipwrecked British sailor, served Kamehameha as a military advisor and governor of the island. These days, all that remains of the homestead are the partial foundations of two of Young's buildings; there are plans to put up an interpretive board with drawings of what the site originally looked like.

KAWAIHAE

Kawaihae has the Big Island's second largest deepwater commercial harbor. The harbor has fuel tanks, cattle pens and a little local beach park – not really much to attract visitors, most of whom stop by just long enough to eat and fuel up on their way to North Kohala.

Kawaihae Shopping Center on Hwy 270 has several restaurants, a pizza-by-the-slice window, an ice cream and shave ice shop, a 7-Eleven convenience store, a gallery and a recommended dive shop called Kohala Divers LTD (☎ 882-1413), which rents equipment and arranges boat trips for divers.

Places to Stay

Makai Hale (☎ 885-4550, 800-262-9912, fax 885-0559, W *www.bestbnb.com*) Single/double $125; additional room for third or fourth person $75. A Japanese woman and her Hawaiian husband run this B&B off Hwy 270. The location, 4 miles from the coast, is convenient both for jaunts to Kohala beaches and to the inland town of Waimea. Both rooms have private bath and access to a small kitchen area. The deck, with swimming pool and Jacuzzi, offers a postcard view of prime Kohala real estate below. During winter and early spring, the 500-ft elevation makes this an excellent whale-watching locale, too. There's a two-night minimum stay.

Places to Eat

Cafe Pesto (☎ 882-1071, *lower level Kawaihae Shopping Center*) Pizzas $10-17, sandwiches $8-10. Open 11am-9pm Sun-Thur,

11am-10pm Fri & Sat. Excellent gourmet pizza, calzones, pastas and salads keep this place packed. The unusual luau pizza has *kalua* pig, sweet onions and pineapple; sundried tomatoes, Japanese eggplant and roasted garlic top the Oriental pizza. Or try the delicious Hamakua calzone ($10) with barbecue chicken, pesto, red onion and Big Island goat cheese. At lunch, served until 4:30pm, you can also get hot sandwiches.

Tres Hombres Beach Grill (☎ 882-1031, *Kawaihae Shopping Center*) Dishes $8. Open 11:30am-9pm Sun-Thur, 11:30am-10pm Fri & Sat. Standard fare includes enchiladas, tacos or tostadas with rice and beans. Two-item combination plates are a few dollars more.

Blue Dolphin (☎ 882-7771, *Hwy 270 south of Kawaihae Shopping Center*) Entrees from $13. Dinner 5:30pm-9:30pm Fri-Sat; drinks until 11pm. Aside from the resorts, nightlife is scarce in Kohala, so locals (even families!) head to this enclosed outdoor space on weekends for dinner and live music. Jazz musicians perform Fridays; rock bands typically play Saturdays. Admission is a $5 *kokua* for the band.

SOUTH KOHALA

North Kohala

The northwest tip of the Big Island is dominated by a long central ridge, the Kohala Mountains.

The leeward side of the ridge is dry and desertlike. The windward side is wet and lush, with steep coastal cliffs and spectacular hanging valleys.

Highlights

- Hiking to Pololu Valley's remote black-sand beach
- Glimpsing humpback whales at the peaceful, historic Mo'okini Heiau
- Discovering the galleries, restaurants and other nooks and crannies of Hawi
- Kayaking down the turn-of-the-century Kohala ditches
- Exploring hills, valleys and waterfalls on the back of a feisty mule
- Driving to the end of scenic Highway 270

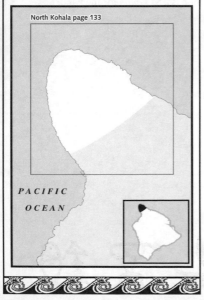

North Kohala page 133

PACIFIC
OCEAN

Though it's off the main tourist circuit and often bypassed by travelers, North Kohala has a couple of impressive historical sites, a few sleepy towns to poke around in and a lovely valley lookout at the very end of the road.

There are two roads to North Kohala: an inland road (Hwy 250) and a coastal road (Hwy 270). Investigate both by going up one and down the other.

Hwy 270 (Akoni Pule Hwy) starts in Kawaihae, takes in the coastal sights of Lapakahi State Historical Park and Mo'okini Heiau and ends at a lookout above Pololu Valley. A trail runs from there down to the valley floor, but even if you're not up for a hike, the view from the lookout is worth the drive.

Hwy 250 (Kohala Mountain Rd) runs south for 20 miles from Hawi to Waimea. This is a very scenic drive along the upland slopes of the Kohala Mountains.

As you head south, the road peaks at 3564 feet and Maui rises out of the mist, with the red crater of Haleakala capping the skyline. Mauna Kea and Mauna Loa are visible before you. Expansive views of the coast and Kawaihae Harbor unfold below, and there's a roadside scenic lookout near the 8-mile marker where you can take it all in. The road goes through rolling green hills dotted with grazing cattle and descends past neat rows of ironwood trees.

LAPAKAHI STATE HISTORICAL PARK

Lapakahi State Historical Park has the feel of a ghost town – which it is. Even the visitors in this desolate spot tend to be few (*no ☎; admission free; open 8am-4pm daily, closed holidays*).

This remote fishing village was settled about 600 years ago; as the terrain was rocky and dry, the villagers turned to the sea for their food. Fish were plentiful, and the cove fronting the village provided a safe year-round canoe landing.

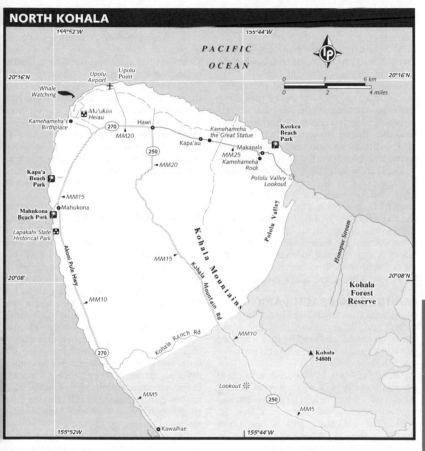

NORTH KOHALA

to the remains of stone walls, house sites and canoe sheds.

Eventually some of the villagers moved to the wetter uplands and began to farm, trading the crops they grew there for fish with those who had stayed on the coast. In the process, Lapakahi grew into an *ahupua'a*, a wedge-shaped division of land radiating from the mountainous interior out to the sea.

In the 19th century, Lapakahi's freshwater table began to drop. This, coupled with the enticement of jobs in developing towns, led to the desertion of the village.

Lapakahi was a big village, and this is a good-size park. A mile-long loop trail leads

The park encourages visitors to imagine what life was like centuries ago. People worshipped at fish shrines, a few of which still remain on the grounds. Displays show how fishermen used lift nets to catch opelu, a technique still practiced today, and how the salt used to preserve the fish was dried in stone salt pans.

Visitors can also try their hands at Hawaiian games. Game pieces and instructions are laid out for *o'o ihe* (spear throwing), *konane* (Hawaiian checkers) and *ulu maika* (stone bowling), the object of the latter being to roll a round stone between two stakes.

The park is just south of the 14-mile marker. Trail brochures are available at the trailhead.

The park is largely unshaded, so it can be hot walking around, and pesky flies are a frequent nuisance. While the park service sometimes keeps a cooler of drinking water available, there's no running water in the park, so bring something to drink. There are a couple of port-a-potties.

Lapakahi's waters are part of a marine life conservation district, and it's immediately obvious when you see this stunning stretch of coast. The fish are so plentiful and the water so clear that you can stand above the shoreline and watch yellow tangs and other colorful fish swim around in the cove below. Alas, you're not allowed to swim with them (since there's no beach to speak of, entry would be a mean feat regardless).

MAHUKONA BEACH PARK

Mahukona Beach Park, a mile north of Lapakahi and half a mile off Hwy 270, is the site of an abandoned landing that was once linked by railroad to the sugar mills on the north Kohala coast.

Veer left (south) as you drive in to reach the small county park, which has rest rooms, picnic tables, a barbecue, a large pavilion and a grassy camping area. Be warned that the area can get a bit buggy and the rest rooms would not win any prizes for cleanliness.

Those planning on **camping** should bring their own drinking water, as the park's water is unfit for consumption. For information on obtaining a county camping permit, see Camping in the Accommodations section of the Facts for the Visitor chapter, or call Hisaoka Gym in Kapa'au (☎ 889-6505) between 1pm-2pm Monday through Friday.

The area beyond the landing makes for interesting snorkeling and diving, although it's usually too rough in winter. Entry, via a ladder, is in about 5 feet of water. Heading north, it's possible to follow an anchor chain out to a submerged boiler and the remains of a ship in about 25 feet of water. Coral lines the bottom and visibility is good when it's calm. You'll find a shower near the ladder where you can rinse off. If you're interested in sunbathing here, bring a chair; there isn't any sand, and you'll have trouble getting comfortable on the concrete slabs.

Also to the north is a navigational heiau that's within walking distance from Mahukona. However, the area has not been deemed a national park or historic site, so there are no placards or brochures to explain the significance of this special place, which isn't designed for excessive foot traffic. If you're curious, get friendly with a local and ask to be taken to this treasured spot.

KAPA'A BEACH PARK

Kapa'a Beach Park is 1¼ miles north of Mahukona and nearly a mile off the 16-mile marker on Hwy 270.

Camping is allowed, but the park is rather dumpy and has neither a sandy beach nor much in the way of facilities. There is a barbecue grill, port-a-potties and a few picnic tables under the rather uninviting pavilion, but no showers or decent restrooms. Don't be surprised to find the teeny 'path' to the water littered with cigarette butts and trash. For information on obtaining a county camping permit, see Camping in the Accommodations section of the Facts for the Visitor chapter, or call Hisaoka Gym (☎ 889-6505) between 1pm-2pm Monday through Friday.

On weekends you'll encounter locals who journey past the rocks into the clear water, which is fairly good for snorkeling. Kapa'a's biggest selling point is its view of Maui, but even that's not enough to waste your time here when there are so many marvelous Kohala beaches to explore.

MO'OKINI HEIAU

Mo'okini is a massive heiau set atop a grassy knoll on the desolate northern tip of the Big Island. One of the oldest and most historically significant heiau in Hawaii, it commands a clear view out across the ocean to Maui. This windswept site has a sense of timelessness and a certain eerie aura.

Chants date Mo'okini Heiau back to 480 AD. This was a luakini heiau, where the *ali'i* (chiefs) offered human sacrifices to the war god Ku. According to legend, it was built in one night with basalt stones gathered in Pololu Valley and passed along a human chain stretching 14 miles.

A kapu that once prevented commoners from entering the heiau grounds wasn't lifted until recent times, and the site (made an historical landmark in 1963) still remains well off the beaten path. Because so few people come this way, there's a good chance it will just be you, the wind and the spirits here. During whale-watching season in the winter months, this is a fantastic spot to observe humpback whales; at the northern-most tip of the coast there's an area of fresh-water where the massive mammals swim to clean off their barnacles. Bring a picnic, along with clothes that offer protection from the wind and other elements.

The heiau is 250 feet long, with rock walls reaching a good 25 feet high. The entrance through the wall into the heiau itself is on the west side. The long enclosure on the right immediately before the heiau entrance was the home of the *mu*, or body catcher, who secured sacrificial victims for the heiau altar. The large scallop-shaped altar on the north end of the heiau is thought to have been added by Pa'ao, a Tahitian priest who arrived around the 12th century and intro-duced human sacrifice to Hawaiian worship. Because the temple was used for this purpose, islanders understandably tried to live a safe distance from the heiau.

The current *kahuna nui* (high priestess), Leimomi Mo'okini Lum, is the most recent in a long line of Mo'okini tracing their lineage back to the temple's first high priest. On the third Saturday of each month (except December), Leimomi runs a **memorable program** at the heiau. She invites Hawaii residents and visitors to the temple to help weed from 9am to noon; bring a lei, work gloves, water, a brown bag lunch and sunscreen. After visitors have invested their sweat and sense of respect, Leimomi pro-vides an oral history about the heiau and answers questions. She also leads a children's day event every November (call ☎ 889-1069 or 373-8000 for more information).

To get there, turn north off Hwy 270 at the 20-mile marker and go 1¾ miles down to Upolu Airport. At the airport, turn left onto the road that runs parallel to the coast. Be aware, however, that this red dirt road is rutted and bumpy and can get very muddy after heavy rains – it's not always passable in a standard car. After 1½ miles you'll come to a fork. The left road leads up to the heiau, a quarter mile farther.

KAMEHAMEHA'S BIRTHPLACE

Hawaiian lore says that Kamehameha the Great was born on a stormy winter night in 1758 on this ruggedly desolate coast.

According to legend, a kahuna told Ka-mehameha's mother that her son would become a destroyer of chiefs and a powerful ruler. The high chief of the island didn't take well to the prophecy, and in a King Herod-like scenario, he ordered the newborn killed.

Immediately after his birth, the baby was taken to Mo'okini Heiau for his birth rituals and then into hiding in the nearby mountains.

If you continue straight ahead at the fork below the heiau for a third of a mile, you'll reach the stone enclosure that marks his birth site.

HAWI

North Kohala's largest town (pronounced Hah-vee) has fewer than 1000 residents, but this little place packs a punch, with several worthy restaurants and some delightful ways to while away a few hours.

North Kohala used to be sugar country, and Hawi was the biggest of half a dozen sugar towns. Kohala Sugar Company, which had incorporated all of the mills, closed down its operations in 1975. Hawi now has a few too many storefronts, but new residents are increasingly drawn this way by the area's lower property values and low-key flavor.

The park on Hwy 250 in front of the post office is cool and shady with giant banyan trees. Behind the park is the old sugar mill tower, a remnant of the town's former mainstay.

Kohala Ditch

Kohala Ditch is an intricate series of ditches, tunnels and flumes that were built to carry water from the rugged wet interior of the Kohala Forest Reserve out to the Hawi area. The source of the water is the Waikoloa Stream, midway between the Pololu and Waipio Valleys.

The ditch was built in 1906 to irrigate Kohala sugarcane fields. The last Kohala cane was cut in the 1970s, but the ditch continues to be a source of water for Kohala ranches and farms.

It was engineered by a sugar man, John Hind, with the financial backing of Samuel Parker of Parker Ranch. Kohala Ditch runs 22½ miles and was built by Japanese immigrant laborers, who were paid about $1 a day for the hazardous work. More than a dozen of those laborers died during the construction.

Much of the ditch runs through 19,000 acres of Kohala land, which the agricultural giant Castle & Cooke sold a few years back to a developer. No development has yet occurred, but the owners have opened up the ditch to guided kayak tours (see Things to Do in the Hawi section of this chapter).

One Hele-On bus leaves daily from Hawi down the Kohala coast to Hilton Waikoloa at 6:35am ($2.25, 65 minutes).

Information

If you enter town via Hwy 270, you'll see a small visitor center, which has a poor map of North Kohala, some brochures on the area and Internet access ($3 for 15 minutes). The hours are 9am-5pm weekdays; weekend hours vary depending on foot traffic and beach weather.

The town also has a post office, grocery store, gas station, and a few galleries and restaurants. For now the town's movie theater sits empty; the projectionist died recently and only a union member can fill the position.

Things to Do

Based in Hawi, **Flumin' da Ditch** (☎ 889-6922; toll-free 877-449-6922, W www.flumin dadich.com; adult/child 5-18 $85/$65) guided tours, led by Kohala natives, take visitors on a wet kayaking tour of Kohala's historic irrigation system. Don't expect rapids or whitewater on the journey, but prepare to get soaked. Morning and afternoon cruises are offered daily; approximate duration is three hours. Tours meet near the intersection of highways 270 and 250 (for more information, see the Kohala Ditch boxed text).

The same company runs Hummer safari tours in the Kohala mountain rainforest; the cost is $95 per person.

The Landing (☎ 889-1000, Hwy 270), North Kohala's very own day spa, is alive and thriving. They offer massages, body treatments and kava.

Places to Stay

Hawi Hotel (☎ 889-0419, W www.hawihotel .com, 55-514 Hawi Rd) Doubles $47, doubles with TV $55, two double beds $72. At the intersection of Hwys 270 and 250 in Hawi center, this is an old-style hotel with 18 simple, clean rooms. Formerly known as the Kohala Village Inn, the place has bounced between trying to attract tourists and being given over to long-term boarders, but its current owner has renovated it as a hotel again. All rooms have private baths, but they don't have fans, air-con or telephones. At press time, the restaurant was closed for business, but it might reopen.

Cardinals' Haven (☎ 884-5550, advance reservations 425-822-3120) Double/triple $55/60, $250 per week (with breakfast supplies). Cardinals' Haven is a homey place with a lovely rural setting 3 miles south of Hawi center. In the winter home of Peter and Sonja Kamber, the single guest unit consists of a bedroom with a comfortable queen bed and a living room with a small sofa bed that could accommodate a third person. It's all quite straightforward, but it does have a TV, microwave, hot plate, toaster, coffeemaker and mini-refrigerator. From the yard, you can look across cattle pastures clear out to Maui. The rental is open only from November 20 to May 10; you can call to make advance reservations when it's closed. The rate includes food supplies to prepare your own breakfast, or you can rent the unit without food for the week for $230. Smoking is not allowed. Originally from Switzerland, the Kambers speak fluent German and French.

Places to Eat

A farmers' market (☎ 889-0618) is held every Saturday from 7:30am-1pm at the park on Hwy 250, mentioned above.

Kohala Coffee Mill (☎ 889-5577, Hwy 270) Open 6:30am-6pm daily, breakfast items $1.25-3. This eatery in the town center serves muffins, pastries, fresh-brewed Kona coffees ($1-1.75) and natural ice cream and sorbets. Postcards, T-shirts and hand-painted coconuts are also on the menu.

Kohala Health Food (☎ 889-0277, Hwy 270) Closed Sun. Adjacent to Kohala Coffee Mill, this shop sells vitamins, shampoos, teas, organic juices and packaged health food items. There are a few tables for patrons.

Hula La's Mexican Kitchen & Salsa Factory (☎ 889-5668, Hwy 270) Open 10am-9pm daily, breakfast served weekends 8am-11am. This hole-in-the-wall has a smattering of tables in close quarters and a few lanai tables. They serve tasty Mexican fare with surprisingly fussy options. Filling burritos ($6.50-7.50), for example, come with flour or spinach tortillas; mild, medium or tropical salsa; mashed pinto beans or black beans. Usual suspects like quesadillas ($4.50-7) and soft tacos ($3.75-4.75) are also available. No credit cards.

Bamboo (☎ 889-5555, Hwy 270) Lunch dishes $8-9, dinner dishes $10. Lunch 11:30am-2:30pm Tues-Sat, 11am-2pm Sun, dinner 6pm-8pm Tues-Sat. In the village center, Bamboo has excellent island food and a pleasant Hawaiian tropical decor. Dishes like chicken satay with rice and

Hawaiian stir-fry appear on the lunch menu; at dinner you'll find pineapple-barbecued chicken and macadamia nut crusted fish of the day, among others. Save room for the hard-to-resist homemade desserts. On Friday and Saturday nights there's live music.

Aunty's Place (☎ 889-0899, Hwy 270) Open 11am-10pm Mon-Sat, noon-10pm Sun. A former waitress at Waimea's popular Edelweiss (see Places to Eat in the Waimea chapter) opened this Hawi newcomer. While the heavily-accented owner doesn't like to compare her 'housewife cooking' to Edelweiss's 'hotel cooking,' she shouldn't be so modest. Try the varied pizzas ($11 and up), served all day, or a traditional German dinner entree like wiener schnitzel ($9) or bratwurst ($10). The small, welcoming restaurant has mostly counter seating.

KAPA'AU

The statue of Kamehameha the Great on the front lawn of the North Kohala Civic Center may look familiar. Its lei-draped and much-photographed copy stands opposite the Iolani Palace in Honolulu.

The statue was made in 1880 in Florence, Italy, by American sculptor Thomas Gould. When the ship delivering it sank off the Falkland Islands, a second statue was then cast from the original mold. The duplicate statue arrived in the islands in 1883 and took its place in downtown Honolulu.

Later the sunken statue was recovered from the ocean floor and completed its trip to Hawaii. This original statue was then sent here, to Kamehameha's childhood home, where it now stands watching the traffic trickle along in quiet Kapa'au. The name Kapa'au, incidentally, means 'wet blanket' after the place where locals say baby Kamehameha and his blanket got deluged with rain.

Information

The town has a courthouse, police station and Kamehameha Park, which includes a large, modern gymnasium and everything from a ballpark to a swimming pool; the facilities are free and open to the public. The town also has a little library, a Bank of

Hawaii and a few interesting shops. Visit Kohala Book Shop (☎ 889-6400, Hwy 270), the biggest used bookstore in Hawaii. Chatty owner Frank Morgan sells a wide variety of used and rare books, plus sheets of song lyrics from old musicals; many of them relate to Hawaii.

Though the area is growing with artists and writers, it's still an aging town that's also attractive to retirees. The only crowd is at the senior center, which is part of the civic center. The senior citizens usually staff a table on the porch with visitor information.

During the annual King Kamehameha Day festivities in June, the park plays hosts to a swingin' soiree that includes a parade and traditional dancing, music and food. Volunteers load down the famous statue with leis.

Kalahikiola Church

Protestant missionaries Elias and Ellen Bond, who arrived in Kohala in 1841, built Kalahikiola Church in 1855. An earthquake damaged it in 1973, but it's since been restored, and the church is still in use today.

If you want to take a look, turn inland off Hwy 270 onto a narrow road half a mile east of the Kamehameha statue, between the 23- and 24-mile markers. The church is half a mile up from the highway.

The land and buildings on the drive in to the church are part of the Bond estate, proof enough that missionary life wasn't one of total deprivation.

The church is typically locked, but the short detour through this lush area is worth a few minutes; only chirping birds mar the solitude.

Kamehameha Rock

Kamehameha Rock is on the right side of the road, about 2 miles east of Kapa'au, on a curve just over a small bridge. It's said that Kamehameha carried this rock uphill from the beach below to demonstrate his strength.

A road crew once attempted to move the rock to a different location; they managed to get it up onto a wagon, but the rock promptly fell off – an obvious sign that it

wanted to stay put. Not wanting to upset Kamehameha's mana, the workers left the rock in place.

Tong Wo Society

Immediately around the corner from Kamehameha Rock is the colorful home of the Kohala Tong Wo Society, founded in 1886. Hawaii once had many Chinese societies, providing immigrants with a place to preserve their cultural identity, speak their native language and socialize. This is the last one remaining on the Big Island. The building is not open to the public.

Organized Tours

ATV Outfitters (☎ 889-6000, Ⓦ *www.out fittershawaii.com*) takes visitors on exciting all-terrain vehicle tours through the rainforest or along the coastline. For tourists who are concerned about the environment, rest assured that the company is too. The ATVs mostly travel on gravel sugar cane roads, and guides don't allow reckless driving that can negatively impact the land.

The seacliff tour ($90, 90 minutes) is the gentlest adventure; the 15-mile waterfall tour ($160) takes several hours and reaches an elevation of 3,000 ft. All the ATVs are automatic.

Places to Eat

Jen's Kohala Cafe (☎ 889-0099) Dishes $4-7.50. Open 10am-6pm Mon-Sat, 11am-5pm Sun. Opposite the Kamehameha statue on Hwy 270, Jen's is the place to eat in town. Options include chicken Caesar salads, good chili and a Greek wrap sandwich with organic greens and feta cheese. Also on the menu are fresh fruit smoothies, deli sandwiches and soups, and daily lunch specials.

Takata Store (☎ 889-5261) Open 8am-7pm Mon-Sat, 8am-1pm Sun. Located on Hwy 270 near the high school in Kapa'au, Takata's is the largest market in North Kohala. It's stocked with produce, meat and all the other edibles you'd want or need.

MAKAPALA

The little village of Makapala has a few hundred residents, a beach park and a couple of places to stay. If you're hiking down to Pololu Valley, the town's little store is the last place to get a soft drink or snack. On several recent visits, however, the store was closed.

Keokea Beach Park

Keokea Beach Park is on a somewhat scenic rocky coast but isn't a real draw for visitors, as there's no sandy beach and it's not great for water activities. Warning signs include dangerous shore break and strong currents; that said, there's a protected – though rocky – cove that makes for gentler swimming. The park does have some amenities, including covered picnic tables, rest rooms, showers, drinking water, barbecue grills and electricity.

The marked turnoff is about 1½ miles before the Pololu Valley Lookout. The park is about a mile in from the highway.

If you head this way, you'll pass an old Japanese cemetery on the way down to the park. Most of the gravestones are in *kanji* (Japanese script), and a few have filled *sake* cups in front of them.

Places to Stay

Camping used to be allowed at Keokea on the grassy section below the pavilion, but it has been discontinued.

Kohala's Guest House (☎ 889-5606, fax 889-5572, 52-277 Akoni Pule Hwy) Studio cottage/2 & 3-bedroom cottages $59/110-125. Nani and Don Svendsen rent four guest cottages near the start of the road down to Keokea Beach Park. The best deals are the two three-bedroom units that sleep 6-8 people; two of the rooms share a bath, while the other room has a private bath. These are modern places, though the bedrooms are simply furnished with just beds and a bureau. These cottages have a shared living room with TV, VCR and stereo, as well as a kitchen with full facilities (head a mile outside of Hawi for groceries).

POLOLU VALLEY

Hwy 270 ends at a viewpoint that overlooks secluded Pololu Valley, with its scenic backdrop of steeply scalloped coastal cliffs spreading out to the east. The lookout has the kind of strikingly beautiful angle that's rarely experienced without a helicopter tour.

Pololu was once thickly planted with wetland taro. Pololu Stream fed the valley, carrying water from the remote, rainy interior to the valley floor. When the Kohala Ditch was built, it siphoned off much of the water and put an end to the taro production. The valley slopes are now forest reserve land, as the last islanders left the valley in the 1940s. One relative island newcomer, however, is singer Kenny Loggins; locals say he has a house near Pololu.

Pololu Valley Trail

The trail from the lookout down to Pololu Valley only takes about 20 minutes to walk. It's steep and can be hot walking, but it's not overly strenuous, and you'll be rewarded with lovely views for the duration of the hike. You will need to be cautious with your footing since much of the trail is packed clay that can be slippery when wet. Some good Samaritans have provided walking sticks for your assistance, but only use them if the trail feels mucky; the sticks are heavy and you'll find them to be more of a hindrance than a help in warm weather.

The black-sand beach fronting the valley stretches for about half a mile and can make an enjoyable stroll. Driftwood collects in great quantities and on rare occasions glass fishing floats get washed up as well. Cattle and horses roam the valley; a gate at the bottom of the trail keeps them in.

Surf is usually high and intimidating in winter, and although it's a bit tamer in summer, there can be rip currents year-round. The beach has no facilities.

Organized Tours

Hawaii Forest & Trail (☎ 331-8505, 800-464-1993, W www.hawaii-forest.com) runs operations all over the island, but one of their outposts is at the end of Highway 270 right before the Pololu Valley lookout point; you'll see the sign on your left as you drive towards the lookout. They offer a Kohala mule trail adventure, birding tours and guided trail hikes through the waterfalls of the Pololu Valley, including Kapoloa Falls. The company runs these excursions on private land with permission from landowners, so they've cornered much of the Pololu Valley market.

Morning mule rides ($95 per person) begin at 8:15am with a local guide who was born and raised in North Kohala. During the three-hour tour, the mules meander across two streams and through ranching pastures to gorgeous lookouts of Waiakalae Falls, Pololu Valley and ridges beyond.

Mules are used for a few reasons: the sure-footed creatures are steadier than horses and they can handle heavier loads. Also, in the early 1900s they helped Japanese laborers build the Kohala Ditch, which you'll see on the tour, so there's a certain symmetry in using them to introduce visitors to the area today.

The mules used to carry fearless riders down the steep Pololu Valley Trail, but permit problems and irritated residents put a stop to that.

Waimea (Kamuela)

Waimea has a pretty setting in the foothills of the Kohala Mountains at an elevation of 2670 feet. It's cooler than the coast, with more clouds and fog. The area has gentle rolling hills and frequent afternoon rainbows.

Headquartered here is the domineering Parker Ranch, Hawaii's largest cattle ranch, which spreads across nearly one-ninth of the Big Island. This is a company town: almost everything in Waimea is owned, run or leased by Parker Ranch.

Waimea has its cowboy influences, but it's rapidly growing in size and sophistication. It's the main town serving the subdivisions popping up on former ranches in the Kohala Mountains. While many of the newcomers are wealthy mainlanders, Waimea is also home to a growing number of international astronomers who work on Mauna Kea.

The WM Keck Observatory office in the town center has a short video and simple displays about the Mauna Kea telescopes, along with information about programs and activities taking place at the volcano. Visitors are welcome to stop by during business hours (8am-4:30pm Mon-Fri).

Waimea won't wow you with a lot of action or fascinating historical sights; the museums are entertaining for a short visit and the green pastures are scenic, but for most visitors Waimea is just a stopover on the drive between Kona and Hilo. That said, this little town does have its advantages: several first-rate galleries, plentiful high-end shopping and an impressive number of excellent restaurants, several of which have received national kudos. Furthermore, Waimea's abundance of reasonable accommodations and its proximity to the Kohala Coast make it a decent alternative for travelers who want to be close to those famous white-sand beaches, but can't afford the steep seaside prices.

Information

Waimea is also referred to as Kamuela, which is the Hawaiian spelling of Samuel.

Highlights

- Enjoying an exquisitely prepared meal at one of several award-winning restaurants
- Seeing a concert, play or dance production at the Kahilu Theatre for less than $25
- Shopping for locally-produced Hawaiian goodies at quaint Waimea stores
- Listening to renditions of Lorenzo Lyons' Hawaiian hymns in Imiola Congregational Church
- Yelling and cheering at a rambunctious rodeo, where homegrown *paniolo* test their mettle roping steer and riding bulls
- Hearing the anecdotes and tragedies of Waimea's influential Parker family while touring Puopelu

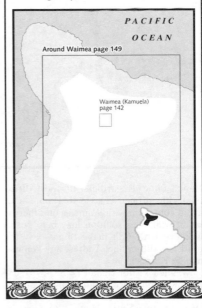

PACIFIC OCEAN

Around Waimea page 149

Waimea (Kamuela) page 142

Although some say the name comes from an early postmaster named Samuel Spencer, most claim it's for Samuel Parker of Parker

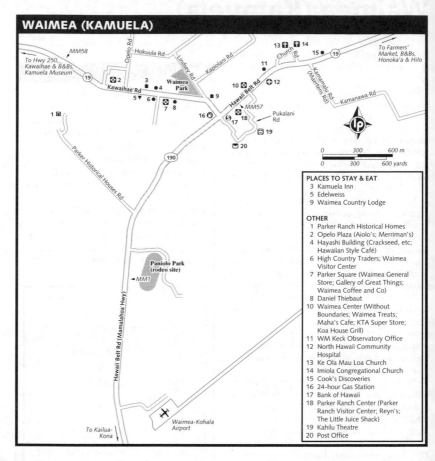

WAIMEA (KAMUELA)

PLACES TO STAY & EAT
3 Kamuela Inn
5 Edelweiss
9 Waimea Country Lodge

OTHER
1 Parker Ranch Historical Homes
2 Opelo Plaza (Aiolo's; Merriman's)
4 Hayashi Building (Crackseed, etc; Hawaiian Style Café)
6 High Country Traders; Waimea Visitor Center
7 Parker Square (Waimea General Store; Gallery of Great Things; Waimea Coffee and Co)
8 Daniel Thiebaut
10 Waimea Center (Without Boundaries; Waimea Treats; Maha's Cafe; KTA Super Store; Koa House Grill)
11 WM Keck Observatory Office
12 North Hawaii Community Hospital
13 Ke Ola Mau Loa Church
14 Imiola Congregational Church
15 Cook's Discoveries
16 24-hour Gas Station
17 Bank of Hawaii
18 Parker Ranch Center (Parker Ranch Visitor Center; Reyn's; The Little Juice Shack)
19 Kahilu Theatre
20 Post Office

Ranch fame. Regardless, the post office made the official change to Kamuela to avoid confusion with Waimeas on other islands; while this solution may help postal workers, it doesn't make things easy for tourists. Bottom line: Address any Waimea mail to Kamuela.

Waimea Visitor Center (☎ 885-6707, 65-1291 Kawaihae Rd, behind High Country Traders) offers free information about Waimea and North Hawaii. Opened in 1999, the office is located in the Lindsey House, which was built in 1909 by Parker Ranch for a five-star employee (those were

the days!). It's open weekdays 8:30am to 3:30pm; closed weekends and holidays. The post office, southwest of the Parker Ranch Center, is open 8am to 4:30pm on weekdays, 9am to 1pm on Saturday.

The Waimea-Kohala Airport, off Hwy 190, 1¾ miles south of the intersection of Hwy 19, has minimal traffic. Private planes mainly use this airport, although the small airline Pacific Wings flies here, with convenient daily service to Honolulu and Kahului, Maui. The airport doesn't have any rental car agencies, but travelers can call for a taxi, or arrange to have one waiting. For more information about the airport, see the Air section of the Getting There & Away chapter.

Parker Ranch Visitor Center

Parker Ranch Visitor Center is a small and not terribly dynamic museum of the ranch's history (☎ 885-7655, ⓦ *www.parkerranch .com, Parker Ranch Shopping Center; adult/ child $6/4.50; open 9am-5pm daily, last ticket sold at 4pm).*

Exhibits include Parker family memorabilia, such as portraits, lineage charts, quilts and dishes; cowboy gear, including saddles and branding irons; and some Hawaiian artifacts – stone adzes, lava bowls, poi pounders, and tapa bed covers. Other Big Island museums have more extensive Hawaiiana collections.

Perhaps most interesting are the old photos and the 25-minute movie on Parker Ranch, which shows footage of cowboys *(paniolo* in Hawaiian) rushing cattle into the sea and lifting them by slings onto the decks of waiting steamers; the video also depicts paniolo roping and branding the cattle.

A ticket that includes this museum and the Parker Ranch Historical Homes costs $12 for adults, $9.50 for children.

At the back of the shopping center, behind the parking lot, there's a picturesque view of Mauna Kea rising above an old wooden corral and pastures.

Parker Ranch Historical Homes

At **Puopelu**, a mini-estate on the Parker Ranch off Hwy 190, just west of Waimea, two historical homes are open to visitors *(adult/child $8.50/6; open 10am-5pm daily, last ticket sold 4pm).* Grandest of the two is the estate's century-old manor, painted pale yellow with white trim, which holds an interesting collection of European art and antique Chinese vases. One room is French provincial, with chandeliers, skylights and walls hung with paintings by French impressionists, including works by Renoir, Degas and Pissarro. Another room is covered with playbills and photos of actor and Parker descendant Richard (Dick) Smart, who opened his home to the public before his

---

Parker Ranch

Parker Ranch claims to be the nation's largest privately owned ranch, and some impressive numbers back those words. It has more than 35,000 cattle on 225,000 acres, contained by 850 miles of fence; the ranch produces a startling 15 million-plus pounds of beef annually.

The first cattle arrived in Hawaii in 1793, a gift to King Kamehameha from British captain George Vancouver. See the History section in the Facts about Hawaii chapter for more information.

Parker Ranch owes its beginnings to John Palmer Parker, a 19-year-old from New England who arrived on the Big Island in 1809 aboard a whaler. He took one look at Hawaii and jumped ship.

Parker soon gained the favor of Kamehameha, who commissioned him to bring the cattle under control. Parker managed to domesticate some of the cattle and butchered others, cutting the herds down to size.

Later, Parker married one of Kamehameha's granddaughters and in the process landed himself a tidy bit of land. He eventually gained control of the entire Waikoloa *ahupua'a* (large wedge-shaped land area) clear down to the sea.

Descendants of the Mexican-Spanish cowboys brought over to help round up the cattle still work the ranches today. Indeed, the Hawaiian word for cowboy, *paniolo*, is a corruption of the Spanish word *españoles*.

---

death in 1992. Word is that the theatrical eccentric greeted tourists in his bathrobe on more than one occasion.

Next door to the manor is the more modest **Mana Hale**, a re-creation of the original 1840s home that John Parker built in the hills 7 miles outside Waimea. Parker constructed his home in essentially the same saltbox style that was popular in his native Massachusetts. The exterior here is a replica, but inside it's the real thing; the original home's interior was dismantled board by board and rebuilt here at Puopelu.

The house is simple and aesthetically striking, with walls, ceilings and floors made entirely of koa wood. It's decorated with period furnishings and eye-catching old photos of the hardy-looking Parker clan.

The turnoff to the homes is on Hwy 190, about three-quarters of a mile south of the intersection with Hwy 19.

Church Row

Waimea's churches are lined up side by side in an area called Church Row. Diverse places of worship are represented in the row, including Buddhists, Baptists and Mormons. **Ke Ola Mau Loa Church** is a green-steepled, all-Hawaiian church, and the one next to it is **Imiola Congregational Church**, which is the oldest. Services are Sundays at 8:30am and 10:15am.

Waimea's first Christian church was a grass hut built in 1830. It was replaced in 1838 by a wood and coral structure, built with coral stones carved out of the reef and carried inland on the backs of Hawaiian Christians. They named it Imiola, which means 'seeking salvation.'

The current Imiola Congregational Church was constructed in 1857 and restored in 1976. The interior is simple and beautiful; it's built entirely of koa, most of it dating back to the original construction.

In the churchyard is the grave of missionary Lorenzo Lyons, who arrived in 1832 and spent 54 years in Waimea. Lyons wrote many of the hymns, including the popular 'Hawaii Aloha,' that are still sung in Hawaiian here each Sunday. Also in the garden is the church bell, too heavy for the church roof to support.

Kamuela Museum

There's a lot of history crammed into the Kamuela Museum (☎ 885-4724, junction Hwys 19 & 250; adult/child under 12 years $5/2; open 8am-5pm daily). Owned by octogenarian Harriett Solomon, a direct descendant of John Parker, the museum contains a treasure trove of Hawaiiana, including tapa beaters, 18th-century feather leis braided with human hair, fishhooks made of human bones, a stone knuckle duster and a dog-toothed death cup. Some items are very rare, and many once belonged to royalty; the museum houses Kamehameha the Great's sacred chair and tables of teak and marble from Iolani Palace. Solomon writes the explanatory text that accompanies each treasure in painstaking longhand.

There's a little bit of everything here, including an eclectic non-Hawaiian collection that includes a Tibetan prayer horn, stuffed moose heads from Canada, a stuffed grizzly bear, a 34-star Union flag with bullet holes, a captured German Nazi flag and a piece of rope used on the *Apollo* 11 mission.

At press time Solomon was less involved in day-to-day operations due to the recent death of her 94-year-old husband, Albert. Her son holds down the fort these days, but Solomon has put the museum and its treasures up for sale. Call first to make sure the museum hasn't closed its doors.

Special Events

Waimea wouldn't be a true cowboy town without a few raucous rodeos. The annual Fourth of July event, with cattle roping, bull riding and all the other traditional rodeo hoopla, just celebrated its 40th anniversary. Another whip-cracking rodeo happens every Labor Day weekend, and smaller paniolo shindigs occur at other times of the year. Peruse W www.rodeohawaii.com for more information.

Home on the range

Waimea's annual Cherry Blossom Festival hits in early February, and the Aloha Festival Paniolo Parade, on the weekend near the first day of autumn, honors local cowboys past and present with ethnic floats and more. In early December, the town gets into the *Kalikimaka* spirit with a Christmas parade and block party.

Places to Stay

Waimea is upcountry, and if you equate Hawaii with beach life and constant sun, you may be disappointed making a base here. But if rolling hills, green pastures and open spaces are what you're looking for, the Waimea area can be an appealing choice.

Barbara Campbell, proprietor of Waimea Gardens Cottage (see B&Bs, below), also runs an upscale B&B service based in Waimea called Hawaii's Best Bed & Breakfasts (W *www.bestbnb.com*). She books other accommodations on the island in the same price range, including eight or nine in the Waimea area. Before approving a new property for her business, she meticulously inspects aspects such as landscaping, hospitality, breakfast, housekeeping and, of course, the rooms.

Hotels Waimea's two hotels are reasonably priced, no-frills lodging options.

Kamuela Inn (☎ 885-4243, 800-555-8968, fax 885-8857, e *kaminn@aloha.net*, W *www .hawaii-bnb.com/kamuela*) Rooms $59-72, suites $89-99. Kamuela Inn is a cross between an inn and a small hotel in both layout and atmosphere. There are 30 rooms with TV and private bath, but no phones. The cheaper standard rooms are comfortable, with cozy patchwork quilts and wood-paneled walls, albeit small; bathrooms are teeny. Suites have refrigerators and stoves and can sleep three or four people. Free pastries and coffee are provided in the morning.

Waimea Country Lodge (☎ 885-4100, 800-367-5004, fax 885-6711, Lindsey Rd) Rooms $90-95, $105 with kitchenette. This small motel has 21 rooms. All have private baths, phones, TVs and views of the Kohala hills out back; many also have pleasant open-beam ceilings. The main drawback is

that there can be early morning noise from trucks unloading at the nearby shopping center.

B&Bs If you're seeking comfort, charm and insidery information, a plethora of B&Bs fit the bill.

Aaah, The Views Bed & Breakfast (☎ 885-3455, fax 885-4031, e *tommare@ aloha.net*, W *www.beingsintouch.com*, 66-1773 Alaneo St) Rooms $65-110; $15 for each additional person; discounts available for longer stays. Mare Grace runs this restful B&B located a few minutes west of Waimea off Hwy 19. Guests can use her yoga room, and Mare will share her knowledge of tai-chi and meditation. The centered attitude shines through in her home, too. Guests can relax in the inviting hammock on the porch overlooking a peaceful stream or in the beautiful wood-lined kitchen. The double bed in the Skylight Room is in a romantic alcove, while the Treetop Suite, with a private deck and entrance, can accommodate a couple or a family of six. All rooms have cable television and phones. A continental breakfast includes island fruits, pastries, Kona coffee and juices.

Mountain Meadow Ranch (☎ 775-9376, fax 775-8033, e *wgeorge737@aol.com*, W *www.mountainmeadowranch.com*) Singles/doubles $65/75, cottage per day/ week $125/600. Located in a quiet eucalyptus grove off the Old Mamalahoa Hwy (Hwy 19), this 7-acre estate 11 miles northeast of Waimea makes a convenient base for exploring Waipio and the Hamakua Coast. Amiable hosts Gay and Bill George have set aside the lower level of their redwood home for guests. There are two bedrooms, a large tiled bathroom, a dry-heat sauna and a lounge with a TV/VCR, microwave and refrigerator. One bedroom has a king bed and the other has a twin and a double bed. Only one party is booked at a time; that is, if you book one bedroom, the other room won't be rented out during your stay. There's also a pleasant cottage on the property that has two bedrooms with queen beds, a full kitchen and a living room with a TV, VCR, woodstove and queen sofa bed. There's no minimum stay for the rooms in the main house; the cottage has a 3-night minimum.

Tina's Country Cottage (☎ 885-4550, *800-262-9912, fax 885-0559,* e *bestbnbs@ aloha.net,* w *www.bestbnb.com*) $115 (based on double occupancy), $20 for each additional person. Tina seems to be Hawaii's version of Martha Stewart: she created the attractive stained glass in her home, which has many other Martha-esque touches, and she's known for her hostessing skills. Her two-bedroom, two-bath cottage is conveniently located just west of town on Hwy 19, plus it has a full kitchen, a porch with a wicker couch, TV and private phone. If your timing is right, you may catch sight of a rodeo next door; the cowboys put on a show about four times a year, and you don't even have to leave the porch to watch it.

Waimea Gardens Cottages (☎ 885-4550, *800-262-9912, fax 885-0559,* e *bestbnbs@ aloha.net,* w *www.bestbnb.com*) Cottages $135-150 (based on double occupancy), plus $15 each extra person. These two charming cottages, 2 miles west of town on Hwy 19, are on the property of Barbara Campbell. Both have hardwood floors, French doors and a deck. The older unit, recently remodeled, has a full kitchen, Jacuzzi and private garden. The newer cottage has more limited cooking facilities, but also has many pleasant touches, including a working fireplace. Both come stocked with breakfast items. There's a three-day minimum stay.

Waimea Suite Bed & Breakfast (☎ 937-2833, e *cookshi@aol.com*) Doubles $125, $25 for each additional person ($15 extra for keiki). Knowledgeable Patti Cook of Cook's Discoveries recently opened for business as a B&B, located 2 miles east of town off Hwy19. Her two-bedroom ground-floor apartment faces Mauna Kea and sleeps up to four guests. Amenities include a full kitchen (stocked with local condiments), cable TV/VCR, telephone, stereo and dining lanai; the apartment also has a private entrance. If you book directly, you'll receive a $20 gift certificate to Cook's Discoveries (see the Shopping section in this chapter). Two-night minimum stay required; 3-night minimum during holidays.

Places to Eat

Budget Despite its high standard of living, Waimea has its fair share of tasty cheap eats.

The Little Juice Shack (☎ 885-1686, *Parker Ranch Shopping Center*) Breakfast $1.50-5, Lunch $4.75-6.25. Open 7am-6pm Mon-Fri; 9am-4pm Sat. Inexpensive fresh food at reasonable prices is the hallmark of this dine and dash spot in the Parker Ranch Shopping Center. Options include the delicious soups, salads, sandwiches and smoothies. All are available to go or to dine in.

Maha's Cafe (☎ 885-0693) Open 8am-4pm Thur-Mon. Maha's, at the north side of the Waimea Center, is a cheerful Hawaiian place serving home-style cooking. At breakfast there are poi pancakes with coconut syrup ($3.50). At lunch, you can get fresh fish with taro on local greens ($9) or sandwiches ($6.50). The cafe is inside Waimea's first frame house, built in 1852; a shop on the side sells Hawaii-made gifts.

Hawaiian Style Café (☎ 885-4295, *Hayashi Building*) Breakfast $5-8, Lunch/Dinner $5-10. Open 6am-12:45pm Mon-Fri, 4pm-7:30pm Tues-Fri, 7:30am-noon Sun. A local-style meal here will blow your cholesterol level for the entire day; prepare for massive portions and fatty ingredients. The restaurant, in a funky pink building, has an old-style counter with cheap chairs and only three booths. Filling fare includes egg dishes ($5.50), French toast ($3.75), beef stew ($5.50) and chicken-fried steak ($6). Almost all the lunch and dinner plates come with two scoops of rice. The Friday special luau plate comes with kalua pig, lomi salmon, pickled vegetables and poi ($9). You may spot the chef wearing his SPAM T-shirt, and you'll find SPAM (and canned sausage) on the menu. It's closed the last Saturday, Sunday and Monday of every month.

For quick treats, stop by the ***Waimea Coffee and Co*** (☎ 885-4472, *Parker Square*), which has sweet snacks and espresso and coffee drinks made with organically grown, 100% pure Kona beans. They're open 7am-5pm Mon-Fri; 8am-4pm Sat.

Waimea Treats (☎ 885-2166, *Waimea Center*) Open daily 10:30am-8pm. This shop serves refreshing shave ice ($2) and a variety of ice cream flavors ($1.50-3.50); tempting local flavors include Kona coffee, Oreo pie, mango and vanilla macadamia nut.

The Waimea Center also has a health food store, a bakery, a deli, and several reasonably priced restaurants.

Mid-Range With such varied dining options, visitors here can eat well without draining the wallet.

Aioli's (☎ 885-6325, Opelo Plaza) Dinner dishes $13-21. Open 11am-4pm Tues, 11am-8pm Wed & Thur, 11am-9pm Fri & Sat, 8am-2pm Sun. This is a popular little spot that bakes its own breads, cakes and pastries and offers good lunchtime sandwiches, salads and soups at reasonable prices. At dinner, there are full meals ranging from Southwest-style goat cheese enchiladas to fresh catch and steaks. Aioli's lacks a liquor license, but you can bring your own beer or wine, and the restaurant doesn't charge a corkage fee.

Koa House Grill (☎ 885-2088, Waimea Center) Lunch dishes $5.25-15, dinner entrees $14-33. Open lunch 11:30am-2pm daily, dinner 5pm-9pm daily. A lot of locals eat the cuisine here, which is best described as eclectic American. Two rooms make up this restaurant. One houses the bar, where smoking is allowed; the nicer dining area, complete with fireplace, is more appropriate for families. As you'd guess, the establishment's name stems from the abundant koa wood in the restaurant. Lunch items include a house burger ($7.50), a fresh fish burrito ($8.25) and a tangy Oriental chicken salad ($9). Many dinner entrees feature local Parker Ranch beef; non meat-eaters can opt for the Thai yellow curry ($14) or the grilled vegetable pizza ($18).

Top End Several award-winning restaurants make Waimea a terrific stopover for foodies.

Merriman's (☎ 885-6822, Opelo Plaza) Lunch dishes $7-12, dinner entrees $17-33. Open lunch 11:30am-1:30pm Mon-Fri, dinner 5:30-9pm daily. Merriman's features Hawaii Regional cuisine, and owner-chef Peter Merriman pioneered the use of fresh, organically grown and chemical-free products from Big Island farmers and fishermen. A specialty is the delicious wok-charred ahi, blackened on the outside and sashimi-like inside. At dinner, there are a few vegetarian meals ($17-19) and seafood and meat dishes ($22-33). At lunch, there are various salads, soups, sandwiches and a few hot grilled dishes, including a tasty coconut chicken with peanut sauce ($9) and beef kabob with Waimea tomatoes ($10).

Daniel Thiebaut (☎ 887-2200, 65-1259 Kawaihae Rd) Lunch dishes $6.50-14.50, dinner entrees $20-30. Open lunch 11:30am-1:30pm Mon-Fri, dinner 5:30pm-9:30pm daily. *Conde Nast Traveler* magazine voted this French-Asian newcomer one of America's top 100 new restaurants in 2001. The restaurant combines casual elegance with a homey atmosphere, and the menu features local produce, fish and meat. Salads are recommended, along with the Kona-style fish with jasmine rice and julienne veggies. A complimentary dessert comes with lunch; if you're lucky, it might be banana cake with cream cheese frosting topped with macadamia nuts in a strawberry sauce and served on a chilled plate. More than 30 wines are available by the glass. If there's a wait, pull up a rattan chair in the bar/lounge area; reservations definitely recommended, especially at dinner.

Edelweiss (☎ 885-6800, Kawaihae Road) Lunch dishes $11.50, dinner entrees $20-26. Open lunch 11:30am-1:30pm Tues-Sat, dinner 5pm-8:30pm Tues-Sat. Also on Waimea's 'restaurant row,' this German restaurant sports dark wood, dim lighting and tons of greenery. The selection of German beers at the small bar isn't as extensive as you might expect; the German wine list is better. Starters include a cup of Manhattan chowder and a simple salad with tarragon dressing, or opt for a salad with Waimea tomatoes, Maui onions and English Stilton cheese ($4.25). Complete dinners are heavy fare; along with the main entree, they include both the soup of the day and a salad, a vegetable and coffee or tea. Weiner schnitzel ($20.50) comes with creamed spinach and a buttery, mustard-based

WAIMEA (KAMUELA)

potato salad. The busy wait staff typically spews out a laundry list of daily specials to a packed house.

Groceries Fresh produce and other grocery items are available at a few locales in town. *KTA Super Store (885-8866, Waimea Center)* is a well-stocked supermarket with a deli and a pharmacy. They're open 6:30am-11pm daily. A new *Foodland* market was set to open in the renovated Parker Square in the spring of 2002.

Farmers' market Open 7am-noon Sat. You can buy fresh local produce at this market that sets up on Saturday mornings at the Hawaiian Home Lands office, on the east side of town at the 55-mile marker. Vendors selling tropical flowers and arts and crafts sometimes make an appearance.

Entertainment

Waimea's entertainment scene is limited, perhaps because cowboys rise at dawn and astronomers work all night!

Kahilu Theatre (☎ 885-6017, Parker Ranch Center) This theater presents plays, classical music concerts, dance troupes and other productions. Broadway leading man and cabaret actor Dick Smart opened the theater in 1981 after returning to the Big Island to run Parker Ranch. He gave himself a starring role in "Oh, Coward!," the first performance here, and the 1989 production of "On Golden Pond." Kahilu was a nickname for his beloved mother, Thelma Parker Smart.

At *Koa House Grill (☎ 885-2088, Waimea Center)* there's live entertainment on Friday and Saturday nights from 9pm until midnight. Thursday nights feature raucous karaoke from 9pm until midnight.

Shopping

Like Waimea's dining scene, shops in the area appeal to locals as well as tourists. Perhaps because of the town's high standard of living, stores here often sell goods of higher quality than you'd find elsewhere on the island. You will spy tacky trinkets, but ubiquitous T-shirt stores and ABC marts that are abundant in towns like Kailua-

Kona have far less prominence in this inland enclave. Most stores are open Mon-Sat from 9am till 5 or 6pm; on Sundays hours are usually shorter.

Buy gifts for family and friends at *Cook's Discoveries (☎ 885-3633, 64-1066 Mamalahoa Hwy)*, where almost everything for sale is made in the islands. Owner Patti Cook caters primarily to a local audience and offers a wide selection of Hawaiian music CDs and tapes (you can demo the CD in the store before you buy it), coasters and note cards, pillows, quilts and slippers. Cookies and other treats are also for sale.

Without Boundaries (☎ 885-1959, Waimea Center) is part gift store and part travel agency, selling merchandise that's mostly nouveau, not Hawaiian. Notables include soaps, body teas, candles, Hawaiian-style bags and fashionable purses. Also look for Hawaiian hand-painted silk scarves and historic note cards featuring Kailua-Kona circa 1895 and JFK's presidential visit to Waikiki in 1963.

Waimea General Store (☎ 885-4479, Parker Square) is terrific for browsing. The store has everything from cookbooks to Christmas ornaments to kids' toys. The book selection includes Hawaiian stories for kids, plus Hawaii-related titles on quilting, travel and other subjects.

For antiques and collectibles, stop by *Gallery of Great Things (☎ 885-7706, Parker Square)*, which contains a collection of Hawaiian, Polynesian and Asian art. Many of the original paintings, sculptures, furniture and Hawaiian quilts run $3000 and up, but some of the store's prints and mounted photos are in the more affordable $25-$250 range, as are mounted maps of Hawaii and Polynesia. Tiny *Crackseed, etc (☎ 885-6966, Hayashi Building)* features an odd combination of candy and treats on one side and wooden bowls, utensils and salt-and-pepper shakers on the other side. You can often find good deals on wood items.

If it's clothing you're after, visit *Reyn's (☎ 885-4493, Parker Ranch Shopping Center)*, known as the 'Brooks Brothers of the Pacific.' Reyn McCullough launched the store on Waikiki Beach more than 40 years ago; now he has a chain of popular stores all over the islands, and the merchandise is marketed on the mainland. Their signature is Hawaiian fabrics in reverse.

At press time, Waimea's renovated Parker Ranch Center was scheduled to open for business in spring of 2002. Look for new stores, a food court, the return of the Parker Ranch Grill and a Foodland supermarket.

Getting There & Away

Waimea is 40 miles from Kailua-Kona along Hwy 190, which turns into Mamalahoa Highway in town. From Honoka'a, Waimea is 15 miles via Hwy 19; the drive from Hilo is about 55 miles via Hwy 19. From Kona, the road climbs out of residential areas into a mix of lava flows and dry, grassy rangeland studded with prickly pear cactus. Along the way you'll see a little one-room church, broad views of the distant coast and blue ocean views, wide-open spaces and tall roadside grasses that have an incredible golden hue in the morning light.

If you come back on this road at night, the highway reflectors light up like an airport runway to guide you along.

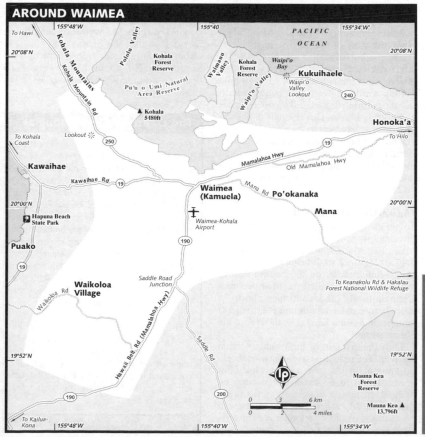

AROUND WAIMEA

One Hele-On bus a day (except Sunday) departs from the parking lot in Parker Ranch Center (near the shops and the visitor center) to Hilo's Mo'oheau bus terminal ($4.50, 100 minutes) at 8am. Going in the other direction, the bus departs Parker Ranch at 3:20pm for Waikoloa (75¢, 25 minutes), Kailua-Kona ($4.50, 75 minutes), Captain Cook ($4.50, 2 hours) and Honaunau ($4.50).

AROUND WAIMEA
Waimea to Honoka'a

Hwy 19 heads east from Waimea to Honoka'a through rolling hills and cattle pastures, with views of Mauna Kea to the south.

For a peaceful, scented back road, turn right off Hwy 19 onto the Old Mamalahoa Hwy just west of the 52-mile marker. (If you're coming from Hilo, turn left at the 43-mile marker opposite Tex Drive In and then take the next immediate right.) This 10-mile detour winds through hill country, with small roadside ranches, old wooden fences and grazing horses. This is a part of Hawaii that tourists have yet to discover. Nobody's in a hurry on this road, if they're on it at all. It can make an interesting alternative route for cyclists, although you'll need to be cautious, as the road is narrow, winding and a bit hilly.

Mana/Keanakolu Rd

To get closer to Mauna Kea for photography or views, you could drive partway down Mana Rd, which leads around the eastern flank of Mauna Kea. It begins off Hwy 19 at the 55-mile marker on the eastern side of Waimea. After 15 miles, the road becomes Keanakolu Rd and continues about 25 miles before reaching Summit Rd (the road leading up Mauna Kea) near the Humu'ula Sheep Station.

Only the first part of the Waimea section is paved. The road is passable on horseback, on a mountain bike or in a 4WD vehicle, but a couple of dozen cattle gates must be opened and closed along the way. Be aware that it's mostly ranchers and hunters who come this way, and it's a long way from anywhere should you get stuck en route.

Hakalau Forest National Wildlife Refuge About 7000 of the 32,700 acres of this koa-ohia refuge are open to the public and will be of particular interest to birders as it protects eight endangered bird species. There are no facilities, no interpretive signs and the locked entrance is 40 rough miles up Keanakolu Rd (good 4WDs only, impassable after rains). Special use permits are obtainable by calling the refuge manager (☎ 933-6915) between 8am and 4pm weekdays. A good time to visit is during National Wildlife Refuge Week (second week in October), when Hawaiian bird experts and refuge rangers introduce the public to the wonders of this native forest.

David Douglas Memorial A memorial to David Douglas, the Scottish botanist for whom the Douglas fir tree is named, is on Keanakolu Rd about halfway between Waimea and the Saddle Rd. Douglas died in 1834 at this spot.

The Death of David Douglas

The circumstances surrounding the death of famed botanist David Douglas in 1834 are somewhat mysterious, as his gored body was found trapped with an angry bull at the bottom of a pit on the slopes of Mauna Kea. Hunters commonly dug such pits and camouflaged them with underbrush as a means of trapping feral cattle, but the probability of both Douglas and a bull falling into the same hole seemed highly suspicious. Fingers were pointed at Australian Ned Gurney, an escaped convict from Botany Bay who had been hiding out in the area and had been the last person to see Douglas alive.

Hilo authorities, unable to solve the case, packed both Douglas' body and the bull's head in brine and shipped them to Honolulu for further investigation. By the time the body arrived in Oahu, it was so badly decomposed that they hastily buried Douglas' remains at the missionary church and the case was closed.

Saddle Road

True to its name, the Saddle Rd runs between the island's two highest points, with Mauna Kea to the north and Mauna Loa to the south.

The road passes over large lava flows and climbs through a variety of terrains and climates. At sunrise and sunset, there's a gentle glow on the mountains and a light show on the clouds. In the early morning, it's crisp enough to see your breath, and if you take the spur road up to Mauna Kea, you'll reach permafrost.

Although most car rental contracts prohibit travel on the Saddle Rd, it isn't because it's a rough road; it's paved the whole way. It's narrow, but it's no big deal – particularly by island standards. Locals looking for the rationale behind the car rental ban come up with things like military convoys or evening fog. The crux of the matter seems to be that the rental agencies just don't want to be responsible for the tow charge (anywhere from $400 to $600) if your car breaks down on Hawaii's most remote road.

The Saddle Rd is 50 miles long and has no gas stations or other facilities along the way, so be sure to start out with a full tank of gas.

Crossing the island on the Saddle Rd is a bit shorter than taking the northern route of the Hawaii Belt Rd, but then again the Saddle Rd is also a bit slower; timewise there isn't much difference either way.

To the west, the Saddle Rd starts out in cattle ranch land with rolling grassy hills and planted stands of eucalyptus trees. It's beautiful, but like the rest of the western side of the island, it's changing. A gated residential community called Waiki'i Ranch divided more than 2000 acres of the area's ranch land into million-dollar house lots of 10, 20 and 40 acres apiece for the region's wealthy urban cowboys.

After about 10 miles, the land starts getting rougher and the pastures and fences fewer. The military takes over where the

Highlights

- Gazing at Mars and stars on a clear night at the Mauna Kea visitor center
- Hiking to Lake Waiau, Mauna Kea's unique alpine mystery
- Skiing or snowboarding on the slopes of a volcano
- Rising above the clouds en route to Hawaii's highest summit
- Taking on the rigors of Mauna Loa's steep and challenging Observatory Trail
- Navigating the twists and turns of the Saddle Road

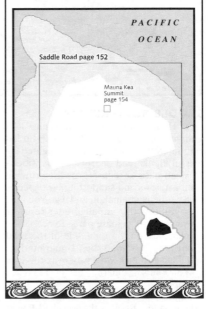

cows leave off, and you'll eventually come to the Quonset huts of the Pohakuloa Military Training Area. Most of the vehicles on the road are military jeeps and trucks, although in hunting season you'll come across a fair number of pickup trucks as well.

SADDLE ROAD

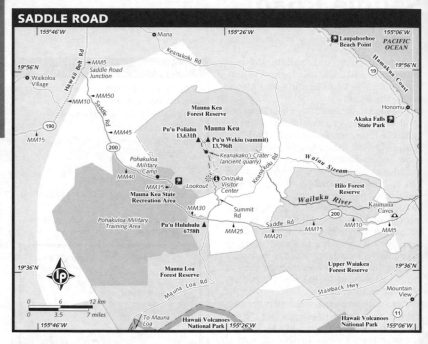

SADDLE ROAD KIPUKA

From Hilo, the approach to the Mauna Kea summit along the Saddle Road is sprinkled with interesting short hikes highlighted by several kipuka and decent birding. **Kipuka 21** is an oasis of dense growth springing from a'a flows and supporting bird species such as apapane, amakihi and iiwi. You may also glimpse the endangered akepa or Hawaii creeper in these parts. To access the kipuka, park on the right side of the road about .2 mile beyond the 21-mile marker; you'll have to pick your way over the lava flow for a short, unmarked distance to reach the kipuka.

Another .1 mile farther west on the left side of Saddle Road is the so-called Power Line road (marked with a PLR sign). This gravel road wends through several kipuka of koa and ohia forest and boasts all the common bird species, plus nene, akiapolaau, Hawaii creeper and the *i'o* (Hawaiian hawk). The best place to glimpse these and

other birds is among the several kipuka dotting the area about 3 miles in from Saddle Road (allow about 90 minutes each way). Alternatively, you can travel another .5 mile beyond the PLR to the trailhead for the **Pu'u O'o Trail**, where there are a handful more kipuka. After about 4 miles on this trail, you'll eventually hook up with the aforementioned kipuka on the PLR road.

MAUNA KEA

Stunning Mauna Kea (White Mountain) is Hawaii's highest mountain, and its 13,796-foot summit has a cluster of important astronomical observatory domes, considered the greatest collection of large astronomical telescopes in the world. And where else in the world can you drive from a sunny beach to the peak of a massive volcano in a few short hours? The freezing temperatures and thin air heighten the singular experience, which makes visitors aware of every labored breath and chilled body part.

The Summit Rd, which climbs up Mauna Kea, begins off Saddle Rd at the 28-mile marker opposite a hunters' check station. It's a well-paved 6¼ miles to the Onizuka visitor center. The road winds up a few thousand feet in elevation. If you've got a small car, it's probably going to labor a bit, but it shouldn't be a problem making it up as far as the visitor center. A standard transmission is preferable.

Surprisingly, you don't really get closer views of Mauna Kea's peaks by driving up to the visitor center. The peaks actually look higher and the views are broader from Saddle Rd. But you'll find other gasp-worthy vistas from Summit Rd, like the majestic views of clouds spread out like a soft feather bed below you; flying above the clouds in an airplane pales in comparison. Mauna Kea doesn't appear as a single main peak but rather a jumble of peaks, some black, some red-brown, some seasonally snowcapped. Once you catch your breath at the summit, look south in the distance for a view of enormous Mauna Loa, the still-active, though less famous, neighboring volcano.

Summit Rd passes through open range with grazing cattle, which were brought to Hawaii in 1793. It's easy to spot Eurasian skylarks in the grass, and if you're lucky you might see the *i'o*, an endemic Hawaiian hawk, hovering overhead. Both birds make their home on the grassy mountain slopes. Mauna Kea is also home to the nene, as well as the *palila*, a small yellow honeycreeper that lives nowhere else in the world. Mouflon (mountain sheep) and feral goats also roam free in the area.

Environmental protection is of great concern here because the mountain is the exclusive home for numerous plants, birds and insects. One of the more predominant plants on the mountain is mullen, which has soft woolly leaves and shoots up a tall stalk. In spring, the stalks get so loaded down with

Mauna Kea Warning

Elevation can be a problem if visitors don't take the time to properly acclimatize.

- The summit air has only about 60% of the oxygen that's available at sea level, and it's not uncommon for visitors to get altitude sickness.

- Unlike Nepal, for instance, where great heights are generally reached only after days of trekking, here you can zip up from sea level to nearly 14,000 feet by car in just two hours.

- Scuba divers who have been diving within the past 24 hours risk getting the bends by going to the summit. It's recommended that children under 16, obese people, pregnant women and those with a respiratory condition, or even a cold for that matter, not go beyond the Onizuka visitor center. Because of the demand that the altitude puts on the heart, people with a heart condition should avoid the summit as well. Remember that there are no medical services on Mauna Kea; the closest hospitals are in Hilo or Waimea.

- Even the astronomers who work up here never fully acclimatize and are always oxygen-deprived in the summit's thin air. Anyone who gets a headache or feels faint or nauseous should head back down the mountain. For more information, see Altitude Sickness under Health in the Facts for the Visitor chapter.

- Bring warm clothing and be prepared for severe weather conditions, as temperatures can drop well below freezing and high winds are common. Mauna Kea can have snow flurries any time of the year, and winter storms can dump a couple of feet of snow overnight. The numbing temperatures may particularly surprise people visiting from the leeward side of the island who are accustomed to shorts, tanks and flip-flops. If you didn't pack appropriate gear, buy some cheap warm clothing; you'll thank us later.

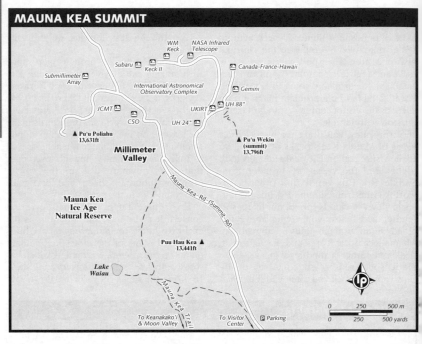

MAUNA KEA SUMMIT

flowers that they bend over from the weight of what look like big yellow helmets. Mullen is not a native plant but was inadvertently brought in by ranchers as a freeloading weed in grass seed. Silversword, a distant relative of the sunflower, is also found at this high elevation. The plant grows for four to 25 years, then dies the autumn after the striking maroon and yellow flowers blossom. Mamane blossoms are abundant, as the mamane forest encircles the mountain between 6500 and 9500 feet.

For information on skiing and snow-boarding on the slopes of Mauna Kea, see the Activities chapter.

Kipuka Pu'u Huluhulu

Across from the turnoff to the summit is a trail to the top of Pu'u Huluhulu ('Shaggy Hill'), a kipuka created more than 10,000 years ago. The 20-minute hike is easy and peaceful and you'll be rewarded with panoramic views of Mauna Loa, Mauna Kea and Hualalai at the top. Around the south side are interesting, overlapping pahoehoe and a'a flows that are between 1500 and 3000 years old. Look for mamane and koa trees and pheasant, turkeys, apapane or hawks while you walk.

Onizuka Visitor Center

The Onizuka visitor center (☎ 961-2180, W www.ifa.hawaii.edu), officially the Onizuka Center for International Astronomy, was named for Ellison Onizuka, a Big Island native and one of the astronauts who died in the 1986 Challenger space shuttle disaster. It's open Monday-Friday from 9am-noon, 1pm-5pm and 6pm-10pm, as well as 9am-10pm Saturday and Sunday.

The center shows a somewhat dated hour-long video on Mauna Kea's observatories, narrated by backyard astronomer Johnny Carson. It also has photo displays of the observatories, information on discoveries made from the summit and exhibits of the mountain's history, ecology and geology. There are computers running astronomy programs, and lots of excellent free literature, including a calendar of meteor showers, sheets about bugs, plants and fauna, volunteer information and more. Catering to Hawaii's large volume of Japanese tourists, the center offers information in Japanese as well.

Coffee and packets of hot chocolate are on hand to warm you up before or after a chilly visit to the summit; a $1 donation is requested. Items for sale include bottled water and Cup O Noodles, along with fun astronaut food like freeze-dried strawberries, ice cream and ice cream sandwiches ($4).

The opening hours are subject to change, so it's a good idea to call before making the trip. The visitor center is approximately one hour's drive from Hilo, Waimea and Waikoloa, and about two hours away from Kailua-Kona.

There are myriad volunteer opportunities at Mauna Kea. See the Volunteer Work section of the Facts for the Visitor chapter.

Across from the visitor center, a 10-minute uphill hike on a well-trodden trail crests a cinder cone offering glorious sunset views.

Stargazing Program Every evening from 6pm to 10pm, the visitor center offers a magnificent cheap thrill: a free astronomy program that includes a presentation about Mauna Kea and stargazing (weather permitting) using a Meade LX-200 16-inch telescope and both 14-inch and 11-inch Celestron telescopes. You'll get a chance to view planets, galaxies, star clusters, supernova remnants and planetary nebulae. On a recent visit, Andromeda, Mars and a globular cluster were on the menu. The instructor also points out all of the constellations visible in Hawaii.

Children are welcome. Wear warm clothing, as night temperatures can sometimes dip to around freezing in winter and into the 40s (°F) in summer. The warm beverages at the visitor center won't help much if you're not bundled up. Also, call to double-check that the program is happening; the

drive is too long to be disappointed by last-minute scheduling changes. Groups of 10 or more should make advance reservations (☎ 961-2180).

For visitors interested in learning more about stargazing, the Bishop Museum puts out a monthly star map that can be accessed via their Web site; you can pick up a copy of the night sky map by visiting the Keck headquarters in Waimea (see the Introduction in the Waimea chapter). The site also features information about sunrise and sunset times throughout Hawaii, moon phases, and other astronomical highlights (planetarium pre-recorded information ☎ 848-4136, ⓦ www.bishopmuseum.org/planetarium/sky.html).

Summit Tours More than 100,000 tourists visit Mauna Kea annually, and most pass through the visitor center, which offers Mauna Kea summit tours on Saturday and Sunday. The tours visit one or two of the summit telescopes, most commonly the University of Hawaii's 88-inch telescope. The tour is free, but you need to provide your own 4WD transportation to the summit. You can go up in 2WD if you insist, but it's not recommended, and you won't be permitted to participate in any station-sponsored programs. If you're lucky, you might be able to catch a ride up with someone from the visitor center, but you can't count on it. Pregnant women and children under 16 are not allowed because of altitude health hazards (see the Dangers & Annoyances section, later).

Check-in is at the visitor center at 1pm; the first hour is spent at the center watching videos about astronomy on Mauna Kea, which also provides an opportunity to acclimatize. The tours usually last until 5pm and are subject to cancellation at any time when there's inclement weather at the summit.

While you're touring the observatories at the summit, don't expect to warm up: the indoor temperatures are kept near freezing to simulate the nighttime temperatures outside.

For commercial tours to the summit, see Organized Tours later in this chapter.

Summit Observatories

The summit of Mauna Kea has the greatest collection of state-of-the-art telescopes on earth and superior conditions for viewing the heavens. Nearing 14,000 feet, the summit is above 40% of the earth's atmosphere and 90% of its water vapor. The air is typically clear, dry and stable.

Not only are the Hawaiian Islands isolated, but Mauna Kea is one of the most secluded places in Hawaii. The air is relatively free from dust and smog. Nights are dark and free from city light interference.

Eight out of 10 nights are perfect for astronomers working at the summit, though rain, freezing fog, snow and high winds can affect viewing the other nights. Only the Andes Mountains match Mauna Kea for cloudless nights, although air turbulence in the Andes makes viewing more difficult there. The air here stays calm because there are no nearby mountain ranges to alter the weather patterns, and the ocean is thermally stable.

The University of Hawaii (UH) holds the lease on Mauna Kea from the 12,000-foot level to the summit, and UH receives observing time at each telescope as one of the lease provisions. Currently, 11 telescopes operate near the summit and one more is in the making.

UH built the summit's first telescope in 1968; it has a 24-inch mirror. The telescope sizes have been increasing by leaps and bounds ever since.

The UK Infrared Telescope (UKIRT), with its 150-inch mirror, was until the early 1990s the world's largest infrared telescope. It can be operated via computers and satellite relays from the Royal Observatory in England.

NASA's Infrared Telescope has measured the heat of volcanoes on Io, one of Jupiter's moons. The most active of Io's volcanoes is now named after the Hawaiian volcano goddess Pele.

Opened in 1992, the WM Keck Observatory, a project of the California Institute of Technology, the University of California and NASA, began operations with Keck I, the world's largest and most powerful optical/infrared telescope. In January 1996, the 390-inch Keck telescope discovered the most distant galaxy ever observed, at 14 billion light-years away. The discovery of this 'new galaxy,' in the constellation Virgo, has brought into question the very age of the universe itself, because the stars making up the galaxy seemingly predate the 'big bang' that is thought to have created the universe.

Keck featured a breakthrough in telescope design. Previously, the sheer weight of the glass mirrors was a limiting factor in telescope construction. The Keck telescope has a unique honeycomb design with 36 hexagonal mirror segments, each 6 feet across, that function as a single piece of glass.

A second Keck telescope (Keck II), a replica of the first, became operational in October 1996. The two telescopes are interchangeable and can function as one – 'like a pair of binoculars searching the sky' – allowing them to study the very cores of elliptical galaxies. The cost for the twin Keck observatories, each weighing 300 tons and reaching a height of 8 stories, was approximately $200 million.

The **Keck Observatory visitor gallery** *(no ☎, W www2.keck.Hawaii.edu:3636/, open 10am-4pm Mon-Fri)* has an informative display, a 12-minute video, rest rooms and a viewing area inside the Keck I dome that allows you to see the telescope.

Just 150 yards west of Keck is Japan's new Subaru Telescope *(W www.subarutelescope .org)*, which opened in 1999 after nearly a decade of construction. Its $300 million price tag makes this the most expensive observatory yet constructed, and its 23-ton mirror, reaching 27 feet in diameter, is the largest optical mirror in existence. Incidentally, the telescope is named for the constellation Pleiades, which in Japanese is called Subaru.

Driving to the Summit

Visitors may go up to the summit in daytime, but astronomers strongly discourage vehicle headlights between sunset and sunrise because the light interferes with observation. What you'll see is mainly the outside of the observatory buildings, where the scientists are at work, although both the University of Hawaii 88-inch telescope and the WM Keck Observatory have visitor centers.

The road to the summit is paved only as far as Hale Pohaku, the buildings just above the Onizuka visitor center, where the scientists reside. From Hale Pokahu there are 5 miles of unpaved road, followed by 4½ miles of paved road. Some say that parts of the road are deliberately kept unpaved to limit access and make it more difficult. People en route to the summit should stop first at the Onizuka center for at least 30 minutes to acclimatize before continuing on.

The road from the Onizuka center to the summit is suitable for 4WD vehicles only; although people occasionally go up in standard cars, this is not recommended due to problems that can occur with poor traction on the slopes. Harper Car & Truck Rentals is the only car rental company that allows its vehicles (4WD jeeps) to be driven to the summit (see the Car Rental section in the Getting Around chapter).

The drive takes about half an hour. You should drive in low gear and loosen the gas cap to prevent vapor lock. The upper road can become covered with ice during winter. Be particularly careful on the way down and watch out for loose cinder. Driving when the angle of the sun is low – in the hour after sunrise or before sunset – can create blinding conditions that make it difficult to see the road and oncoming cars.

About 4½ miles up is an area called **Moon Valley**, where the Apollo astronauts rehearsed with their lunar rover before their journey to the real moonscape.

At 5½ miles up, look to the left for a narrow ridge with two caves and black stones. That's **Keanakako'i**, 'Cave of the Adze,' an ancient adze quarry. From this spot, high-quality basalt was quarried to make adzes and other tools and weapons, which were traded throughout the islands. For people interested in archaeology, it's an impressive site. This is a protected area and nothing should be removed.

Dimming the Light

You might notice, as you tour around the Big Island, that the streetlights have an unusual orange glow. In order to provide Mauna Kea astronomers with the best viewing conditions possible, streetlights on the island have been converted to low-impact sodium. Rather than using the full iridescent spectrum, these orange lights use only a few wavelengths, which the telescopes can be adjusted to remove.

Call ☎ 974-4203 for a recording on current road conditions.

Hiking to the Summit

The daunting 6-mile **Mauna Kea summit trail** starts near the end of the paved road above the Onizuka visitor center. Instead of continuing on the main 4WD road, take the road to the left; park at the visitor center and walk about 200 yards to the trailhead. The trail begins up through wooden posts and more or less parallels the summit road (some of the hike is actually along the road to the observatories). It's marked with posts and stone cairns. Detailed maps are available at the visitor center.

The trail starts at 9200 feet and climbs almost 4600 feet in a mere 6 miles. Altitude, steepness and weather combine for a triple threat, making the hike quite strenuous. Dress in layers of warm clothing and bring plenty of water. Also remember to lather on the sunscreen; it's easy to forget that you can get badly sunburned in these conditions. Get an early start if you're braving this climb and give yourself the maximum daylight hours; most people need four to five hours to reach the summit and you'll need time to get back down before dark..

Walking on cinders adds another difficult element, but there are incredible vistas and strange moonlike landscapes en route to the highest peak. The trail passes through the **Mauna Kea Ice Age Natural Area Reserve**. There was once a Pleistocene glacier here, and scratchings on rocks from the glacial moraine can still be seen.

The ancient adze quarry Keanakako'i, at 12,400 feet, is two-thirds of the way up. Lake Waiau is a mile farther.

You might be tempted to hitch a ride from someone at the Onizuka visitor center who's going to the summit and then walk down. But if you haven't spent the previous night in the mountains, there's a danger in doing this, as you won't have as much time to acclimatize. Also, don't attempt the hike in inclement weather.

Lake Waiau

Lake Waiau is a unique alpine lake that, at 13,020 feet, is the third-highest lake in the USA. It sits inside the Pu'u Waiau cinder cone in a barren and treeless setting.

Lake Waiau is rather mysterious. It's a small, strangely green lake, no more than 10 feet deep and set on porous cinder in desert conditions that receive less than 15 inches of rainfall per year. It's fed by permafrost and meltwater from winter snows, which elsewhere on Mauna Kea quickly evaporates. Chilly Lake Waiau has no freshwater springs and yet it's never dry.

Hawaiians used to bring the umbilical cords of their babies here and place them in

---

Pu'u Poliahu

Just below Mauna Kea summit is the hill Pu'u Poliahu, home of Poliahu, the goddess of snow.

Poliahu is said to be more beautiful than her sister Pele. According to legend, during conflicts over men, Pele would get miffed and erupt Mauna Kea; Poliahu would cover it over with ice and snow. Then Pele would erupt again. Back and forth they would go. The legend is metaphorically correct. As recently as 10,000 years ago, there were volcanic eruptions through glacial ice caps here.

Because of its spiritual significance, Pu'u Poliahu is off-limits to astronomical domes, so you won't find observatories here.

---

the lake to give their children the strength of the mountain.

Three different trailheads take visitors to Lake Waiau. The 30-minute trek from the visitor center is the most challenging because it's uphill the whole darn way. Alternatively, from the parking lot a mile farther up the road, cross over to the beaten path, which is a fairly easy 20-minute hike. The third and final option is at the hairpin turn just before the observatories; look for the 10mph sign and you'll see the trailhead. This last one is 15-30 minutes, depending on your fitness level and acclimatization. As always, drink a lot of water and take your time.

Organized Tours

Mauna Kea Summit & Stars Adventure (☎ 331-8505, 800-464-1993, Ⓦ *www.hawaii -forest.com*) Tour $145. A gourmet dinner at the Parker Ranch sheep station precedes this sunset Mauna Kea summit tour, which includes stargazing. Pick-ups are in Kailua-Kona and Waikoloa. Hawaii Forest & Trail runs this adventure, and they also have bird-watching adventures on Saddle Rd.

Paradise Safaris (☎ 322-2366, Ⓦ *www .maunakea.com*) Tour $144. Paradise Safaris conducts sunset tours of Mauna Kea summit. The tour includes stargazing from the company's own portable telescope and pick-up in Kailua-Kona, Waikoloa or Waimea.

Arnott's Lodge (☎ 969-7097, Ⓦ *www .arnottslodge.com, see Places to Stay, Hilo*) Tour for Lodge guests/nonguests $48/$96. This company offers sunset tours, stargazing tours and a daytime outing to Mauna Kea; the cost is the same for all three.

See also Summit Tours, earlier.

Places to Stay

At press time, the ***Mauna Kea State Recreation Area*** (*bookings: Division of State Parks*, ☎ 974-6200, *75 Aupuni St, Hilo*) was closed to campers so that the park could upgrade its equipment to comply with EPA regulations. For the time being camping options are limited to spots outside Mauna Kea State Recreation Area (see the Big Island Camping map in the Facts for the

Visitor chapter for ideas); the closest hotels and B&Bs are in Waimea and Hilo (see relevant chapters).

However, the park, 7 miles west of Summit Rd near the 35-mile marker, may reopen. Call the number above to get the latest information.

Before its closure, the recreation area had housekeeping cabins complete with basic kitchens, bathrooms, hot showers and bed space for up to six people. The park also contains picnic tables and rest rooms.

Nearby military maneuvers can be noisy, and with an elevation of 6500 feet, the area commonly experiences cool days and cold nights. But should it reopen, the park is a good base for those planning to hike Mauna Kea or Mauna Loa.

MAUNA LOA'S NORTHERN FLANK

The road to Mauna Loa starts just east of Summit Rd and climbs 18 miles up the northern flank of Mauna Loa to a weather station at 11,150 feet. There are no visitor facilities at the weather station, so be sure to use the rest rooms before you set out.

The narrow road is gently sloping and passable in a standard car. As it's a winding, nearly single-lane drive with some blind spots, give yourself about 45 minutes to drive up. It might be wise to loosen your gas cap before you start in order to avoid vapor lock problems. Park in the lot below the weather station; the equipment used to measure atmospheric conditions is highly sensitive to vehicle exhaust.

The summit and domes of Mauna Kea are visible from here, and when conditions are just right you can glimpse the 'Mauna Kea shadow' at sunset. It's a curious phenomenon in which Mauna Kea sometimes casts a blue-purple shadow behind itself in the sky.

Observatory Trail

The weather station is the trailhead for the steep and difficult Observatory Trail, which connects up with the Mauna Loa Summit Trail after 3.8 miles. From there it's 2.6 miles around the western side of Mauna Loa's caldera, Mokuaweoweo, to the summit at 13,677 feet, or 2.1 miles along the eastern side of Mokuaweoweo Caldera to Mauna Loa cabin at 13,250 feet.

The hike to the cabin takes four to six hours for strong hikers. Anyone who is not in top shape shouldn't even consider it.

Overnight hikers need to register in advance with the Kilauea Visitor Center in Hawaii Volcanoes National Park. See Backcountry Hiking & Camping in the Hawaii Volcanoes National Park chapter for details.

Mauna Loa to Hilo

Heading eastward from the hunters' check station at the foot of Summit Rd, the terrain along Saddle Rd gradually becomes ohia-fern forest, shrubby at first, but getting thicker and taller as Hilo gets closer.

This section of road has been upgraded and the ride onward to Hilo is a fairly good one, but be cautious of oncoming drivers who take to the center of the road to cut curves.

About 4 miles outside Hilo, Akolea Rd leads off to the left and connects in 2 miles to Waianuenue Ave, which passes Pe'epe'e Falls, Boiling Pots and Rainbow Falls (see the Around Hilo section in the Hilo chapter). Alternatively, if you stay on Saddle Rd, you'll soon come to Kaumana Caves on the left. For information on all of these sites, see the Hilo chapter.

Hamakua Coast

The Hamakua Coast winds along the northeastern shoreline, from the dramatic cliffs and valleys of Waipi'o and neighboring sacred spots down to Hilo. The 45-mile stretch has been dubbed the Hamakua Heritage Coast in a marketing effort to highlight its history.

Highlights

- Hiking, camping and reveling in the legendary Waipi'o Valley
- Backcountry camping in the Waimanu Valley
- Catching a Hamakua Music Festival headliner in laidback Honoka'a
- Feeling the spray of towering Akaka Falls
- Gorging yourself on heaven-sent *malasadas*
- Losing yourself in the s-curves of Pepe'ekeo 4-Mile Scenic Drive

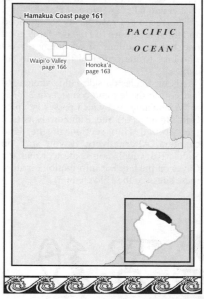

Hamakua Coast page 161

PACIFIC OCEAN

Waipi'o Valley page 166

Honoka'a page 163

From Waimea, it's 15 miles east on Hwy 19 to the quaint town of Honoka'a, from where it's a quick and pretty 9 miles to the Waipi'o Valley Lookout. You'll be blown over with a whisper gazing upon that verdant valley with its waterfalls and black-sand beach. Imagine descending into and being enveloped by it. (You can: see the Waipi'o Valley section later in this chapter.)

The Hamakua Coast is the heart of the defunct Hawaiian sugar industry, and feral cane, some eight feet tall, blows in the trades. The Pacific sparkles a seductive blue from almost every vantage up this way, contrasting brilliantly with the green monkeypod crowns and orange African tulip tree blossoms that grow all around. Streams and waterfalls pulse through many of the gulches on the way.

The Hawaii Belt Rd (Hwy 19) is an impressive engineering feat spanning lush ravines with a series of sweeping cantilevered bridges. It's a picturesque drive and the back roads are worth wending around if you have time to dawdle.

Hwy 19 passes small towns and unmarked roads that will reward the curious with unfrequented pockets of beach and genuine aloha. If you're just passing through on the Kona-to-Hilo circuit, at least make time for Waipi'o Valley Lookout, majestic Akaka Falls and the Pepe'ekeo 4-mile scenic drive.

There are many lovely B&Bs along this stretch of coast, but only a few budget places worth recommending. There are, however, campsites at several public beach parks.

HONOKA'A

Like the tides of the Pacific below, Honoka'a rises and falls with the times: from cattle and sugar to soldiers and tourists, this town has had to reinvent itself after each crashing wave. Most recently and famously, the Honoka'a Sugar Company (opened in 1873) processed its last harvest in 1993 and shuttered its mill.

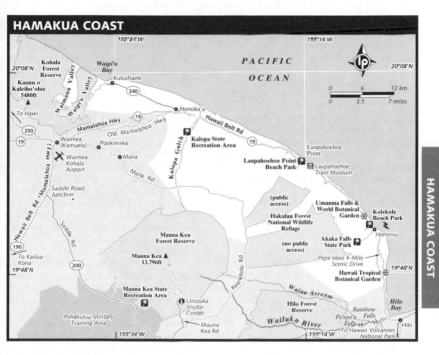

HAMAKUA COAST

At times reflective and progressive – antique shops and aura photographers share storefronts along the historic main street – Honoka'a is the biggest town (population 2186) on the Hamakua Coast. This makes for good people watching when Waipi'o Valley residents come 'topside' to stock up. You'll know them by their muddy, beat-up trucks, and the passel of hounds scrambling around in the back.

Information

All services but the post office are strung along Mamane St (Hwy 240), Honoka'a's main thoroughfare. The First Hawaiian Bank has an ATM and there are two gas stations (though you'll pay around 20¢ more per gallon up here). You can check email at the library which is only open weekdays. The entire town sleeps on Sundays.

The visitor center may not be staffed when you show up, but feel free to take advantage of the clean public toilet out back. Nearby, **Hawaiian Walkways** (☎ 775-0372, 800-457-7759, W www.hawaiianwalkways .com) leads informed, guided hikes to surrounding natural wonders including Waipi'o Valley and Kilauea; half-day hikes are $85 per person and include gear and lunch.

Things to See & Do

The renewed economic and creative spirit of Honoka'a shines at the **Live Arts Gallery** (☎ 775-1240, 45-368 Lehua St; admission free; open 9am-5pm daily) where painters, glass blowers, ceramists and other artists work in open studios, allowing visitors a peek at the creative process. Many pieces are for sale if something strikes your fancy. Also here is **Hamakua Coffee Roasters** (☎ 775-0118), roasting up beans to rival their Kona neighbors. Not all artists are always in residence, so call for the events calendar.

Do you possess the coveted purple aura? You can find out at **Starseed** (☎ 775-9344,

45-3551A Mamane St; open 10am-5pm Mon-Sat). For $10 (or $20 with analysis), they'll photograph your aura. There's also an espresso bar here, if your aura needs a jolt.

The **Annual Taro Festival** is a one day affair each November that's jam-packed with everything that can be done with taro (and some things that probably shouldn't!). Check this out for some homegrown fun – especially the poi eating contest.

Beside the library is the **Katsu Goto Memorial**. A Japanese cane field worker, Goto was hanged by Honoka'a sugar bosses and accomplices in 1889 for his attempts to improve conditions on Hamakua plantations. He's considered one of the first union activists.

Places to Stay

If you're watching your budget, the rustic group cabins at Kalopa State Recreation Area just south of Honoka'a are an affordable, enticing option (see that section later).

Hotel Honoka'a Club (☎ 775-0678, 800-808-0678, W *home1.gte.net/honokaac, PO Box 247, Honoka'a, HI 96727, Mamane St)* Dorm beds $15, singles with shared shower $25, rooms with private bath $45-65, suites $80. Reception: 8am-1pm & 4pm-8pm. The basic Hotel Honoka'a Club is the only game in town. Visitors can share a dorm-style room or have a small private room with a sink and bed. These cheaper rooms share a shower and toilet, but they're at the quieter end of the hotel. There are also nicer rooms with private bathrooms and a bit of a view; the more expensive room has a queen bed and TV.

Waipi'o Wayside B&B (☎/fax 775-0275, 800-833-8849, W *www.waipiowayside.com, PO Box 840, Honoka'a, HI 96727)* Moon Room $95, rooms with private bath $115-145. Waipi'o Wayside B&B, between the 3- and 4-mile marker on Hwy 240 heading towards Waipi'o Valley, is a 1932 plantation house nestled in a macadamia nut orchard. There are five rooms, each cozy in their own way – antique furnishings, sprays of flowers, plush linens and bath goodies make it. The cheaper Moon Room has a private de-

tached bath. All rates include a gorgeous breakfast that includes homegrown fruit and Big Island coffee. Relax in the garden gazebo, on the sprawling lanai or swinging in a hammock; life doesn't get much better than this.

Places to Eat

For such a small town, Honoka'a has some terrific eats.

Taro Junction Natural Foods (☎ 775-9477, *Mamane St)* Open 10am-5:30pm Mon-Fri, 9am-5pm Sat. This is Honoka'a's resident health food store. Friendly and packed with all good things, head here for picnic fixings. **TKS Supermarket**, on the corner of Mamane and Lehua Sts is another good option for DIYers, as is the *farmers' market* (6am-3pm Saturdays).

Simply Natural (☎ 775-0119, *Mamane St)* Dishes $3.50-6.50. Open 9am-4pm daily. From banana taro pancakes and omelettes, to smoothies that make a meal, this is the place to sate your breakfast cravings. They also do lunch.

Mamane Street Bakery & Café (☎ 775-9478, *Mamane St)* Open 6:30am-5:30pm Mon, 6:30am-5pm Tues, Wed & Sat, 6:30am-6pm Thur & Fri. Mingle with local old-timers, freaks and farmers over some coffee and sweets on any given day at this Honoka'a favorite.

Jolene's Kau Kau Korner (☎ 775-9498, 45-3625 Mamane St)* Lunch $4.50-7.95. Open for lunch only, Mon-Fri. If you've always wanted to try a plate lunch, take this chance. The local beef industry is well represented on Jolene's menu also; try the mushroom burger.

Café Il Mundo (☎ 775-7711, 45-3626A Mamane St)* Pizzas $8.75-17, sandwiches $4.75-7.85. Open 10:30am-8:30pm. You'll dream of these pizzas all the way into Waipi'o and back. Made fresh to order and by the slice (until 5pm), the combinations are wholesome and yummy. Also on offer are toothsome sandwiches, soups and generous salads. Bring your own wine and enjoy.

New Moon Café (☎ 775-0877, *Mamane St)* Breakfast from $3.50, lunch from $4.50. Open 9am-4pm, Sat 9am-1pm. Serving the

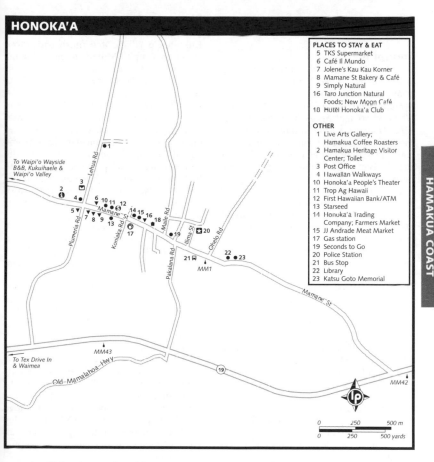

HONOKA'A

PLACES TO STAY & EAT
5 TKS Supermarket
6 Café Il Mundo
7 Jolene's Kau Kau Korner
8 Mamane St Bakery & Café
9 Simply Natural
16 Taro Junction Natural
   Foods; New Moon Café
18 Hotel Honoka'a Club

OTHER
1 Live Arts Gallery;
   Hamakua Coffee Roasters
2 Hamakua Heritage Visitor
   Center; Toilet
3 Post Office
4 Hawaiian Walkways
10 Honoka'a People's Theater
11 Trop Ag Hawaii
12 First Hawaiian Bank/ATM
13 Starseed
14 Honoka'a Trading
   Company; Farmers Market
15 JJ Andrade Meat Market
17 Gas station
19 Seconds to Go
20 Police Station
21 Bus Stop
22 Library
23 Katsu Goto Memorial

To Waipi'o Wayside
B&B, Kukuihaele &
Waipi'o Valley

To Tex Drive In
& Waimea

MM43

MM1

Mamane St

Old-Mamalahoa Hwy

19

MM42

0   250   500 m
0   250   500 yards

HAMAKUA COAST

typical café fare in a mellow, hipster atmosphere just behind Taro Junction Natural Foods, this place has a patio and occasional live music. Try the decked out taro burger, with impressive side salads for $5.50 or chill out and people watch while sipping some kava.

Tex Drive In (☎ 775-0598) Open 6am-9pm daily. Just up on Hwy 19, Tex's famous malasadas will send you to the fat farm and the poor house, but not before taking a pit stop in heaven. Never again will a doughnut crumb pass your lips after tasting one of these Portuguese pastries. Tex's *malasadas*

come in plain (75¢ each) or filled varieties, like hot pepper jelly, or papaya-pineapple ($1). Tex also has good sandwiches, burgers and plate lunch, but honestly, who cares? Bring on the fried dough!

Entertainment

On Friday, Saturday and Sunday nights, you can catch a movie at the historic **Honoka'a People's Theater** (☎ 775-0000, *Mamane St; adults/senior/child $6/4/3; open Fri-Sun*). Built in 1930, this theater also hosts the **Hamakua Music Festival** and the **Hawaii International Film Festival**, both held annually in November. For information on the latter call ☎ 775-3378.

Shopping

Honoka'a has some wicked good shopping; pick your way down Mamane St and see what jumps out at you.

Honoka'a Trading Company (☎ 775-0808, *Mamane St*) and *Seconds to Go* (☎ 775-9212, *Mamane St*) are antique stores both chock-a-block full of vintage aloha wear, books, glassware and all manner of Hawaiiana; the Barbie hula outfits are particularly snazzy.

Trop Ag Hawaii (☎ 775-9730, 45-3610 *Mamane St*) are purveyors of delicious Hamakua coffee beans, while *JJ Andrade Meatmarket* (☎ 775-0741, *Mamane St*) proudly sells happy beef from cows grazed naturally on Big Island grass. Make no mistake, you can taste the difference.

Getting There & Away

The Hele-On Bus ('7 Downtown Hilo') has morning departures opposite the 76 gas station in Honoka'a to the Mooheau Terminal in Hilo ($3.75, 75 minutes) at 5:50am and 8:30am; afternoon buses leave from in front of the old gym complex at 3:15pm, 5:10pm and 5:25pm. The bus only operates weekdays.

KUKUIHAELE

About 7 miles beyond Honoka'a heading toward Waipi'o Valley on Hwy 240, a loop to the right curves down into the tiny village of Kukuihaele.

In Hawaiian Kukuihaele means 'Traveling Light,' and refers to the ghostly Night Marchers, who are said to pass through this area carrying torches on their way to Waipi'o. You'll hear them before you see them.

Though there's little to Kukuihaele proper, this is the setting-off point for most tours into Waipi'o Valley, and many B&Bs are off village side roads. In Kukuihaele, *Waipi'o Valley Artworks* (☎ 775-0958) sells fine local crafts, from blown glass to hand carved koa bowls, and has a particularly large book selection.

Places to Stay

These listings start with places to stay in Kukuihaele village and finish with those closer to Waipi'o Valley, though all sport great views and locations.

Hale Kukui Orchard Retreat (☎ 775-7130, ⓦ *www.halekukui.com*, *PO Box 5044, Honoka'a, HI 96727*) Studio $95, 2-bedroom $145, cottage $160. These deliciously tranquil and secluded cottages are tucked in an orchard, offering spectacular views (some partial) for which the area is famous. The cottages are wood paneled, with private baths and kitchenette. Each has a lanai and guests are welcome to harvest as much of the dozen varieties of fruit grown here as they can eat.

Cliff House Hawaii (☎ 775-0005, 800-492-4746, ⓦ *www.cliffhousehawaii.com*, *PO Box 5045, Kukuihaele, HI, 96727*) 2-bedroom house $150, two night minimum. This gorgeous home on 40 acres has great big windows and a wraparound lanai, providing unforgettable views of the sapphire waters and cliffs surrounding Waipi'o. The house has tile floors, comfortable bedrooms, a fully equipped kitchen and TV/VCR.

Waipio Lookout (☎ 775-1306, ⓦ *www.interpac.net/~waipiohi*, *PO Box 5022, Kukuihaele, HI 96727*) 1-bedroom apartment $75/450/1600 daily/weekly/monthly. This cute apartment is on the 1st floor of a contemporary two-story house on the ridge about 200 yards before the Waipi'o Valley Lookout. There's a futon, queen bed, full kitchen, phone, TV and lanai with sweeping valley views.

Waipi'o Ridge Vacation Rental (☎ 775-0603, ⓔ *rlasko3343@aol.com*, *PO Box 5039, Kukuihaele, HI 96727*) Cottage $85/$450 daily/weekly double occupancy. Almost teetering on the cliff above the valley, this one-bedroom cottage has the location of a lifetime. If the view doesn't make you dizzy, the riot of aloha and tribal décor will. Avail yourself of the fully equipped kitchen and dine with an ethereal view. There's a queen bed, sofa bed, private bath, TV and VCR.

Also on this property is a funky, but comfortable Airstream trailer with lanai that sleeps three ($75/night or $390/week). There's a bath, outside shower and kitchenette. Access to these are just below the lookout.

Places to Eat

Luckily Honoka'a is just up the road because food pickings in Kukuihaele are slim.

The *Last Chance Store* (open 9am-3:30pm Mon-Sat) is aptly named as it's your last chance to stock up before Waipi'o Valley. This small grocery has what you might expect: snacks, canned chili, beer, water and wine.

The shop adjacent to *Waipi'o Valley Artworks* (☎ 775-0958, fax 775-0551, 800-492-4746) sells Tropical Dreams ice cream (the jury is still out whether this is better than Hilo Homemade), muffins, sandwiches and coffee; the shop is open 8am-5pm daily.

WAIPI'O VALLEY

Hwy 240 ends abruptly at the cliffs looming over Waipi'o Valley. The view is glorious on clear days, disappointing if there's haze. Multiple waterfalls burst from the cliff face during winter rains.

The largest and southernmost of the seven spectacular amphitheater valleys on the windward side of the Kohala Mountains, Waipi'o is a mile wide at the coast and nearly 6 miles deep. Some of the near-vertical *pali* (cliffs) wrapping around the valley reach heights of 2000 feet.

Everything in Waipi'o ('Curving Water' in Hawaiian) is a fertile tangle of jungle, flowering plants, taro patches and waterfalls. The mouth of the valley is fronted by a black-sand beach, which is cleaved by Waipi'o Stream. The whole place pulsates with *mana* (spiritual power), beckoning visitors to venture down.

Until very recently, there were two hotels tucked in the valley, and there may be one up and running when you arrive; otherwise you can camp in Waipi'o or Waimanu Valley beyond.

History

Waipi'o is called the 'Valley of the Kings' because it was once the political and religious center of Hawaii and home to the highest *ali'i* (chiefs or royalty). Caucuses convened here to appoint successors, mediate disputes and maintain harmony between the spiritual and earth-bound worlds. Waipi'o's sacred status is evidenced by the number of important heiau. The most

Valley of Kings, Gods and Shark-Men

Waipi'o Valley is considered sacred for many supernatural and regal reasons. Not only was this where the god Lono wooed his beautiful maiden Kaikilani and King Kamehameha I received the war god Ku, it was also where the progenitor gods Kane and Kanaloa debauched themselves on the land's bounty – including *awa*. According to legend, Kanaloa ('the awa-drinker') and his followers revolted following a prohibition upon the narcotic beverage and were consequently banished to the underworld. The portal to this land of the dead is said to be carved into the steep cliffs above Waipi'o.

Other powers that once – and perhaps still – called Waipi'o Valley home include Uli, the goddess of sorcery and the legendary shark-man Nenewe. The Waipi'o version of this popular legend holds that Nenewe was fed meat as a youth to make him a strong and accomplished warrior. He quickly developed a taste for richer flesh, however and started eating humans. He lured residents by warning them of shark attacks, but folks started disappearing and Nenewe topped the suspect list. Shark-men always have a shark's mouth marked on their back and Nenewe's exposed him as the homicidal culprit, whereupon he hauled tail to Maui to feast there.

Liloa was a chief who dwelled in Waipi'o Valley, very near the sacred heiau of Paka'alana. Liloa made several contributions to ancient Hawaiian culture: he introduced homosexual practices and sired Umi, the farmer and fisherman responsible for laying out Waipi'o's taro patches.

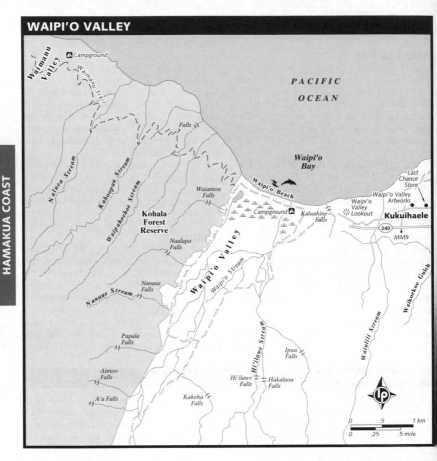

WAIPI'O VALLEY

sacred, Paka'alana, was the site of one of the island's two major pu'uhonua (the other is the Place of Refuge). It's hidden amongst the trees on the southern end of the beach.

Umi, who was the Big Island's ruling chief in the early 16th century, is credited with laying out Waipi'o's taro fields, many of which are still in production today. Waipi'o is also the site where Kamehameha the Great received the statue of his fearsome war god, Kukailimoku.

According to oral histories, at least 10,000 people – and possibly many times more – lived in Waipi'o before the arrival of Westerners. It was the most fertile and productive valley on the Big Island.

In 1823, William Ellis, the first missionary to visit the valley, guessed the population to be about 1300. Later in that century, immigrants, mainly Chinese, began to settle Waipi'o. At one time, the valley supported schools, restaurants and churches, as well as a post office and jail. In 1946, Hawaii's most devastating tsunami slammed great waves far back into the valley. Coincidentally or not, no one in this sacred place perished (likewise, all valley residents were also spared during the great 1979 flood). After the tsunami, most people resettled 'topside' and Waipi'o has been sparsely populated ever since.

Today, taro remains important in Waipi'o. Many of the valley's 50 or so residents have taro patches, and you may see farmers knee-deep in the muddy ponds.

Other Waipi'o crops include lotus (for its roots), avocados, breadfruit, oranges, limes and *pakalolo* (marijuana). There are *kukui* (candlenut) and mahogany trees, Turk's cap hibiscus, air plants and noni.

Hiking

From the Waipi'o Valley Lookout at the end of Hwy 240, you can see the switchback trail ('Z-trail' to locals) that leads to Waimanu Valley on the opposite cliff face. From the lookout you'll also glimpse the rugged coastal cliffs that stretch out to the northwest and on the clearest days, you can see Maui outlined darkly in the distance.

The mile-long, paved sinew of road that leads down into Waipi'o Valley is so steep (25% grade) that it's open only to hikers and 4WD vehicles (though standard cars with good drivers can make it). Tour companies do the run daily, but the trek down is easier than it looks. It's pretty easy to hitch a ride back up. There are toilets topside at the lookout, but the water isn't potable, so stock up in Honoka'a.

The roundtrip hike (30 minutes down, one hour up) from the lookout to the valley floor isn't terribly arduous, but forgotten muscles will tingle the next day if you're out of shape and old knees will knock with the steep grade. It's shady most of the way. Nevertheless, you'll work up a sweat, so be sure to carry water. From the bottom of the hill, walk to the left for about five minutes, for a chance to see the wild horses that graze along the stream here. It's a beautiful Hawaiian tableau, with precipitous cliffs as a backdrop.

You'll also get a distant view of **Hi'ilawe Falls**, which is Hawaii's highest free-fall waterfall – a sheer drop of more than 1000 feet. According to legend, Lono, the god of abundance and excess, slid down from the heavens and discovered Kaikilani, the beautiful woman who became his wife, sitting beside Hi'ilawe Falls.

Hiking to Hi'ilawe Falls is possible, but it's challenging, as there's no real trail – another of those bushwhacking, 'whose idea was this anyway?' type of hikes. You'll spend most of the 90 minutes or so rock hopping slippery boulders and trying to dope out which way to go (even the GSPS sheet for the valley isn't much help). Only goats will make it to the falls in the heart of the rainy season.

Keep in mind that many valley residents living so far removed from life's normal rigors are doing so with good reason, so there are a lot of 'Keep Out' signs. Generally the farther back in the valley you go, the less friendly the dogs become.

Waipi'o Beach It's about a 10-minute walk from the bottom of the hill to the beach, but tack on an extra 10 minutes and a pound of mud if it has rained recently.

Waipi'o Beach is lined with graceful ironwood trees serving as a barrier against the winds that sometimes whip through here. Surfers catch wave action at Waipi'o, but mind the rip currents and if the sea seems too rough, it is. Rogue waves and a treacherous undertow are features of the roiling ocean here. When it's calm, Waipi'o Beach is sublime and you might encounter spinner dolphins.

Walk along the beach toward the stream mouth for a good view of **Kaluahine Falls**, which cascade down the cliffs to the east. Getting to them is easier said than done, as the coast between Waipi'o Beach and the falls is loose lava rock and a nightmare on the ankles. If you go for it, respect the sea as high surf can be dangerous and if she really wants you, she'll have you.

Local lore has it that Night Marchers periodically come down from the upper valley to the beach and march to *Lua o Milu,* an entrance to the netherworld hidden among the cliffs.

Switchback Trail to Waimanu Valley

The switchback trail up the northwest cliff face is an ancient Hawaiian footpath. It

HAMAKUA COAST

looks harder than it actually is – unless you're heavily burdened with a backpack. It's a well-beaten path, worn a few feet deep in places – almost like walking in a little trough. If you are laboring along, take heart: once you reach the ridge, the trail gets much easier.

Doing part of the trail makes a nice day hike from Waipi'o, but hoofing it all the way to Waimanu Valley and back in a day is unrealistic. It takes about 90 minutes from the floor of Waipi'o Valley to the third gulch, where there are little pools and a small waterfall. The trail is used by hikers and hunters, who come up this way to bag wild boar.

The trail continues up and down a series of ravines to Waimanu Valley. From Waipi'o Valley to Waimanu is about 8 miles in all, but because the switchbacks make for slow going, it will take about seven hours (though gung-ho Hawaiians have been known to do it in four!).

Waimanu is a mini-Waipi'o, less the tourists. This too is a stunning deep valley framed by escarpments, waterfalls and a black-sand beach. On any given day, you will bask alone amongst all this beauty, as most visitors only behold this valley from a helicopter.

Waimanu Valley once had a sizable settlement and contains many ruins, including house and heiau terraces, stone enclosures and old taro ponds. In the early 19th century, Waimanu was inhabited by an estimated 200 people, but by the turn of the 20th century, only three families remained. Since the 1946 tsunami, the valley has been abandoned.

Because it represents an unaltered Hawaiian freshwater ecosystem, Waimanu Valley has been set aside as a national estuarine sanctuary, and the removal of any plant or aquatic life (except for freshwater prawns and ocean fish) is forbidden.

The mighty taro

All freshwater available on this hike must be treated before drinking.

Rumor has it that you can hike through the valleys beyond Waimanu all the way to Polulu; If any of you survive it successfully, please drop us a line.

Dangers & Annoyances Even though waterfalls are full and gorgeous, the winter rainy season is hardly the optimum time to hike anywhere along the Hamakua Coast, and this is especially true in these valleys. During heavy rains, streams in Waipi'o can swell to impassable, usually for just a few hours at a time, although occasionally for longer periods. Flash floods are also possible (for more on those nasties, see the Dangers & Annoyances section of the Facts for the Visitor chapter). Don't succumb to macho hiker syndrome: it's dangerous to attempt crossing swollen streams if the water reaches above your knees.

Because feral animals roam the area, precautions against leptospirosis are advisable (see the Health section in the Facts for the Visitor chapter), though the only 100% fool-proof way of avoiding contamination is not venturing into freshwater. Taro farmers in Waipi'o have one of Hawaii's highest incident rates of this waterborne ailment.

Don't drink from any creeks or streams without first boiling or treating the water.

Organized Tours

You can hike, horseback ride, bounce around in a wagon or be chauffeured in a 4-WD on organized tours into and around Waipi'o Valley. All tours leave from either the Last Chance Store or Waipi'o Valley Artworks, both in Kukuihaele.

Waipi'o Valley Shuttle (☎ 775-7121) Adult/child $40/20. Tours depart 9am, 11am, 1pm, 3pm Mon-Sat. This company offers 90 minute tours in 4WD vans. These are essentially taxi tours for those who don't want to walk, though the driver does point out waterfalls, identify plants and throw in a bit of history. The tours leave from The Last Chance Store.

Waipi'o Valley Wagon Tours (☎ 775-9518) Adult/child $40/20. Tours depart

9:30am, 11:30am, 1:30pm Mon-Sat. An alternative to the van tours is this one-hour jaunt across the valley floor in an open mule-drawn wagon (clients are spirited to the valley floor via 4-WD). The tour guide gives commentary on the valley's history as he carts visitors along Waipi'o's rutted dirt roads and fords rocky streams. Tours leave from the Last Chance Store.

Waipi'o on Horseback (☎ 775-7291) Trail ride $75. A more adventurous possibility is touring the valley on horseback. This friendly outfit offers a 2½-hour ride in the valley at 9:30am and 1:30pm, Monday to Friday and ranch rides on Sundays. Tours depart form the Last Chance Store.

Waipi'o Na'alapa Trail Rides (☎ 775-0419) Trail ride $75. This operator has a 2½-hour trail ride in the valley at 9:30am and 1pm. There are no rides on Sunday or during bad weather. Check in 30 minutes before scheduled departure at Waipi'o Valley Artworks.

Waipi'o Ridge Stables (☎ 775-1007, **w** *www.topofwaipio.com*) Trail ride $145. This outfit offers more extensive 5-hour tours that follow the usual route along the valley rim, followed by a trot to Hi'ilawe Falls, ending with a picnic and a swim at a hidden waterfall. Tours leave from Waipi'o Valley Artworks.

Places to Stay

Camping is permitted at designated sites in Waipi'o Valley, and backcountry camping is allowed in Waimanu Valley.

Bishop Estate, which owns most of Waipi'o Valley, allows camping at four primitive sites (no toilet, no water; campers are required to bring their own chemical toilets) inland from the beach. The maximum stay is four days, and you must apply for a permit at least two weeks in advance (summer and weekends are in high demand, so reserve your spots as early as possible). The permit requires each camper to sign a liability waiver. The permits are free and the camping well worth the rigmarole. Obtain permits in advance by calling or writing the Bishop Estate (☎ 322-5300, fax 322-9446), 78-6831 Ali'i Drive, suite 232, Kailua-Kona,

HI 96740. The office is in the Keauhou Shopping Center just south of Kailua-Kona and is open 7:30am-4:30pm, Monday to Friday.

In *Waimanu Valley*, which is managed by the state, camping for up to six nights is allowed free by permit. Facilities include fire pits and a couple of composting outhouses. Camping reservations are taken no more than 30 days in advance by the Division of Forestry & Wildlife (☎ 974-4221, PO Box 4849, 19 E Kawili, Hilo, HI 96720). You can apply for the permit by phone; with enough advance notice (two weeks or so), the permit can be mailed to you. Otherwise, the actual permit can be picked up during office hours either at the forestry office in Hilo or at the state tree nursery on Hwy 190 in Waimea.

KALOPA STATE RECREATION AREA

Kalopa State Recreation Area is a few miles southeast of Honoka'a and about 3 miles *mauka* (inland), from the marked turnoff on Hwy 19.

Not many folks make it out to this 100-acre park of native rain forest, with its picnic sites and sweet camping cabins. At an elevation of 2000 feet, it's cooler and wetter than the coast, averaging about 90 inches of rain a year.

The park has a 2-mile trail to the Kalopa Gulch in the adjoining forest reserve. Begin trekking along Robusta Lane, on the left between the caretaker's house and the campgrounds. It's about a third of a mile to the edge of the gulch through a thick forest of tall eucalyptus trees. The gulch was formed eons ago by the erosive movement of melting glaciers that originated at Mauna Kea. A trail continues along the rim of the gulch for another mile, and a number of side trails along the way branch off and head west back into the park.

Kalopa State Recreation Area also has a nature trail, beginning near the cabins, which loops for three-quarters of a mile through an old ohia forest where some of the trees measure more than 3 feet in diameter. Kalopa's woods are habitat for the *elepaio*, an easily spotted native forest bird about the size of a sparrow. It's brown and white and makes a loud whistle that sounds like its name.

Tent camping is in a pleasant, grassy area surrounded by tall trees. There are rest rooms and covered pavilions with electricity, running water, barbecue grills, picnic tables – the works! The air takes on a nighttime chill, but this still rates as one of the Big Island's best camping spots; you might even have it all to yourself.

The simple **group cabins** are one of the greatest values going: for $55 you get a cabin for eight people with bunk beds, sheets and towels. Additionally, there are shared hot showers, a fully equipped kitchen and tables and chairs for that late night poker game.

Permits are required for the cabins and *technically* for the campsites as well. For details, see Camping in the Accommodations section of the Facts for the Visitor chapter.

LAUPAHOEHOE

It would be misleading to actually call Laupahoehoe (pronounced lau-pa-hoy-hoy) a town, what with its 2100 residents spread out over a dozen miles. But what it lacks in size it makes up for in spunk. Case in point is the **Laupahoehoe Train Museum** (☎ *962-6300, fax 962-2221,* ⓦ *www.geocities.com/trainmuseum; adults/seniors & children $3/2; open 9am-4:30 Mon-Fri, 10am-2pm Sat).*

This all-volunteer museum is a labor of community love. Housed in a historic home once belonging to a railroad employee, the museum collects all the ephemera, knick-knacks and nostalgia of the bygone Hawaiian railroad era. The docents are amazingly knowledgeable and burst with pride when speaking of the restored length of track, 'Rusty' the switch engine and the other pieces of train history that keep rolling in. Look for 'Rusty' in front of the museum between the 25-and 26-mile markers on Hwy 19.

Self-starters, and motivated individuals are encouraged to contact the museum about volunteer opportunities.

People interested in visiting the **Hakalau Forest National Wildlife Refuge** should see the Waimea chapter, as there is no makai access to this pristine chunk of green. Birders will be particularly interested in this remote area, which protects at least eight endangered species.

Laupahoehoe Point

Midway between Honoka'a and Hilo, Laupahoehoe Point is 1⅓ miles down a steep, winding road to the coast. There are cliff views and waterfalls springing to life from all directions after heavy downpours.

Laupahoehoe means 'leaf of pahoehoe lava,' which is appropriate for this flat peninsula-like point that was formed by a feisty Mauna Kea eruption. Lava slithered down a ravine and out into the sea, eventually hardening into Laupahoehoe Point.

Tragedy hit Laupahoehoe on April 1, 1946, when tsunami waves up to 30 feet high pounded ashore, killing 20 children and four adults. After the tsunami, nearly the whole town moved uphill, not wanting to push their luck. A monument on a hillock above the water lists those who died. Every April, there's a community festival at the Point with food, music and old timers 'talking story.'

Laupahoehoe is a rugged coastal area not suitable for swimming. The surf is usually rough and sometimes crashes up over the rocks and onto the lower parking lot (roll up those windows).

Interisland boats once landed here. Indeed, many of the immigrants who came to work the sugarcane fields along the Hamakua Coast first set foot on the Big Island at Laupahoehoe.

The county beach park on the point has rest rooms, *campsites*, showers, potable water, picnic pavilions and electricity, and it's relatively secluded. All this makes it convenient for camping, but ideal for late-night partying, too. Locals keen to throw back a few or 10 sometimes use the park as a drinking hangout and it can get fairly rowdy.

For information on a camping permits, see Camping in the Accommodations section of the Facts for the Visitor chapter.

UMAUMA FALLS & WORLD BOTANICAL GARDENS

At the 16-mile marker, is the World Botanical Gardens (☎ 963-5427; adult/child $7/free; 9am-5:30 Mon-Sat). If you're a gardener or have visited other Hawaiian gardens, this place will probably disappoint. The big draw is their unadulterated view of **Umauma Falls**: a tripartite waterfall cascading to the river below. Free admission is available to hikers (see below) on Sundays, when the gardens are closed. Take the left across from the garden entrance and drive 6 miles, or follow the road past the garden entrance to the little stone wall on the left (about a quarter of a mile).

Hardy (some would say foolhardy) visitors can try to hike up Umauma Stream to the falls, but beware: It's a neck-risking, ankle-wrenching, boulder-hopping trial if it has rained lately. Otherwise, it's a walk in the park – just wade on up.

To set out, drive past the World Botanical Gardens for about half a mile to just before the narrow bridge.

Descend the slippery slope on the near side of the bridge and start heading up river (with the bridge at your back). it's less than a mile to the falls, but plan on a 90-minute to two-hour hike (yes, it's that bad!) and wear the most grippy reef shoes you can find.

Hike with a buddy, bring water and plan on getting wet. There's no access along the banks, so you'll have to wade upriver or rock hop over slimy boulders. It can flash flood here before you can yell 'run!' so get up and out fast if it starts to rain. Famished mosquitoes add to the fun.

KOLEKOLE BEACH PARK

This grassy park is at the side of Kolekole Stream, which flows down from Akaka Falls. There are small waterfalls that swell to gushers when it rains, picnic tables, barbecue pits, rest rooms and showers, all of which make the park a popular weekend picnic spot for families.

Ocean swimming is dangerous here, but locals **surf** and **boogie board**. Assess the currents and breaks before paddling out. The shore is a jumble of tide-smoothed boulders and not good for chilling at the beach in the classic sense.

Camping is allowed with a permit from the county, though weekend and summer days the park hops with picnicking families and teenage sweethearts leaning into their libidos. For information on obtaining a camping permit, see Camping in the Accommodations section in the Facts for the Visitor chapter.

To get to the park, turn inland off Hwy 19 at the south end of the Kolekole Bridge, about three-quarters of a mile south of the 15-mile marker.

HONOMU

Honomu is an old sugar town that might have been forgotten, if not for its location on Hwy 220 en route to Akaka Falls. As it is, things are pretty slow here and almost sickeningly cute: nestled amongst the galleries and antique peddlers, there's all the tourist claptrap you can imagine, including the Teddy Bear Store of Hawaii.

Still, there's at least one superb gallery. **Hawaii's Artist Ohana** (☎ 963-5467) on Hwy 220 has a broad collection of fine Big Island art and handiwork, including fiber baskets, wooden bowls, pottery, jewelry and paintings. The gallery is open Tuesday to Saturday 10:30am to 5:30pm.

There are no places to stay in Honomu proper, but the nearby Palms Cliff House on the makai side of Hwy 19 is one option, as is Akiko's Buddhist Bed & Breakfast in Hakalau, just two miles up the road from Honomu.

Palms Cliff House (☎ 963-6076, fax 963-6316, ⓦ www.palmscliffhouse.com, PO Box 189, Honomu, HI 96728) Single or double $175-375. If you're rich and in love, let the good times roll at this place for a night or three. Each of the eight rooms is different, but all have a private lanai, views overlooking Pohakumanu Bay, plush linens and marble baths. The more expensive rooms have Jacuzzis with views and gas fireplaces. All guests can use the garden hot tub and rates include a gourmet breakfast on the dining lanai. Non-guests can also avail

HAMAKUA COAST

themselves of this breakfast feast for $25; reservations recommended. Look for the sign just after the 13-mile marker on the makai side of Hwy 19.

Akiko's Buddhist Bed & Breakfast (☎/fax 963-6422, W *www.alternative-hawaii.com/akiko, PO Box 272, Hakalau, HI 96710*) Daily singles/doubles $40/55, weekly $265/365, monthly $550/750. This is a gem for the spiritually inclined. There are three types of rooms: spare, but comfortable spaces with futons leading to the meditation room; proper beds in a small plantation house; or a self-contained studio (two-week minimum). All the options are clean, cozy and marked by the style of the proprietress (eg, altars, incense and paper lanterns). Akiko's is not for everyone: silence is observed daily between 6:30pm and 6am in the main house, all bathrooms are shared and it's away from any town. Still, if you're on the wavelength, the air of peace permeating the place, daily meditation sessions (5:30am) and family feel will not disappoint.

Akiko also has the Montanaga Garage Gallery adjacent. This funky, grand gallery and performance space is in a converted mechanic's garage. Past events have included photography and sculpture exhibits and gigs by ukulele masters. The calendar is varied; visit the Web site for the latest.

Yoga classes are also on offer in Akiko's beautiful studio out back; classes are drop-in and open to the public on Sundays at 8:30am ($8).

AKAKA FALLS STATE PARK
Turn onto Hwy 220 from Hwy 19 (between the 13-and 14-mile marker) to visit the Big Island's most impressive, easy-to-view waterfall. It shouldn't be missed.

The waterfall lookout is along a half-mile rain forest loop that's a 20-minute stroll from the parking lot. The unevenly paved trail passes through dense and varied vegetation, including massive philodendrons, fragrant ginger, dangling heliconia, orchids and gigantic bamboo groves. Looking upon the last – some of which soar to 40 feet – you'll believe the saying that 'bamboo grows six inches a day.'

Start the loop trail by going to the right, and you'll come first to the 100-foot **Kahuna Falls**. It's a pretty waterfall, but kind of wimpy when compared to its neighbor. Up ahead is **Akaka Falls**, dropping a sheer 420 feet down a fern-draped cliff. Its mood depends on the weather – sometimes it rushes with a mighty roar, and at other times it gently cascades. Either way it's beautiful. With a little luck, you might catch a rainbow winking in the spray.

A word to the worldly: though Akaka Falls are truly big and breathtaking, the approach is almost *too* easy for folks with some falls under their belt. Sights like these feel like they should be earned – perhaps you'll agree as you gaze upon the falls while a fellow nearby squawks inanely into his cell phone.

PEPE'EKEO 4-MILE SCENIC DRIVE
The 4-mile scenic loop between the 7- and 8-mile markers en route to Honomu from Hilo makes for a majestic, tropical cruise. The road crosses a string of one-lane bridges spanning little streams. In places the African tulip canopy meets, casting a lacy net across the sky, while the orange blossoms bejewel the road. Squashed lilikoi (passion fruit) and guava are mingled among the flowers and mango trees soar over it all. Harvest from the roadside if the fresh fruit urge strikes. There are many small paths leading to babbling rivers and the shore along here: look for one on the right about 2½ miles along, just after the one-lane wooden bridge.

The road is well marked on the highway at both ends, with the south end about 7 miles north of Hilo. Towards the north end is the often raved about smoothie stop called *What's Shakin'* (☎ 964-3080) Smoothies are $3.85-4.25, and it's open 10am-5pm daily.

Hawaii Tropical Botanical Garden
If your wallet is bursting with green and you crave more scenery, stop in at the Hawaii Tropical Botanical Garden (☎ 964-5233, W *www.hawaiigarden.com; adult/child 6-16*

years $15/5; open 9am-5pm daily, last entry 4pm) a nature preserve with 2000 species of tropical plants and a couple of streams and waterfalls.

Buy your ticket at the yellow building on the inland side of the road, then walk down to the valley garden at nearby Onomea Bay. Note that it is a steep incline, so it can be challenging for little feet and tired knees.

Onomea Bay Trail

For a quick and pretty hike down to photogenic Onomea Bay, take the Na Ala Hele trailhead on the right just after the Hawaii Tropical Botanical Garden. After a 10-minute hike down a trail that's steep and slippery when wet, you'll come to a finger of lava jutting into the sea. A spur to the right goes to a couple of small waterfalls and a cove where the fresh and salt water meet. Continuing straight on brings you to the diminutive bluffs overlooking the batik blues of Onomea Bay. Look for the rope tied to the almond tree for secluded, low tide beach access. The mosquitoes here are ravenous, but the views compensate.

Hilo

Hilo (pronounced hee-lo) is the county capital and the Big Island's commercial and population center. But before Hilo puffs up in your mind's eye like an irate blowfish, consider that most folks call it 'old Hilo town,' befitting its pace; original wood facades with corrugated eaves make up the waterfront business district; and the population is just 47,000.

Then there's Hilo's graceful beauty, which seeps into the subconscious as you catch sight of Mauna Kea standing guard over Hilo Bay's sinuous shoreline, a paradisiacal tableau dotted with outrigger canoes and swaying palms. On a clear day, Hilo beguiles. And therein lies the rub, for the problem is finding a clear day: according to official statistics, measurable rain falls in Hilo 278 days of the average year, adding up to just over 129 inches annually. Indeed, this estimate seems optimistic and has led to the saying that 'in Hilo, people don't tan, they rust,' to which we'd append 'and molder.'

But while such copious rainfall means perpetually damp towels, it also means gushing waterfalls, tropical fruits thudding to the ground, verdant thickets of orchids and lush valleys and gardens galore. Toto, I have a feeling we're not in Kona anymore.

These conditions are ideal for growing tropical plants, flowers and fruit and are responsible for the Big Island nicknames of the Orchid Isle and the Anthurium Isle. Though anthuriums as a major industry may be on the wane as Latin American growers move into the market with cheaper product, over 20,000 orchid varieties still grow with conviction here. In fact, the orchid industry based in good old Hilo town is the world's largest.

The rains also serve to keep developers and spun sugar tourists away. Though they try, resorts have never been able to make a go of it on the windward side, and in many ways Hilo is the last Hawaiian city unaffected by mass tourism. The 'rainiest city in the US' just can't compete with the sun-

Highlights

- Strolling amongst the regal grounds of the Lili'uokalani Gardens with majestic Mauna Kea in the background
- Catching your first wave at Honoli'i Beach Park
- Checking out the Lyman Museum and Pacific Tsunami Museum
- Thrift shopping for vintage aloha wear and Sonny Chillingworth LPs
- Hip swaying to the world's finest hula performances at the Merrie Monarch Festival
- Picnicking and splashing about at beautiful Rainbow or Pe'epe'e Falls

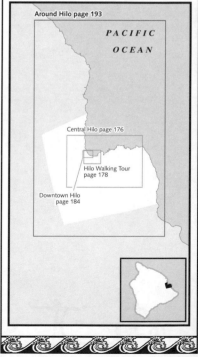

Around Hilo page 193

PACIFIC OCEAN

Central Hilo page 176

Hilo Walking Tour page 178

Downtown Hilo page 184

HILO

drenched beaches of the Kona coast. As a result, Hilo is one of Hawaii's best-kept secrets.

Hilo provides easier access to Hawaii Volcanoes National Park, is more affordable than the Kona side, has a sophisticated, diverse cultural scene, and boasts more hot tubs and saunas than swimming pools.

What's more, Hilo is an ethnic montage, with residents of Japanese, Korean, Filipino, Portuguese, Puerto Rican, Hawaiian and Caucasian descent living harmoniously together (sometimes in the same body!). There's also an alternative community that's taken root since the 1970s, attracted by Hilo's cheap rents, mellow pace and gorgeous scenery. Hilo is super pedestrian friendly: distances aren't too onerous, drivers are courteous and wide, pleasant streets run through with mysterious back alleys invite strolling.

Information

Tourist Offices The Big Island Visitors Bureau (☎ 961-5797), on the corner of Haili and Keawe Sts, is open 8am to 4:30pm Monday to Friday.

Pick up camping permits in the County Offices at the County Department of Parks & Recreation (☎ 961-8311), 25 Aupuni St, Rm 210, from 8:30am to 4pm Monday to Friday or the Division of State Parks (☎ 974-6200), 75 Aupuni St, Rm 204 in the State Offices, from 8am to 3:30pm Monday to Friday. Both are near Wailoa River State Park.

Money The Bank of Hawaii has branches at 120 Pauahi and 417 E Kawili; First Hawaiian Bank has branches at 1205 Kilauea Ave in the Hilo Shopping Center and downtown on Waianuenue Ave near Keawe St.

Post Befitting a county capital, Hilo has two post offices. The main one, (where general delivery mail is held), is on the road into the airport. It's open 8:15am to 4:45pm Monday to Thursday, 8:15am to 5pm Friday and 8:30am to 12:30pm Saturday. The zip code is 96720.

The more convenient downtown post office is in the federal building on Waianuenue Ave. It's open 8am to 4pm Monday to Friday and 12:30pm to 4pm on Saturday.

For Federal Express, UPS and packing supplies, PostNet (☎ 959-0066) at the Prince Kuhio Plaza, 111 E Puainako St, No 585, is the place to go. It's open 9am to 7pm on weekdays, 9am to 4pm on Saturday and 10am to 4pm on Sunday. These folks also offer Internet access at competitive prices.

Email & Internet Access You can check your email at the very friendly and centrally located Beach Dog Rental & Sales (☎ 961-5207), 62 Kinoole St. It cost $2 for 20 minutes with a fast connection. Also available are printers, scanners and free coffee. It's open 10am to 7pm Monday to Friday and 10am to 2pm on Saturday.

Another option for Internet access is Mail Boxes Etc (☎ 959-9330) in the Puainako Town Center. Rental costs are $3 for 15 minutes or $10/hour.

With a library card ($10 for visitors), you can check your email free, once a week, at the Hilo library (see that section later).

Travel Agencies Cut Rate Tickets (☎ 969-1944), behind the Minit Stop gas station at Leilani St and Hwy 11, sells interisland coupons. It's open 8am-7pm Monday to Friday, 9am-5pm Saturday and 9am-2pm Sunday. Coupons are also sold at the KTA Superstore in the Puainako Town Center or at Bank of Hawaii ATMs.

Hawaiian Airlines (☎ 935-0858) has an office at 120 Kamehameha Ave; it's open 8am to noon and 1:15pm-4pm Monday to Friday.

For a full-service agency, try Regal Travel (☎ 935-5796) in the Hilo Shopping Center.

Bookstores Basically Books (☎ 961-0144, 800-903-6277, W www.basicallybooks.com), 160 Kamehameha Ave, is a terrific book store specializing in maps and Hawaiiana, including out-of-print books, activity guides and literature. The store also carries many guidebooks and USGS topographic maps of Hawaii and the Pacific.

HILO

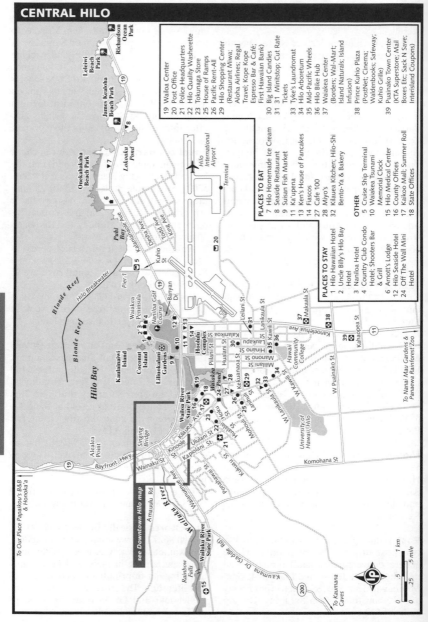

There's a Borders (☎ 933-1410) book-store on Hwy 11 in the Waiakea Center, with a good selection of newspapers, maga-zines and local music CDs. They host special events and have a café inside. There is also a Waldenbooks in the Prince Kuhio Plaza.

Library The Hilo library (☎ 933-8888), 300 Waianuenue Ave, is a honey, with an open interior garden flanked by desks and read-ing tables, an awesome Hawaiiana section, a good selection of CDs and movies and two Internet terminals. Internet access is free with a library card, but patrons are limited to one reserved and one walk-in session per week; sessions last 50 minutes.

The library is open 10am-5pm Mon and Tuesday, 9am-7pm Wed and Thur, 9am-5pm Fri and 9am-4pm Saturday. For information on obtaining a library card, see the Libraries section in the Facts for the Visitor chapter.

Laundry Hilo Quality Washerette, 210 Hoku St, is directly behind the 7-Eleven on Kinoole St. More low-key is Tyke's Laun-dromat at 1454 Kilauea Ave, next to the Kilauea Kitchen. Both are open 6am to 10pm daily.

Emergency For police, fire and ambu-lance, dial ☎ 911. The hospital, Hilo Medical Center, is at 1190 Waianuenue Ave, near Rainbow Falls; for information, dial ☎ 974-4700; for the emergency room, dial ☎ 974-6800. The police department headquarters (☎ 935-3311) is at 349 Kapiolani St.

Hilo Walking Tour

This leisurely 90-minute walk will ignite your imagination, particularly on a sunny day. When it's clear, you'll see the astron-omy observatories atop Mauna Kea out-lined like meringue peaks against the blue sky, drawing the heavens closer to earth and the summit closer to Hilo.

Begin at Kamehameha Ave near Manono St, where time stands still at the **Waiakea Tsunami Memorial Clock**. The clock is stuck on 1:05, the exact moment in the predawn hours of May 23, 1960 when Hilo's last major tsunami swept ashore.

Walking northwest towards downtown, you can duck into the **Suisan Fish Market** for some poke as fresh as it comes and head to the peaceful grounds of the **Lili'uokalani Gardens** to enjoy your pupus. This 30-acre garden named for Hawaii's last queen is filled with koi ponds, little Japanese pago-das, stone lanterns, arched bridges and clutches of bamboo. Many of the lanterns and pagodas were donated by Japanese re-gional governments and sister cities in honor of the 100th anniversary of Japanese immigration to Hawaii. The two miles of paths here are perfect for a sunset stroll or early morning jog.

If you like, detour from the walking tour (or abandon it altogether) and walk over to **Coconut Island** or **Banyan Drive**. For more on those sites, see their individual headings later.

Continuing on Kamehameha Ave across the Wailoa River and Bridge, veer towards the shoreline of **Bayfront Beach Park**. Loads of birds and pretty palms dance along the water and there are expansive views of Hilo Bay and Hilo town, with Mauna Kea and Mauna Loa in the distance; the lush cliffs curving north up the coast are also visible.

Walking along the shore you'll see several **outrigger canoe clubs**, with their rigs propped up on grassy expanses. On week-ends especially, regional rivals may be train-ing or competing with these seafaring marvels. A couple of hundred feet on, the shore ends in a rocky jumble and you'll have to walk on the shoulder between northbound traffic (such as it is) and the sea – don't worry, it's not as bad as it sounds.

At the first opportunity, cross over Kamehameha Ave to the northwest corner of Waianuenue St and check out the **F Koehnen Building**. Here's a recently refur-bished, typical example of Hilo's early 20th century bayfront architecture.

Heading east, you'll come to the **Pacific Tsunami Museum** at the corner of Kame-hameha Ave and Kalakaua St. Designed by renowned Honolulu architect CW Dickey (considered the creator of the Hawaiian Regional architectural style) and completed in 1930, this building miraculously survived

HILO

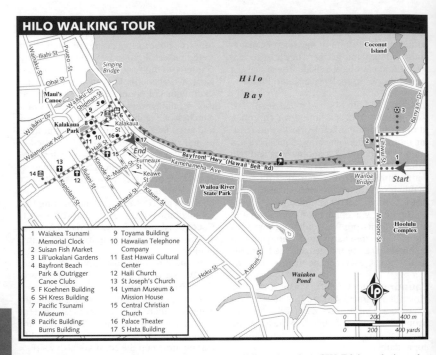

HILO WALKING TOUR

1 Waiakea Tsunami Memorial Clock
2 Suisan Fish Market
3 Lili'uokalani Gardens
4 Bayfront Beach Park & Outrigger Canoe Clubs
5 F Koehnen Building
6 SH Kress Building
7 Pacific Tsunami Museum
8 Pacific Building; Burns Building
9 Toyama Building
10 Hawaiian Telephone Company
11 East Hawaii Cultural Center
12 Haili Church
13 St Joseph's Church
14 Lyman Museum & Mission House
15 Central Christian Church
16 Palace Theater
17 S Hata Building

both the 1946 and 1960 tsunamis. Notice the tsunami-cam on the roof of the building, which projects live surf images 24/7/365. For more information on the museum, see its individual entry later.

Just east on Kamehameha Ave is the **SH Kress** building with its art deco accents done up in institutional pastels (puke yellow, penitentiary blue, etc). Now a movie theater, you might pop in for a $4.75 matinee.

Walking up Kalakaua St and across Keawe, look north and you'll see the **Pacific Building** (1922) and the **Burns Building** next door. The earth toned, geometric accents of the former epitomize understated elegance. Across Waianuenue is the **Toyama Bldg** (1908), recently painstakingly restored to show off its jester fringe and rose windows. This part of town has trim that would make San Francisco's painted ladies blush.

Follow Kalakaua St to the west and you'll come to the jewel in Hilo's architectural crown: the **Hawaiian Telephone Company** building. Another CW Dickey design, the details on this building are amazing. There's the hipped roof and terra cotta tiles most obviously, but notice the metalwork details on the windows, the painted panels on the underside of the eaves, the hearts on the crossbeams and the copper drain spout with floral catchment.

Next door is the **East Hawaii Cultural Center** (☎ 961-5771; ⓦ www.lastplace.com/EXHIBITS/EHCC; 141 Kalakaua St; admission by $2 donation; open 10am-4pm Mon-Sat). Completed in 1932, this building also has a hipped roof and other features (like the covered lanai) typical to island homes of the 1800s. On the National Register of Historic Buildings and Places, this was the Hilo Police station until 1975. Gallery openings, plays and performances are periodically held here. They also offer language, culture and craft courses.

Both buildings face **Kalakaua Park** and the neoclassical federal building beyond.

The center of the park is dominated by a majestic banyan that makes you wish trees could talk. Nearby sits the **King Kalakaua statue** (the Merrie Monarch). The taro leaf by the King's side symbolizes his connection with the land, while the *ipu* (hula drum) on his right stands for the Hawaiian culture that he helped revive. The park also has a Korean War veterans memorial, a reflecting pool choked with lilies and a time capsule sealed on the last total solar eclipse (July 11, 1991). It's due to be opened on the next one (May 3, 2106).

Heading away from the park and federal building on Kinoole St brings you to Haili St. Once known as Church Street for all the houses of worship lining it, it has a stretch of interesting sites. Make a right and walk to the Congregational **Haili Church** on the corner of Ululani St. This yellow clapboard cutie was built in 1859 and looks like it was transplanted straight from the New England countryside. Services are held here in Hawaiian and English.

Across Haili at the corner of Kapiolani Sts is **St Joseph's Church**. A pink paean to the Catholic faith built in 1919, it has stained glass windows with trumpeting angels and other inspirational designs.

A few steps away across Kapiolani St is the venerable **Lyman Museum & Mission House**. See the individual heading later for information on this excellent museum.

If you still have some gas in your tank, you can walk down Haili St towards the bay, stopping at the Victorian-style **Central Christian Church** on the corner of Kilauea and the 1925 **Palace Theater** a little farther along.

Around the corner is the **S Hata Building** (1912) at 308 Kamehameha Ave. This is a fine example of Renaissance revival architecture and is an interesting piece of history in that it was expropriated from the original Japanese owners by the US government during WW II.

Lyman Museum & Mission House

The Lyman Museum is a first-class museum and a great place to spend a rainy afternoon (☎ 935-5021, fax 965-7685, ☑ *www.lyman museum.org, 276 Haili St; adult/senior/child 6-17 years/family $7/5/3/12.50; open 9am-4:30pm Mon-Sat)*.

The Earth Heritage Gallery immediately sucks you into the heart of the volcano that marks the museum's newest and greatest installation: Hawaii Before Humans. Through the lava tube you go, escorted by the sights and sounds of volcanic eruptions, curtains of fire and molten lava, delivered via hidden speakers and TV monitors. The well-written exhibit takes you through Hawaii's geological history from the first volcanic cone that broke the sea's surface, to the Loihi Seamount. Visually and intellectually stimulating, it's a great addition to an already singular museum.

Elsewhere, you'll learn how adzes were made of volcanic clinker, kukui nuts were skewered on coconut-frond spines to burn as candles, and other aspects of life in ancient Hawaii. Exhibits include fine feather leis, tapa cloth and a pili grass house. Mana, kahuna and *awa* (kava) drinking are all succinctly explained.

The museum has a world-class mineral exhibit with thousands of rocks, crystals and gemstones. There are explanations of volcanic eruptions and lava formations with samples of spatter, olivine, Pele's tears and Pele's hair.

The astronomy exhibit has celestial displays, plus an introduction to the latest happenings in the world of astronomy via two computers linked to Mauna Kea summit observatories.

Adjacent to the museum is the **Mission House**, built by the Reverend David Lyman and his wife, Sarah, in 1839. The two missionaries had seven children and boarded a number of island boys who attended their church school.

The docent-led Mission House tour will give you a good sense of the people who lived here. The house has many of the original furnishings, including Sarah Lyman's melodeon, china dishes and old patchwork quilts. The tours are given at 10:30am and 11:30am and 1pm, 2pm, 3pm and are included in the museum admission price.

HILO

The Mission House encourages interested volunteers (long-term or for special events) to call for an application.

Pacific Tsunami Museum

The newest addition to Hilo's cultural collection is the Pacific Tsunami Museum (☎ 935-0926, fax 935-0842, Ⓦ *www.tsunami .org, 130 Kamehameha Ave; adult/senior/ student $5/4/2; 9am-4pm Mon-Sat*).

This well-curated, multimedia museum captures the destructive horror and triumphant survival left in the wake of Pacific tsunamis. Although tsunamis have killed more Hawaiians than all other natural disasters combined, this museum covers the entire Pacific region.

Oral histories, survivor stories and documentary pieces (including those about the David Douglas murder and Mark Twain's

---

Little Tokyo & Big Tsunamis

On April 1, 1946, Hilo Bay was inundated by a tsunami that had raced across the Pacific from an earthquake epicenter in the Aleutian Islands. It struck at 6:54am without warning.

Fifty-foot waves jumped the seawall and swept over the city. They ripped the first line of buildings from their foundations, carrying them inland and smashing them into the rows behind. As the waves pulled back, they sucked splintered debris and a number of people out to sea.

By 7am the town was littered with shattered buildings. The ground was not visible

COURTESY OF PACIFIC TSUNAMI MUSEUM

Aftermath of a tsunami

through the pile of rubble. Throughout Hawaii the tsunami killed 159 people and caused $25 million in property damage. The hardest hit was Hilo, with 96 fatalities.

Hilo's bayfront 'Little Tokyo' bore the brunt of the storm. Shinmachi, which means 'New Town' in Japanese, was rebuilt on the same spot.

Fourteen years later, on May 23, 1960, an earthquake off the coast of Chile triggered a tsunami that sped towards Hilo at 440 miles per hour. A series of three waves washed up in succession, each one sweeping farther into the city.

Although the tsunami warning speakers roared this time, many people didn't take them seriously. The tiny tsunamis of the 1950s had been relatively harmless, and some people actually went down to the beach to watch the waves.

Those along the shore were swept inland, while others farther up were dragged out into the bay. A few lucky ones who managed to grab hold of floating debris were rescued at sea. In the end, this tsunami caused 61 deaths and property damage of over $20 million.

Once more the Shinmachi area was leveled, but this time, instead of being redeveloped, the low-lying bayfront property was turned into parks and the survivors were relocated to higher ground.

shipwreck), are projected on videos and in a mini-theater inside an old bank vault; computers are available for those who want to know more about these gigantic 'harbor waves.' The docents are superbly informed, probably because some are tsunami survivors themselves.

Naha & Pinao Stones

On the front lawn of the Hilo library are the Naha and Pinao Stones. The **Pinao Stone** was an entrance pillar to an old Hawaiian heiau. The **Naha Stone**, from the same temple grounds, is estimated at 2½ tons. According to Hawaiian legend, anyone who had the strength to budge the stone would also have the strength to conquer and unite all the Hawaiian Islands. Kamehameha the Great reputedly met the challenge, overturning the stone in his youth.

Maui's Canoe

At the north end of Keawe St, just beyond Wailuku Drive, is the Puueo St Bridge, which crosses over the Wailuku River. The large rock in the river upstream on the left is known as Maui's Canoe.

Legend has it that the demigod Maui paddled his canoe with such speed across the ocean that he crash-landed here and the canoe turned to stone. Ever the devoted son, Maui was rushing to save his mother, Hina, from a water monster who was trying to drown her by damming the river and flooding her cave beneath Rainbow Falls.

Wailoa River State Park

Located on the grassy expanses where Shinmachi once stood, this park can be reached from Pauahi St. There are two **memorials** here, one dedicated to the tsunami victims and the other, an eternal flame, dedicated to the area's Vietnam War dead.

The Wailoa River flows through the park, and most of **Waiakea Pond** is within the park boundaries. This spring-fed estuarine pond has both saltwater and brackish water fish species, mostly mullet, but also papio ulua. There's a boat launch ramp near the mouth of the river for motorless boats. No fishing licenses are required, but there are

regulations; see Fishing in the Activities chapter for details.

Near the memorials is the **Wailoa Center** (☎ 944-0416; admission free; open 8am-4:30pm Mon & Tues, Thur & Fri, noon-4:30pm Wed, 9am-3pm Sat). This state-run art gallery has fascinating rotating exhibits. Recent offerings included Hawaiian AIDS quilt contributions, masks from Guatemala and a local all-women goddess show. An interesting photo presentation of the tsunami damage is on display downstairs. It's best to arrive early, as the gallery staff sometimes lock up by 4pm. Courses such as Hawaiian language, hula and quilting are occasionally offered here; call the center for a schedule.

Banyan Drive

Banyan Drive wraps around the edge of the Waiakea Peninsula, which juts into Hilo Bay. The road skirts the Lili'uokalani Gardens, the nine-hole **Naniloa Country Club Golf Course** (☎ 808-935-3000, $20/25 weekdays/weekends for nine holes) and Hilo's bayfront hotels.

While Banyan Drive is not all that interesting per se, the sprawling banyan trees that were planted in the 1930s by royalty and celebrities are impressive. Look closely and you'll see plaques beneath the trees identifying the arborists – Babe Ruth, Amelia Earhart and Cecil B DeMille among them.

Coconut Island Connected to land by a footbridge, Coconut Island protrudes into the bay opposite the Lili'uokalani Gardens. The island is a county park with picnic tables and swimming, but it's most popular as a recreational fishing spot. Hilo's Fourth of July fireworks display is shot off from the island, and the Easter-time Merrie Monarch Festival has its opening ceremonies here.

In ancient times, Coconut Island was called Moku Ola, 'Island of Life,' in part due to the powers of a healing stone on the island that was used by kahuna to cure the sick. Moku Ola also had pure spring water, which was said to bring good health, and a birthing stone that instilled mana in the children born on the island.

HILO

Hilo Arboretum

This 19.4-acre spread of trees administered by the Department of Land and Natural Resources is free to the public. Established in 1920, there are over 1000 species of trees here, including some 12 types of palms and many varieties of fruit trees including starfruit, figs, tamarind, breadfruit, pineapple guava and mangosteen. Visitors are allowed to harvest one sack each. You can also purchase saplings from the on-site nursery. This is a shady, quiet place to read on a balmy day. The arboretum is open 8am-3pm Monday to Friday; enter on W Kawili Street, just off Kilauea.

Beaches

Make no mistake: Hilo is not a beach town. Still, there are some decent pockets for snorkeling, catching a break or watching the sunrise along Kalanianaole Ave, a 4-mile-long coastal road on the eastern side of Hilo. All these beaches can get fairly rough with rip currents and surf, so talk to folks and assess conditions before venturing out. The buddy system is a good idea for any water activities here.

Venturing farther east of Richardson Ocean Park on Kalanianaole Ave is unpleasant as the folks living back there don't take kindly to strangers.

Puhi Bay This bay, about 1.4 miles from the intersection of Hwys 11 and 19 is the first you'll come to. It's not much for swimming (and is teeth-rattling cold due to the cold-water spring that feeds the bay until you're out about 100 feet or so), but it's a good beginner **dive site**. If you enter from the grassy outcropping on the eastern side, you'll come to an interesting reef, 'Tetsu's Ledge,' at 30 feet.

Onekahakaha Beach Park The next beach up is Onekahakaha, which is about a quarter mile north from Kalanianaole Ave.

The park has a broad sandy-bottomed pool formed by a large boulder enclosure. As the water's just a foot or two deep in most places, it's popular with families with young children.

On the Hilo side of the park, an unprotected cove attracts snorkelers on calm days, but mind the seaward current. The park department cautions swimmers and snorkelers not to venture beyond the breakwater at any time. There are rest rooms, showers and a picnic area.

James Kealoha Beach Park Kealoha is a roadside county park known locally as 'Four-Mile Beach' because of the distance between the park and the downtown post office. There are showers and rest rooms.

For **swimming** and **snorkeling**, most people go to the eastern, sheltered side of the park, which is protected by an island and a breakwater. It's generally calm there, with clean, clear water and pockets of white sand.

The Hilo side of the park is open ocean and much rougher. Locals sometimes net fish here and it's a popular winter surfing spot, although there are strong rip currents.

Leleiwi Beach Park The next park, almost a mile eastward along Kalanianaole, is Leleiwi. This is another good **dive site**, but the entrance is a bit trickier than at Puhi Bay (see that section earlier). The best place to enter is to the left of the third pavilion, where the wall jogs towards the ocean. From there walk to the level area beyond the gap in the wall.

Richardson Ocean Park This park, just before the end of the road, has a small black-sand beach fronting Hilo's most popular **snorkeling site**. The surf can be hectic here, which means decent bumps for **boogie boarding** and **surfing**. The west side of the bay tends to be colder due to subsurface freshwater springs. On the east side, fewer springs make for better snorkeling.

The eastern side of the park also has a lava shoreline and tide pools that can be fun to explore. There are rest rooms, showers, picnic tables and a lifeguard.

Activities

Though Hilo is not the watersport capital of the Big Island, there are still some aqua activities available here.

If you're interested in **kayaking, snorkeling** or getting certified for SCUBA (or want to do a dive), head to *Planet Ocean Water sports* (☎ 935-7277, fax 933-1125, W www .hawaiidive.com, 100 Kamehameha Ave). Snorkel rental is $6/24 for the day/week; a single kayak is $25/100 and PADI certification is $159. Guided, one-tank shore dives cost $75/60/50 per person for groups of one/two/three.

Also renting gear, guiding dives and offering certification at more competitive rates is *Nautilus Dive Center* (☎ 935-6939, W www .nautilusdivehilo.com, 382 Kamehameha Ave).

If you're a sidewalk surfer and want to **skateboard**, roll into *House of Ramps* (☎ 961-2557, 20 A Lanihuli St). This warehouse space has a half-pipe, ramps and jumps, for both boarders and BMX bikers. They rent protective gear ($1), build boards and do repairs, but you'll have to bring your own ride. It's open 10am-9pm Mon-Sat and noon-6pm Sundays; it can be crowded weekends. Entrance is $8/day.

There's affordable **golfing** at the Hilo Municipal Golf Course (☎ 959-7711, 340 Haihai St). Fees are $20/25 for 18 holes on weekdays/weekends and the pro shop rents clubs ($15 for a round of 18 holes).

Special Events

Since 1964, the world-famous **Merrie Monarch Festival** has featured the most talented hula halau from far and wide in a variety of competitions. It begins on Easter Sunday and lasts three days. This is definitely a festive time to be in Hilo.

Places to Stay

Partially due to the weather, Hilo has no self-contained resorts. People don't come to Hilo to hang around a pool, but to visit the sights and then head on. Consequently, the 'vacation rental' condo market that's so common on the Kona Coast is virtually non-existent here.

Budget Though camping is the only way to keep your nightly housing costs under double digits, there are few budget places in Hilo offering decent value.

Arnott's Lodge (☎ 969-7097, fax 961-9638, W www.arnottslodge.com, 98 Apapane Rd) Tent sites $9 per person, bed in 4-bed dorm $17, singles/doubles without bath $37/47, doubles with bath $57, 2-bedroom unit $120. Though a bit removed from town, this is *the* place to connect with other travelers. This clean, friendly, hostel-style lodge has 36 dorm beds in gender-specific, wheelchair accessible rooms and a slew of private rooms. Rooms come with shared or private baths and shared kitchen facilities. An adjacent house has a two-bedroom unit that accommodates up to five people. In addition, tenting is allowed in a grassy space adjacent to the hostel. There's a common TV/VCR room, free local calls, Internet connection, a coin laundry, free airport pick-up (until 8pm) and a scheduled daily shuttle service ($3 return) into town. Other extras include delicious barbecues ($7) and bike rentals for $10 a day.

Arnott's offers popular, well-run tours ($48/96 for guests/non-guests) to Puna, South Point and Green Sands Beach, Hawaii Volcanoes National Park, and Mauna Kea. MasterCard and Visa are accepted. To get to Arnott's, go east 1½ miles on Kalanianaole Ave from Hwy 11 and turn left onto Keokea Loop Rd. The lodge is about 100 yards down the road.

Dolphin Bay Hotel (☎ 935-1466, fax 935-1523, W www.dolphinbayhilo.com, 333 Iliahi St) Singles/doubles $66/72, superior rooms $76/79, 1-bedroom units $89, 2-bedroom unit $99, rental units per week $400. The popular Dolphin Bay Hotel, on a hill just above downtown, is an aloha-filled, family-run place. All 18 units have full kitchens, TVs and bathrooms, and all except the standard rooms have sunken bathtubs. Fresh-picked fruit from the backyard is available, along with free morning coffee. There are also four large one-bedroom units and a two-bedroom unit, for either singles or doubles. There's an annex on the opposite side of the street with six rental units, each with a queen bed, kitchen and TV; these units rent by the week. This is one of Hilo's most popular hotels, so reservations are advised.

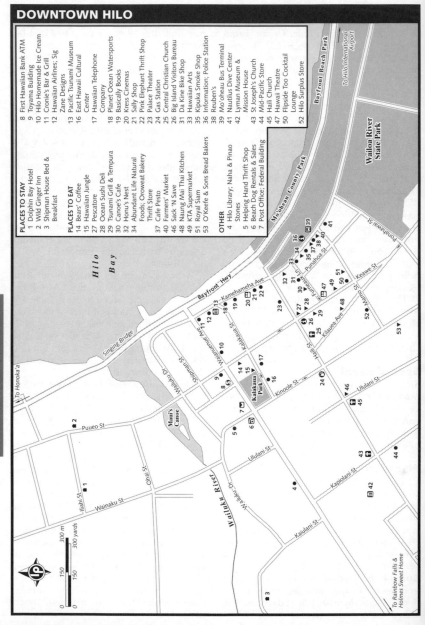

DOWNTOWN HILO

PLACES TO STAY
1 Dolphin Bay Hotel
2 Wild Ginger Inn
3 Shipman House Bed & Breakfast

PLACES TO EAT
14 Bears' Coffee
15 Hawaiian Jungle
27 Pescatore
28 Ocean Sushi Deli
29 Tsunami Grill & Tempura
30 Canoe's Cafe
32 Honu's Nest
34 Abundant Life Natural Foods; Oroweat Bakery Thrift Store
37 Cafe Pesto
40 Farmers' Market
46 Sack 'N Save
48 Naung Mai Thai Kitchen
49 KTA Supermarket
51 Royal Siam
53 O'Keefe & Sons Bread Bakers

OTHER
4 Hilo Library; Naha & Pinao Stones
5 Helping Hand Thrift Shop
6 Beach Dog Rentals & Sales
7 Post Office; Federal Building
8 First Hawaiian Bank ATM
9 Toyama Building
10 Hilo Homemade Ice Cream
11 Cronie's Bar & Grill
12 Hawaiian Airlines; Sig Zane Designs
13 Pacific Tsunami Museum
16 East Hawaii Cultural Center
17 Hawaiian Telephone Company
18 Planet Ocean Watersports
19 Basically Books
20 Kress Cinemas
21 Sally Shop
22 Pink Elephant Thrift Shop
23 Palace Theater
24 Gas Station
25 Central Christian Church
26 Big Island Visitors Bureau
31 Da Kine Bike Shop
33 Hawaiian Arts
35 Kipuka Smoke Shop
36 Information; Police Station
38 Reuben's
39 Mo'oheau Bus Terminal
41 Nautilus Dive Center
42 Lyman Museum & Mission House
43 St Joseph's Church
44 Mid-Pacific Store
45 Haili Church
47 Hawaii Theatre
50 Flipside Too Cocktail Lounge
52 Hilo Surplus Store

Hilo Bay

Mo'oheau County Park

Bayfront Beach Park

To Hilo International Airport

Wailoa River State Park

Wailoa River

Bayfront Hwy

Kamehameha Ave

Ponahawai St

Punahoa St

Keawe St

Kalakaua St

Kinoole St

Haili St

Furneaux Ln

Kilauea Ave

Kaumana Ave

Waianuenue Ave

Shipman St

Mamo St

Ululani St

Kapiolani St

Kaiulani St

Kaiakaua Park

Maui's Canoe

Singing Bridge

Mauloa Dr

To Honoka'a

Puueo St

Ohai St

Ilihai St

Wainaku St

Wailuku River

W Wailuku Dr

To Rainbow Falls & Holmes Sweet Home

300 m
300 yards
150
150
0
0

HILO

Wild Ginger Inn (☎ 935-5556, 800-882-1887, www.wildgingerinn.com, 100 Puueo St) Dorm bed $17, singles/doubles $45, superior $49, executive suite $59, grand suite $75. This friendly place amidst exuberant gardens with a creek meandering through is a good value. The rooms have private baths and either a double or two twin beds; most have small refrigerators and the suites have sitting rooms, kitchenettes and views; breakfast is included in room prices. The dorm rooms were being renovated at the time of writing. There are discounts for stays of three nights or more. There are laundry facilities, and Internet access and bike rentals are also available.

Off The Wall Mini-Hotel (☎ 934-8000, 10 Wilson St) Dorm bed $15, singles/doubles $35. This casual, well-located place is the most basic and affordable of any in Hilo. Just off Kilauea Ave (which can be noisy), it's a 15-minute walk into downtown Hilo and convenient to shops and restaurants. Nothing fancy here – there are bunk beds and industrial carpeting in the dorm rooms – but the singles are cozy and clean. Ask about weekly discounts.

Lihi Kai (☎ 935-7865, 30 Kahoa Rd) Rooms with breakfast; single or double occupancy $60. Lihi Kai is a laid-back B&B in Amy Gamble Lannan's home, perched on a cliff above Hilo Bay. The two guest rooms share a bath and a half. There's a swimming pool and a large living room with a wonderful ocean view.

Mid-Range Hilo's mid-range accommodation offer less character, but more amenities, than the budget places.

Holmes Sweet Home (☎ 961-9089, fax 934-0711, e homswhom@gte.net, 107 Koula St) Rooms $60-75. With just two rooms, this B&B retains a genuine, familial atmosphere. One room is larger than the other, but both are clean and wheelchair accessible with queen beds, private entrances and baths. They also share a sitting room and breakfast nook.

Our Place Papaikou's B&B (☎/fax 964-5250, www.ourplacebandb.com, PO Box 469, Papaikou) Rooms $60-80, including tax.

The two rooms in this sweet, exposed-beam home beside Kaieie Stream in Papaikou, 6 miles north of Hilo, are a good value. The smaller room shares a bath, while the larger, master bedroom has a king bed and private bath. Rates include breakfast. It's a pretty spot here and guests share the lanai overlooking the garden and stream and a grand living room with a fireplace, library and piano.

Country Club Condo Hotel (☎ 935-4918, fax 935-7575, w www.alakairealty.com/countryclub/, 121 Banyan Drive) Furnished studio daily/weekly/monthly $65/280/450. This place is primarily used for local housing, but they do rent furnished studios by the day and well-kept deluxe studios with so-so views of Hilo port for $670/month. The units suffer from the largely schmaltzy décor, but some have little balconies, which are a nice plus.

Uncle Billy's Hilo Bay Hotel (☎ 935-0861, 800-367-5102, fax 935-7903, w www.unclebilly.com, 87 Banyan Drive) Standard/superior/oceanfront rooms $84/94/104. Uncle Billy's Hilo Bay Hotel is a Hawaiian-owned 130-room hotel with a rough-around-the-edges Polynesian theme. The standard rooms are pricey for what you get; the superior and oceanfront rooms are much nicer. You can save more than 25% if you book via the Internet and there are tons of other discounts available. The dinner and hula show makes a nice outing for Auntie's birthday (see Entertainment later).

Hale Kai Bjornen (☎ 935-6330, fax 935-8439, w www.interpac.net/~halekai, 111 Honoli'i Pali) Rooms $90-100, suite $110. Just off Hwy 19 near the 5-mile marker north of Hilo, this lovely, well-appointed B&B has a terrific setting and fine views across Hilo Bay. Each of the comfortable four ocean-facing rooms has a private bath, cable TV and either a queen or king bed. The suite has a kitchenette (4 night minimum). Guests have use of the swimming pool, the lanais, a refrigerator, the living room and the hot tub overlooking the ocean.

Hilo Seaside Hotel (☎ 935-0821, 800-560-5557, w www.hiloseasidehotel.com, 126

HILO

Banyan Drive) Rooms $98-130. This is a 145-unit complex of two-story motel-style buildings. The carpeted rooms have air-con, ceiling fans, louvered windows, TVs and refrigerators. Avoid the rooms around the swimming pool and the streetside Hukilau wing, both of which can get noisy. The nicest rooms are in the deluxe ocean wing and have balconies overlooking the hotel's carp pond and Reeds Bay. The most expensive rooms have kitchenettes. Always ask what discounts are available here and visit the Web site for current deals.

Top End You won't find the luxury digs on this side like those that have made the Kona and Kohala coasts famous, but there are still a handful of serviceable, high-end hotels.

Naniloa Hotel (☎ 969-3333, 800-367-5360, fax 969-6622, 93 Banyan Drive) Rooms $100-140, suites $240. With 325 rooms, the Naniloa Hotel is Hilo's only 'skyscraper.' The rooms have air-con, TVs and phones, but are rather straightforward for the rates, which range depending on the view. Only the top-end rooms have lanais; the suites have living rooms and wrap-around lanais. The Naniloa is popular with Japanese tour groups and there's a full-service spa.

Hilo Hawaiian Hotel (☎ 935-9361, 800-367-5004, fax 961-9642, ⓦ www.castleresorts .com, 71 Banyan Drive) Garden-/ocean-view rooms $115/145. This 285-room sprawler near Coconut Island is Hilo's best hotel. Rooms are comfortable with nice enough decor, either a king or two smaller beds, air-con, TV and phone; most have private lanais. Garden-view rooms look across the parking lot to the golf course, while ocean-view rooms gaze on Hilo Bay. Ask about adding a rental car for no extra cost when you book your room, or visit their Web site for other promotions. For breakfast pastries, muffins and coffee for around $1 apiece, hit the *Hilo Hawaiian Hotel Bakery (☎ 969-7143),* open 6am-6pm daily. It's just in front of the hotel on Banyan Drive.

Shipman House Bed & Breakfast (☎/fax 934-8002, 800-627-8447, ⓦ www.hilo-hawaii .com, 131 Kaiulani St) Rooms with breakfast; single or double occupancy $145-175.

This B&B, on a knoll above town, is a beautiful Victorian mansion that has been in the Shipman family since 1901; past visitors have included Queen Liliuokalani and Jack London. The congenial owners, Barbara-Ann and Gary Andersen, have thoroughly renovated the property, which is on the National Register of Historic Places. There are three B&B rooms in the main house; the downstairs room has two antique koa twin beds, while the two upstairs rooms both have queen beds. In addition, two more rooms are in the adjacent 1910 guest cottage. All have private gorgeous baths with tubs, fans, small refrigerators and beautiful furnishings. Endearing touches include guest kimonos, fresh flowers and the library and grand piano which are available for guest use.

Places to Eat

Hilo has such a dazzling choice of places to eat, from drive-ins to fine Asian dining, even if you're watching your budget, try and splash out for a meal or two.

Budget Hilo fairly bursts at the seams with cheap and tasty grub and there are many more places than those described here; ferret out your favorites and spread the word.

Cafe 100 (☎ 935-8683, menu hotline 935-6368, 969 Kilauea Ave) Loco Mocos $1.75-3.99, sandwiches $1.95-$3.15, plate lunch $3.95-$5.95. Open 6:45am-8:30pm Mon-Fri, 6:45am-9:30pm Sat & Sun. For a thoroughly loco local experience, head to this drive-in. Cafe 100 is the original home of loco moco (rice topped with a hamburger, fried egg and a cardiac arresting amount of brown gravy) and has 17 different varieties from which to choose. It also has sandwiches, full breakfasts ($3) and plate lunches. Call the menu hotline for the day's specials.

Bears' Coffee (☎ 935-0708, 106 Keawe St) Dishes $1.75-6. Open 6:30am-5pm Mon-Sat, 8am-noon Sun. From hippies and car mechanics to surfers and bankers, there's always an interesting crowd here. In addition to coffee, they also have pastries, good Belgian waffles and egg dishes (until

11:30am), and from 10am on, there are deli sandwiches, burritos and bagels with a choice of more than a dozen fillings.

Canoe's Cafe (☎ 935-4070, 14 Furneaux St) Sandwiches $5.95-6.50. Open 9:30am-3pm Mon-Fri, 10am-2pm Sun & holidays. This casual spot with good food has a dizzying array of delicious sandwiches that can be tailored to your taste. The large selection includes Indian-style Tandoori chicken sandwiches or a grilled vegetable panini number. The café also has interesting fresh salads, stuffed potatoes of many types and soups made fresh daily. Breakfast is served until 10:30am.

Kope Kope Espresso Bar and Café (☎ 933-1221, 1261 Kilauea Ave) Bagels 90¢-$1.50. Open 6:30am-6pm Mon-Thur, 6:30am-7pm Fri, 7:30am-3pm Sat. This relaxed place encourages lingering with decent tunes, good magazines and jigsaw puzzles for the truly idle. Choose from an incredible variety of cream cheese flavors including lilikoi, coconut or lomi salmon. They also do wraps, sandwiches and soups.

Summer Roll (☎ 969-9907, 777 Kilauea Ave) Lunch buffet $3.25-5.75. Open 10am-8pm Mon-Sat. This family-run hole-in-the-wall at the east side of the Kaikoo Mall does good Vietnamese and Chinese food. The summer rolls ($3.25) make a tasty appetizer, and there is an extensive choice of hot *(phô)* and cold *(bun)* noodle dishes ($5.75-6.85) and the lunch buffet is renowned. They're in the process of expanding the menu, so the selection is due to grow.

Miyo's (☎ 935-2273, 400 Hualani St) Open lunch 11am-2pm, dinner 5:30pm-8:30pm Mon-Sat. Miyo's has a great location overlooking Waiakea Pond and the food to match. Enjoy a filling lunch combo (miso, salad, rice, ahi rolls, tempura and salmon, all for $10.50) as the breeze wafts through the casual wooden dining room. More affordable tempura and sashimi ($7.95) or tempura and sesame chicken ($7.50) combos with all the extras are also available. The same meals at dinner cost around two dollars more. Miyo's is upstairs behind the Karaoke Box in the Waiakea Villas complex.

Kuhio Grille (☎ 959-2336) Open 6am-10pm Sun-Thur, 6am-2am Fri & Sat. This casual eatery at the north side of the Prince Kuhio Plaza is the 'home of the one-pound laulau' and a local favorite for Hawaiian food. For $10.95 you can get the Hawaiian laulau plate made with local taro leaves, poi, lomi salmon and *haupia* (coconut pudding). Since that's more food than anyone should be able to eat, perhaps go for the laulau plate lunch ($6.50). The menu also includes omelettes, burgers, saimin and specials for kids.

Ka'upena (☎ 933-1106, 1710 Kamehamehu Ave) Open 9am-6pm Mon-Sat. Another local favorite for *ono* Hawaiian food, Ka'upena is the 'home of the foot-long laulau' ($6.95), which comes full of tender fish and pork wrapped in a ti leaf. Side orders of poke, poi or kalua pig are available for $1.55 if you want to try just a taste. Don't miss their original haulolo desert: half haupia and half taro pudding.

Island Infusion (☎ 933-9555), in the foodcourt of the Waiakea Center, is another of Hilo's tastiest Hawaiian eateries. It's open 10am-9pm daily.

Honu's Nest (☎ 935-9321, 270 Kamehameha Ave) Soups $4.25-8.25, Bento $3-6, mains $6.95-9.50. Open lunch only Mon-Sat. This sweet, teeny place facing the bay serves Japanese comfort food. Grab a colorful bento for the beach or settle in for a gaping bowl of soba noodle soup. Also on offer are donburi, tempura and teishoku with your choice of chicken, fish, squid or tofu.

Hawaiian Jungle (☎ 934-0700, 110 Kalakaua St) Lunch $4.95-7, dinner $7.50-15.95. Open 11am-9pm Mon-Fri, 11am-3pm special lunch menu, 7am-9pm Sat & Sun. The tiki torches, big, lazy ceiling fans and large windows overlooking Kalakaua Park create a warm atmosphere that complements the wholesome Mexican and Peruvian food here. The tamales, *lomo saltado* (the classic Peruvian beef dish) and *papas rellenos* (stuffed potatoes) are particularly delicious. Drop in on a Friday or Saturday evening when there's live music.

Reuben's (☎ 961-2552, 336 Kamehameha Ave) Combination plates $8-9.50. Open

HILO

11am-9pm Mon-Fri, noon-9pm Sat. The décor at this local favorite is strictly Oaxaca cantina: festively painted cinderblock, piñatas galore and folding tables and chairs, and the food is just as authentic. The salsa will kick your butt, the chips are freshly fried and the fish taco and tamale combination plate ($9.50) will not soon be forgotten. Come with an appetite.

Kilauea Kitchen (☎ 935-6665, 1438 *Kilauea Ave*) Breakfast $4.50-5.75, lunch $5.95-7.25, dinner $5.50-9.95. Open breakfast 7am-10:30, lunch 11am-2:30pm, dinner 5pm-8pm daily. During breakfast this place serves solid fare like omelettes and pancakes with all manner of meats accompanying. Lunch means salads and soups mostly, but the kitchen really shines during dinner. Choose from sushi, seared ahi or mahimahi with caper and anchovy sauce. Attached is the superlative *Hilo-Shi Bento-Ya and Bakery*, with large, delicious bentos ($4 and up), a hot bar and sinful baked goods including brownies, palmiers and muffins.

Hilo Homemade Ice Cream (☎ 933-9399, 1477 Kalanianaole Ave) Open 10:30am-5pm Mon-Sat (☎ 969-9559, 41 Wainuenue Ave) Open 9:30am-5pm Mon-Sat. Hilo's best ice cream is now obtainable at two locations: on the road to Richardson Beach and smack in the middle of downtown. Flavors include tasty *poha* (gooseberry), zesty ginger and a killer kona coffee. Single scoops are $1.88, doubles are $2.88.

Ken's House of Pancakes (☎ 935-8711, 1730 Kamehameha Ave) Open 24 hours daily. The glory that is Ken's: always open, with hundreds of menu items including huge SPAM omelettes with potatoes, toast and coffee ($7), luscious macadamia nut pancakes ($5.65), and milkshakes like ambrosia ($2.95). Dinner offerings like kalua pig and cabbage with all the trimmings for $7.95, plus a kids' menu, make this the perfect spot following Mauna Kea stargazing.

Ocean Sushi Deli (☎ 961-6625, fax 935-2555, 239 Keawe St) Sushi $1.50-4, sushi chirashi $6.95-9.95, sashimi $6.75/13.50/17.95 for 7/15/21 pieces. Open 10am-2:30pm & 4:30pm-9pm Mon-Sat. This perky place offers both traditional and contemporary

sushi, with scores of special rolls ($4.50-5.50) including an ahi-avocado and kukui nut treasure and poke mac nut roll. I dare you to try the plantation roll (hamburger, onion and gravy). There are lots of veggie rolls if you're not into raw fish.

These folks also have the wicked popular *Tsunami Grill & Tempura* (☎ 961-6789, fax 935-2555) across the street. The menu is huge, there's a daily lunch and dinner buffet ($10.95/$14.95) and they're open until 1am Fri & Sat.

Royal Siam (☎/fax 961-6100, 68 Mamo St) Mains $5.25-8.95. Lunch 11am-2pm, dinner 5pm-9pm Mon-Sat. Royal Siam has good Thai food at reasonable prices. Choose from salads, soups and noodle dishes, as well as a selection of tasty red, green and yellow curries. There are beef, chicken and seafood dishes and a page of not very imaginative vegetarian dishes.

Naung Mai Thai Kitchen (☎ 934-7540, 86 *Kilauea Ave*) Lunch buffet $4.75-6.25, dinner $6.95-9.95. Open lunch 11am-2pm Mon, Tues, Thur, Fri and dinner 5pm-8:30pm Mon-Thur, 5pm-9pm Fri & Sat . This intimate and comfortable place tucked on the forgotten reaches of Kilauea is a keeper: yummy fish specialties (market price), big, bold soups and a variety of curries are all prepared with care and no MSG.

Mid-Range & Top End For a few extra bucks, you can experience Hilo's finest dining, often in lovely settings.

Fiascos (☎ 935-7666, 200 Kanoelehua Ave) Open 11am-10pm Sun-Thur, 11am-11pm Fri & Sat. Fiascos feels like a chain, but with a more imaginative menu and better waitstaff. The massive salad and soup bar ($5/9 with a meal/as an entrée) is definitely a bonus. They have 33 beers on offer: Hilo's biggest selection.

Restaurant Miwa (☎ 961-4454, 1261 Kilauea Ave) Sushi $2.75-5.50, lunch $5.95-8.95, dinner $8.95-$19.50. Lunch 11am-2pm, dinner 5pm-10pm Mon-Sat; dinner 5pm-9pm Sun. Restaurant Miwa in the Hilo Shopping Center serves good, quality food at decent prices. It has a sushi bar, good sashimi and a full range of Japanese dishes.

They serve a full-meal teishoku at lunch and dinner that is tasty and filling. A children's menu is also available. If you're at all nostalgic for Japan, this place will twang the heartstrings.

Pescatore (☎ 969-9090, 235 Keawe St) Breakfast 7:30am-11am Sat & Sun, lunch 11am-2pm & dinner 5:30pm-9pm daily. Pescatore has attentive service and excellent Italian food, though the atmosphere is a bit Little Italy social club. Breakfast ($4.25-$5.75) and lunch are particularly good deals. At lunch, try the spaghetti Bolognese ($5.95) or scampi alfredo ($10.95). At dinner, pasta dishes are about double the lunch prices, while meat and seafood main courses average $21.

Cafe Pesto (☎ 969-6640, 308 Kamehameha Ave) Lunch $7.95-$11.95, dinner $9.95-$28.95, pizzas $9.95-$17.95. Open 11am-9pm Sun-Thur, 11am-10pm Fri & Sat. Cafe Pesto is considered one of the Big Island's star restaurants. Serving creative Hawaii Regional cuisine that features local jewels like Kona lobster, Kamuela beef and Pahoa corn, you'll pay for your memorable meal here, but it will be worth it. Their gourmet wood-fired pizzas and innovative salads are reliably tasty too. Lunch is an attractive option if you want the taste sensation without the price tag.

Seaside Restaurant (☎ 935-8825, 1790 Kalanianaole Ave) Full meals $17.95-$23.95. Open 5pm-8:30pm Tues-Thur, 5pm-9pm Fri & Sat. This family-run operation serves the island's freshest fish in a faux panel dining room. The outdoor tables, however, sit prettily above the family's aquafarm. Pick from fresh rainbow trout, perch or several other types of fish, all of which are raised in the pond. Everything is delicious; try the mullet steamed in ti leaves with lemon and onions. Meals include rice, salad, apple pie and coffee. It's kind of pricey, but the service and portions are stellar. Call ahead for reservations.

Groceries & Markets If you're sick of restaurants, Hilo has lots of places where you can pick up the raw materials for a great meal.

Abundant Life Natural Foods (☎ 935 7411, 292 Kamehameha Ave) Open 8:30am-7pm Mon, Tues, Thur, Fri, 7am-7pm Wed & Sat, 10am-5pm Sun. This health food store has all the quality cheeses, juices and bulk foods you'd expect. It also has a simple deli and smoothie bar and some of the best prices on the island. Live music and other special events are also occasionally hosted here. Two doors away, *Oroweat Bakery Thrift Store* has slightly dated breads at discount prices.

Farmers market (cnr Mamo St & Kamehameha Ave) Open 7am-noon Wed & Sat. At Hilo's farmers market you can pick up papayas for 25¢, as well as Ka'u oranges and other island fruits, veggies and flowers direct from the growers at bargain prices. Be careful they don't coerce you into buying overripe or otherwise bogus product.

O'Keefe & Sons Bread Bakers (☎ 934-9334, 374 Kinoole St) Loaves $2.75-3.95. Open 6am-4pm Mon-Fri, 6am-3pm Sat. These folks bake gorgeous artisan breads that will start your mouth watering. Choose from rye, focaccia, garlic sourdough, apple raisin – you get the idea. Pastries and sandwiches are also available.

Island Naturals (☎ 935-5533, 303 Maakala) Open 8:30am-8pm Mon-Sat, 10am-7pm Sun. This natural food store in the Waiakea Center has an amazing smoothie and deli counter, plus a hot food bar with rotating selections including the likes of ahi in coconut, vegetarian pad Thai and curries ($6.95/lb).

Suisan Fish Market (☎ 935-9349, 85 Lihiwai St) Open 8am-5pm Mon-Sat. Even though the century-old fish auction no longer happens here, you can still come here to get your fresh fish. Marlin, ahi, mahimahi and oysters are among the options. Don't miss the delicious selection of poke.

KTA Supermarket (323 Keawe St; open 7am-9pm Mon-Sat, 7am-6pm Sun) is a convenient downtown grocery store. There's a *Safeway* supermarket at the Prince Kuhio Plaza on Hwy 11 and both a *Sack N Save* and *KTA Superstore* in the nearby Puainako Town Center. The latter has 30 types of poke. If you're heading for Volcano early in the morning, Sack N Save has coffee and doughnuts from 5am.

Entertainment

Locals and visitors alike gripe about Hilo's lack of nightlife. Still, if you're into art flicks, gallery openings, local music, karaoke, billiards or sports, there's usually something happening. Check out the free newspaper *Hawaii Island Journal* and bulletin boards for goings on about town.

Fiascos (see Places to Eat, earlier) This establishment is one of the first to be locally recommended when you ask around for after-dark fun stuff. There's country line dancing on Thursday evenings and jazz on Friday – and that gives you an idea of how slow things can get around here!

Hilo Hawaiian Hotel (see Places to Stay – Top End) The lounge at this hotel sometimes has live contemporary Hawaiian music.

Hilo Bay Hotel (see Places to Stay – Mid-Range) Live music and hula show 6pm-7:30pm & 8pm-9:30pm daily. Uncle Billy's hotel presents an enthusiastic little hula show during dinnertime at the restaurant (dishes like something from a low-budget wedding start at $10.95).

East Hawaii Cultural Center (see the Walking Tour section, earlier) Periodically there are community plays, dances and concerts at this center; check the *Hawaii Tribune Herald* for the current schedule.

Cinemas For such a humble town, Hilo has a shockingly good film scene; snuggle up with some popcorn and catch a flick one rainy winter night.

Palace Theater (detailed recorded information ☎ 934-7777, W www.hilopalace.com, 38 Haili St) This repertory house shows foreign films, documentaries, director's cuts and the like Friday-Sunday ($6). There are also special events here including concerts, plays, and readings. The local intelligentsia comes out of the woodwork for events here and it makes a fun night out.

Hawaii Theatre (detailed recorded information ☎ 969-3939, 291 Keawe St) Adult/

senior/child $5/4/3. This funky film house shows rare prints, classic oldies, horror B-movies, foreign films and all the other stuff the big guys won't touch. Price of admission includes free coffee, and that just rocks.

Kress Cinemas (recorded information ☎ 961-3456, 174 Kamehameha Ave) This cinema in the art deco–style Kress Building, is an atmospheric place to take in a little celluloid. It shows standard first-run Hollywood films and has a good bargain matinee for $4.75.

Similar fare is screened at the movie theaters at; *Prince Kuhio Plaza* (recorded information ☎ 961-3456, Hwy 11); and *Waiakea Shopping Plaza* (recorded information ☎ 961-3456, 88 Kanoelehua Ave).

Bars *Cronies Bar & Grill* (☎ 935-5158, 11 Waianuenue Ave) Open 11am-2am Mon-Fri, 3pm-2pm Sat. This place has an atmosphere as stimulating as its name, but the live music (Hawaiian and local especially) is worth a listen. There are also dirt cheap drink specials like $2 pitcher night; granted it's Budweiser, but still!

Flipside Too (☎ 961-0057, 94 Mamo St) If you like dive bars, this is the place. Sticky floors, a couple of pool tables, darts and shadowy characters are all fixtures here. Every third Saturday is 'alternative' night; check the flyer in the window for details.

Shooters Bar & Grill (☎ 969-7069, 121 Banyan Drive) Connected to the Country Club Condo Hotel, this is a sleepy chrome-and-linoleum watering hole by day, but a drunken train wreck waiting to happen by night (maybe that's why it's reminiscent of an Australian pub). Still, it's open until 3:30am on Fridays and Saturdays, has DJs, bands, pool tables and pinball, and a decent kitchen grilling up pub fare.

Spectator Sports

The University of Hawaii at Hilo **volleyball** and **basketball** teams play at the *Afook Chinen Civic Center* (also called Hilo Civic). The former are quite competitive and play in the fall, while the basketball squad is, well, let's just say you really have to love hoops to keep coming back. Still, it's a lively crowd and is something fun to do on a winter night. The **baseball** team plays in the spring at the *Victor Baseball Complex*. Tickets are $5/4 for reserved/general admission for all events. Both these venues are located at the Hoolulu Complex on Manono St; for schedule and ticket information, contact the UH Athletic Department (☎ 808-974-7520) or see their helpful Web site: **w** vulcans.uhh.hawaii.edu/index.shtml.

Shopping

Hilo has terrific, cheap thrift stores that are great for cool aloha wear or vintage clothing. Hands down, the best selection is at *Mid-Pacific Store* (☎ 935-3822, 76 Kapiolani St). Bring a fat wallet for the silk and crepe kimonos, genuine palaka *paniolo* shirts and terrific aloha wear (including swimsuits). You might also pop into the *Sally Shop* (188 Kamehameha Ave), the *Helping Hand Thrift Shop* (42 Kinoole St) with its killer 25¢ rack or the *Pink Elephant Thrift Shop* (216 Kamehameha Ave). Another slew of thrift stores are clustered on Kilauea Ave between Ponahawai and Furneaux Sts.

Sig Zane Designs ☎ 935-7077, 112 Kamehameha Ave). This place designs its own aloha wear with sophisticated style. Their clothing makes great souvenirs, as do the original t-shirt designs made and screened at *Hawaiian Arts* (☎ 935-1860, 284 Kamehameha Ave).

Smokers should make a beeline for the *Kipuka Smoke Shop* (☎ 961-5082, 308 Kamehameha Ave). The cigar selection is respectable, as is the choice of rolled and loose tobacco (including American Spirit), but nothing matches the mind-boggling variety of rolling papers.

Big Island Candies (☎ 935-8890, 585 Hinano St) Open 8:30am-5pm daily. When you're done with the aforementioned rolling papers, head straight to this shop, which makes and sells chocolate-covered macadamia nuts, cookies and other sweet treats. Free samples and coffee are pressed upon you while you watch candy being hand-dipped in chocolate.

Whatever fishing supplies you may need can be purchased at *Tokunaga Store* (☎ 935-

Clown Princess of Hawaii

Clara Inter was a Hawaiian schoolteacher on a glee club trip to Canada in 1936 when she first performed 'Hilo Hattie (Does the Hilo Hop),' to a delighted Canadian crowd. A year or so later in the Monarch Room at Waikiki's Royal Hawaiian Hotel, Clara approached bandleader (and author of the song) Don McDiarmid Sr and asked him to play it. McDiarmid was uncertain that it would go over well at the ritzy hotel, since it was a 'low class' hula, alluding to Hattie doing a dance that 'no law would allow.'

Well, with a taste of applause and fame already under her muumuu from her Canadian experience, Clara wasn't going to be deterred. She convinced him to do the tune and the rest, as they say, is history. Clara Inter was catapulted to international stardom on the wings of this song (with worldwide tours and appearances in several movies including *Song of the Islands* and *Ma & Pa Kettle in Waikiki*), legally changed her name to Hilo Hattie and eventually lent it to the now famous chain of Hawaiian stores. She's known as the Clown Princess of Hawaii.

6965, 26 Hoku St). Information is also available here about local competitions, seasons and regulations.

There are also several shopping centers, such as *Prince Kuhio Plaza (Hwy 11)* which has 75 stores (including a one-hour photo place), *Puainako Town Center* and *Waiakea Center*.

GETTING AROUND
Bus

Within Hilo The Hele-On Bus (☎ 961-8744) has a few intra-city routes, all costing 75¢. The bad news is they only operate Monday to Friday. Here are details for the most important routes and stops:

No 4 Kaumana – this bus goes five times a day (the first leaves at 7:45am, the last at 2:20pm) from Mo'oheau Bus Terminal-Hilo Library-Hilo Medical Center (and Rainbow Falls).

HILO

No 6 **Waiakea-Uka** – this bus goes five times a day (the first leaves at 7:05am, the last at 3:05pm) from Mo'oheau Bus Terminal-Hilo Shopping Center-the University of Hawaii-Prince Kuhio Plaza-Walmart.

Inter-District There *are* buses that make their way around the island, but again, they only run Monday to Friday. This is one of the reasons hitchhiking is so prevalent here. The following list summarizes Hele-On buses serving other districts (all buses leave from Mo'oheau Bus Terminal unless noted):

No 31 Honoka'a – Six departures to Honoka'a ($3.75, 75 minutes) stopping in Laupahoehoe and Pa'aulio; the first three departures leave from the parking lot just east of the terminal.

No 16 Kailua-Kona – One departure at 1:30pm ($6, three hours), this bus goes north, stopping all along the Hamakua Coast, and Waimea before reaching the Lanihau Center in Kona. Continues to Captain Cook and Honaunau.

No 9 Pahoa – Departures at 2:40pm and 4:45pm ($2.25, one hour), this goes to Pahoa via Kea'au.

No 23 Ka'u – One departure at 2:40pm ($5.25, 2½ hours) to Ocean View. This bus stops in Kurtistown, Hawaii Volcanoes National Park, Punalu'u, Na'alehu and Waiohinu.

Schedules are available at the Big Island Tourist Bureau and the information kiosk at the Mo'oheau Bus Terminal.

Bicycle

Getting around town on a bike is totally feasible, and longer tours are possible for the fit and/or game. The following shops rent bicycles, safety gear and car racks and do repairs:

Da Kine Bike Shop (☎ 934-9861), 12 Furneaux St, from $5/day rusty cruisers to $50 pro models with trailer and pack, this friendly place rents them all. They also run cycling tours to 'anywhere on the Island.'

Mid-Pacific Wheels (☎ 935-6211), 1133-C Manono St, rents 21-speed bikes for $15/day, open seven days a week.

Hilo Bike Hub (☎ 961-4452), 318 E Kawili St, Rents cruisers/rock hoppers/full suspension bikes for $25/30/35 day and has a super seven days for the price of four deal.

AROUND HILO
Honoli'i Beach Park

Honoli'i Cove is a protected pocket with Hilo's best surfing. The park has showers and toilets and is popular with local surfers and boogie boarders. If you want to learn to surf on the windward side, this is probably as good a place as any (another possibility is Pohiki Bay in Puna, see that chapter later).

To get to Honoli'i, take Hwy 19 north out of Hilo. Between the 4- and 5-mile markers, make a right onto Nahala and a left onto Kahoa. Join all the other cars parked on the side of the road and head down to the park. For a little variety, you can return to Hwy 19 by following Kahoa downhill on a one lane road that winds through an enchanting forest for a mile or so before dumping you back on Hwy 19 just past the 5-mile marker.

Rainbow Falls

Rainbow Falls is a quick 5-minute drive outside of Hilo and worth it for the massive banyan tree alone.

Waianuenue, literally 'rainbow seen in water,' is the Hawaiian name for this lovely 80-foot cascade ringed by palms, ohia and African tulip trees. The gaping cave beneath the falls is fit for a goddess and indeed, is said to have been the home of Hina, mother of Maui.

A trail to the left of the upper viewing platform leads down to the water and some good swimming and picnic spots. Take the upper portion of this trail for an encounter with the grand dame of banyans, supporting a canopy so thick it blocks the sun and roots so vast it swallows children. The trail ends at the water's edge; swimmers and rock hoppers can explore upriver for private aquatic delights Be prepared for voracious mosquitoes.

Pe'epe'e Falls & Boiling Pots

Pe'epe'e Falls and Boiling Pots are further up Waianuenue Ave, about 1½ miles past Rainbow Falls and are another good spot for a dip and a picnic.

Pe'epe'e (pronounced peh-eh peh-eh) Falls drops over a sheer rock face. As the water cascades downstream over a series of

HILO

basalt depressions in the river, it swirls and churns into bubbling pools – hence the name Boiling Pots. The viewpoints here are wheelchair accessible.

Follow the well beaten path just beyond the 'No swimming' sign for some good swimming.

Kaumana Caves

The Kaumana Caves were formed by an 1881 lava flow from Mauna Loa. As the flow ebbed, the outer edges of the deep lava stream cooled and crusted over in a tunnel-like effect. The hot molten lava inside then drained away, creating these caves.

The caves are wet, mossy and thickly carpeted with ferns and impatiens. If you have a flashlight, you might want to explore them, although they tend to be quite drippy.

The caves, which are signposted, are 3 miles up Kaumana Drive (Hwy 200) on the right.

Nani Mau Gardens

Nani Mau Gardens is a stop on the tour bus headless chicken circuit. The gardens encompass more than 20 acres of flowering plants, including a lovely orchid section (☎ 959-3500, adult/child 6-17 years $10/6; open 8:30am-5pm daily). Unlike many Hawaiian gardens, this one isn't terribly naturalized or charmingly overgrown. Instead, it's formally designed, with sculpted plantings and wide asphalt paths. Narrated tram rides are available ($7 extra), and there's a *restaurant*.

Nani Mau is about 3 miles south of Hilo. The turnoff from Hwy 11 onto Makalika St is marked with a sign. The garden is accessible to the disabled.

Panaewa Rainforest Zoo

It's not the biggest or the baddest or the most lovely, but at least the Panaewa Rainforest Zoo (☎ 959-7224, ⓦ www.hilozoo.com; open 9am-4:15pm) is free. Loaner umbrellas are also free, so it's not a bad place to stroll around for an hour, though some of the cages are painfully small.

There are monkeys, reptiles, a pygmy hippo, axis deer and feral pigs and goats.

Among the many birds here are the endangered nene and the Hawaiian duck, hawk and owl. Free-roaming peacocks have the run of the place. The pride of the zoo's collection is a cross-eyed Bengal tiger from Las Vegas. Kids might enjoy the petting zoo, open on Saturdays from 1:30pm-2:30pm. For voyeuristic travelers, feeding times are 9am and 3:15pm daily.

To get there, turn off Hwy 11 a few miles south of town at W Mamaki St, which almost immediately turns into the Stainback Hwy. The zoo is a mile west of Hwy 11.

Mauna Loa Macadamia Nut Visitor Center

Mauna Loa Macadamia Nut Visitor Center is on Macadamia Rd off Hwy 11, about 5 miles south of Hilo (☎ 966-8618; open 8:30am-5:30pm). The 2½-mile entrance road cuts across macadamia trees as far as the eye can see, making you wonder why they're so expensive.

HILO

C Brewer Co, which owns Mauna Loa Macadamia Nut, produces most of Hawaii's macadamia nuts. The large visitor center caters to tour-bus crowds and is essentially just a gift shop and snack bar.

To the side is a working factory, which has an outside walkway with windows that allow visitors to view the large, fast-paced assembly line inside, where the nuts are shelled, roasted, packaged and readied for your gustatory pleasure. Unfortunately, there are no free samples available!

The little planted area behind the visitor center, with its labeled fruit trees and flowering bushes, is worth a stroll if you've come this far.

Puna

Pocked with hidden delights, the Puna district encompasses the easternmost knob of the Big Island. Many of the main attractions revolve around lava: black-sand beaches, lava tide pools, a forest of lava tree molds and ribbons of the red hot stuff flowing into the sea.

Kilauea's active East Rift Zone slices clear across Puna. The most recent series of eruptions has been sending lava this way since 1983. In 1990, lava buried Hwy 130 and the village of Kalapana on the southeastern shores; going there is eerie evidence of Pele's destructive ways. But head a couple of miles to the southwest and you can see lava cascading into the sea, forming new land.

Puna is the maverick district, with an alternative temperament perpetuated by individuals and groups attracted to the cheap, coastal land. Here you'll find sovereignty activists, communists, hippies and marijuana growers. Despite Draconian police measures aimed at curtailing cultivation (including raids, aerial sprayings and infrared surveillance), Puna is still the Big Island pot capital and proud of it. Locals proffer 'Puna buds' or 'Puna butter' with boastful delight.

Other crops that take well to lava and flourish in Puna are anthuriums, papayas, and orchids. Indeed, many of the orchids that get credited to Hilo are actually grown in Puna. Kava *(awa)*, noni and avocado are also raised here.

Puna is not known for its beaches – partly because many remain hidden to all but the most dogged explorers. What's more, a few people die every year on Puna's beaches: swimmers cannot be too cautious with the rough seas on this part of the coast.

Puna is also a hotbed for grass roots organization and protest, as residents try to keep the district wild and out of the hands of big business. The Puna Geothermal Venture has been providing 25% of the Big Island's energy for years, and residents aren't happy about it. Not only does the

Highlights

- Beholding lava flowing into the sea
- Kicking it on a black-sand, nude beach
- Relaxing in a natural sauna or hot pool, both volcanically heated
- Catching a set at the Isaac Hale Beach Park break
- Snorkeling in tide pools thick with coral and fish
- Melting your stress away with a cup of kava and a massage at the Pahoa Farmer's Market

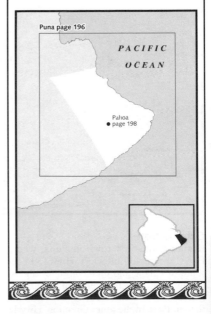

drilling tap into the heart of Pele, it releases nasty gases including sulfur dioxide, hydrogen sulfide and ammonia, threatening the health of residents. Puna activists are also fighting to block the construction of a 494-acre sport/spa complex on Red Road (Hwy 137) that will decimate native rain forest.

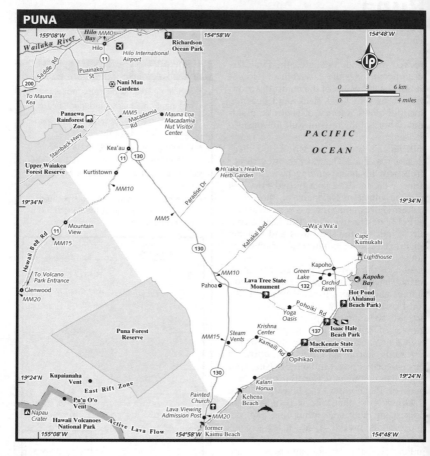

PUNA

Orientation

Kea'au is the first town in Puna, where Hwys 11 and 130 intersect. Hwy 130 goes south to Pahoa, and then continues almost to the coast. The road ends at 21.2 miles, where lava covered the lower reaches of the road in 1990. In the other direction, Hwy 11 climbs up through several small towns before reaching Volcano and the Hawaii Volcanoes National Park.

KEA'AU

Kea'au is the small town at Puna's northern end. The district's main sightseeing area is to the southeast and southwest, leading up to the national park, but there are some points of interest in Kea'au proper if you're over this way. It also has some of the cheapest gas on the island, so fill up here to save a few dimes. There's also a post office, laundromat and ATM in the Keaau Shopping Center. The Internet terminal at the library is usually available for walk-in appointments (a real rarity).

In the Paradise Park subdivision to the southeast of Kea'au is **Hi'iaka's Healing Herb Garden** (☎ 966-6126, ⓦ www.hiiakas .com, 15-1667 2nd St; self-guided tour adult/

child $10/5, fully guided tour $15/8; open 1pm-5pm Tues, Thurs & Sat). This lovingly tended, one-acre garden collects scores of Western, Hawaiian, Chinese and Ayurvedic herbs. You can take the informative and often funny, self-guided audio tour or have owner and herbalist Barbara Fahs give you the personalized version. Barbara also sells tinctures, offers classes, workshops and a residency program, plus rents the fully equipped *cottage* on the grounds (single/double $50/75).

All of the places to eat are in or beside the Kea'au Shopping Center at the intersection of Hwys 11 and the spur that jogs southwest to Hwy 130.

Charley's Bar & Grill (☎ 966-7589) Pub grub $4.50-9.50. Open 11am-midnight Mon & Tues, 11am-2am Wed-Sat, 9am-1am Sun. This place does decent burgers, pizza and other familiar bar food, but its real draw is the fully stocked bar, ice cold beer and live music Thur-Sat ($3 cover).

Verna's Drive Inn (☎ 966-9288) Open 6am-8pm Mon-Sat, 7:30am-4pm Sun. This is one of five Verna's islandwide, serving the same dirt-cheap egg and meat breakfasts, saimin and plate lunch as the others.

Kea'au Natural Foods (☎ 966-8877) Open 8:30am-8pm Mon-Fri, 8:30am-7pm Sat, 9:30am-5pm Sun. This small health food store has a good bulk selection, fabulous coffee, decent organic produce and loads of perpetually discounted items.

PAHOA

The heart of Puna is Pahoa, a scruffy little town with raised wooden sidewalks, cowboy architecture and an untamed edge. Alternative influences from the '60s and beyond lend it a bohemian, ragamuffin feel. Pahoa is caught in a wrinkle in time, with the sights and smells of bygone days mingling with the beeps of ATM machines and the convenience of drive-thru espresso shacks.

Orientation

Roads in and around Pahoa take many names. For example, the road through town is called Government Main Rd, Old Government Rd, Main St and Pahoa Rd, while

it's signposted as Pahoa Village Rd. You'll hear Pahoa Road and Main St most often; addresses are usually written as Government Main Rd.

It's quite easy to hitchhike in and around Pahoa. If you have room in your rental, you might make a few friends.

Information

Both the Bank of Hawaii and the First Hawaiian Bank in the center of town have ATMs.

The post office accepts general delivery mail and is open 8:30am-4pm Mon-Fri and 11am-2pm Sat.

The library (☎ 965-8574) is open 10am-8pm Monday, 10am-5pm Tuesday-Thursday, 9:30am-4:30pm Friday and 9am-noon Saturday. They have a superb Hawaiiana collection and decent CDs and movies. There is one Internet terminal in constant use.

For a decent selection of new and used books with an emphasis on Hawaiiana and area activity guides, check out Pahoa Home Video in the Pahoa Village Center; they also sell maps.

Things to See & Do

Pahoa has an **Olympic-size pool** in the heart of town. It's open from 1:45pm-4:30pm daily; there's also a kiddie pool (free admission).

The weekend Aloha Center **farmers market** is truly an event. Here, you can sip kava, have your palm read, get a massage, boogie to a local band, fondle a crystal, peruse quality used books and buy organic goat cheese. It's held on Saturday and Sunday from 8am until it breaks up, but Sunday is usually more robust.

Places to Stay

Punahometel (☎ 965-0317, 965-9666, ⓔ ed vensure@cs.com, 13-3345 Kumukahi in Leilani Estates) Camping $7, double with shared/private bath $15/20. More like the Hippie Econolodge than the Hippie Hilton, the Punahometel is a crash pad with the nice price, just 3 miles south of Pahoa town. Rooms are pretty battered, but there are always loads of guests to party with and the

PUNA

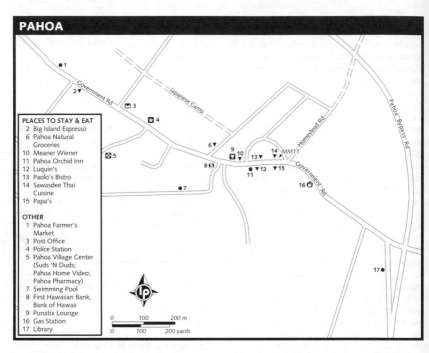

PAHOA

PLACES TO STAY & EAT
2 Big Island Espresso
6 Pahoa Natural
     Groceries
10 Meaner Wiener
11 Pahoa Orchid Inn
12 Luquin's
13 Paolo's Bistro
14 Sawasdee Thai
     Cuisine
15 Papa's

OTHER
1 Pahoa Farmer's
     Market
3 Post Office
4 Police Station
5 Pahoa Village Center
     (Suds 'N Duds;
     Pahoa Home Video;
     Pahoa Pharmacy)
7 Swimming Pool
8 First Hawaiian Bank,
     Bank of Hawaii
9 Punatix Lounge
16 Gas Station
17 Library

0   100   200 m
0   100   200 yards

communal kitchen means your budget can stretch a mile. At the time of writing there were plans to move the hotel near Isaac Hale Beach (see that section under Around Pahoa later), but folks looked pretty bleary at that point and weren't going *anywhere* fast.

Pahoa Orchid Inn (☎ 965-6444, W www .pahoaorchidinn.com, PO Box 1415, Pahoa, HI 96778) Doubles with shared/private bath $40/60. This inn has eight cozy, 2nd-story rooms in a historic wooden building on Main St. Recently renovated, this place is cute and quiet, with the rooms arranged around an inner lanai that makes you feel miles away from the hustle and bustle of Pahoa. The carpeted rooms are small, but nicely furnished with antiques. Most rooms have cable TV and mini-refrigerators. Ask about weekly discounts.

Steam Vent Inn (Volcano Ranch; ☎ 965-8800, W www.hawaiivolcanoinn.com) Bunk $15, doubles in bunkhouse $30, doubles

with private bath in main house $60-125, all prices include tax. This place is perfectly perched on 25 acres with views overlooking the ocean. The main-house rooms are tiled, sparkling clean and comfortable; the pricier rooms have ocean-facing lanais. Guests can use the kitchen (though rates include continental breakfast) and hot tub. Downhill a bit is the bunkhouse, a basic, funky place with bunk beds and one private room sharing a bath and kitchen, but a good value considering the location. Perhaps the greatest part of this place is the on-site volcanic vent and steam house. It seats eight and has a cold and hot shower inside; the steam here is much hotter than those at the vents nearby on Hwy 130.

Places to Eat

Big Island Espresso (no ☎, Government Main Rd, near the post office) Open 6:30am-noon Mon-Fri, 7am-3pm Sat & Sun. You can't miss this little pink shack on the way

PUNA

into town and you shouldn't: the generous Breyer's milkshakes come in 47 flavors and are buried in whipped cream ($2/2.50/3 small/med/lrg). There are also 75¢ espresso shots, mochas, lattes and good old coffee; all are available iced or spiced with the flavored syrup of your choosing.

Pahoa Natural Groceries *(965-8322, 15-1403 Government Main Rd)* Open 7;30am-8pm Mon Sat, 7.30am-6pm Sun. Serving as the nexus for Pahoa's healthy, hippy contingent, this large, well-stocked natural foods store has so much good stuff, it's hard to stay away (despite the painful prices). The sandwiches ($3.50) are wholesome and the delicious hot-food bar ($4.99/lb) switches regional cuisines daily; there's a respectable wine selection as well. Those with the sweet tooth munchies will be delighted with their baked items.

Meaner Wiener *(☎ 965-6644, 15-2929 Government Main Rd)* Open 11am-2pm & 5pm-10pm Mon-Fri, 5pm-10pm Sat & Sun. You won't believe the size of the hot dogs nestled in a potato bun and buried under a mound of chili and parmesan cheese that is the Meaner Wiener ($2.75). Too much? Try the turkey sausage Leaner Wiener or the veggie Beaner Wiener ($2.50each). Coffee here is just 50¢ a cup, with three free refills. Nice!

Papa's *(☎ 965-7100, 15-2950 Government Main Rd)*. Dishes $4.25-6. This very laid-back café keeps loose Monday to Saturday hours, but is worth catching open for their fabulous falafel, veggie burgers and Indian-inspired fare. The sweets ($2) are handmade by the attentive owner and go all too well with the coffee and chai. The outdoor patio fronts Main St, which is great for people watching.

Sawasdee Thai Cuisine *(☎ 965-8186, 15-2955 Government Main Rd)* Dishes $4.95-$11.95. Open noon-8pm daily. In a field crowded with Thai places, this place leads the pack. There are the usual curries, but interesting Muslim varieties of curry, panang and pineapple varieties as well. Also vying for your attention are fresh salads and sublime appetizers. Organic produce, locally raised meat and poultry and homegrown herbs are used whenever possible. The presentation is gorgeous and the service so friendly, you can eat here two nights in a row guilt-free. They also do take-out.

Luquin's *(☎ 965-9990, Government Main Rd)* Breakfast $3-6, à la carte dishes $2.75-5.75, combination plates $6.50-10.50 Open 7am-9pm daily. Can this even be called Mexican food? Anemic salsa, bland guacamole and off-tasting fish tacos were just the start. To be fair, folks rave about the gigantic breakfast burritos ($3) at this Pahoa institution. Still, the cocktail bar hops most nights and is an interesting place to check out a slice of life Puna-style.

Paolo's Bistro *(☎ 965-7033, Government Main Rd)* Mains $8.95-$16.95, specials $18.95. Open dinner 5:30pm-9pm Tues-Sun. This eatery serves Northern Italian fare in a subdued, intimate atmosphere, though waitstaff can get overwhelmed weekends. There are pasta dishes, served with minestrone or try the cioppino; save room for dessert.

Entertainment

Pahoa is pretty dead, except when some special event flares up. Then it hops high because everyone is desperate for something different to do.

Punatix Lounge *(Pahoa Lounge; ☎ 965-1514, 15-2929 Government Main Rd)* Open noon-1am daily. Now here's a dive with charm. There's a dance floor, lots of tables to sprawl and brawl over, a back patio and a couple of pool tables and dart boards. One night it may be packed with drag queens striking a pose, while the next might find the local biker club tattooing each other out back.

Other Pahoa entertainment is below the radar. ***Full moon parties*** are held each month and while the location rotates around the island, Puna is a likely locale and folks here definitely know where they're happening; ask around.

Getting Around

One Hele-On bus (No 7 'Downtown Hilo') passes through Pahoa on its way to Hilo at 6:05am, Monday to Friday ($2.25, 90 minutes).

PUNA

It's a pretty easy hitch to either Hilo or Volcano from Pahoa.

AROUND PAHOA

The usual route for exploring the Pahoa area is a triangle heading down Hwy 132 past Lava Tree State Monument to Kapoho, then continuing on Hwy 137 along the shore to the lava flow at Kalapana, returning to Pahoa via Hwy 130, (with a detour to the active lava flow at the end of that road). If possible, try to time it so you arrive at the flow near sunset so you can see it firing up the night. Conveniently, Hwys 137 and 130 still connect, but who knows? Pele could get frisky and change it all by the time you read this book.

From Pahoa, Hwy 132 passes through a tropical reserve. It's like an enchanted forest and will give you an idea of Puna's allure. This entire area presents a great opportunity to ditch your guidebook and poke around. But always respect any private property and no trespassing signs – you'll see lots of them here. Perhaps one of the best ways to gain access around here is to stay in one of the inns sprinkled about the area, availing yourself of your host's insider status.

Lava Tree State Monument

The approach to Lava Tree State Monument is like a dreamscape, with a tight-knit canopy of monkey pod trees arching overhead, letting through dappled bits of sun and sky. This beautiful stretch is called the Tree Tunnel and cloaks this road in mystery.

The park itself makes for a quick diversion, with a 20-minute loop trail through thickets of bamboo orchids, passing interesting lava tree molds on the way. The tree molds here were created in 1790, when this ohia rain forest was engulfed in pahoehoe from Kilauea's East Rift Zone. The lava was free-flowing and moved quickly, like a river flooding its banks.

As the molten lava ran through the forest, some of it started congealing around the moisture-laden ohia trunks, while the rest of the flow moved on through and quickly receded.

Although the trees themselves burned away, the molds of lava that had formed around them remained. Now, 200 years later, there's a ghost forest of phallic lava shells. Some of the 'lava trees' are some 10 feet high, while others are short enough to look down into, sheltering ferns and frogs within their hollows.

Be careful if you walk off the path, as the ground is crossed by deep cracks in places, some hidden by new vegetation. It's speculated that one deep fracture, (caused by an earthquake at the same time as the flow), may have drained much of the lava back into the earth. You can check out the crack to the left of the bathrooms.

The park is on Hwy 132, 2½ miles east from its intersection with Hwy 130. The mosquitoes can be wicked. These are the last public toilets for a piece.

Lava Tree Inn (☎ 965-7441, 877-390-9200, fax 965-7410, e hapa1234@aol.com, PO Box 6300, Hilo, HI 96720) Singles $45, doubles $65-85, doubles with Jacuzzi $125. This 2-story home in a quiet, peaceful setting just past the park on the entrance road, is a good option with a great location. The rooms are affordable, there's an upstairs lanai and everything fronts the lush grounds.

Kapoho

Hwy 132 heads east through orchards of papaya and vanda orchids to what was once Kapoho, a farming town of about 300 people.

On January 13, 1960, a fountain of fire half a mile long shot up just above Kapoho. The main flow of liquid pahoehoe lava ran toward the ocean but a slower moving offshoot of a'a lava crept toward the town, burying orchid farms in its path. On January 28 the lava entered Kapoho and buried it. A hot springs resort and nearly 100 homes and businesses succumbed to the lava.

Then a bizarre thing occurred when the lava approached the sea at **Cape Kumukahi**. Within a few feet of the cape's lighthouse, the lava flow split in two and circled around the structure, sparing it from destruction. Coincidence, natural phenomenon or charity reciprocated on the part of Pele? You be the judge.

Puna & Pele

In the Hawaiian language, there are several axioms linking Puna with Pele. For example, to express anger, someone might say *Ke lauahi maila o Pele ia Puna*, 'Pele is pouring lava out on Puna.' Equally common are both historic and modern stories of a mysterious woman traveling alone through Puna. Sometimes she's young and attractive, other times she's old and wizened, and often she's seen just before a volcanic eruption. Those who stop and pick her up hitchhiking or show some other kindness are protected from the lava flow

After the 1960 lava flow destroyed the village of Kapoho, stories circulated about how the light-keeper in the spared Kapoho lighthouse had offered a meal to an elderly woman who had showed up at his door on the eve of the eruption.

The lighthouse has been replaced by a modern light behind cyclone fencing, so there's not much to see down the 1¾ miles of dirt road leading to it from the intersection of Hwys 132 and 137 (often called 'four corners' locally). However, Cape Kumukahi, which means 'first beginning' in Hawaiian, is the easternmost point in the state and has some of the freshest air in the world, known as **virgin air**, according to scientists who monitor such things.

Farms are gradually returning to the area and just past the 4-mile marker on the right you'll see a sign offering orchids for $2.50-5. This is the Bonelli family **orchid farm** (☎ 965-2613). Head here to pick up some beautiful dendrobiums or oncidiums for your condo or ship them to friends on the mainland ($25 for shipping and plant).

Wa'a Wa'a

At the intersection of Hwys 132 and 137 (Red Road), most people hook a right to explore Red Road's coastal diversions. If you go left instead, however, you'll be spirited away to a time when the land was thick with pandalus and breadfruit too tall to topple and no sound was heard but offshore breezes. Although there are lots of folks living an off-the-grid lifestyle back in here, it really feels like you're in a different century.

Wa'a Wa'a is loaded with kapu and 'Keep out' signs and that's largely because the area is peppered with ancient Hawaiian burial grounds. You will be adversely affected if you fuss around here where you

shouldn't. Still, you can pop in for a 3-hour **coconut weaving** class with Bruddah Joe ($5 donation, 10am Wed, 11am Sat). Look for his sign on the left about a mile down the road from the intersection of Hwys 132 and 137. There's also coastal access at **Orr's Beach** a further mile or so down the road.

ALONG RED ROAD (HWY 137)

In reality, very few people call this coastal road anything but Red Road. That's because it was once brilliantly paved with well-tamped red cinder from the 1960 Kapoho lava flow. It's now mostly basic black tarmac, but you can see ribbons of red along the shoulders and a short stretch near the 8-mile marker is still red. Other names for this road (in order of usage) include Hwy 137, Kalapana-Kapoho Rd and Beach Rd.

The road is flanked by barren lava for the first few miles, but gives way to thick groves of hilo, hala and mango trees that are so gorgeous it's hard to get concerned about their invasive nature. In low-lying parts, the road floods during winter storms and high tide. There are many little tracks leading from the road to the cliffs and coast in this area that might reap generous rewards if you feel like exploring.

Visit this beautiful corner of the Big Island before the proposed mega-resort starts construction between Isaac Hale Beach Park and the hot pond. The attendant bulldozers, cement mixers and road-widening machines will certainly ruin the heretofore peaceful effect.

PUNA

Nasty Noni

Unparalleled among traditional restoratives is *noni* (Indian mulberry), which grows with wild abandon all along Red Road. Noni is effective against everything from diarrhea to diabetes and tastes bad enough to prove it. While noni has received little serious attention from the scientific community (although that is changing), Hawaiians have used it topically for generations to treat sores and wounds. Noni is also said to be a natural alternative to Viagra, so sharpen those shovels, boys.

You'll know the tree by its dark green, waxy leaves and baseball-sized fruit with alien 'eyes' dimpling its flesh. To prepare noni, pick the fruit when it's still hard and just ripening white. Wash and put the fruit in a jar just covered with water and set it in partial shade to ferment. When the water is nearly evaporated and the noni look like decomposing brains, press the pulp through a sieve and transfer to the refrigerator. Take a tablespoon each morning on an empty stomach. Practitioners maintain the empty stomach directive has nothing to do with noni's flavor, but we wonder. Prepared noni can be purchased in Big Island health food stores for $11 for 8oz. Be sure to check with your doctor first.

For more on this wondrous plant, see *Noni* by Diana Fairechild (Flyana Rhyme).

Green Lake

A freshwater crater lake ensconced among breadfruit, guava, avocado and rustling bamboo: here's just another reason for all that Puna pride. The placid green waters here are ideal for (clothing-optional) swimming and there's a rope swing and wooden raft for your aquatic romping pleasure.

To get here, park opposite Kapoho Beach Rd, just after the 8-mile marker. You'll know the spot by the fence and the other parked cars (there are usually a few, though you may get lucky). Technically this is private property and there are 'No Trespassing' signs, but the gate to the right is almost always open and it's a favorite local spot. Enter through the gate and walk on the road for about five minutes, (always bearing right), after which you'll take the little path through a garden on the left and a homestead on the right. Beyond the garden, the trail continues down and to the left; the lake sits prettily at the bottom. Be courteous and respectful in this area, please.

Hale O Naia (☎ 965-5340, Ⓦ *www.hale -o-naia.com, Kapoho Beach Rd*) Room $75, suite $150. This sanctuary, in the gated community down Kapoho Beach Rd opposite Green Lake, is a little slice of paradise. The two rooms are in Sally Whitney's beautifully detailed home, right on the lip of Kapoho Bay. The more basic room is hardly that, featuring a lovely canopy bed, private sea-facing lanai and a private detached bath with a Jacuzzi tub. The suite is incredible, with a king-size bed, his and her baths, a sitting room, sauna and huge lanai. There are hammocks and a hot tub and you have access to kayaks, snorkel and boogie boards. Rates are based on double occupancy and include breakfast. Reservations are a must.

Kapoho Tide Pools

These tide pools are in the Kapoho Vacationland subdivision, a mile south of the lighthouse. The sprawling network of tide pools is formed in lava basins, some of which are deep enough for **snorkeling**. There are several rich spots (the best on the windward side) with lush coral gardens supporting saddle wrasses, Moorish idols, urchins, sea cucumbers and many varieties of butterfly fish. The pools are too shallow during low tide to permit gliding about inside them.

To get there, turn off Hwy 137 onto Kapoho Kai Drive, at the end, turn left on Wai Opae, drive for about 500 feet and park in front of the house festooned with all manner of found artifacts (don't worry, you can't miss it). Take the rocky trail across smaller pools for about 75 feet to a large cove that flushes to the ocean. Following the rocky channel along the left-hand side minimizes the currents here, which can be really strong. This is a great place for hydrophobes to snorkel because they can just lie on the lava and poke a mask into the water; lying on an old boogie board makes for comfortable underwater viewing.

Hot Pond (Ahalanui Beach Park)

One glorious swimming spot in Puna is the Hot Pond (written as Ahalanui Beach Park or Secrets Beach on maps), on Red Road a mile north of Isaac Hale Beach Park. This is a lovely thermal spring-fed pool set in lava rock and edged by swaying palms. It's roughly 60 feet in diameter and deep enough for swimming.

The water temperature averages about 90°F. The pool has an inlet to the ocean (which pounds upon the seawall rocks at the makai side of the pool, bringing in many tropical fish during high tide and providing snorkeling opportunities), so the water stays clean. It's usually hotter during low tide.

The park has picnic tables, pit toilets and a lifeguard. There's plenty of parking, but as always, don't leave anything valuable in your car. Nighttime soaks under the moon and stars is also a possibility.

Isaac Hale Beach Park

Isaac Hale Beach Park, on Pohoiki Bay, has a chunky lava shoreline and a good surfing break. On weekends, there's usually a frenzy of local activity.

The Pohoiki boat ramp here is Puna's only put-in, so there's lots of sea traffic. Still, this is the best place for **surfing** and **scuba diving** in the district. Enter to the left of the boat ramp, but beware of passing boats.

Soaking fans are in for a treat as there's a small **hot pond** hiding back in the growth along the shore. To reach this 10-foot oasis, pick up the beaten path just beyond the house bedecked with No Trespassing signs. Moments later, you'll see the pond gleaming to your right.

Camping is allowed, but it's not a very attractive option, as the camping area is virtually in the parking lot and it's the preferred site for long term squatters. For information on obtaining a county camping permit, see Camping in the Accommodations section in the Facts for the Visitor chapter.

The park has toilets but little else.

Pohoiki Road

As you veer around the bend to continue following Red Road, you have the option of staying straight on Pohoiki Rd back to Pahoa. This is yet another of Puna's shaded, mystical roads that winds through thick forest dotted with papaya orchards and noni growing wild. It's a good shortcut up to Pahoa town.

Yoga Oasis (☎ 965-8460, 800-274-4446, W *www.yogaoasis.org, 13-683 Pohoiki Rd*) single/double room or tentalow $75/95, single/double deluxe tentalow $125/225, single/double house $175/225. This yoga retreat nestled on 26 acres of orchards is about 2 miles up Pohoiki Rd from the coast. All room prices include daily yoga and an organic breakfast. The spotless rooms in the main house are tastefully decorated and share a spectacular marble bath. Basic tentalows farther back on the property share this bath, but the deluxe model has private facilities and a gorgeous black bamboo bed. There are drop-in yoga classes at 8am ($10) and all-inclusive yoga retreats featuring room and board, daily yoga, herbal detoxification, massage and more.

MacKenzie State Recreation Area

There's no beach at MacKenzie State Recreation Area, but the 40-foot cliffs and dramatically surging surf are wild. Fishing from the cliffs may land you some *ulua*, a big old jack fish that favors turbulent waters.

This 13-acre park in a grove of ironwood trees is eerily quiet and secluded. The needles underfoot provide a spongy carpet, but also prevent anything else from growing here. Both tent and trailer *camping* are allowed with a state permit, but the facilities, which include picnic tables and latrines, are run-down, and drinking water is unavailable. For information on obtaining a camping permit, see Camping in the Accommodations section of the Facts for the Visitor chapter.

Locals believe Night Marchers like to prowl around here, so if you start hearing drums and see torches bobbing along in the distance, show your reverence by lying face down while they pass.

Opihikao & Around
The village of Opihikao is marked by a little Congregational church and a couple of houses.

Kalani Honua, a New Age conference and retreat center on 113 beautiful acres, is 2½ miles southwest of Opihikao village, between the 17- and 18-mile markers. The center has a diverse workshop menu, including tai chi retreats, alternative health and fitness courses, Hawaiian culture programs and workshops geared to the gay and lesbian community. Nature tours taking in waterfalls, caves or remote beaches and valleys are on offer as well. They also have daily drop-in yoga classes ($10) and a spa day pass ($10) that allows access to the pool, Jacuzzi, sauna and watsu pool.

Kalani Honua (☎ 965-7828, 800-800-6886, **ⓦ** www.kalani.com, RR2 Box 4500, Pahoa, HI 96778) Tent sites singles/doubles $20/30 (add $10 for Nov-Apr), rooms with shared bath $105/110, rooms with private bath $125/135, cottages with private bath $110/130, tree house with private bath $210/240. Buffet breakfast $8, lunch $10, dinner $16. Dining room open breakfast 7:30am-8:30am, lunch noon-1pm, dinner 6pm-7:15pm. While this retreat caters mostly to groups, it welcomes individual travelers on a space-available basis. There are dozens of rooms, most in two-story cedar lodges with exposed-beam ceilings; a screened common area contains a shared kitchen. Also available are private cottages with one bedroom, bath and living room and three tree houses.

Tents can be pitched on the grounds and there's a sauna, Jacuzzi, and a large swimming pool for guests.

The center has a volunteer-resident program that provides room, board, pool and spa access, yoga and retreat classes in exchange for 30 hours of work per week; a three-month commitment is required. This is a great alternative for those willing and able to work while they learn and play. There's a fairly rigorous application process. Kalani also has an artist-in-residence program open to artists of nearly all media (stipends available).

The *dining room*, which serves buffet-style vegetarian meals, is open to the public. The food is divine, but dining room hours are short and sweet. The separate ***Puna Olelo Café*** serves coffee, ice cream and snacks and serves as host for occasional poetry readings and live music; it's open Mon-Sat 6:30pm-10:30pm.

Up on Opihikao Rd about 2 miles from the turn off on Red Road is the local Krishna gathering, happening every Sunday night at 6:30, and sometimes on Wednesdays (look for the shingle announcing the shindigs). You don't have to be a believer and they won't give you the hard press to become one, but the house bursts with devotees. The night starts out with energetic chanting and leaping about to a live band, followed by some prayers and a sermon of sorts delivered by the pontificating host. A huge dinner follows (donation suggested), highlighted by the best pizza in Puna. You aren't required to leap and pray to partake of the dinner and many local bohemians skip the chanting and show up for dinner around 8pm.

Kehena Beach
Kehena Beach, at the base of a cliff, is a sweet black-sand beach created by a 1955 lava flow. Shaded by coconut and ironwood trees, this beach is a free-spirited, nude sunbathing spot attracting a mixed crowd of hippies and Hawaiians, families and seniors. Even when it rains in Pahoa, it's usually sunny here.

When the water is calm, swimming is usually safe, but mind the currents and undertows. In the morning, it's not unusual for dolphins to venture close to shore.

On Sundays, Kehena pulsates to the beats of a well-established drum circle, as percussionists and musicians of all shapes, sizes and abilities jam and dance amongst wafts of blue smoke.

Kehena is on Red Rd, immediately south of the 19-mile marker. Look for the little parking lot on the right and you'll see the path down to the beach, a five-minute walk over jagged lava rock. Don't leave valuables in your car.

Dangers & Annoyances Good, strong swimmers die at Kehena every year. At the time of writing, two choppers within a week had to buzz in and pluck folks from the surf. One made it, one didn't. Respect the ocean here and do not venture beyond the rocky point on the southern end. Rip currents, undertows and rogue waves are all possibilities, especially in winter.

Kalapana (Former Village)

For years, the village of Kalapana sat precariously atop Kilauea's restless east rift. When the latest series of eruptions began in 1983, the main lava flow moved down slope to the west of Kalapana. Much of the early flow passed through a series of lava tubes, which carried the molten lava down to the coast and into the sea. During pauses in the eruption in 1990, the tubes cooled long enough to harden and block up. When the eruption started anew, the lava flow, no longer able to take its previous course, turned toward Kalapana. By the end of 1990 the entire village, including 100 homes, was buried.

Today Red Rd (Hwy 137) ends abruptly at the former site of Kaimu Beach on the eastern edge of Kalapana. Kaimu was the most famous black-sand beach in Hawaii, but is now encased under a sea of hardened lava. A few houses were spared, including Uncle Robert's, where you can take a **nature walk** (suggested donation) and peruse photos of the devastating event that buried Kalapana.

Keep Uncle Robert's at your back and a 10-minute walk across the lava leads to a new **black-sand beach**. You'll need to watch your footing, as there are cracks in the lava and potential thin spots, but it's a fairly well-trodden walk. Towards the end of the flow, the pahoehoe turns to coarse granules and hundreds of baby coconut palms form a natural promenade to the sea. The beach is only an apostrophe of sand, but you can have it all to yourself, even on a Sunday.

Verna's V Drive-In (☎ 965-8234) Dishes $2.50-5. Open 10am-5pm Mon-Fri, 9am-5pm Sat & Sun. If you're hungry, this branch of the mini-empire serves the cheap

She could be a goddess – best give her a lift!

burgers, sandwiches and plate lunch they're famous for. It also has a kicking selection of ice cream.

HIGHWAY 130

From the edge of the Kalapana lava flow, a side road leads up to Hwy 130, which returns to Pahoa. There are a couple of sights along the way.

Once on Hwy 130 proper, backtrack about a mile to view the **live lava flow**. In August 2001, the county cut a controversial road through the hardened lava to allow access to the area where lava pulses downhill and into the sea. People were already driving out there before the road, but now the park charges $5 entrance fee per car (free for hikers). While the new road has been bad for residents, it's phenomenal for visitors as there's nothing like beholding hot lava hitting the sea, boiling the water and shooting up tall steam plumes into the night sky.

Some nights are more dramatic than others and it's really anti-climactic during the day, so try to get there as it grows dark to watch the show unfold.

After paying the entrance fee, it's a 2½-mile drive over lava to where you park and walk for another 30 minutes to the viewing area. Bring flashlights, water and durable

PUNA

shoes. The first two are sometimes sold by young entrepreneurs at the trailhead. Heed the warning signs, as the lava shelf is fragile and volcanic fumes can be harmful, especially to the very young, old or pregnant. Vehicle access to the flow is open noon-8:15pm daily, though you are welcome to remain until 10pm.

Painted Church

The Star of the Sea (1929) is a little white Catholic church noted for its interior trompe l'oeil murals that create the effect of being in a large cathedral. The painting style is primitive, but the illusion of depth is amazingly effective. The church also has an accomplished stained-glass window of Father Damien, who was with the parish before he moved to the leprosy colony on Molokai.

The church, which was in Kalapana, was moved by community members just before lava flows swept over the town. It now sits along Hwy 130 at the 20-mile marker.

Recently deconsecrated, the church is in the process of being turned into a cultural center by the Kalapana Ohana Association. Even if it's locked, you're free to walk up and peek at the interior through the front windows. Call ☎ 965-7429 for visiting hours.

Steam Vents

At the 15-mile marker, 3½ miles from Pahoa, there's a big sign screaming 'Scenic View' with an arrow pointing into the bushes. There's absolutely zilch to view unless you know what you're looking for. In this case, it's puffs of steam from several low spatter cones with hollowed out natural steam baths inside, perfect for a sauna.

Take the track into the overgrowth for a few minutes: the first right fork leads to a two-person sauna with wooden planks for seats. Keep heading back on the path, though, and there's a much larger one that accommodates a few people lying down. The vents are pretty hot – not Swedish or professional athlete hot – but still delicious as the sulfurous grog mixes with the sweet coastal air. Nighttime brings hundreds of hungry roaches (how relaxing!). The vents

are – like many Puna activities – clothing optional.

ALONG HWY 11
Kurtistown

Heading up past Kea'au to Volcano on Hwy 11, the first burg you come to is Kurtistown. There isn't much to it but a gas station and post office, but there are some affordable places to stay on the backroads.

For a look at some amazing artistry, stop in at **Dan De Luz's Woods** (☎ 968-6607). Stunningly beautiful bowls, picture frames, platters and more are made from mango, koa, sandalwood, banyan and other native woods by this master craftsman. The prices are totally reasonable for such works of art. To get there, turn right onto Ahuahu Pl, just after the 12-mile marker. It's open 9am-5pm Monday to Friday.

Pineapple Park Hostel (☎/fax 968-8170, 800-877-8652, Ⓦ www.pineapple-park.com, PO Box 639, Kurtistown, HI 96760) Camping $12 per person, dorm beds $20, doubles with shared bath $50-65, doubles with private bath $75-85. This quiet, well-kept place is a good option if you have wheels. There are sex-segregated dorms, with bed linen included; there are also four pleasant private rooms, two with private baths and a lanai (breakfast included). Hostelers can prepare their own meals in the big guest kitchen. Other amenities include a pool table, horseshoes, big-screen TV, laundry facilities, and lockers. There may be some camping cabins available for rent by the time you arrive.

Pineapple Park is off the beaten track but is still a convenient base for exploring the region. From Kea'au, head west on Hwy 11. Turn left onto S Kulani Rd just past the 13-mile marker. Turn right on Pohala St and left on Pikake St, then look for the sign. It's a total of 2½ miles from Hwy 11.

Butterfly Inn (☎ 966-7936, 800-546-2442, Ⓦ www.thebutterflyinn.com, PO Box 6010 Kurtistown, HI 96760) Singles/doubles $55/65. Staying here feels like you live in Hawaii: the two comfortable rooms are on the top floor of a house and share an ample kitchen and sitting room. The shared bath adjacent features a tub that gazes upon the gardens. There's a hot tub and wood burning sauna ($10) tucked amidst the landscaped grounds. This inn is for women only and it's far off the beaten track, so forget it if you don't have a car.

The Butterfly Inn also has a work-exchange program (20 hours/week, one month minimum in exchange for lodging in a plywood palace without plumbing) that has received decidedly mixed reviews – some people dig it, others flee under the cover of night.

Koa Kaffee (☎ 968-1129, *Across from Dan De Luz's Woods*) Open 5am-8pm Wed-Mon, 5am-2pm Tues. This little diner serves wholesome food (try the Portuguese bean soup) at good prices; early birds will appreciate the pre-dawn hours.

Mountain View

Oops! You missed Mountain View. That was it, the two gas pumps and mini-mart receding in your rearview at the 14-mile marker. Actually, there's a *Verna's Too Drive In* (☎ 968-8774) branch next to the mini-mart that's good for saimin or plate lunch if you're peaked.

The *Mountain View Bakery* (☎ 968-6353) on spooky Old Volcano Road just behind this teeny strip, bakes fresh and sinful butter rolls (rolls of butter would be more appropriate) and is the 'home of the famous stone cookies.' True to their moniker, these rock-hard sweeties are great with coffee and last *forever*: the perfect backpacking snack at $4.50/bag.

Glenwood

Here's yet another one-store town, en route to the national park. But like the others before it, there are reasons to stop and poke around.

Hirano's Store, just before the 20-mile marker has gas and food stuffs, but the real reason to pull over here is to see the fuming Pu'u O'o vent from the clearing across the way. On a clear day you can see this active vent (the one responsible for the lava flowing to the sea at the end of Hwy 130; see that section earlier) huffing and puffing away.

If you continue up Hwy 11 (a half mile drive past the 22 mile marker), you'll come to **Akatsuka Orchid Gardens** (☎ 967-8234, *fax 967-7140; admission free; open 8:30am-5pm daily*). This major orchid concern has been growing an incredible number of species here since 1974. There's a gift shop and garden walk; it ships worldwide.

PUNA

Hawaii Volcanoes National Park

Hawaii Volcanoes National Park (HVNP; W www.nps.gov/havo) is unique among US national parks. The huge preserve contains two active volcanoes and terrain ranging from tropical beaches to the subarctic Mauna Loa summit.

The centerpiece of the park is Kilauea Caldera, the sunken center of Kilauea Volcano, the youngest and most active volcano on earth. This still-steaming crater, where molten magma boils just beneath the surface, makes a great day hike – or you can drive around the entire rim. Within the caldera is the Halema'uma'u crater, another smoking, fuming beast that's green around the gills from sulphurous gases. This crater is the home of Madame Pele.

The park's landscape is phenomenal, with dozens of craters and cinder cones, hills piled with pumice, and hardened oceans of lava frozen rock-solid on the hillsides. Dotting the lava landscape are rain forest and fern grove oases called *kipuka*, plus newer thickets of green that have taken root in the rugged black rock. These islands provide a protected habitat for a number of native bird species. Completing the scene are the massive blue flanks of Mauna Loa in the distance.

The park is one of Hawaii's best places for camping and hiking, and those who leave the car behind will be rewarded with an unforgettable experience. It has 140 miles of amazingly varied trails and both drive-up campsites and backcountry camping. You can also hike to the active lava flow at the end of Chain of Craters Rd. The park encompasses about a quarter-million acres of land – more than the entire island of Molokai – and it's still growing; in the past 15 years, lava pouring from Kilauea has added more than 500 acres of land to the Big Island.

Kilauea's has been active since 1983, destroying everything in its path. The coastal road to Puna was blocked by lava in 1988. The Wahaula Visitor Center on the south

Highlights

- Trekking to and camping at the Pu'u O'o vent, the most active part of the world's most active volcano
- Exploring the Kilauea Caldera and paying respects to Madame Pele in her Halema'uma'u Crater home
- Hoofing it over miles of lava to where the hot flow pours into the ocean
- Checking out the unique species in the Kipuka Puaulu
- Browsing the world-class offerings at the Volcano Art Center
- Relaxing in the lap of luxury in one of Volcano town's many B&Bs, retreats or vacation homes

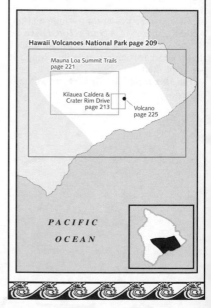

Hawaii Volcanoes National Park page 209

Mauna Loa Summit Trails page 221

Kilauea Caldera & Crater Rim Drive page 213

Volcano page 225

PACIFIC OCEAN

coast went under the next year, and the entire village of Kalapana was buried in 1990. Since that time, the flows have crept

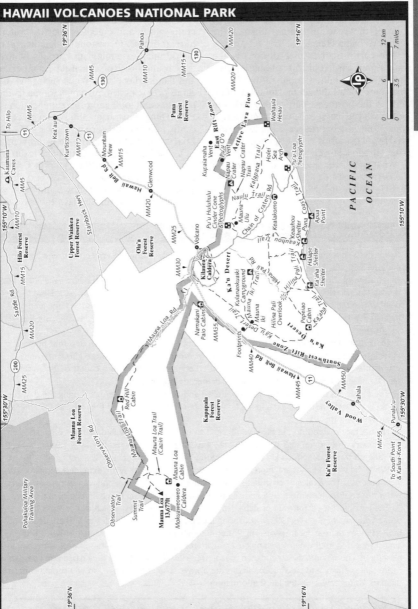

HAWAII VOLCANOES NATIONAL PARK

To Hilo

Kaumana Caves

Kea'au

Kurtistown

Mountain View

Glenwood

Volcano

Pahoa

Puna Forest Reserve

Ola'a Forest Reserve

Upper Waiakea Forest Reserve

Hilo Forest Reserve

Saddle Rd

Stainback Hwy

Hawaii Belt Rd

East Rift Zone

Kupaianaha Vent

Napau Crater

Napau Vent

Pu'u O'o

Active Lava Flow

Wahaula Heiau

Pu'u Loa Petroglyphs

Holei Sea Arch

Kalapana Trail

Napau Crater Trail

Pu'u Huluhulu Cinder Cone & Petroglyphs

Naulu Trail

Mauna Ulu

Chain of Craters Rd

Kealakomo

Keauhou Trail

Keauhou Shelter

Apua Point

PACIFIC OCEAN

Kilauea Caldera

Ka'u Desert

Halape Shelter

'Ka'aha Shelter

Hilina Pali Rd

Puna Coast Trail

Hilina Pali Trail

Kulanaokuaiki Campground

Mauna Iki Trail

Mauna Iki

Hilina Pali Overlook

Pepeiao Cabin

Ka'u Desert Trail

Footprints Trail

Namakani Paio Cabins

Ka'u Desert

Southwest Rift Zone

Hawaii Belt Rd

Wood Valley

Pahala

Punalu'u

To South Point & Kailua-Kona

Ka'u Forest Reserve

Kapapala Forest Reserve

Mauna Loa Rd

Red Hill Cabin

Mauna Loa Trail

Mauna Loa Trail (Cabin Trail)

Mauna Loa Cabin

Mauna Loa 13,677ft

Mokuaweoweo Caldera

Summit Trail

Observatory Trail

Observatory Rd

Mauna Loa Forest Reserve

Pohakuloa Military Training Area

0   6   12 km
0   3.5   7 miles

farther west, engulfing Kamoamoa Beach in 1994 and later claiming an additional mile of the road, including most of the sacred Wahaula Heiau.

The current series of eruptions is the longest in recorded history and has ejected more than 2.5 billion cubic yards of lava. The center of all the action is the Pu'u O'o vent, in the northeast part of the park. On clear days you can see the vent's smoldering cone from just before the 20-mile marker on Hwy 11; there's a little pullout across from Hirano's Store.

What you'll be able to see depends on the current volcanic activity, but remember that Hawaiian shield volcanoes lack the explosive gases of more dramatic volcanoes (eg, Mt St Helens) that spew mud, ash or lava into the air. Instead, the lava here generally oozes and creeps, while the craters huff and puff. Occasionally, Kilauea gets melodramatic sending up curtains of fire, lava fountains, Rorschach-type spattering and flaming lava balls. When such rare volcanic events occur, everyone zooms to the park to get a look and offer supplication to Pele. Things have been almost too quiet recently and scientists are monitoring Mauna Loa, which is slowly filling up with magma.

Volcanoes are pretty anticlimactic during the day. From the end of Chain of Craters Rd, you can see steam clouds and that's about it. Once the sun is down and the stars wink to life however, the lava tubes on the

Go to the Flow

Giving in to visitor demands, the Park Service somewhat reluctantly allows people to hike from the end of Chain of Craters Rd to the active lava flow.

It's a pretty strenuous trek over hardened lava, and there's no established trail. As the coastline is unstable, hikers should stay about a quarter mile inland. The walk eventually leads close to the point where the lava flows dramatically into the sea (but not quite as close as the flow near Kalapana in Puna; see the Hwy 130 section of the Puna chapter). For safety reasons, the Park Service suggests getting no closer than half a mile.

In all, the roundtrip hike covers a distance of about 6 miles and takes around four hours. It's most interesting to begin late in the afternoon in order to view the orange glow after dark. If you're interested in joining a guided trek, Arnott's Lodge makes the hike a couple of days a week; see Organized Tours in the Getting Around chapter for information.

The trail is not only unmarked, it's unpatrolled and potentially dangerous. During the day, the black lava reflects the sun's heat and the temperature commonly gets into the high 90s (°F); there's no shade along the way.

No matter how you do the hike, you'll need to be prepared. The Park Service suggests each person carry a minimum of 3 quarts of water, a flashlight (you can sometimes purchase them at the ranger's trailer), a first-aid kit, sunscreen, sturdy boots and long pants.

While the steam plumes are impressive to see from a distance, they are extremely dangerous to view up close. The explosive clash between seawater and 2100°F molten lava can spray scalding water hundreds of feet into the air and can throw chunks of lava up to a half mile inland.

The lava crust itself forms in unstable ledges called lava benches, which can collapse into the ocean without warning. In 1993, a collapsing lava bench sent one islander to his fiery death and burned more than a dozen people in the ensuing steam explosion. In March 1999, the scene almost repeated itself when seven onlookers scattered to safety after a series of explosions began blasting lava bombs into the air and then collapsed the 25-acre lava bench they'd been standing on.

Volcanic activity and viewing conditions are always subject to change, so you should contact the park visitor center for the latest information.

mountainside glow red in the night sky, and lava lakes at the top of vents reflect light onto passing clouds. If the ceiling to a tube collapses, you can see 'skylights' (punctures in the earth's surface that reveal the molten lava below). You can also make a trek across hardened lava to within a quarter of a mile from where the lava hits the sea (see the boxed text Go to the Flow).

ORIENTATION

The park's main road is Crater Rim Drive, which circles the moonscape around Kilauea Caldera, taking in many interesting sites sprinkled around the rim. You can quickly buzz the drive-up sites in an hour – and if that's all the time you have it's unquestionably worth it. Still, it's far better to give yourself three hours or so to allow time for a few short walks and stops at the visitor center and museum.

The park's other scenic drive is the Chain of Craters Rd, which leads south 20 miles through the volatile East Rift Zone to the coast, ending at the site of the most recent lava activity.

While you can get a good sense of the place in one full day, it's easy to spend days, if not weeks, exploring this fascinating park. If you can, take advantage of the fact that the price of admission allows you access for a full week.

Hikers and campers will want to flip right to the Hiking section later in this chapter. In addition to camping, there are a couple of places to stay within the park boundaries (see the Volcano section near the end of this chapter for details).

INFORMATION

One of the many beauties of HVNP is that it's open 24 hours a day, 365 days a year. This allows you to take advantage of celestial events including eclipses and meteor showers.

The park's 24-hour eruption hotline (☎ 985-6000) tells you what the volcano is doing that day and where to best view the action. For more detailed information, talk to one of the helpful rangers at the visitor center directly (☎ 985-6017). Updates on eruptions, weather conditions and road closures are available at 530 AM on your radio dial.

You can obtain the main park brochure in advance, along with camping and hiking information if you specifically request it, by writing to Hawaii Volcanoes National Park, PO Box 52, Hawaii National Park, HI 96718. The park's Web site is also a font of information.

If you're interested in working in the park, see the Volunteer section of the Facts for the Visitor chapter.

Drivers should note that the nearest gas is in Volcano town, so fill up if you plan on driving the many interesting roads contained within the park.

Fees

Park admission permits multiple entries within a seven-day period. Hikers, bikers and motorcyclists are charged $5 per person, while cars are charged $10. If volcanoes are your thing, consider purchasing the annual HVNP pass for $20. Visitors on foot or bicycle enter through the check station (staffed from 8am to 4:30pm daily).

National park passes are also sold here, including an annual pass for $50 that covers Haleakala on Maui and all other US National Park sites. US citizens with disabilities can obtain a Golden Access Passport (free), and those age 62 or older can buy a Golden Age Passport ($10); both allow unlimited and free lifetime access to all US National Parks. Such a deal.

Access for the Disabled

Many of the park sites – including the Visitor Center, Jaggar Museum, Volcano Art Center and Volcano House hotel – are wheelchair accessible. Many of the pull-ups along Crater Rim Drive and the Chain of Craters Rd are curb-free. A few of the park's shorter trails, including Devastation Trail and an eastern section of the Crater Rim Trail near Waldron Ledge, are wheelchair accessible as well. Hand rails or rope cordons are also used to demark short paths like the one to the Halema'uma'u Overlook and Steam Vents.

Climate

Rain, wind and fog typify the moody weather up here. From mistings to downpours, chilly conditions move in fast, and on any given day it can change from hot and dry to cool and soaking in a flash. As a result, many people shiver their way around this park in shorts like so many San Francisco tourists in summer. Throw some long pants, socks and a jacket in the trunk just in case.

Near Kilauea Caldera, temperatures average about 15°F cooler than in Kona. Get a recorded weather forecast by calling ☎ 961-5582 (closed 4pm-midnight).

Road Closures

During periods of prolonged drought, both Mauna Loa Rd and Hilina Pali Rd are subject to closure due to fire-hazard conditions. Alternatively, Hwy 11 between Pahala and Ocean View Estates is prone to flooding, washouts and closures during tempestuous storms.

Dangers & Annoyances

Hawaiian volcanoes are seldom violent, and most of the lava that flows from cracks in the rift zones is slow moving and provides plenty of warning. The eruptions don't spew out a lot of ash or poisonous gases either, which is what accounts for most volcano-related deaths in other parts of the world.

Still, fatalities happen here. Recent deaths have resulted from collapsing benches on the edge of the active flow, steam explosions where the lava hits the ocean and lava tubes caving in.

Another hazard is the toxic cocktail pumping from steam vents. This stuff contains sulfuric and hydrochloric acid and minute glass particles. Everyone should take care around these fumes, but especially people with respiratory and heart conditions, moms-to-be, infants and young children. These higher-risk folks are advised to avoid the areas where fumes are most highly concentrated, including Sulphur Banks and the Halema'uma'u Overlook.

Other potential hazards include deep cracks in the earth and thin lava crust, which may mask hollows and lava tubes. If you stay on marked trails, you shouldn't have any problems. All park warning signs should be taken seriously.

The tales are legendary of folks pocketing chunks of lava or strands of Pele's hair, only to sorely regret it upon returning to real life.

KILAUEA CALDERA & CRATER RIM DRIVE

Crater Rim Drive is a field trip in vulcanology. This amazing 11-mile loop road skirts the rim of Kilauea Caldera, with pull outs and scenic points at steam vents and vast, smoking craters. From roadside parking areas, short trails lead through various landscapes, including a lava tube and a native rain forest. There are also trailheads for longer hikes into and around the caldera (see the Hiking section, later).

Natural forces have rerouted Crater Rim Drive more than once and will undoubtedly continue to recreate the landscape in the future. For example, earthquakes in both 1975 and 1983 rattled it hard enough to knock sections of the road into the caldera. Quakes come with the territory: there are over 1200 earthquakes of measurable magnitude on this island per week.

The most interesting stops are at Jaggar Museum, Halema'uma'u Overlook, Devastation Trail and Thurston Lava Tube. This section is organized according to the most typical route around the caldera, which works counterclockwise from the visitor center.

Unlike the Chain of Craters Rd, Crater Rim Drive is relatively level, making it a good road for cyclists.

Kilauea Visitor Center

The visitor center is a good place to get oriented to the park. It's open every day from 7:45am-5pm. There are bathrooms, drinking water and public phones. The friendly staff here have the latest information on volcanic activity, interpretive programs, guided walks and backcountry trail conditions; the bulletin board lists special events.

There are free pamphlets for some trails and the shop sells an excellent selection of

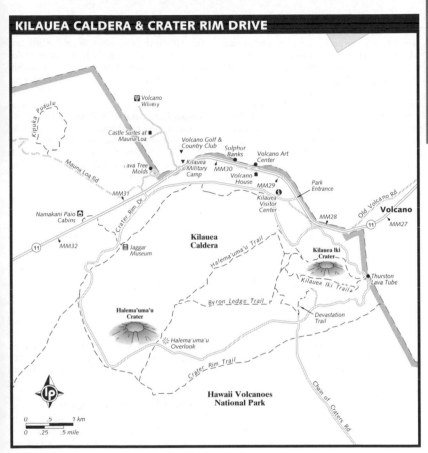

KILAUEA CALDERA & CRATER RIM DRIVE

Kipuka Puaulu

Volcano Winery

Castle Suites at Mauna Loa

Mauna Loa Rd

Lava Tree Molds

Volcano Golf & Country Club

Sulphur Banks

Volcano Art Center

Kilauea Military Camp

MM30

Volcano House

MM29

Park Entrance

Old Volcano Rd

Volcano

Kilauea Visitor Center

MM28

MM27

MM31

Crater Rim Dr

Namakani Paio Cabins

11

MM32

Jaggar Museum

Kilauea Caldera

Halema'uma'u Trail

Kilauea Iki Crater

Kilauea Iki Trail

Thurston Lava Tube

Byron Ledge Trail

Devastation Trail

Halema'uma'u Crater

Halema'uma'u Overlook

Crater Rim Trail

Chain of Craters Rd

Hawaii Volcanoes National Park

0   .5   1 km
0   .25   .5 mile

books and videos. The *Road Guide to Hawaii Volcanoes National Park*, by Barbara and Robert Decker, will be particularly helpful for auto junkets.

There's a very cool, educational junior ranger program for kids five to 12. Kids complete an activity book ($1.95) while making a self-guided tour of the park, earning a badge in the process.

The center contains a small theater where a 25-minute film on the geology of Kilauea is played on the hour from 9am to 4pm (free). Although the films change periodically, you're likely to see some of the most explosive lava footage ever caught on film, including coursing rivers of lava, lava fountains, curtains of fire and lava-sparked forest fires engulfing everything in its path.

Tuesdays nights at 7pm, the park hosts **After Dark in the Park**, a program series led by area experts on issues of cultural, historical and geological importance (free).

Volcano Art Center

The Volcano Art Center (☎ 967-7565, fax 967-7511, ⓦ www.volcanoartcenter.org; open 9am-5pm daily), next to the Kilauea Visitor Center, sells an incredible array of quality local art in a gallery setting. Here you'll find pottery, Hawaiian quilts, paintings, weavings, woodwork, sculpture, jewelry and more. Many pieces are one-of-a-kind, and it's worth a visit just to admire the artistry, even if you're not a shopper.

The center is in the original Volcano House lodge, built in 1877. The nonprofit organization that runs it offers workshops on crafts and hula and sponsors concerts, plays and other activities.

Look for their monthly publication, the *Volcano Gazette*, for a calendar of art center events, After Dark in the Park topics and other local happenings.

Sulphur Banks

The first stop beyond the art center is the Sulphur Banks, where the yellow, red and brown piles of steaming rocks feel like something from a particularly good *Star Trek* set.

This is one of many areas where Kilauea lets off steam, releasing hundreds of tons of sulfuric gases daily. As the steam reaches the surface, it deposits sulfur around the mouths of the vents, crusting them over with a fluorescent yellow froth. The rotten egg smell is from the hydrogen sulfide wafting from the vents. Other gases in the mix include carbon dioxide and sulfur dioxide. Don't breathe deep in this gathering gloom.

Steam Vents

There are a few open, nonsulphurous steam vents at the next pull-off, though they're just wisps compared to the chuffing bluffs nearby. Rainwater that sinks into the earth is heated by the hot rocks below and rises back up as steam.

The two-minute walk beyond the vents leads out to a part of the crater rim aptly called **Steaming Bluff**. The cooler it is, the more warm steam there'll be streaming off the bluffs and whistling over the caldera. Peek into the cracks and chasms beside the trail here to see the sacred bundles *(ho'okupu)* left for Pele by past visitors. Tasty, tart ohelo berries also grow nearby if you feel like noshing. Just be sure to offer a few to Pele before indulging.

Jaggar Museum

This museum (☎ 985-6049; open 8:30am-5pm) is worth a visit both for its displays and the fine view of Pele's home, the Halema'uma'u Crater. Halema'uma'u sits within Kilauea Caldera and is sometimes referred to as the 'crater within the crater.' When the weather is clear, there's a rapturous view of Mauna Loa to the west, 20 miles away.

Interesting museum exhibits include the Herb Kawainui Kane mural showing the Hawaiian pantheon, the seismic signals recording island earthquakes and the history of the museum and its founder Dr. Thomas A. Jaggar (no relation to Mick, but with rock star-style nonetheless: don't miss the photo of Professor Jaggar in his 'wheeled boat'). Jaggar founded the **Hawaiian Volcano Observatory** (HVO; closed to the public) beside the museum.

Drivers should be careful of the endangered nene that congregate in the museum parking lot (see boxed text Those Wild Nene).

After leaving the museum, you'll pass the **Southwest Rift**, where you can stop and take a look at the wide fissure slicing across the earth. The Southwest Rift is one gigantic crack extending from the caldera summit to the coast and out to sea beneath the ocean floor.

Halema'uma'u Overlook

The next attraction is Halema'uma'u Overlook, which is perched on the crater rim, just beyond the parking area. On any given day the floor of this crater sends volcanic gases heavenward, tainting the air all around. Of the stink Mark Twain commented: 'the smell of sulfur is strong, but not unpleasant to a sinner.'

For at least a hundred years (from 1823, when missionary William Ellis first recorded the sight in writing), Halema'uma'u was a boiling lake of lava that alternately rose and fell, overflowing its banks before crawling back down the crater slopes in a scorching ebb tide.

This fiery lake attracted people from all over the world. Some observers compared it to the flaming pits of hell, while others saw

Those Wild Nene

The native nene, Hawaii's state bird, is believed to be descended from a clutch of Canadian geese that flew off course (those wayward Canadians again!). Once numbering in the tens of thousands, the nene have rebounded from the brink of extinction – they were down to 30 on the Big Island at one point – by a captive breeding and release program. Today, there are some several hundred nene, about 125 or so that live in Hawaii Volcanoes National Park.

Nene are curious, social birds; they mix with two-legged friends whenever they get the opportunity. From crater floors to parking lots and camping areas, you're likely to see Hawaiian geese heading your way for a handout.

Obviously, most Lonely Planet readers know that feeding wild animals (no matter how cute and tame they seem) is detrimental to their sustainability. Still, for those not in the loop: please don't feed the nene. Also, one of the greatest immediate threats to the struggling nene population is careless drivers, so please drive attentively in nene lands.

primeval creation. Whatever primordial images this liquid inferno engendered, it never failed to inspire. Again, gazing upon the incredible site Mark Twain declared: 'here was room for the imagination to work!'

In 1924, seeping water sparked a massive steam explosion that blew up the lava lake, causing boulders and mud to rain down and setting off a lightning storm. When it was over, the crater had doubled in size and the lava activity had ceased. The crust has since cooled, although the crater continues to steam with conviction and the area is pungent with the smell of sulfur. Currently the crater measures about 3000 feet across and 300 feet deep.

All of the Big Island is Pele's territory, but Halema'uma'u is her home. During special ceremonies, the hula is performed in her honor here, and throughout the year those wishing to appease Pele leave flowers, bottles of gin and other offerings at the crater rim.

The Halema'uma'u Overlook begins the **Halema'uma'u Trail**, which runs 3.2 miles across Kilauea Caldera to the visitor center

(see the Hiking section later) and makes a terrific half-day hike.

If your itinerary is cramped, at least check out the easy half-mile walk (30 minutes roundtrip) from the overlook to the site of the 1982 lava flow.

Devastation Trail

Beyond the Halema'uma'u Overlook, Crater Rim Drive continues across the barren Ka'u Desert and then through the fallout area of the 1959 eruption of Kilauea Iki Crater. At that time, ash and pumice blown southwest of the crater buried a mile of Crater Rim Drive 8 feet deep in a blizzard of volcanic residue. Tractors had to be hauled in to plow the road clear of the burnt flotsam.

The Devastation Trail is a 1-mile roundtrip walk across a former rain forest devastated by cinder and pumice from that eruption. This trail gets its name from the dead ohia trees, stripped bare and sunbleached white, which stand stark against the black landscape. You can't keep good flora down, however, and slowly, ohia trees, ohelo berry bushes and ferns started colonizing the area anew. There are also some tree molds along the way.

The trail is paved and has parking lots on each end. The prominent cinder cone along the way is Puu Puai, 'Gushing Hill,' formed during the 1959 eruption. The 0.4 mile boardwalk trail to the Puu Puia Overlook is a quick, worthy aside, providing good views into the Kilauea Iki Crater.

Chain of Craters Rd intersects Crater Rim Drive opposite the west side parking area for the Devastation Trail.

Thurston Lava Tube

On the east side of the Chain of Craters Rd intersection, Crater Rim Drive passes through the magical rain forest of native tree ferns and ohia that covers Kilauea's windward slope.

The Thurston Lava Tube Trail is an enjoyable 15-minute loop walk (0.3 miles) that starts out in ohia forest, passes through an impressive lava tube and then enters a fern grove. All the organized tours stop here, so it might be loud and cramped in the tube when you drop in.

Lava tubes are formed when the outer crust of a river of lava starts to harden but the liquid lava beneath the surface continues to flow on through. After the flow has drained out, the hard shell remains. Thurston Lava Tube, created between 300 and 500 years ago, is a grand example – its tunnel formation is almost big enough to run a train through.

You'll likely be accompanied by a soundtrack of birdsong along this walk. The *apapane*, a native honeycreeper, is easy to spot at the upper end of the trail. It has a red body and silvery-white underside and flits from the yellow flowers of the mamane tree to the red pom-pom blossoms of the ohia. You may also hear strains of the *omao* (a type of thrush) or the common *amakihi*, another type of honeycreeper whose yellow and green feathers were used in the regal capes once worn by Hawaiian royalty.

Kilauea Iki Crater

When Kilauea Iki ('Little Kilauea') burst open in a fiery inferno in November 1959, it transformed the whole crater floor into a pool of molten lava 400 feet deep. Its fountains reached record heights of 1900 feet, lighting the evening sky with a bright orange glow for miles around. At its peak, it gushed out 2 million tons of lava an hour.

From Kilauea Iki Overlook there's a good view of the mile-wide crater below. A trail runs across the crater floor, providing another exciting opportunity to get close to the earth's raw power. Crossing the crater is not unlike walking on ice – here, too, there's a lake below the hardened surface, although in this case it's molten magma, not water. Recent plumb tests reveal that the lava is a mere 230 feet beneath the surface. For more information, see Hiking section later in this chapter.

CHAIN OF CRATERS ROAD

Chain of Craters Rd winds 20 miles down the southern slopes of Kilauea Volcano, ending abruptly at the edge of the most recent lava flow on the Puna Coast. It's a good paved two-lane road, although there are no services along the way. Lots of sinuous curves and slow moving sightseers make it a longer drive than you might expect.

The road provides striking vistas of the coastline far below, and for miles the predominant view is of long fingers of lava reaching down to the sea. This is the region called the East Rift Zone and it's where all the most recent lava action happens.

In some places the road slices through lava, while elsewhere the lava has won out, paving over the road. You'll see both a'a lava, which is crusty and rough, and pahoehoe lava, which is as shiny and black as fresh tar. You can sometimes also find thin filaments of volcanic glass known as Pele's hair in the lava cracks and crevices. Chartreuse ferns against the dark reddish-burnt lava poke through too.

In addition to endless lava expanses, the road takes in an impressive collection of sights, including a handful of craters that you can literally pull up to and peer into. Some are so new they're devoid of life, while others are thick with ohia lehua, wild orchids and ferns.

Chain of Craters Rd once connected to Hwys 130 and 137, allowing traffic between the volcano and Hilo via Puna. Lava flows closed the road in 1969, but by 1979 it was back in service, albeit slightly rerouted. Flows from Kilauea's active east rift cut the link again in 1988 and have since buried a 9-mile stretch of the road.

Hilina Pali Rd

All along the 2¼-mile approach to Hilina Pali Rd, you'll see **pit craters** of varying size and age. The most interesting is the forested oasis of Koko'olau Crater, a bit before the turn for Hilina Pali Rd.

Hilina Pali Rd leads 4 miles to the **Kulanaokuaiki Campground**. It's another 5 miles to the end of the road and the site of Hilina Pali Overlook, a lookout at 2280 feet with a view of the southeast coast. Just beyond the overlook is the trailhead for the Ka'u Desert Trail and for the Ka'aha and Hilina Pali Trails, which lead down to the coast. They are all hot, dry, backcountry trails.

Mauna Ulu

In 1969, eruptions from Kilauea's east rift began building a new lava shield, which eventually rose 400 feet above its surroundings. It was named Mauna Ulu, 'Growing Mountain.'

By the time the flow stopped in 1974, it had covered 10,000 acres of parkland and added 200 acres of new land to the coast.

It also buried a 12-mile section of Chain of Craters Rd in lava up to 300 feet deep. A half-mile portion of the old road survives, and you can follow it to the lava flow by taking the turnoff on the left, 3½ miles down Chain of Craters Rd. Just beyond this is Mauna Ulu itself.

The **Pu'u Huluhulu Overlook Trail**, a 3-mile roundtrip hike, begins at the parking area, crosses over lava flows from 1973 and 1974 and climbs to the top of a 150-foot cinder cone. On clear days, you'll have panoramic views taking in Mauna Loa, Mauna Kea, the tempestuous Pu'u O'o vent, Kilauea, the East Rift Zone and the ocean beyond. In 1984, the Pu'u O'o started

shooting up lava fountains while Mauna Loa exploded in a separate eruption in the background. These were the first concurrent eruptions in Hawaii in 165 years and hikers on this trail bore witness to the extraordinary event. Expect this beautiful, moderate hike, to take about two hours roundtrip.

As you continue down Chain of Craters Rd, you'll be passing over Mauna Ulu's extensive flows.

Kealakomo

About halfway along the road, at an elevation of 2000 feet, is Kealakomo, a covered shelter with picnic tables and a superb ocean view. In 1975, a 7.2-magnitude earthquake rocked Kealakomo, dropping the entire shelf five feet and touching off a tsunami. Two campers drowned at the Halape Shelter, though many more somehow survived being swept inland by the great waves. You can learn more about this event at the Jaggar Museum.

From here, the road begins to descend along a series of winding switchbacks, some deeply cut through lava flows. As you make your way down the 1000 feet to the coast, you leave the trade winds behind and things dry out and warm up. This is the trailhead for the Naulu-Kalapana-Napau Crater Trail leading to the Pu'u O'o vent (see Napau Crater Trail in the Hiking section).

Pu'u Loa Petroglyphs

The Pu'u Loa Trail leads 1 mile to a field of petroglyphs carved into pahoehoe lava by early Hawaiians. The site, which is along an ancient trail that once ran between Ka'u and Puna has more than 15,000 drawings – perhaps the greatest concentration of petroglyphs in Hawaii. A boardwalk runs along a large group of them and offers some fine photo opportunities.

Pu'u Loa (Long Hill) at the southeastern edge of the boardwalk, was the place where Hawaiians buried the umbilical cords of their babies so their children would enjoy long lives. The thousands of dimpled depressions in this petroglyph field were pounded out as receptacles for the umbilical cord (piko).

Petroglyphs

The ancient Hawaiians had no written history, but cut petroglyphs into smooth lava rock. Many of these carved pictures are stylized stick figures depicting warriors, canoe paddlers, dogs, birds and other decipherable images. Some are linear marks, which may have been made to record important events or represent calendars or genealogical charts.

The meanings and purposes behind Hawaiian petroglyphs are not well understood. Some may have been intentionally cryptic, while others may just be random graffiti or the carvings of a budding artist.

Most petroglyphs are found along ancient footpaths and may have been clustered at sites chock full of mana. The Big Island has the greatest concentration of petroglyphs in all of Hawaii.

The marked trailhead begins on the Chain of Craters Rd midway between the 16- and 17-mile markers. It makes for an interesting, easy 75-minute roundtrip walk.

Holei Sea Arch

Look for the sign marking the Holei Sea Arch just before the 19-mile marker. This rugged section of the coast has sharply eroded lava cliffs, called Holei Pali, which are constantly being pounded by crashing surf.

The high rock arch carved out of one of the cliffs is impressive, though Na Maka O Kahai, goddess of the sea and sister to Pele, will eventually knock these cliffs down with waves as powerful and destructive as lava.

End of the Road

Chain of Craters Rd ends abruptly at the coast, where hardened lava flows seal off the tarmac. From around 1pm to 7pm, park rangers staff a station where you can get information. They also sell flashlights ($3) and bottled water ($1).

In recent times, most of the lava flowing from Kilauea's east rift has been coming

from the Pu'u O'o Vent. When the molten lava, which is carried downhill in lava tubes, hits the ocean, it boils the water and sends skyward immense acidic steam plumes.

Park rangers have marked a trail over the hardened lava to an observation point that offers a good, though distant, view of the billowing coastal steam cloud. After dark, pulsing surface flows and the billowy steam cloud take on an orange glow. The trail is only about 300 yards, but give yourself about 30 minutes roundtrip. The walk is over crisp, shiny lava, and you need to watch your footing, as there are sharp jags as well as cracks and holes in the brittle surface. Wear sturdy shoes with good traction. Nighttime offers the most dramatic viewing, but a flashlight is a necessity for navigating the ankle-wrenching lava trail.

For information on hiking closer to the action, see the boxed text 'Go to the Flow.'

MAUNA LOA ROAD

Mauna Loa Rd leads off Hwy 11 about 2¼ miles west of the visitor center. The road provides access to the eastern approach of Mauna Loa, the world's most massive active volcano. Mauna Loa has erupted more than 18 times in the past century; the last eruption was in March 1984 and lasted 21 days.

The Mauna Loa Trail, a challenging trek which climbs the slopes of Mauna Loa, begins at the end of the road, 13½ miles from Hwy 11. For details, see the Hiking section, later.

Near the start of Mauna Loa Rd there's a turnoff to some **lava tree molds**. These deep, tube-like apertures were formed when a lava flow engulfed the rain forest that stood here. Because the trees were so waterlogged, the lava hardened around them instead of burning them on contact. As the trees disintegrated, deep holes where the trunks once stood were left in the ground.

Kipuka Puaulu

Kipuka Puaulu, a unique sanctuary for native flora and fauna, is about 1½ miles up Mauna Loa Rd. The mile-long **Kipuka Puaulu Loop Trail** runs through this 100-acre oasis of Hawaiian forest.

About 400 years ago, a major lava flow from Mauna Loa's northeast rift covered most of the surrounding area. Pele took pity on this bit of land, parting the flow and creating an island forest in a sea of lava, called a *kipuka* in Hawaiian.

Kipuka Puaulu is an ecopreserve of rare endemic plants, insects and birds. The lava that surrounds the kipuka serves as a protective barrier against intruding foreign species (eg, kahili ginger, banana poka and faya trees) that are taking over other parts of the park.

Koa is the largest of the trees here. The young koa trees have fernlike leaves that are replaced with flat, crescent-shaped leaf stalks as the koa matures and rises above the forest floor. The tree provides a habitat for the ferns and climbing peperomia that take root in its moist bark.

Kipuka Puaulu is delightfully quiet, except for the chirping of birds (and the occasional helicopter). Native species include the inquisitive elepaio and three honeycreepers – the *amakihi*, *apapane* and *i'iwi*. All of these birds are sparrow-size and brightly colored. The trees soar here, so bring your binoculars or you'll see little.

Also along the trail is a lava tube in the dark depths of which a unique species of big-eyed spider was discovered in 1973. A free flora and fauna trail guide is available at the visitor center.

HIKING

The park has an extensive network of hiking trails, rising from sea level to over 13,000 feet. The hikes range from short, easy walks to serious backcountry treks. If your boots are made for walking, you'll unlock much of the Big Island's mystique that otherwise remains hidden.

In addition to the hikes that follow, information on a number of shorter hikes is given earlier in this chapter. Except at the camping cabins and shelters, there is no drinking water available along any of the trails.

Crater Rim Trail

The Crater Rim Trail is an 11-mile hiking trail running roughly parallel to Crater Rim Drive. On the north side, the trail skirts the crater rim, while on the south side, it runs outside the paved road.

Because the vehicle road is designed to take in the main sights, you'll actually miss a few of them by hiking, but you'll gain in other ways. First, you can create a nice loop by setting off south on the Crater Rim Trail through misty ohia forest from where you can descend into the Kilauea Caldera or the Kilauea Iki Crater. Second, walking allows you to nosh on ohelo berries while birds chirp upbeat melodies all about you. Last, it lets you truly appreciate the meaning of changeable weather (okay, so that's not such a bonus). This hike will take between five and six hours with a leisurely lunch break thrown in.

Halema'uma'u Trail

Diagonally across the road from the visitor center are several trailheads, including one for the Halema'uma'u Trail.

The first section of the Halema'uma'u Trail passes briefly through a moist ohia forest, with tall ferns and flowering ginger. It then descends about 500 feet to the floor of Kilauea Caldera and continues for 3 miles across the surface of this still-active volcano, pocked with smoking vents.

In ancient times, the caldera was much deeper, but in the past century overflows from Halema'uma'u Crater and eruptions from the caldera floor have built it up.

The process is easy to visualize, as the trail crosses flow after flow, beginning with one from 1974 and continuing over lava from 1885, 1894, 1954, 1971 and 1982, each distinguished by a different shade of black. The trail is marked with *ahu*, lava rock cairns.

Shortly after breakfast on April 30, 1982, geologists at the Hawaiian Volcano Observatory watched as their seismographs and tiltmeters went haywire, warning of an eruption. The Park Service quickly closed off Halema'uma'u Trail and cleared hikers from the crater floor. Before noon a half-mile fissure split open in the crater and began spewing out a million cubic meters of lava. There hasn't been another major eruption here since 1982.

Halema'uma'u Trail ends about 3½ miles from the visitor center at Halema'uma'u Overlook, which provides inspiring, sulfur-laced views into this smoking, foreboding crater believed to be the home of Pele. On clear days this is a hot, dry hike; the rest of the time it's cold and damp. Carry water with you as there's none on the way; a trail guide to flora, fauna and history is available at the visitor center.

Kilauea Iki Trail

When Kilauea Iki Crater exploded in 1959, its magnificent lava fountains set a new height record of 1900 feet. When the eruption finally subsided, a huge expanse of the park southwest of the crater was buried deep in ash. Today, the crater floor is crossed by a popular 4-mile loop hike.

Kilauea Iki Trail begins near the parking lot of the Thurston Lava Tube and descends 400 feet through glistening, fairy tale ohia forest to the crater floor. Here and there you'll espy the massive gape of Kilauea Iki and tiny hikers making their way across the crater. Once on the crater floor, shots of steam and smoke pulse from the ground and stubborn ohelo berries, ohia trees and ferns break through the hard surface that glints black, red, brown and blue. Rainbows often hang around here too. Like many trails in the park, the way is delineated with *ahu* (rock cairns).

Keep to the right at the far side of the crater to connect with the loop trail to the parking lot or to the Byron Ledge or Crater Rim Trails. The former hooks up with the Halema'uma'u Trail after a mile.

Footprints Trail

The Footprints Trail is the beginning of the Mauna Iki Trail, which leads to a network of trails through the Ka'u Desert. The trailhead is between the 37- and 38-mile markers on Hwy 11, 9 miles southwest of Kilauea Visitor Center (read: no entrance fee). The footprints are an easy three-quarter-mile hike in from the highway.

In 1790, a tremendously violent and queer steam explosion at Kilauea choked the area in hot, poisonous gasses, leaving a blanket of ash several inches thick. A regiment of warriors, who were retreating to Ka'u after attacking Kamehameha's sacred Waipi'o Valley, tried to outrun the deadly concoction, but failed. The men were literally stopped in their tracks and suffocated by gas clouds. A shower of hot mud and ashes hardened around them, leaving a permanent cast of their footprints in mid-sprint.

Two hundred years later, you can still count the toes in a few of the prints – although it takes some imagination these days, as most of the trailside footprints have been seriously damaged by vandals. Every so often, wind and erosion expose more footprints, and since it's a pleasant walk anyway, it makes a decent diversion.

Backcountry Hiking & Camping

Free hiking shelters and rustic cabins are available along some of the park's backcountry trails. These trails lead in and around the world's most active volcano provide a wild and unparalleled Hawaii experience. There is no trail signage on the lava flows, where you'll be relying on ahu; pack the compass.

In addition to the two cabins along the Mauna Loa Summit Trail, there's a small cabin at Kipuka Pepeiao along the Ka'u Desert Trail and primitive three-walled shelters on the coast at Keauhou, Halape and Ka'aha. All have pit toilets and limited catchment water that should be treated before drinking. The current water level at each site is posted on a board at the visitor center.

There are also two primitive camping areas that have pit toilets but no shelter or water. The seaside Apua Point campsite is along the Puna Coast Trail, while the fabulous Napau Crater campsite, just 3 miles west of the erupting Pu'u O'o Vent, is reached via the Napau Trail or a combination of the Naulu and Kalapana Trails. For more information about backcountry camping, see the individual trail sections.

All overnight hikers are required to register and obtain a free permit at the visitor center before heading out. Permits are issued on a first-come, first-served basis, beginning no earlier than noon on the day before your intended hike. There's a three-day limit at each backcountry camping site, and each site has a limit of eight to 16 campers.

The Park Service considers the following essential backpacking equipment: first-aid kit, a flashlight with extra batteries, a minimum of four quarts of water, an extra stash of food, a compass, a mirror (for signaling), broken-in boots, complete rain gear, a cooking stove with fuel (open fires are prohibited), sunscreen and a hat. Note that the desert and coastal trails are extremely hot when the sun is shining and sometimes even under cloud cover.

On both the Mauna Loa Summit and the Observatory Trails, it's important to acclimatize, as altitude sickness is a real danger. Common symptoms are headache, nausea and shortness of breath. For minor symptoms, deep breathing brings some relief, as does lying down with your head lower than your feet. If the symptoms are more serious, relief will only come with immediate descent. Even 1500 feet can help alleviate altitude sickness (for more information, see the Health section of the Facts for the Visitor chapter).

Hypothermia is another hazard. A good windproof jacket, wool sweater, winter-rated sleeping bag and rain gear are all essential. Sunglasses and sunscreen will provide protection from snow glare and the sun's strong rays that prevail in the thin atmosphere.

More information on backcountry hiking can be obtained at the visitor center or by writing to Hawaii Volcanoes National Park, PO Box 52, Hawaii National Park, HI 96718. Specifically inquire about their backcountry trail map series. In addition, avid hikers might want to pick up a book dedicated to Big Island trails (see the Books section of the Facts for the Visitor chapter for some ideas).

Mauna Loa Summit Trails The Mauna Loa Trail begins at the end of Mauna Loa Rd, 13½ miles north of Hwy 11 (about an hour's drive from the visitor center). It's possible to summit Mauna Loa from the Mauna Loa Weather Observatory, but it's not recommended unless you're acclimatized like an Andean (see the Observatory

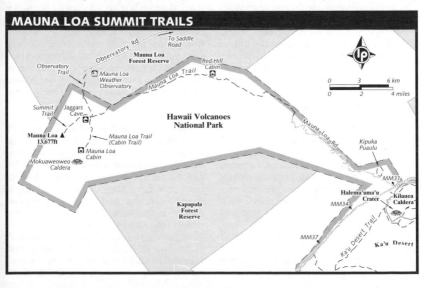

MAUNA LOA SUMMIT TRAILS

Trail section later). Overnight hikers are required to register at the visitor center, which also has the latest information on trail and cabin conditions.

This is a rugged 19.1-mile trail that ascends 6600 feet. The ascent is gradual, but the elevation and arctic conditions at the summit make it a serious hike for which you must be fit and well-equipped. Plan on at least three days, but four will allow for proper acclimatization and time at the summit.

Two free cabins are available on a first-come, first-served basis (obtainable one day before you set out, but no earlier) and are good places to break the hike: Red Hill cabin has eight bunks with mattresses, and Mauna Loa summit cabin has 12. Potable water is available at both.

The trail rises out of an ohia forest and above the tree line, climbing 7.5 miles to Red Hill (Pu'u Ulaula) at 10,035 feet. This leg of the hike takes four to six hours. From Red Hill there are fine views of Mauna Kea to the north and Maui's venerable Haleakala to the northwest.

It's 11.6 miles and a full day's hike from Red Hill to the summit cabin at 13,250 feet. The route is barren, with gaping fissures cleaving the lavascape that includes spatter ramparts and cones. At the 9.5-mile mark, you come to the Makuaweoweo Caldera and a fork in the trail: as you might expect, the Cabin Trail (2.1 miles) leads to your night's resting place. If you absolutely can't push on to the Mauna Loa cabin, Jaggar's Cave (just beyond the fork), can provide shelter for a night.

The other fork is the Summit Trail (2.6 miles) leading to guess where? At 13,677 feet, the Mauna Loa summit has a subarctic climate, and temperatures normally drop to freezing every night. Winter snowstorms can last a few days, bringing white-out conditions and snow packs as deep as 9 feet. Occasionally, snow falls as low as Red Hill and covers the upper end of the trail. Consult the rangers at the visitor center about weather before setting out as it can get nasty up here, leading to chopper rescues and similar inconveniences.

Observatory Trail This steep, strenuous alternative approach to the Mauna Loa summit starts at the Mauna Loa Weather Observatory (11,150 feet). The Observatory is reached along an 18-mile paved spur off the Saddle Rd. As the trail gains 2527 feet in just 6.4 miles, you must be properly acclimatized and equipped to even think about this hike (for more on acclimatizing, see the introduction to this section). You can try sleeping overnight near the Observatory to become adjusted, but even that may not be enough. Heavy weather conditions (including freezing wind, fog, snow and other unpleasantness) are also considerations in assessing this hike.

The Observatory Rd may be closed during winter and for this and other aforementioned foul weather issues, this hike is better left to the summer months. Remember: you must register at the visitor center in HVNP (a 2½-hour drive from the trailhead) before setting out – another disincentive to this summit approach.

The actual trailhead is about a half mile below the Observatory, down a 4WD road. Set out early – either before or with the rising sun. The trail crisscrosses a series of a'a and pahoehoe lava flows and the way is (hopefully) marked frequently with rock cairns. If there has been recent heavy snowfall, the cairns may be obscured, in which case you're screwed. After summiting, you can either circle around to the other side of the Mokuaweoweo Caldera to the Mauna Loa Cabin (4.7 miles) or head back to the Observatory.

Ka'u Desert Trail The Ka'u Desert Trail network is the most extensive in the park, but so much of it makes for hot, boring and otherwise undesirable hiking that it's best to pick up the trail at the end of Hilina Pali Rd instead of from Hwy 11. From Hilina Pali Rd, you can hike southwest to the **Pepeiao Cabin** via the Ka'u Desert Trail and continue to the **Ka'aha shelter** on the coast.

In theory, you could head southeast from Hilina Pali Rd on the Hilina Pali Trail to the south coast shelters, though by all accounts this is punishing. Better to access those

Fragile Paradise

Halape was an idyllic beachfront campground bordered by coconut trees until November 29, 1975, when the strongest earthquake in 100 years shook the Big Island. Just before dawn, rock slides from the upper slopes sent most of the 36 campers running toward the sea, where the coastline suddenly sank. As the beach submerged beneath their feet, a series of tsunamis swept the campers up, carrying them first out to sea and then coughing them back on shore. Miraculously, only two people died.

The earthquake left a fine sandy cove inland of the former beach, and despite its turbulent past, Halape is still a lovely spot. Swimming is good in the protected cove, but there are strong currents in the open ocean beyond.

Halape is one of only eight Big Island nesting sites for the endangered hawksbill sea turtle, though they haven't been seen around lately. Still, some guidelines to observe include: not setting up tents in areas identified as turtle nesting sites and keeping sites clean of food scraps and minimizing the use of night lighting, which can disorient the turtles. Hawksbill turtles also nest at the park's Keauhou and Apua Point backcountry camping areas.

shelters from the Puna Coast (see that section later) or the Keauhou Trail. As with all the trailheads in the park, there is no water here, though there is drinking water at the cabin.

The trailhead is 9 miles down Hilina Pali Rd. The hike isn't hard, with an elevation gain of fewer than 750 feet over the 4.8-mile trail. Still, the cabin is isolated and will offer all the privacy you could ever want (maybe too much for some!). As always, the way is over lava and is marked with rock cairns. The hike should take about 4½ hours, longer if you're carrying gear.

From the cabin to the Ka'aha shelter, it's 6 miles over a tricky route peppered with a'a chunks that look deceptively like cairns. Just keep heading towards the sea. Depending on current trail conditions, you may have to retrace your steps to Hilina Pali Rd, rather than continuing on the loop north. Check at the visitor center for the latest.

Puna Coast Trail The Puna Coast Trail starts almost at the end of the Chain of Craters Rd, at about the 19.5-mile mark, near the Pu'u Loa Petroglyphs. This is the best way to hike to the **Apua Point campsite**. Farther west, the **Keauhou** and **Halape** shelters could also be incorporated into a multi-day loop that returns via the Keauhou Trail.

The entire stretch of this hike is on coastal cliffs. It's gorgeous and hot, so come prepared for photo ops and nagging thirst (there's water at the shelters, but not the campsite). Apua Point is 6.6 miles from the trailhead, along a flat, decently marked trail. Camp responsibly here (it's a popular turtle nesting ground) among the palms or push on to Keauhou shelter.

The Keauhou shelter is another 3.1 miles farther along over – you guessed it – more lava. You can camp in the shelter or pitch a tent on the beach, barring gale force winds.

The Halape Shelter is 1.6 miles farther west and a bit inland. There's a sprinkling of palm trees here and a brackish lagoon for rinsing off. Turtles used to nest here, but rangers haven't observed any in a while.

You can return the way you came or head north on the 6.8-mile Keauhou Trail.

Napau Crater Trail You have two choices for this unforgettable hike to the active **Pu'u O'o vent** and the **Napau Crater campground**.

You can take the well marked Napau Trail (18 miles roundtrip, about 9 hours) or the Naulu-Kalapana-Napau Trail (14.4 miles roundtrip, about 7 hours). Combining the two into a loop is a good alternative, though it involves hitchhiking back to your car on Chain of Craters Rd. Any way you cut it, this is an awesome hike; bring lots of film and a pair of binoculars.

The Napau trailhead is at the 3.5-mile mark of Chain of Craters Rd, near the Mauna Ulu Lava Shield. The first 5 miles of the trail follows what was the Chain of Craters Rd, before pahoehoe lava covered it in 1973 and 1974. There are great examples of pumice and Pele's hair strewn all over the flows here.

Further on, you pass lava trees and the Pu'u Huluhulu cinder cone (see the Mauna Ulu section earlier), before coming to the Makaopuhi crater. On clear days the view is religious, as you find yourself in the middle of a triangle formed by Mauna Loa to the northwest, Mauna Kea to the north and the fire-breathing Pu'u O'o straight ahead. At the Makaopuhi Crater you duck into a cool fern forest where new purple fiddle heads look like staffs from a Dr Seuss musical score. Twenty minutes along is the Naulu Trail fork leading to the Kealakomo parking area.

At the other end of the fern forest, you'll come to the rock walls of the 'pulu factory.' This is the old depository for *pulu* – the silken clusters encasing the stems of *hapu'u* ferns (which you can examine closely on this hike). Pulu was used as mattress ticking and pillow stuffing, and an industry in the fluff flourished until it was discovered pulu turns to dust after a few years tucked inside a mattress. Ooops! The ancient Hawaiians used pulu to embalm their dead.

Ten minutes past the pulu factory, there are fantastic views of the partially collapsed cone. Though the Mayans believe the navel of the world lies on the volcanic shores of Lake Atitlán, you'll beg to differ after gazing upon the singular Pu'u O'o from the rim of the Napau Crater.

The primitive campground is five minutes from the junction for the Napau Crater lookout. The two sites on the rise gaze directly on the vent. If you've come this far, ignore your blisters and hike up towards the toilet (there's a sign), swing around it and follow the almost indistinguishable trail to the floor of the Napau Crater. This is the new 2-mile bit opened in December 2001 that heads across the crater and right to the base of the mighty Pu'u O'o. The trail is very faint in places and the rock cairns are a work in progress.

VOLCANO

The village of Volcano, about two miles east of the park, is a charming town in a storybook setting. Giant tree ferns unfurl their fuzzy heads, ohia trees droop with red, puffy blossoms and the mist dances among sunbeams. No wonder so many artists remove themselves to Volcano.

There's a post office on Old Volcano Rd and Internet access at the Lava Rock Cafe. Gas is sold at a couple of pumps beside the cafe. Tourist and accommodation information is provided at a little shack outside the Thai Thai Restaurant, a bit west on Old Volcano Rd. There are so many B&Bs and rental cottages here, however, you might want to consult an island-wide booking service to help focus your search (for agencies, see the B&B section of the Facts for the Visitor chapter).

Despite the disproportionate number of B&Bs, there's too much mana coursing through this hamlet to call it quaint. Still, it does have the little **Volcano Winery** *(☎ 967-7772, W www.volcanowinery.com, End of Pii Mauna Dr)* Open 10am-5:30pm daily. Stop in here to taste locally-made wines in the shadow of Mauna Loa. These friendly folks make a selection of interesting grape, tropical fruit and honey wines ($13-16/bottle).

There's also **golf** in a superlative setting at the ***Volcano Golf & Country Club*** *(☎ 967-7331, Pii Mauna Dr)* 18 holes and cart $62.50. These have to be some of the world's most majestic links. Set beneath the grand Mauna Loa and Mauna Kea volcanoes, golfing here truly will be a good walk spoiled! Ask about local (including Neighbor Island) discounts.

SPECIAL EVENTS

The national park hosts several annual events that become truly special in such an

Lava flowing into the sea, Hawaii Volcanoes National Park

Natural fireworks, courtesy of Kilauea

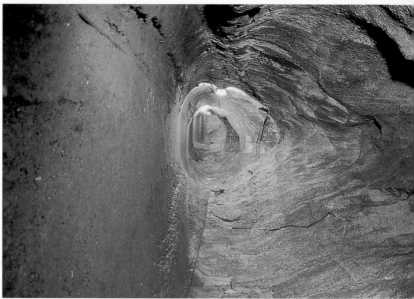

MARK PARKES

Inside a lava tube, Kilauea

JANICE MARIE SHELDON

Lava flow from Kilauea

JANICE MARIE SHELDON

Devastation Trail, Kilauea

inspired setting. Park entrance fees apply to the following selection of the most popular events:

Annual Dance & Music Concert – celebrating over 10 years, this annual event hosted by the Volcano Art Center presents works by Big Island choreographers, dancers and musicians; last weekend in March.

Na Mea Hawaii Hula Kahiko Series – this series of free outdoor hula performances takes place at the end of May and beginning of June.

Annual Kilauea Volcano Wilderness Runs – a marathon, 5- and 10-mile runs in one of the most sublime competition sites, there's also a 5-mile walk. Held for more than 20 years in the last weekend in July. For more information see w www.volcanoartcenter.org.

Aloha Festivals Ka Hoola Ana – this brilliant Royal Court procession and celebration on the Halema'uma'u Crater rim at the end of August is a must-see.

PLACES TO STAY
Volcano (Town)
Volcano town is rife with places to stay, from cute guest cottages to dorm beds.

Holo Holo In (☎ 967-7950, 800-671-2999, fax 967-8025, w www.enable.org/holoholo, 19-4036 Kalani Honua Rd) Dorm bed HI members/nonmembers $15/17, doubles $40, plus $15 each extra person. Holo Holo In, which is affiliated with Hostelling International, is a small hostel and lodge run by Yabuki Satoshi. Two of the rooms have five beds each and are used as dorms, which are clean, but darkish. Another is a private room with a double bed and two twins. There's a shared kitchen, complimentary coffee and tea, a TV room, laundry facilities and a sauna. The atmosphere is friendly and mellow. Yabuki has a day job, so it's best to call after 4:30pm.

Kulana Artist Sanctuary (☎ 985-9055, PO Box 190, Volcano, HI 96785) Cabin $20 per person, camping $15 per person. This artist's retreat in a quiet, women-centric environment encourages exploration of creative horizons. Accommodation is in simple cabins and guests share the main house (bathroom, fully-equipped kitchen and

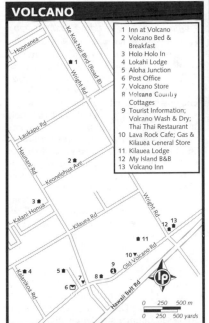

VOLCANO

1 Inn at Volcano
2 Volcano Bed & Breakfast
3 Holo Holo In
4 Lokahi Lodge
5 Aloha Junction
6 Post Office
7 Volcano Store
8 Volcano Country Cottages
9 Tourist Information; Volcano Wash & Dry; Thai Thai Restaurant
10 Lava Rock Cafe; Gas & Kilauea General Store
11 Kilauea Lodge
12 My Island B&B
13 Volcano Inn

0   250   500 m
0   250   500 yards

library) with Cristina, Kulana's founder. In the cooperative spirit of her vision, participation by guests in the caretaking of Kulana is required. Don't worry: you won't be wielding a circular saw unless you want to. Monthly artist-in-resident program ($250 plus electricity) is also available. Unlike some places on the Big Island, Kulana lives up to its motto: 'no smoking, alcohol, drugs or drama.' Call for guidelines.

My Island B&B (☎ 967-7216, fax 967-7719, w www.myislandinnhawaii.com, PO Box 100, Volcano, HI 96785) Singles/doubles with breakfast $45-90/60-120, studio units $70-80/85-95, houses $125 (double occupancy). At this B&B in the former Lyman summer digs, Gordon and Joann Morse rent out two cramped bedrooms with private baths and an attic room (toilet only). There are also a couple of studio units in the garden with kitchens, TVs, phones, bathrooms and lanais. They also own several bigger houses in different locations around Volcano.

Volcano Inn (☎ 967-7293, 800-997-2292, fax 985-7349, Ⓦ www.volcanoinn.com, PO Box 963, Volcano, HI 96785) Singles/doubles cottages $75-95/$95-145, rooms $55-105. This wooden beauty has cozy rooms ensconced in an ohia forest. Take a delicious breakfast (included in the price) on the covered lanai or chill in a hammock. The self-contained cedar cottages tucked away in the fern forest feature loads of windows and views. Stained glass, skylights, fireplaces, quilts, robes and heat are among the perks. Even the affordable Lava Room ($55) is inviting, despite being on the ground floor *and* next to the laundry room.

Volcano Rainforest Retreat (☎ 985-8696, 800-550-8696, Ⓦ www.volcanoretreat.com, PO Box 957, Volcano, HI 96785) Cottages $95-170. Tiptoeing through the tree ferns and flowers of the beautiful Volcano Rainforest Retreat, Peter Golden may aver that he and wife Kathleen have the best digs in Volcano. He's not being a braggart, he's being *accurate*. These three unique cedar cottages harmonize structure with nature so lyrically your heart will sing an aria upon check-in. The guest cottage ($170) is a lovely, full-on home with sleeping loft, reading nook, dining area and a bathroom (and tub) gazing upon the grounds. The Forest House ($140) is a cedar and redwood octagon with fireplace, kitchenette, skylights and a queen bed made for romping. The Sanctuary (single/double $95/110) is just that, with a separate Japanese soaking tub and shower. All prices include breakfast and use of the hot tub nestled amongst the green. The retreat oozes love, positivity and warmth. Reservations are a must.

Hale Ohia (☎ 967-7986, 800-455-3803, fax 967-8610, Ⓦ www.haleohia.com, PO Box 758, Volcano, HI 96785) Doubles with breakfast $95-140, cottages $110-150. This old timer on the Volcano B&B scene (but for sale at the time of writing), has pleasant grounds and a hot tub in the backyard. All the units are tastefully decorated, with clean, spare lines. The cottages are lovely and have fireplaces, lanais and kitchen facilities. Cottage No 44 ($150) is particularly sweet and secluded.

Kilauea Lodge (☎ 967-7366, fax 967-7367, Ⓦ www.kilauealodge.com, PO Box 116, Volcano, HI 96785) Rooms $125-145, cottages $145-155, all with breakfast, all non-smoking. Kilauea Lodge has a variety of solid, comfortable accommodations on their lush 10-acre spread, plus a couple of cute cottages nearby. Choose from a room in the annex with terrific beds and garden views ($125) or one of the four pleasantly renovated rooms with fireplaces, quilts, bathtubs and other cozy amenities ($135). A bit more luxurious are the honeymoon suite with fireplace, lanai and shower for two (ooooh!) and the 1-bedroom cottage (both $145). None of the rooms on the main property have TVs or phones, but who needs them, what with the beautiful garden hot tub? They also have two 2-bedroom cottages off the main grounds ($155 each).

Other places to stay include **Aloha Junction** (☎ 967-7289, 800-967-7286, Ⓦ www.bbvolcano.com), with singles/doubles for $60/75 in the heart of the host's home and **Volcano Country Cottages** (967-7960, 800-967-7960, Ⓦ www.volcanocottages.com), with self-sufficient cottages for $95-120.

Chalet Kilauea Collection (☎ 967-7786, 800-937-7786, fax 967-8660, Ⓦ www.volcanohawaii.com, Wright Rd, PO Box 998, Volcano, HI 96785) The Chalet Kilauea Collection is a group of accommodations – from affordable rooms with shared bath to exclusive honeymoon suites – sprinkled around town. The contact information above applies to all the properties detailed below.

Their primary property is the **Inn at Volcano**, a B&B with four theme rooms including the Out of Africa and Oriental Jade options ($139-199) and two suites ($299-399). The rooms are tasteful and the suites singular. All prices include gourmet breakfast and afternoon tea. There's a hot tub in the garden gazebo and all the amenities you should expect for the price.

Volcano Vacation Homes Five 1-BR to 3-BR houses $139-379. If privacy and creature comforts are what you're after, these are a good option. Done in upscale resort style, the houses are spotless and attractive, if a bit beige. They all have fireplaces, TV and VCR and fully equipped kitchens; some have views, others are wheelchair accessible. Guests can use the Inn at Volcano's hot tub.

Volcano Bed and Breakfast Rooms $49-69. This is the Collection's thrifty option: a cozy B&B on Keonelehua Rd, just north of the village center. It has six guest rooms, ranging from a small room with a double bed ($49) to larger rooms with queen beds ($69). Bathrooms are shared, as is the common space (which includes a fireplace, TV and VCR, and fully equipped kitchen). The rates include a buffet-style continental breakfast.

They also administer the ***Lokahi Lodge*** (doubles $129-149) and the ***Castle Suites at Mauna Loa*** (doubles $159-249), near the Volcano Golf and Country Club.

In the Park

The park has two drive-up campgrounds. Additionally, there is backcountry camping in cabins, shelters and campsites. (For more information see the Backcountry Hiking & Camping section, earlier). Camping is free and the campgrounds are not usually crowded, although, like anywhere, things heat up in summer. There's no reservation system – it's first-come, first-served. Officially, camping is limited to seven days per campground per year.

Namakani Paio Campground The park's busiest campground, is just off Hwy 11, about 3 miles west of the visitor center. If you're stuck between Hilo and Kona, it's a convenient place to stop for the night. The open tent sites are in a meadow that offers little privacy but is surrounded by fragrant eucalyptus trees. There are rest rooms, water, fireplaces and picnic tables. From the campground, it's about a 1-mile hike to the Jaggar Museum and Crater Rim Trail. Crashers note: if rangers come through here and you haven't registered *and paid* at the visitor center, you'll be asked to leave. Technically, they can arrest you, but this is the Big Island, so that's exceedingly unlikely.

Kulanaokuaiki Campground *(Hilina Pali Rd)* This new campground, 3½ miles southwest of Chain of Craters Rd, has three sites. It's the less developed of the two campgrounds, but has toilets, a water catchment system and picnic tables.

Namakani Paio Cabins *(bookings: Volcano House ☎ 967-7321)* 4-person cabins $40. These 10 windowless A-frame cabins are at the national park's Namakani Paio Campground. Each has a double bed, two bunk beds and electric lights, but there are no power outlets or heating. There are communal showers and rest rooms. It gets cold at night, so bring a sleeping bag. (Or tent camp in the adjacent campground for free!)

You must book the cabins through Volcano House, where you pay and pick up your bag of linen. You'll pay refundable deposits of $12 for keys and $20 for linen.

Volcano House *(☎ 967-7321, fax 967-8429, PO Box 53, Hawaii National Park, HI 96718)* Annex rooms $85, 2nd-story rooms $165-185, kids 12 and under free. Volcano House is perched right on the rim of Kilauea Caldera, opposite the park's visitor center. Although many of the room views are disappointing, the common area vistas (including from the restaurant, snack bar and cocktail lounge) are delicious. By and large, the lower-level rooms look out onto a walkway and even some of those on the upper floor have only a partial caldera view. The rooms themselves are small but otherwise pleasant, with koa furnishings, small libraries, stacks of cool stationary and heat. There are no TVs, but the hotel maintains a terrific game library with everything from Monopoly to mankala. The best rooms are the pricey 2nd-story ones in the main building, while the cheapest are in the annex.

Kilauea Military Camp *(☎ 967-8334, fax 967-8343, W www.kmc-volcano.com/, Crater Rim Dr)* 1-bedroom apartment $45-86, 3-bedroom apartment $69-101, 1-bedroom cottage $48-89, 2-bedroom cottage $57-109, 3-bedroom cottage $85-117. This is a resort for active and retired military personnel. Price depends on your division and rank; some units have Jacuzzis.

PLACES TO EAT
Volcano (Town)

Volcano town, small as it is, has some fine dining.

Kilauea Lodge (☎ 967-7366, see Places to Stay) Dinner mains $22-27. Open dinner 5:30-9pm daily. Kilauea Lodge does upscale dining in a warm, country setting. The atmospheric dining room has high wooden ceilings, a stone fireplace and windows looking out onto a fern forest. Braised rabbit, venison medallions in brandy, Parker Ranch beef and fresh fish in a papaya ginger sauce are a sample of what may be on offer when you turn up.

Thai Thai Restaurant (☎ 967-7969, 19-4084 Old Volcano Rd) Dishes $8.99-12.99. Open 5pm-9pm. The extensive menu here features many vegetarian choices and a staggering array of noodle, rice and curry dishes. Go wild, it's all fresh, tasty and spicy (if you like) and the portions are generous. The owners hail from Thailand, which is evident the moment you walk in.

Volcano Golf and Country Club (☎ 967-7331, Pi'i Mauna Dr) Breakfast $3.50-5.95, lunch $7.25-9.25. Open 8am-2pm Mon-Fri, 6:30am-2pm Sat & Sun. This place caters to the local golfing crowd with standard egg and pancake breakfast fare. Things get a little more interesting at lunch when there's saimin, mahi mahi and kalua pork available.

Lava Rock Cafe Open 7:30am-5pm Mon, Tues-Sat 7:30am-9pm, Sun 7:30am-4pm. Lunch dishes $6-8.50, dinner dishes $8-11. This little cafe behind Kilauea General Store is the favorite breakfast spot in town, but then again, it's the *only* breakfast spot in town. Stick to the French toast with lilikoi butter ($5) to avoid disappointment. Plate lunches start at around $6, and the burgers are good, but steer clear of the saimin. At dinner you can get fried chicken, lasagna or teriyaki beef, served with soup and salad ($8-10). The cafe also offers inexpensive Internet access.

You can pick up groceries, coffee and snack items like Spam musubi at **Volcano Store**. Slimmer pickings are available at the **Kilauea General Store**, next to the Lava

Rock Cafe. One or the other is open 5am to 7pm daily.

In the Park

A picnic in the park on a nice day is unbeatable, so consider packing your own and dining whenever and wherever the feeling strikes.

Volcano House (☎ 967-7321, see Places to Stay) Breakfast/lunch buffet $9.50/12.50, dinner mains $13.25-22. Breakfast 7am-10:30am, lunch 11am-2pm, dinner 5:30pm to 8:30pm. The Volcano House restaurant serves up good coffee and a cafeteria-quality breakfast buffet and lunch buffet. The food is better at dinner with main courses ranging from pasta ($13.25) to shrimp scampi ($22). While the dining-room view overlooking Kilauea Caldera is magnificent, it can be matched at much cheaper prices in the adjacent **snack shop** (open 8:30am-4:30pm) which has chili, sandwiches, yogurt, juice and coffee. Chill out next to the living room fire, which has been burning continuously for more than 126 years or take a cocktail at **Uncle George's Lounge** (open 4pm-9pm daily).

Kilauea Military Camp (KMC; ☎ 967-8333, Crater Rim Dr)Breakfast & Lunch $3-7, dinner $9.25-12.95. Open daily for breakfast 5:30am-8am, lunch 11am-1pm, dinner 5:30pm-8pm. This military installation in the park is open to civilian diners. It's cafeteria style, but better than the mess you might remember. Call ahead to get your name on the list at the guardhouse. This isn't always necessary, but with certain recent events, they're pretty skittish these days.

GETTING THERE & AWAY

The park is 29 miles from Hilo and 97 miles from Kailua-Kona. It takes about 45 minutes to drive from Hilo and 2½ hours from Kailua-Kona, with no stops.

The public bus running between Hilo and Ocean View in Ka'u stops at the visitor center (and at Volcano village) once in each direction Monday to Friday. It leaves the visitor center for Hilo at 8:10am and returns from Hilo at 2:40pm ($2.25, 1 hour).

VOLCANOES:
FIREWALK WITH THE GODDESS

Here the days are made splendid by secluded black-sand beaches, challenging summit attempts, primordial gases belching from the earth's belly and live lava action. But all of these fascinations exist solely because this 4030-sq-mile hunk of rock called the Big Island is actually the surface of five volcanoes (with a sixth ascending fast). Two of these volcanoes are wicked active and one – the mighty Kilauea – is among the planet's most feisty. The eruption has been *continuous* since 1983, making it the longest known eruptive event in Hawaiian history, and it shows no signs of slowing.

With volcanoes come earthquakes, tsunamis, lava and landslides, and the Big Island has them all. But when you're actually here, it's kind of like living with the earthquake threat in San Francisco: you try not to dwell on it, instead reveling in the beauty surrounding you. In the case of the Big Island, the more you learn, the more intriguing its volcanism becomes.

VOLCANISM 101
As you may not care to remember from some long-ago science class, the earth is made up of a molten core, a mostly solid mantle and a crust that is springy below the seafloor, firmer above. The crust, or lithosphere, floats about the surface of the earth as a series of plates. When these plates collide, bits of crust collapse back into the earth's core, where it's so hot, it boils those old rocks, resulting in volcanic eruptions. When plates drift apart, the molten mantle, called magma, bubbles up to fill the gap, also creating volcanic eruptions. All this herky-jerky movement is called plate tectonics. Is that a high school bell ringing?

Right: The road to Mauna Loa winds past the snow-covered craters.

ANN CECIL

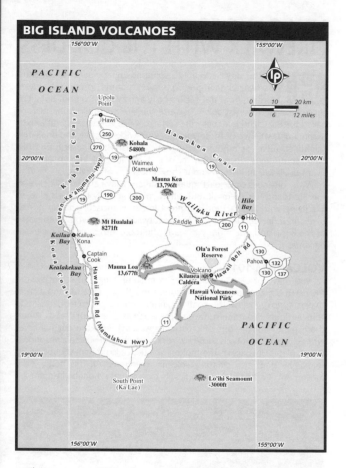

BIG ISLAND VOLCANOES

There are some 1500 active volcanoes on earth. About 95% of these are located on plate edges (the path of least resistance for the flowing magma). The spectacularly volatile 'Ring of Fire,' for instance, is a series of the world's most active volcanoes (eg, Mount Pinatubo in the Philippines, Mount St Helen's in Washington state and Japan's Mount Unzen), rimming the edge of the Pacific Plate.

So what does this all have to do with Hawaiian volcanoes? Next to nothing, because the volcanoes here fall into that special 5% that are nowhere near the plate margin. (From the Big Island to the nearest plate edge is about 2500 miles.) Instead, these volcanoes are part of the Hawaiian Island–Emperor Seamount chain, created by somewhat mysterious 'hot spots' in the earth's mantle. When the Pacific Plate passes over the hot spot, magma is forced through the submarine plate, lava spills onto the ocean floor and over time, builds into a volcanic mass. Continuously fed by magma, the mass eventually breaches the ocean surface to become an island. Because the Pacific Plate is moving to the northwest at 2 to 4 inches a year, volcanoes that pass beyond the hot spot are cut off from the magma wellspring and become extinct. Others still drifting above it remain active or dormant.

The Big Island, once again in a league all its own, straddles the hot spot and so has active, dormant and extinct volcanoes, while all the other, older, Hawaiian islands have moved beyond the hot spot. Experts estimate that the Big Island is a youthful one million years old, while Kauai is the kupuna of the group at a wizened 6 million years.

THE FAB FIVE

The five volcanoes making up the Big Island are **Kilauea, Mauna Loa, Hualalai, Mauna Kea** and **Kohala**. The first two are active, the second two are dormant (meaning they may still erupt) and the last, however glorious, is kaput or extinct. All Big Island volcanoes are shield volcanoes – or 'hot spot' volcanoes – which differ in form and function from volcanoes on the plate margins. If you come to Hawaii hoping to see a conical classic like Mount St Helen's spewing gases and ash, you'll be disappointed – at first.

Shield volcanoes (as opposed to their flamboyant Ring of Fire counterparts), are discreet drama queens: they don't blow, they flow. Typically, magma builds up in a reservoir below the summit and spills out through weak spots along the flanks called rift zones.

Since shield volcanoes lack the enormous amounts of explosive gases that produce the deadly eruptions of other volcanoes, you can explore Hawaiian volcanoes at will. For instance, volcanoes here mostly ooze lava instead of ejaculating it, so you can hike right out to the live flow in relative safety.

Also, since shield volcanoes build up magma in a slow, almost consistent way, experts at the Hawaiian Volcanoes Observatory (HVO) are able to provide warning about impending volcanic events. This allows volcano watchers plenty of time to get a good seat. Lucky are those who have witnessed a curtain of fire dancing from a fissure or a lava fountain shooting sky high. Early warning signs mean you can also summit active volcanoes here.

Still, the destructive power of volcanoes cannot be underestimated. On the one hand, the uninterrupted lava flow means new earth and black-sand beaches are being created daily. The other side of that coin, however, is sobering: leveled villages, displaced families, forests, businesses and beaches once thriving are buried under a blanket of lava, erasing memories and landscapes with swaths of fire. There's a reason Hawaiians call Pele *ka wahine ai konua*: 'the woman who devours the land.'

From time immemorial to right now, Hawaiians have recognized and respected the power of the volcano. Through prayer, worship and offerings, ancient Hawaiians and other contemporary suppliants petition the benevolent side of Madame Pele, the goddess of volcanoes and fire (see The Power of Pele section, later).

Running the Numbers

Volcanic statistics for the Big Island are staggering, and some of the numbers are just unfathomable. Here's a collection of the most impressive:

• Highest recorded lava temperature: 2192°F

• Fastest speed at which lava runs downhill: 35 mph

• Amount of lava pouring into the sea: 90,000 gallons per minute, on average

• Average number of Big Island earthquakes weekly: 1200

• Approximate number of acres added to the Big Island in the current eruption: 510

• Number of square miles buried under lava in current eruption:64.3

• Number of homes lost in current eruption: 187 (with losses totaling $61 million)

• Number of times Hawaii Volcanoes National Park has been expanded: 5

• Oldest lava flow on the Big Island: approximately 375,000 years

• Years the Hawaiian Island–Emperor Seamount chain has been in the making: 70 million (at least)

• Years until the Lo'ihi Seamount pokes above the ocean surface: 60,000 (at current rate), 10,000 if it gets a move on, but 100,000 if it switches to 'Island time'

• Last time a fatality resulted from a volcanic eruption: 1924

Kilauea Caldera

At present, the Kilauea Caldera is the Big Island's major volcanic force. Indeed, it's the planet's youngest, most active volcano (ah, to be like Kilauea!), sending out 600,000 cubic yards of lava daily.

The latest eruption episode started in 1983 in the Napau Crater along the East Rift Zone of the caldera. Three years of non-stop spattering and fountaining lava created an 835-foot tall cone called the Pu'u O'o (the Hill of the O'o; pronounced Poo-oo Oh-oh). This mighty mite belched lava, gas and fumes until 1997 when the cone suddenly collapsed in a 'now you see it, now you don't,' 3-hour event and stopped producing lava. The cone was only filling up with new magma, as it turned out: 24 days later it resumed its spew and hasn't quit since.

Hikers can get good looks at smoking Pu'u O'o by hitting the Napau Crater trail; see the Backcountry Hiking & Camping section of the Hawaii Volcanoes National Park chapter. Alternatively, on clear days, you can see Pu'u O'o smoke from the makai side clearing just before the 20-mile marker on Hwy 11.

Mauna Loa

Ah, Mauna Loa. Calling it 'superlative' would be redundant. Measured from its base on the ocean floor to its summit above Hilo, it dwarfs

Mt Everest by thousands of feet. Purists and summit chasers don't like that, but hey, the base of the mountain *is* on the ocean floor. Furthermore, with an area of over 18,000 cubic miles, it's the most massive mountain on earth and you'll know that just by looking at it.

If you're still not convinced, consider the fact that it takes baby Kilauea an entire day to produce the volume of lava Mauna Loa can put forth in an hour. And you thought Mauna Loa was just a brand of mac nut!

The last time Mauna Loa erupted was in March 1984, putting the fear of Pele into Hilo and environs as the lava inched its way closer to town. Luckily, it fizzled out some 4 miles away. With Kilauea pumping out its usual copious amounts of lava, this was the first time two Hawaiian volcanoes had erupted concurrently in 165 years. The latest word on Mauna Loa is that it's filling up with magma and could blow sooner rather than later; the volcanologists at HVO have their eyes and tilt-meters trained on it.

With no written language, the ancient Hawaiians had a way with words and Mauna Loa means 'Long Mountain.' Indeed, this mountain is so long and broad, it's hard to imagine you're on one of the world's most tremendous volcanoes. It looks like a hillock from Hilo and only slightly bigger from the Jaggar Museum scenic point in Hawaii Volcanoes National Park.

Serious trekkers wanting to experience more intimate contact with mighty Mauna Loa should consider one of the two summit hikes (see the Backcountry Hiking & Camping section of the Hawaii Volcanoes National Park & Around chapter).

LO'IHI SEAMOUNT

Save for the reincarnated, none of us will be around to see the Lo'ihi Seamount push its way above sea level. Still, the thought of a sixth volcano rising from the ocean floor to fuse with the other five already gracing the Big Island is pretty exciting.

Located about 20 miles off the southeast coast, the Lo'ihi Seamount is an active volcano that sits over the hot spot and is continuously fed by molten magma. At its highest point, the Lo'ihi Seamount rises about 12,500 feet from the ocean floor, but is still some 3200 feet underwater.

Scientists estimate it will take another 10,000 to 100,000 years for it to finally appear, though if it continues growing at its current rate, it will pierce through in 60,000 years. Of course, these figures do not account for whatever effects global warming may have on worldwide ocean levels. Scientists projecting the appearance of Lo'ihi in a century or two due to violent volcanic events are dreaming.

Above Right: Argue all you want, but Mauna Loa is still taller than Everest!

THE LANGUAGE OF LAVA

Two of the most important words in the lava lexicon are **a'a** and **pahoehoe** (pronounced pa-hoy-hoy), the two types here on the Big Island. A'a is the rough, clinkery stuff that wrenches your ankles when you walk on it, making you exclaim 'ah! ah!' Pahoehoe is the smooth, ropey blanket that shines red, brown and blue up close, but looks like the charred surface of the moon from afar. The difference in how the two form depends on the gas content and how the lava cools. Lava that starts as pahoehoe can cool unevenly, lose gas and turn to a'a. But once a'a, always a'a. These Hawaiian terms have been adopted worldwide as lava classification terms.

KIM GRANT

Another important distinction is that between magma and lava: the first is the molten hot stuff within the earth. As soon as it breaks the surface, however, it's called lava. Here are some other words you'll come across in your volcanic explorations:

caldera – bigger than a crater, a caldera is created when the vent region collapses from the top, leaving a bowl-shaped depression at the summit

crater – a volcanic depression smaller than a caldera that can form by explosion *or* collapse

kipuka – an oasis of green, spared by lava flows, where unique species often develop

Pele's hair – strands of basalt ejecta spun by the wind into golden, thready glass with a steel wool–type texture

Pele's tears – fast-cooling, basalt ejecta that form droplets of ebony glass

pit crater – a crater with steep walls formed when magma is subducted, causing the ground to collapse; Halema'uma'u is a pit crater

pumice – solidified lava foam; some pumice is so light and airy, it floats

pu'u – hill: Pu'u O'o is hill of the O'o, Pu'u Loa is long hill, etc

reticulite – frothy pumice ejecta

seamount – an underwater mountain; when it breaks the ocean's surface it becomes a volcano or island

tephra – anything thrown into the air during an eruption

vog – volcanic smog created by sulfur dioxide and other gases

THE POWER OF PELE

Mythical understandings intertwine with geological explanations to create a volcanic reality here that is uniquely Hawaiian. The goddess of volcanoes and fire is Madame Pele and she is one bad-ass, touchy deity. Placate her and everything should be cool, but watch out if you piss her off. How else to explain homes and lives miraculously spared and flows diverting and skirting inches from sacred heiau, while everything else for miles around goes up in flames?

Left: Pahoehoe patterns at Hawaii Volcanos National Park

Legend holds that Pele rules over everything hot on the Big Island: fire, volcanoes and the leeward side. She ascended as the fiery ruler after a lover's spat with the pig-god Kama-pua'a. They dueled to a draw and decided to cleave the island in two: she got the hot, dry Kona side, he the wet, rainy windward side.

Worship and reverence of Pele are alive and well on the Big Island (when you can't get homeowner's insurance against lava, you'll take all the help you can get!). She's said to appear on the volcanoes as a beautiful young woman, but down-slope, away from her home, she appears as an old hag. You may see her youthful visage in a lava flow or notice the old crone hitchhiking on Hwy 11 as you approach the national park (you're advised to give her a lift). Indeed, more than one Lonely Planet author has reported Pele sightings. It's also completely kapu to take away lava rocks from Hawaii, for to do so risks upsetting the goddess.

The area all around Halema'uma'u Crater (which the goddess calls home) is dotted with leis, anthuriums and *ho'okupu*, offerings wrapped in ti leaves. In this century, she has developed a taste for gin, and you may espy a bottle or two of Tanqueray nestled in a fissure. Furthermore, it's common practice to offer a couple of heavily laden ohelo branches to the goddess before partaking of this fruit yourself.

Everywhere in your travels here, you'll see art, literature, artifacts and offerings to the fiery goddess. There are also two types of volcanic ejecta named for her: Pele's tears and Pele's hair (see the Language of Lava section, earlier).

Ka'u

The Ka'u district encompasses the entire southern flank of the Big Island and acts as a buffer zone between the densely touristed area of South Kona and the steaming, sulphurous landscape of Hawaii Volcanoes National Park. This stretch of Hwy 11 is prone to flooding, washouts and road clo-

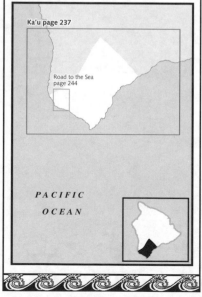

Ka'u page 237

Road to the Sea page 244

PACIFIC
OCEAN

sures during heavy winter storms. In this case, your route choices between the two sides of the island are reduced to the Saddle Road and the Waimea-Hamakua Coast-Hilo option. During the worst storms, even the latter might be closed due to rockslides.

Ka'u is sparsely populated, with only about 5000 people and three places worthy of the word town. Much of it is dry and desert-like, with lots of hardened lava to go around. Ka'u can be harsh on the eyes, but it must have looked like Eden to the Polynesian voyagers who first set foot on Hawaii at South Point. This coastal area is dotted with exotic green- and black-sand beaches that distinguish the Ka'u coastline from all others. Ka'u also radiates a mana that is surprising considering its sere landscape, but completely understandable considering its history.

HAWAII VOLCANOES NATIONAL PARK TO PAHALA

From the western edge of Hawaii Volcanoes National Park it's 12 miles to Pahala. Hwy 11 cuts across an 11-mile stretch of the park. There's no charge to drive through on the highway nor to explore the Mauna Loa side of the park. Many of the park's longer, more challenging hikes, including the Observatory Trail and the Mauna Loa Summit Trail, are in this section. Between the 37- and 38-mile markers, you can also access the Footprints Trail, which leads to the Mauna Iki Trail and a large network of trails through the Ka'u desert (see the Hawaii Volcanoes National Park chapter for details on all these hikes).

Kilauea's southwest rift zone runs through this part of the Ka'u Desert, on the seaward side of the road. The rift runs for 20 miles, all the way from the Kilauea summit to the coast.

WOOD VALLEY

About 4 miles up the slopes from the small town of Pahala is remote Wood Valley and the Buddhist temple and retreat center of

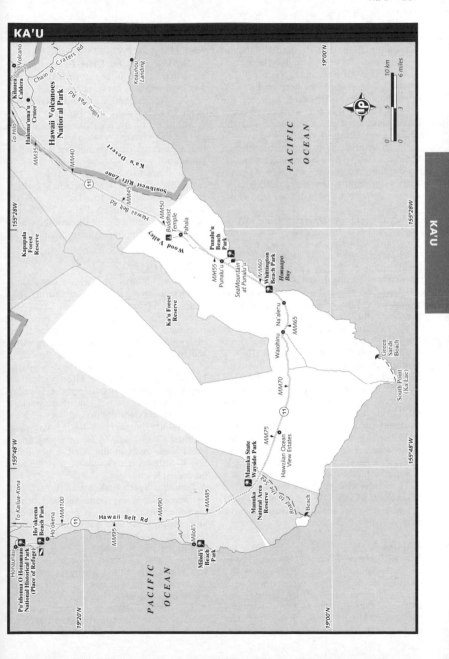

Nechung Dorje Drayang Ling. The temple, which sits in a quiet, verdant 25-acre setting, was built in the early 20th century by Japanese sugarcane laborers who lived here.

In 1975 a Tibetan lama, Nechung Rinpoche, took up residence here, and in 1980 the Dalai Lama visited to dedicate the temple. Since that time, many Tibetan lamas have conducted programs here and the Dalai Lama himself returned to visit in 1994. In addition to its Buddhist teachings, the center is also used by groups conducting meditation, yoga classes and New Age and spiritual programs. If you're interested, the center can send you a list of upcoming workshops.

Nechung Dorje Drayang Ling (Wood Valley Temple & Retreat Center; ☎ *928-8539, fax 928-6271,* W *www.nechung.org, PO Box 250, Pahala, HI 96777)* Dorm beds $35, singles/doubles $50/70. The center owns a two-story building that has a meditation hall and two pleasant guest rooms on the upper floor. One room has a queen platform bed and Japanese decor, the other has a king bed and Hawaiian decor. The ground floor also has a few simpler rooms and three dormitories with a total of 14 beds. There's also a separate guest house with five doubles tucked back on the grounds. There's a two-day minimum stay, and all rooms share a bath. A kitchen is available, but guests must bring their own food. There's a library of books on Buddhist culture, and you're welcome to join in morning services. Day visitors are welcomed on weekends. For those seeking a peaceful retreat, the temple is a special place.

The center also produces organic coffee that sells for $35/lb – if the old axiom 'you get what you pay for' holds true, this java must deliver enlightenment!

PAHALA

Pahala, on the north side of Hwy 11, is really two little hamlets side by side. Down by the old mill is the original sugar town, with rickety homes flanked by coffee can planters, cars rusting in the yards and 'Beware of Dog' warnings. In contrast, the north side of town has tract homes, gas sta-

tions, a bank with ATM, a post office, a community center and a convenience store. The Ka'u Hospital (☎ 928-8331) is also here.

The legendary *Tex Drive In* was opening a branch in Pahala at the time of writing. Malasada addicts, come and get 'em!

Ka'u Agribusiness, which once had 15,000 acres of sugarcane planted for 15 miles in either direction from Pahala, closed its mill in 1996. The company introduced groves of macadamia nut trees on much of the former cane land.

There are two entrances to Pahala. The northern access is via Kamani St, which passes the hospital before heading directly into town. Alternatively, Pahala can be accessed via Maile St to the south, which winds up past the shuttered sugar mill to the commercial part of town.

PUNALU'U

Punalu'u is a small bay with a black-sand beach famous for the green sea turtles that trundle out from the sea to bask in the sun after gorging on *limu* (seaweed). Feel very fortunate if there isn't a tour bus or three disgorging breathless honeymooners willy-nilly when you arrive.

Punalu'u was once the site of a major Hawaiian settlement, and later became an important sugar port. The most popular section of the beach is the northern pocket, lined with coconut palms and backed by a duck pond. The ruins of the Pahala Sugar Company's old warehouse and pier are a short walk away at the north end of the beach. Sitting on a rise above it is the Kaneeleele Heiau.

Punalu'u Beach Park, a county park just to the south, has rest rooms, showers, drinking water, electricity outlets, picnic pavilions and *camping*. Its flat, grassy area right on the beach and protected by low-lying trees is a nice place to camp, although it's very exposed and has zero privacy. At night you'll be serenaded to sleep by the melodies of crashing surf, but come daybreak, the whole area is abustle with sightseers.

The real treat here are the turtles that come to feast and sprawl on the beach to catch some rays. On any given day, your chances are very good of hanging out with these gentle giants. Most days, the swimming leaves a lot to be desired and it's funny to watch *malihini* (newcomers) in tropical swimwear braving the icy, spring-fed waters. There's also a strong undertow, fierce rip currents pulling seaward near the pier and lots of natural flotsam floating about (eg coconut husks, driftwood, almond pits). Still, strong snorkelers probably can't resist the opportunity to swim with the turtles; use the buddy system just in case. Conversely, sometimes it's quite calm here and wonderful for swimming, snorkeling and lazing about.

Just past Punalu'u on Hwy 11, you'll reach the entrance to SeaMountain, Ka'u's only condo complex. To get to the beach park, take either this turnoff or the next one, less than a mile farther along and marked Punalu'u Park.

Punalu'u is a county park; for information on obtaining a camping permit, see Camping in the Accommodations section in the Facts for the Visitor chapter.

Places to Stay & Eat

SeaMountain at Punalu'u (☎ 928-6200, fax 928-8075, 800-344-7675, W *www.seamtn hawaii.com, PO Box 460, Pahala, HI 96777)* Low/high season rates; studios $78-90/95-108, 1-bedroom units $100-115/120-135, 2-bedroom units $133-150/155-174. This condominium complex is a bit scary: it's really remote for starters, there's no restaurant and the balding golf course ($45 for 18 holes and cart) has sand patches that are not hazards by design. And in this day and age of Martha Stewart everything, everywhere, there is *no* excuse for such heavy reliance on rattan. But for a condo in the middle of nowhere, it's fairly cheap. There's also a pool, Jacuzzi and tennis courts.

Supposedly, the golf course pro shop serves snacks and sandwiches from 10:30am to 2:30pm, but it looked like something from *The Shining* at the time of research. Good luck.

WHITTINGTON BEACH PARK

Not far from Punalu'u, there's a pull-off with a scenic lookout above Honuapo Bay.

From here you can see the cement pilings of the old Honuapo Pier, which was used for shipping sugar and hemp until the 1930s.

Honuapo Bay is the site of Whittington Beach Park; the turnoff is 1 mile beyond the lookout. Although there are tide pools to explore, there's no beach at Whittington, and the ocean is usually too rough for swimming or fishing. Endangered green sea turtles, which can sometimes be seen offshore, apparently have been frequenting these waters for a long time, as Honuapo means 'caught turtle' in Hawaiian.

Camping is allowed with a permit, and it's far enough from the highway to offer a little privacy. This park makes a pretty good choice for camping, and mid-week it will probably just be you, the crash of the surf and perhaps a long-term camper or two. Camp beyond the reach of the streetlight by the parking lot, as the light burns all night. Whittington has rest rooms and sheltered picnic tables, but there's no potable water.

This is a county campground; for information on obtaining a camping permit, see Camping in the Accommodations section of the Facts for the Visitor chapter.

NA'ALEHU

Na'alehu is a sweet little town jumbled along the highway, with an exotic feel reminiscent of more foreign climes. It's also the southernmost town in the USA, which is something.

Modest as it is, Na'alehu is the region's shopping and worshipping center (the population of around 2500 supports no fewer than six churches). It has a grocery store, an ATM, a library, post office and the Ka'u police station, just east out of town. The 76 gas station here is open 5am-10pm weekdays and 6am-10pm Saturday and Sunday.

Becky's Bed & Breakfast (☎/fax 929-9690, 866-422-3259, W *http://1bb.com/Beckys, PO Box 673, Na'alehu Hi 96772)* Singles/doubles $60/65, includes all-you-can-eat breakfast. This home on Na'alehu's 'main drag' rents three clean, comfortable rooms, all with private bath and lanai. Guests have limited kitchen access; drop in – or book in advance to receive a 25% discount.

Na'alehu Fruit Stand (☎ 929-9009, Hwy 11) Open 9am-6pm Mon-Thur, 9am-7pm Fri-Sun. Pizzas small/large $8/10, sandwiches $3.95-4.95. The best place to eat in town is this friendly produce stand, health food store, pizzeria and sandwich shop all in one. The food is tasty, wholesome and everything sold here has been made on site. The ovens crank out bread in the morning and pizzas to order starting at 11am. The shop makes sandwiches on homemade whole-wheat bread, or you can get a submarine sandwich with the works. Macadamia nut bars and other pastries cost about a dollar. There are a few picnic tables out front where you can eat and 'talk story' with the locals.

Shaka Restaurant (☎ 929-7404, Hwy11) Breakfast $4.75-7.50, lunch $5.25-8.50, dinner $9.95-14.95. Open 10am-9pm Tues-Sun. For full, hearty meals in a proper restaurant setting, this is your choice in Na'alehu. Breakfast treats include eggs Benedict and Punalu'u sweet bread French toast (yum!), while dinner is a carnivore's delight: choose from Big Island T-bones, filet mignon or porterhouse steaks, chicken, ribs or chops. There's a kids' menu, beer and wine and live music most Friday, Saturday and Sunday nights.

Punalu'u Bakeshop and Visitor's Center (☎ 929-7343, Hwy 11) Open 9am-5pm daily. The baked goods from this place are justly renowned. The sweet bread and taro rolls are heavenly and hip-bulging and the turnovers and malasadas are respectable (though lacking the swoon factor of Tex's in Honoka'a). There's also a counter with plate lunch, saimin and sandwiches and covered tables where you can eat. Everything is made on the premises. The tourist info is more of the same glossy flyers, but the bathrooms are clean.

WAIOHINU

Hwy 11 winds down into a pretty valley and the sleepy hamlet of Waiohinu, which sits nestled beneath green hills.

The town's claim to fame is the **Mark Twain monkeypod tree**, planted by the author in 1866. The original tree fell in a hurricane in 1957, but hardy new trunks sprung up and it's once again full grown. The tree is in the center of town, beside the souvenir shop also carrying the Twain name.

The last weekend in August is a great time to visit this part of the island, when the **Ka'u Hula Festival** happens in Waiohinu Park. Highlights include hula halaus dancing traditional and modern forms, terrific Hawaiian and local food and music. It's free, too.

Also in the village center is **Wong Yuen's Chevron gas station** which has a small convenience store at the side; there's a 76 station down the road in Na'alehu keeping late hours if Yuen's is dark.

Shirakawa Motel (☎/fax 929-7462, 95-6040 Hwy 11, Na'alehu, HI 96772) Singles/doubles $30/35, kitchenette units $42. In the very center of town, this green, weather-beaten motel is tucked behind a big, new house. There are a dozen basic units in a lovely setting beneath verdant hills. Rooms have private baths and twin beds.

Margo's Corner (☎ 929-9614, Wakea St, PO Box 447, Na'alehu, HI 96772) Tent sites $25 per person, single/double cottages $60/75 (two night minimum). This establishment, at the home of Margo Hobbs and Philip Shaw, offers bicyclists and backpackers a place to pitch a tent or lay their heads while exploring the Ka'u area. All prices include largely organic vegetarian or vegan breakfast and there's a small *health food store* on site.

There are a couple of tent areas with pebbly mounds to allow drainage, or you can pitch your tent on the grass; tenters share a bathroom. There's also a pentagonal, free-standing private cottage out back with a private bath and queen bed. Smoking is prohibited. Margo's is on Wakea St, a couple of miles southwest of Waiohinu center, off Kamaoa Rd. Call ahead for reservations.

Macadamia Meadows Bed and Breakfast (☎/fax 929-8097, 888-929-8118, W www.macadamiameadows.com, PO Box 756, Na'alehu, HI 96772) Doubles with breakfast $65-110, 2-bedroom suite $120. Half a mile south of Waiohinu center, this B&B is on the 8-acre macadamia farm of Charlene and

Cortney Cowan. Centered around a contemporary, country home with open-beam ceilings, it has four large guest rooms, all with private entrance, lanai and cable TV. The continental breakfast features nuts and fruit grown on the farm. A good choice at the lowest rate is the Mokupuni Room, which has a private bath, queen bed, microwave and refrigerator. The suite can accommodate four people; one of the rooms has a king-size water bed (vavavavoom!). There's a pool and tennis court with ocean views.

Hobbit House Bed & Breakfast (☎ 929-9755, Ⓦ *http://hi-hobbit.com, PO Box 269, Na'alehu, HI 96772*) Doubles $170, including breakfast. This place is a fairy tale realized, and if ever a temptation arose to break the 'Lonely Planet writers do not accept discounts' golden rule the Hobbit House is it. This one-of-a-kind home is high on a bluff up a steep half-mile 4WD track with expansive views to South Point. Romantic and whimsical in a classy, accomplished way, your soul will smile when you realize it's all yours for three days (minimum). There are sloping roofs, huge windows inlaid with stained glass and bent-branch casements, a double Jacuzzi surrounded by more stained glass, an antique poster bed, a lanai, a full kitchen and not a straight line in the place. Did someone say 'I do?'

SOUTH POINT

The end of the line, you can't get any farther south in the USA than South Point. In Hawaiian, it's known as Ka Lae, which means simply 'the point.'

South Point has rocky coastal cliffs and an ocean so turbulent it makes you realize how desperately the sea voyaging Polynesians must have been to set foot on land here (if this is indeed where they alit as most scholars theorize). What

The delicious mahi mahi

isn't in question is that South Point was the site of one of the earliest Hawaiian settlements, which seems incredible in light of the harsh terrain here. However, South Point was a sustainable place to settle, because of the fishing largesse just offshore and the fresh water available up the road at Punalu'u. Much of the area is now under the jurisdiction of Hawaiian Home Lands.

The turnoff to South Point is midway between the 69- and 70-mile markers on Hwy 11. South Point itself is 12 miles from the turnoff, at the end of a one-lane, paved road; there are no facilities.

South Point Rd starts out in scattered house sites and macadamia nut farms, which soon give way to grassy pastures. The winds are whipping here, as evidenced by the trees, some bent almost horizontal with their branches trailing along the ground.

Kamaoa Wind Farms

After a few miles, you crest a hill and come face to face with row upon row of huge high-tech windmills plopped in a pasture beside the road. With cattle grazing beneath, it's a surreal scene, and combined with the unearthly whirring sound, it feels like something from the imagination of George Lucas.

Each of these wind turbine generators can produce enough electricity for 100 families. It's thought, theoretically at least, that by using wind energy conversion, the state could produce more than enough electricity to meet its needs. However, with the controversial Puna geothermal plant cranking out enough energy for 25,000, it's unlikely wind power will ascend to supremacy anytime soon.

Four miles south of the windmills, you'll pass a few abandoned buildings wasting away. Until 1965, this was a Pacific Missile Range station that tracked missiles shot from California to the Marshall Islands in Micronesia.

Ka Lae

Ten miles down from the highway, South Point Rd forks and the road to the left goes to Kaulana boat ramp and a small cove.

KA'U

The Big One

Ka'u was at the epicenter of the massive 1868 earthquake (7.9 on the Richter scale), the worst Hawaii has ever recorded. For five straight days from March 27, the earth rattled and rolled almost continuously by a series of tremors and quakes. Then, on the afternoon of April 2, the earth rocked violently in every direction and an inferno burst loose from beneath the surface.

Those fortunate enough to be uphill watched as a river of lava poured quickly down the hillsides and swallowed up everything in its path, including people, homes, trees and cattle. Within minutes, the coast was inundated by a tsunami, and villages near the shore were swept away. A total of 77 people died in the disaster, 46 due to the tsunami and 31 from the landslide.

This triple whammy of earthquakes, lava flows and tsunamis permanently changed Ka'u's landscape. Huge cinder cones came crashing down the slopes, and one landslide buried an entire village and seriously damaged parts of Ninole and Punalu'u. You can see the 1868 lava flow along the highway 2 miles west of the South Point turnoff. The old village of Kahuku lies beneath it.

There may be a sign saying 'Ka Lae Info Center,' which is a euphemism for 'get bilked here' (see Green Sands Beach later for more information).

The road to the right leads to the craggy South Point cliffs. The confluence of ocean currents just offshore makes this one of Hawaii's most bountiful fishing grounds. Locals fish from the cliffs, and many of the bolder (or hungrier) ones precariously hang out over the edge of the steep lava ledges. Red snapper and ulua fish are particularly plentiful.

Ruins at Ka Lae include the Kalalea Heiau, a small, stone enclosure that is usually classified as a *ko'a* – a small, stone pen designed to encourage fish and birds to multiply. Corralled inside the heiau is a well-preserved fishing shrine where ancient Hawaiians left offerings to Ku'ula, the god of fisherman, in hopes of currying favor for a bountiful catch. Both these sites are just beside the light tower; head straight towards the sea from the light and you're at the most southern point in the USA. It's an awesome sight, with sets of violent waves crashing into the rocks at physics-defying angles.

The outcrop on the west side of the fishing shrine is a good place to see scores of the canoe mooring holes that were long ago hammered through the rock ledges. Ancient Hawaiians used to anchor one end of a rope through these cleats and tie the other end to their canoes. The strong currents would pull the canoes straight out to deep turbulent waters, where the enterprising Hawaiians could fish, still tethered to the shore, without getting swept out to sea.

The wooden platforms built on the edge of the cliffs have hoists and ladders that are used to get things to and from the small boats that anchor below. This is a popular fishing spot and folks around the island boast of Caribbean-style cliff jumping here and it *seems* possible. You may see a sea turtle or two gliding around in the relatively calm waters below the hoists.

There's a large unprotected puka in the lava directly behind the platforms where you can watch water rage up the sides and recede again with incoming waves. Keep an eye out for it, particularly if you have kids in tow, as it's not obvious until you're almost on top of it.

Green Sands Beach

For another singular Big Island beach experience, return to the fork and take the road to the right, with the Ka Lae Info Center sign. This is neither at Ka Lae, nor an info center, but these are just details, right? In reality, there's a shack and some folks charging each car five bucks for 'secure parking' in the lot nearby so you can proceed to the beach with an easy mind. Because shore access in Hawaii is always free to the public, they can't legally charge you to go to the beach; hence the secure parking ruse. It's foxy in that capitalist way, but irksome in that same way. You can pay it or not and see what happens. They do have the only toilet for miles, which will be priceless for some.

From the 'secure parking lot,' it's a few minutes to the Kaulana boat ramp. Beside the ramp you'll notice pockets of green sand sparkling in the sun. These are semi-precious olivine crystals chipped from the lava cliffs and worn smooth by a relentless and pounding surf.

The highest concentration of green sand in Hawaii is at Green Sands Beach, a 2½-mile hike along the 4WD road heading northeast from the boat ramp. The walk is not difficult, though once you reach Green Sands you'll need to scramble down the cliffs to get to the beach. If you have a high-riding 4WD vehicle, you could consider driving in, but the road is rough and the drive takes about 25 minutes.

Try and visit on a calm day, as high surf can flood the entire beach and the wind will deposit green sand sparkles in every exposed orifice. A couple of minutes beyond Kaulana boat ramp the trail passes the site of Kapalaoa, an ancient fishing village.

By now, this small beach is squarely on the beaten path and there's a good chance of hearing the jangle of a cell phone on any given day. For a more intimate setting, check out the Road to the Sea (see that section earlier).

HAWAIIAN OCEAN VIEW ESTATES

A few miles before Manuka you'll come to the last services for the long stretch between here and Honaunau. There's a gas station, post office, grocery store, hardware store and a couple of places to eat. This is the commercial center, such as it is, for Hawaiian Ocean View Estates (HOVE) and a couple of other small, isolated south-side subdivisions.

This area remains one of the last sunny expanses of land in Hawaii to be totally resort-free. Controversial proposals for large developments occasionally pop up, but so far all have been defeated by local activists. Thanks ya'll. No resorts means, in part, that the places to stay here are friendly, family-owned affairs.

Bougainvillea Bed & Breakfast (☎/fax 929-7089, 800-688-1763, 🅦 www.hi-inns.com/bouga, PO Box 6045, Ocean View, HI 96737) Singles/doubles with breakfast $65/69. This B&B, in the home of Martie and Don Nitsche, has some of the best guest amenities in HOVE. The comfortable rooms each have a private bath, private entrance and TV/VCR. There's a swimming pool with ocean views and a hot tub set back behind the house: come hither and stargaze. These folks know the Big Island and can hook you up with tips and advice. The B&B is between the 77- and 78-mile marker on the makai side of Hwy 11.

South Point Bed & Breakfast (☎ 939-9049, PO Box 6589, Ocean View, HI 96737) Units per double $55, ocean-view unit per double $65. South Point B&B is just past the 76-mile marker on the mauka side. There are three comfortable units, each with a private entrance and bath. The units are better than the outside might suggest and the larger unit has a kitchen and a private lanai with a distant ocean view. All rates include a continental breakfast and use of the Jacuzzi.

Ohana House Rural Retreat (☎ 929-9139, 888-999-9139, 🅦 www.alternative-hawaii.com/ohana, PO Box 6351, Ocean View, HI 96737) Doubles per day/week in house $60/$300, doubles day/week in cottage $40/200. These are rustic, off-the-grid digs, but with nice perks and a divine price. The house sleeps five, has a lanai, a fireplace and a steam bath (two night minimum, 3rd night free). The cottage is one of those plywood palaces near and dear to guidebook writers, with outside facilities and a solar shower. All linens are provided, both places have full kitchens and you can rent out the entire compound for your group. There's also a cabin on the property ($100/week) and work-exchange possibilities.

Leilani Bed & Breakfast (☎ 939-7452, 🅔 leilanibb@aol.com, PO Box 6037 Ocean View, HI 96737) Singles/doubles $45/50, Ohana Room $60. This unique home is located on the mauka side of Hwy 11 at the

78-mile marker. Three rooms share a bath, while the Ohana room has private facilities and can sleep up to six. The landscaping is beautiful, there's an atrium in the center and a gorgeous stone-paved patio out back; the owners lead spelunking tours.

Ocean View Pizzaria (☎ 929-9677, *Ocean View Town Center*) Pizzas small/large $10/12, regular toppings $1.25/1.50, deluxe toppings $2.25/2.50, Sandwiches $3.75-5.20. Open 11am-7pm Sun-Thur, 11am-8pm Fri & Sat. What an extraordinary island: here you are in the middle of nowhere and just when the craving hits, there's tasty, fresh, quality pizza made to order. This place wins the Big Apple seal of approval: there's a little dining room, fresh coffee (85¢, with 40¢ refills), killer milkshakes, the aforementioned pizzas and submarine sandwiches. Delicious from start to finish.

Also, check out the tacos and tamales at ***Café Ohia*** (*929-8086, Ocean View Town Center*). Across the highway there's the ***Desert Rose Café*** (*939-7673*), a plate lunch cum diner affair.

ROAD TO THE SEA

If there was ever a reason to rent a 4WD, the pair of isolated **green-** and **black-sand beaches** at the end of this 'road' are it. This is *rough* going over lava, ledges and cracks that threaten to suck you in.

Access to the first beach presents only a few precipitous drop-offs and you might give it a go with a 2WD drive; it's the second sandy stretch that really requires the stalwart wheels and driver. Of course, you can always park off to the side and hike into the second beach (about 1½ miles). Trekking around here presents some intriguing opportunities as there are surely more coves and beach pockets to be discovered. Low tide maximizes exploration opportunities. Bring as much water as you can carry as it's hot and shadeless, with no potable water.

The green sand comes from olivine pulverized by the surf, while the black sand is crushed, surf-worn lava. Olivine is a type of volcanic basalt rich in iron, magnesium and silica; both Mauna Loa and Kilauea eject these green crystals.

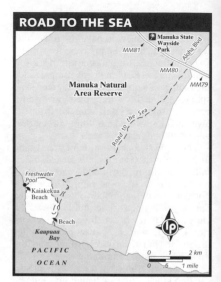

ROAD TO THE SEA

Few people venture down this way, especially mid-week, and you'll likely have both beaches to yourself. They're so isolated, romping in the liquid sapphire sea and curling your toes in the soft, psychedelic sand, it feels like the entire island is yours alone.

There's good fishing off the cliffs at the second beach and opihi a-popping at both. There are 130 words for wind in Hawaiian and you'll experience around 125 here most days, when even your inner ears will be exfoliated by flying sand; calm days descend every so often.

To get there, turn in at the mailboxes between the 79- and 80-mile markers on Hwy 11. It gets tricky further on, so set your trip odometer at the turnoff. From here it's 6 long, hard miles over a rudimentary track through lava to **Kaupua'a**, the first and smaller of the two beaches. It takes about 45 minutes and is pretty much straight on; you access the beach from the left.

The second beach is reached by taking a right-hand turn at the 5.5 mark. Don't take the right fork at the 5.4 mile mark: only a mule could make it up there, and don't take the right-hand fork *beyond* the 5.5 mark or you'll be lost, fast. The track jogs around to the right before heading towards the shore again and the way isn't always readily apparent. Get out and assess the route often. If you're carrying a lot of weight in the back, have them get out and walk to improve clearance.

Park just before the red *pu'u* (hill) and walk down the slope to **Kaiakekua**, the bigger of the two beaches. Alternatively, you can just brutalize your rental and pick your way over the lava and down to the shore. Remember that cars tend to sink in sand. There's a bit of shade here, and the colorado cliffs looming over the beach are stunning. If you walk to the north end of the beach, you'll come to a lime-green freshwater pool with a couple of hot pockets. A beautiful place for a soak. There is also a heiau up on the makai side ridge above it.

MANUKA STATE WAYSIDE PARK

Manuka State Wayside Park is a 13½-acre arboretum off Hwy 11 just north of the 81-mile marker. The trees and bushes, planted here between the mid-1930s and the 1950s, include 48 native Hawaiian species and 130 introduced species; many are labeled.

Camping is allowed by permit in the three-sided covered shelter, which has space for about five sleeping bags. In a pinch it will serve for an overnight break between Hilo and Kona, but is a bit forlorn with an odd vibe and it's close to the road; push on to the much more inviting Whittington to the east or Miloli'i Beach Park to the west if you can. While camping under the trees looks tempting, it's prohibited. There are rest rooms and picnic tables, but no drinking water.

The park is in the 25,500-acre Manuka Natural Area Reserve, which reaches from the slopes of Mauna Loa down to the sea. The reserve encompasses a couple of heiau and other ruins.

The **Manuka Nature Trail**, a 2-mile interpretive loop, begins above the parking lot. The trail crosses ancient lava flows and traverses varied terrain including both rain forest and dry lowland plants. A detailed brochure explaining the trail's flora can be obtained from the state parks office in Hilo.

KA'U

South Kona

Hwy 11 meanders north towards Kailua-Kona through a number of small unhurried upland communities: Honaunau, Captain Cook, Kealakekua, Kainaliu and Honalo. Surrounded by coffee farms, macadamia nut groves and tropical fruit trees, these towns get frequent afternoon showers that are useful both for their all-important agriculture and their overheated local and mainland visitors.

Side roads off Hwy 11 lead to the villages of Miloliʻi and Hoʻokena, along with better known spots like Kealakekua Bay and Puʻuhonua O Honaunau National Historical Park (commonly called Place of Refuge). South Kona is short on beaches, but there are a couple of excellent spots for snorkeling and diving.

MILOLIʻI

Miloliʻi means 'fine twist.' Historically, the village was known for its skilled sennit twisters who used bark from the *olona* shrub to make fine cord and highly valued fishnets.

While Miloliʻi is one of the most traditional fishing villages in Hawaii, this is more in spirit than in appearance. Old fishing shacks have been replaced with modern homes, and fishers now zip out in motorized boats to do their fishing. The small village consequently holds little of direct interest to most visitors. Furthermore, Miloliʻi residents generally prefer their isolation and the simple life they lead, and do not exhibit the Hawaiian hospitality so evident elsewhere on the island.

Miloliʻi sits at the edge of an expansive 1926 lava flow that covered the nearby fishing village of Hoʻopuloa. It's 33 miles south of Kailua-Kona and 63 miles from Volcano; the turnoff is just south of the 89-mile marker on Hwy 11, from where it's 5 miles down a paved but steep and winding single-lane road that cuts across the lava flow. The drive provides unusual photo opportunities of lava dotted with modest, corrugated tin-roof houses.

Highlights

- Sipping a homebrewed cuppa joe at one of many Kona coffee farms
- Roaming and exploring the special sanctuary of the Place of Refuge
- Spying pygmy dolphins at Hoʻokena bay
- Attending a play or indie film at Kainaliu's charming Aloha Theatre
- Cooling off during an afternoon drizzle in the South Kona hills

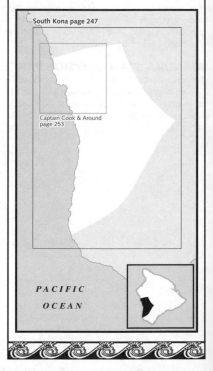

South Kona page 247

Captain Cook & Around page 253

PACIFIC OCEAN

Beaches

Miloliʻi Beach Park is the main beach here. It has rocky entry points into the water, but you'll find decent swimming past the rocks.

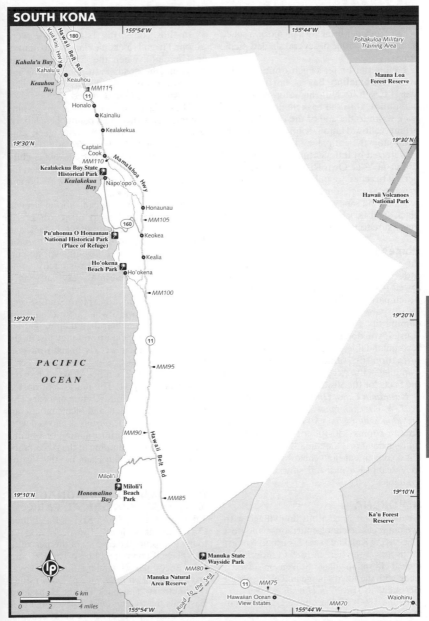

SOUTH KONA

Pohakuloa Military
Training Area

Mauna Loa
Forest Reserve

Hawaii Volcanoes
National Park

Hawaii Belt Rd

Kuakini Hwy

180

Kahalu'u Bay

Kahalu'u

Keauhou
Bay

Keauhou

MM115

11

Honalo

Kainaliu

Kealakekua

Captain
Cook

MM110

Mamalahoa Hwy

Kealakekua Bay State
Historical Park

Kealakekua
Bay

Nāpo'opo'o

Honaunau

MM105

160

Pu'uhonua O Honaunau
National Historical Park
(Place of Refuge)

Keokea

Kealia

Ho'okena
Beach Park

Ho'okena

MM100

Hawaii Volcanoes
National Park

Hawaii Volcanoes
National Park

PACIFIC
OCEAN

11

MM95

MM90

Hawaii Belt Rd

Miloli'i

Honomalino
Bay

Miloli'i
Beach
Park

MM85

Ka'u Forest
Reserve

Manuka State
Wayside Park

MM80

Manuka Natural
Area Reserve

Road to the Sea

11

MM75

Hawaiian Ocean
View Estates

MM70

Waiohinu

0   3   6 km
0   2   4 miles

155°54'W

155°44'W

19°30'N

19°20'N

19°10'N

SOUTH KONA

Weekdays are very quiet, though you might spot a few surfers doing battle with the ocean. Consider bringing a picnic or a snack to munch on at one of several shaded picnic tables.

By far the better beach option in this area, **Honomalino Bay** is fairly easy to access via a trail along the water. Park in the main lot next to the basketball court, then walk south to the end of the road (past the bright yellow Hauoli Kamanao Church) and follow the path along the water. Don't be deterred by intimidating 'Keep Out' and 'Enter at Your Own Risk' signs – remember, all beaches are public here. You'll have to wade through some shallow water before reaching the sandy stretch of nearly empty black-sand beach. If you've come this far, make sure to investigate the small cave.

Places to Stay

At Miloli'i Beach Park, past the village's little boat ramp, *camping* is officially allowed with a county permit. However, the beach park is right in the village, without a lot of space or privacy, and this is also the community's playground and volleyball court. If you don't have village ties, it's not a recommendable place to camp. But for information on obtaining a permit, see Camping in the Accommodations section of the Facts for the Visitor chapter.

Kaimama Guest House & Hostel (☎ *328-2207,* **w** *www.kaimanavacations.com, corner of Akahi St and Elima St*) Bunks $20, single/double rooms $30/40, cottage $55. Most tourists don't rest their heads in Miloli'i, but it is a convenient (and cheap) stop en route to Volcano. Kayaks and snorkel gear are available.

HO'OKENA

Ho'okena was once a bustling village with two churches, a school, courthouse and post office. King Kalakaua sent his friend Robert Louis Stevenson here in 1889 to show him a typical Hawaiian village. Stevenson stayed a week with the town's judge and wrote about Ho'okena in *Travels in Hawaii*.

In the 1890s, Chinese immigrants began to move into Ho'okena, setting up shops and restaurants. A tavern and a hotel opened, and the town got rougher and rowdier.

In those days, Big Island cattle were shipped from Ho'okena's landing to market in Honolulu. When the circle-island road was built, the steamers stopped coming and the townspeople moved away. By the 1920s, the town was all but deserted.

These days, Ho'okena is a tiny fishing community with a small county beach park. The beach itself has very soft black sand and minimal rocks. Trees provide shade in the bay, which is backed by lava sea cliffs. Kayakers paddle around here, and when the winter surf is up, local kids with boogie boards hit the waves.

When it's calm, you can snorkel straight out from the landing. It drops off pretty quickly, from 10 feet to about 30 feet, and there's an abundance of coral. Don't go too far out or you may encounter strong currents. Pygmy dolphins occasionally come into the bay, sometimes as many as a hundred at once.

If you have time to explore South Kona, Ho'okena is a worthwhile detour, and the locals are far friendlier than their neighbors in Miloli'i; chat them up and they just might invite you to their weekly beachfront potluck dinner.

Ho'okena is 2¼ miles down a narrow road from Hwy 11. The marked turnoff is between the 101- and 102-mile markers. The beach park has toilets and picnic tables, but no drinking water. *Camping* is allowed with a county permit; for information on obtaining a permit, see Camping in the Accommodations section of the Facts for the Visitor chapter.

PU'UHONUA O HONAUNAU NATIONAL HISTORICAL PARK

Take your time at South Kona's Pu'uhonua O Honaunau National Historical Park; it's tough to capture the essence of this peaceful, vast place if you're in a hurry. The 180-acre park encompasses ancient temples, royal grounds and a *pu'uhonua*, a place of refuge or sanctuary. The park fronts Honaunau Bay, thus the tongue-twister of a name that simply means 'place of refuge at Honaunau.'

Kapu keeper at the Place of Refuge

In old Hawaii, breaking any of the many kapu that strictly regulated all daily interactions was thought to anger the gods, who might retaliate with a natural disaster or two. To appease the gods, the offender was hunted down and killed.

Commoners who broke a kapu, as well as defeated warriors and ordinary criminals, could have their lives spared by reaching the sacred ground of the pu'uhonua.

This was more of a challenge than it might appear. Since royals and their warriors lived on the grounds immediately surrounding the refuge, kapu breakers were forced to swim through open ocean, braving currents and sharks, to get to the pu'uhonua. Once inside the sanctuary, priests performed ceremonies of absolution that apparently placated the gods. Kapu breakers could then return home with a clean slate.

Hale O Keawe Heiau, the temple on the point of the cove, was built around 1650. The bones of 23 chiefs were buried there. It's thought that the *mana* (spiritual power) of the chiefs remained in their bones and added a spiritual power to those who came into the grounds. The heiau has been authentically reconstructed. The carved wooden ki'i that stand close to 15 feet high beside it are said to embody the ancient gods.

Leading up to the heiau is a large stone wall built around 1550. It's called the **Great Wall** and is more than 1000 feet long and 10 feet high. The west side of the wall contained the pu'uhonua, and the east side held the royal grounds.

A self-guided walk, detailed in the park brochure, passes by Hale o Keawe Heiau, two older heiau, a petroglyph, legendary stones, a fishpond, lava tree molds and a few thatched huts and shelters. The canoe on display is hand-carved from koa wood.

Also fun to explore are the **tide pools** in the pahoehoe lava at the south end of the park. The tiny black speckles dotting the shallow pools behind the heiau are *pipipi*, a kind of periwinkle. Even better are the tide pools near the picnic area farther south, which harbor coral, black-shelled crabs, small fish and eels, sea hares, and sea urchins with rose-colored spines.

Information

Admission to Pu'uhonua O Honaunau National Historical Park (☎ 328-2288, W www .nps.gov/puho; adult/family $3/5; open 6am-8pm Sun-Thur, 6am-11pm Fri & Sat) is good for repeated visits over one week. Fees are generally collected between 7:30am and 5pm, but visitors are free to enter and stroll the grounds from 6am. On several recent visits, fees were inexplicably waived. Arrive early for better weather, or risk the cloudier afternoon skies in favor of fewer tourists.

Twenty-minute orientation talks, somewhat geared to people on tour buses who don't have time to see the whole park, are given at 10am, 10:30am and 11am and at 2:30pm, 3pm and 3:30pm daily.

A free program in Hawaiian studies is held monthly in the park's amphitheater, usually at 7:30pm on the first Wednesday of the month. A festival with traditional displays and food, *hukilau* (net fishing) and a 'royal court' is held on the weekend closest to July 1.

MARK NEWMAN

SOUTH KONA

Kona Coffee

Missionaries introduced the first coffee trees to Hawaii in 1827, and by the turn of the 20th century, it was an important cash crop throughout the state. However, the erratic rise and fall of coffee prices eventually drove coffee farmers out of business on the other Hawaiian Islands. Only the Big Island's Kona coffee was of high enough quality to sell at a profit during gluts in world markets. Also, great marketing and a few hardcore farmers contributed to Kona's successful coffee export.

Coffee production in Hawaii had dropped dramatically by 1980, when a rising interest in gourmet coffee sparked sales of the highly aromatic Kona beans. Today, Kona coffee is the most commercially successful coffee grown in the USA. Almost the entire harvest comes from the upland towns of South Kona, from Holualoa in the north to Honaunau in the south. The coffee trees thrive in the rich volcanic soil and under the cloud cover that moves in nearly every afternoon.

A relative of the gardenia, coffee has fragrant white blossoms in the spring. In the summer, the trees have green berries, which turn red as they ripen.

The berries (or 'cherry,' as they're called) don't all ripen at once, so they must be picked by hand several times a season. Harvest season begins in August. Coffee farmers at the lowest elevations may finish by December, while those at the 2000-foot level might harvest into March.

Hiking

Hiking to Ki'ilae Village along the **1871 Trail** takes an enjoyable hour or so. The park office lends out an informative booklet for a self-guided tour, and they'll direct you to the nearby trailhead.

On the way to the abandoned village you'll pass a collapsed lava tube and temple ruins before reaching the steep Alahaka Ramp, which once allowed riders on horseback to travel between villages. Halfway up the ramp is Waiu-O-Hina lava tube; bring a flashlight if you want to explore it because the floor is rough and jagged rocks jut out overhead. The far end opens to the sea, and some intrepid travelers plunge about 20 feet into the water from the cliff, then climb back up the rocks.

At the top of the ramp, incredible vistas spread out below. Keep going until you reach the spot where Ki'ilae Village once stood, then head back to avoid winding up in Ho'okena.

The trail is tree-lined but not shaded, and it meanders through lava flows, so a morning or late afternoon excursion is advised. Come equipped with water, sunscreen and a hat regardless.

Beaches

Swimming is allowed at **Keoneele Cove** inside the Place of Refuge. Shallow with a gradual decline, the cove was once the royal canoe landing. Snorkeling is best when the tide is rising, as the water is a bit deeper and the tide brings in fish. The park discourages sunbathing, and visitors are asked not to leave towels or mats on the ground.

Just north of the Place of Refuge is **Two-Step**, a terrific place to snorkel and dive. From the park's parking lot, take the narrow road (marked with a 15mph sign) to the left and go down about 500 feet. Incidentally, the little park on the inland side of the road was the original site of St Benedict's Painted Church, now in Honaunau.

Snorkelers step off a lava ledge immediately north of the boat ramp into about 10 feet of water. It then drops off fairly quickly to about 25 feet. Some naturally formed lava steps, which gave the beach its nickname, make it fairly easy to get in and out of the water, but there's no beach here, so the site is best suited for those who are comfortable jumping into deep waters.

Visibility is excellent, especially if you come midday when the sun is directly overhead; this cuts down on glare and cloudiness, and you'll see good-sized reef fish and a fine variety of corals close to shore. The predatory 'crown of thorns' starfish can be seen here feasting on live coral polyps.

SOUTH KONA

Divers can investigate a ledge a little way out that drops off about 100 feet. In winter, high surf can create rough waters.

HONAUNAU
Honaunau's main attraction is Pu'uhonua O Honaunau National Historical Park, commonly called the Place of Refuge, but there are other things to see in this area as well.

Hwy 160 connects with Hwy 11 at the store Merv's Place, then leads down to the Place of Refuge, passing Painted Church Rd and some rural scenery with grazing horses, stone walls and brilliant bougainvillea.

Macadamia Nut Factory
The Kona Coast Macadamia Nut & Candy Factory (☎ 328-8141, open 8am-5:30pm Mon-Fri, 8am-4pm Sat, 10:30am-4pm Sun), on Middle Keei Rd near Hwy 11, has a little display with a husking machine and a nutcracker. You can try it out free of charge, one macadamia nut at a time, and eat the final product.

The showroom overlooks the real operation out back, where nuts by the bagful are husked and sorted. The shop sells both raw and roasted macadamia nuts, and provides fun facts for visitors (for example, the Big Island is responsible for more than 90% of the worldwide macadamia nut production).

St Benedict's Painted Church
John Berchmans Velghe, a Catholic priest who came to Hawaii from Belgium in 1899, is responsible for the unusual painted interior of this notable church (☎ 328-2227).

Father John painted the walls with a series of biblical scenes as an aid in teaching the Bible to natives who couldn't read. He designed the wall behind the altar to resemble the Gothic cathedral in Burgos, Spain. In true Hawaiian style, painted palm leaves look like an extension of the slender columns that support the roof of the church.

When Father John arrived, the church was on the coast near the Place of Refuge, but he decided to move it 2 miles up the slopes to its present location. It's not clear whether he did this as protection from tsunamis or to rise above – both literally

and symbolically – the Place of Refuge and the old gods of 'pagan Hawaii.'

The tin-roof church still holds daily mass at 7am; the 7:15am Sunday service includes hymns sung in Hawaiian. The church is on Painted Church Rd; turn north at the 1-mile marker on Hwy 160 and go a quarter mile – a small sign points the way.

Places to Stay
Dragonfly Ranch (☎ 328-2159, 800-487-2159, fax 328-9570, w www.dragonflyranch.com) Outdoor lanai cubby $85, main house room $100, suites $150, honeymoon suite $200. Dragonfly Ranch, on Hwy 160 west of Painted Church Rd, is a cosmic New Age retreat with a gardenlike (and buggy!) setting where Pomeranian dogs and outdoor cats roam freely. 'Soul' proprietor Barbara Moore has been running the place for close to 30 years. Accommodation options include standard rooms in the main house, a conventional studio adjacent to the main house and an open-air Honeymoon Suite with a king-size bed on a platform deck without walls; netting keeps out the large but harmless spiders that share the gardens. Make sure to walk the labyrinth, a maze of rainbow colors behind the house overlooking the sea.

A Place of Refuge (☎ 328-0604, e crhawaii@kona.net, 83-5440 Painted Church Rd) Doubles $65-75. Located between Kealakekua Bay and the Place of Refuge, this B&B and working farm rents three rooms in a decidedly no-frills atmosphere. The two upstairs rooms have queen beds, while the downstairs room has a queen and a twin; none of the rooms have TVs, but guests can gaze at the terrific ocean view from the lanai instead. Owner Roger Dilts, a part-time Sierra Club activist, lends snorkel gear; also inquire about his kayak. There's no highway noise, but quacking geese make their presence known. Rates include full breakfast, and guests can use the kitchen.

Places to Eat
Bong Brothers (no ☎, Hwy 11) Closed Saturday. Bong Brothers, on Hwy 11 just south of Middle Keei Rd, sells its own coffee as

well as organic produce, smoothies and a few deli items. At lunchtime a vegetarian chef cooks up homemade soups and healthy specials such as bean burritos or lasagna for $5 or less.

Wakefield Gardens Restaurant (☎ *328-9930, Hwy 160*) Dishes $8. Open 11am-3:30pm daily. Recently remodeled, this soothing place, on Hwy 160 just west of Painted Church Rd, has an open-air dining patio that makes for a pleasant lunch stop. There are sandwiches, salads and plenty of vegetarian options. The restaurant also features boxed lunches for tourists on the go.

Keei Café (☎ *328-8451, Hwy 11*) Dishes $10-20. Open 5:15pm-9pm Tues-Sat. Keei Café, on Hwy 11 at the 106-mile marker, is a simple place with plastic chairs, but it has a credentialed gourmet chef who serves up the area's best dinners. The menu includes chalkboard specials such as delicious fresh ahi or *ono* (wahoo, a kind of mackerel) ($21). Creative vegetarian selections and good homemade desserts are also available. At press time, Keei Café was planning to move to Kainaliu in late fall 2002.

CAPTAIN COOK

The town named for the Pacific navigator is on Hwy 11, above the bay where Cook met his untimely end. It's a small, unpretentious town with a few county and state offices, a shopping center, a hotel and a couple of restaurants. The Chevron gas station at the north side of town is open 24 hours a day.

As you continue south from town, you'll pass a handful of roadside coffee-tasting rooms that sell locally grown coffee and provide free freshly brewed samples.

If you just want to examine coffee trees, there's an unmarked pull-off for that purpose midway between the 107- and 108-mile markers, on the seaward side of the road. Coffee trees are planted in the front and macadamia trees beyond.

About a mile farther south is **Royal Kona Museum & Coffee Mill**, the latest incarnation of a complex that has undergone several transformations in recent years *(open 7:45am-5pm daily)*. More of a gift shop than a museum, the store offers free

coffee samples and displays interesting period photos. Out back there's a working coffee operation where you can observe the pulping mill, wash station and drying bins. There's also a walk-through lava tube.

Places to Stay

Manago Hotel (☎ *323-2642, fax 323-3451, Hwy 11*) Singles/doubles $25/28, single/double motel-style rooms $42-47/45-50. This family-run hotel started in 1917 as a restaurant, serving bowls of udon to salespeople on the then-long journey between Hilo and Kona. Those wanting to stay overnight paid $1 for a futon on tatami mats – the atmospheric Japanese Room ($64) still has the mats. These days, the basic rooms with shared baths in the original roadside building show their age with spartan furnishings, thin walls.

The newer wing has 42 ordinary but sufficient motel-style rooms, with radios and private baths (no television). The highlight is the unobstructed lanai view of Kealakekua Bay a mile below; the higher rates are for better views. There's a common TV room near the restaurant.

Pineapple Park (☎ *323-2224, 877-865-2266,* W *www.pineapple-park.com, Hwy 11 between 110 & 111 mile markers*) Camp site/dorm bed/private room $12/20/55-65. This new hostel and B&B, located next to an exotic fruit stand, primarily draws a European clientele. Accommodations include seven private rooms (the rate includes a continental breakfast), 14 bunks and campsites out back (campers have access to the kitchen and showers). The hostel has a big kitchen, laundry facilities and a large common area. At the bus stop across the street, there's service to Hilo and Kona. For $15 the proprietors will pick you up from Kona Airport.

Pomaikai (Lucky) Farm Bed & Breakfast (☎ *328-2112, 800-325-6427, fax 328-2255,* W *www.luckyfarm.com, 85-5465 Mamalahoa Hwy*) Room $55, converted barn $65, duplex units $65. This B&B is on Hwy 11 overlooking Keei Bay about 3 miles south of Captain Cook. Host Nita Isherwood, who speaks fluent French, offers

CAPTAIN COOK & AROUND

PLACES TO STAY
9 Banana Patch
17 Pineapple Park
21 Manago Hotel & Restaurant
27 Lucky Farm Bed & Breakfast
28 A Place of Refuge
34 Dragonfly Ranch

PLACES TO EAT
3 Teshima's Restaurant
4 Aloha Angel Cafe
5 Evie's Natural Foods
7 Seven Senses Restaurant
8 Philly Deli
12 Kona Mountain Café
14 Chris' Bakery
25 Coffee Shack
30 Super J's
31 Keei Cafe
33 Bong Brothers
35 Wakefield Gardens Restaurant

OTHER
1 Daifukuji Soto Mission
2 Aloha Kayak Company
7 Hospital
10 Post Office
11 Bank of Hawaii
13 Library
15 Greenwell Farms
16 Kona Historical Society Museum
18 Kona Coffee Living History Farm
19 Amy BH Greenwell Ethnobotanical Gardens
20 State & County Offices
22 Post Office
23 Kealakekua Ranch Center (Choice Mart; Pasta Kitchen; Hong Kong Chop Suey)
24 Captain Cook Monument
26 Coffee Trees
29 Royal Kona Museum & Coffee Mill
32 Kona Coast Macadamia Nut & Candy Factory
36 St Benedict's Painted Church
37 Merv's Place Store

SOUTH KONA

casual accommodations: there is one simple room in the main house, a rustic converted coffee barn with an outdoor shower and two open-air duplex units behind the house. All units have private toilets. Guests have access to a common kitchen area with refrigerator, microwave and barbecue grill. Rates include an all-you-can-eat breakfast with homegrown coffee, fruit and macadamia nuts. There's a two-night minimum and as the place is near the highway, expect some traffic noise.

Cedar House (☎/fax 328-8829, **w** www.cedarhouse-hawaii.com) Shared bath $65-

70; private bath $80-90. Diana and Nik von der Luehe rent four guest rooms in their lovely, contemporary home. Perched on a quiet 5-acre coffee farm a mile up from the town center, the house has lots of windows and natural wood, and a deck with a distant ocean view. The two pleasant rooms on the ground floor each have a king and a twin bed, private entrance, private bath and TV; one has a kitchenette. The smaller two rooms, upstairs in the main house, have queen beds, TV and shared bath. Rates include a full breakfast. Nik speaks fluent German, as well as some French and Cantonese.

Places to Eat

Manago Restaurant (☎ 323-2642, Manago Hotel, see Places to Stay) Open breakfast 7am-9am, lunch 11am-2pm, dinner 5pm-7:30pm Tues-Sun. This is a Japanese version of a meat-and-potatoes eatery. It's not health food, but the portions are large, and the old-style local atmosphere is fun. Pork chops are the specialty. Two big chops, rice, potato salad and side dishes such as tofu curd cost $8, while sandwiches are around $4.50.

Super J's (☎ 328-9566, Hwy 11, south of the 107-mile marker) Open 10am-6pm Mon-Sat. Named for owners Janice and John (and their six kids with 'J' names), this Hawaiian take-out find offers only a few menu items, including a kalua pig and cabbage plate ($6). There are a handful of tables, but few people use them.

Coffee Shack (☎ 328-9555, Hwy 11, south of the 109-mile marker) Open 7am-5pm daily; breakfast served till 11am. Most of the tables sit on the lanai overlooking the ocean and the grassy slopes below. Try the fried egg sandwich ($6) or a tempting breakfast pastry ($2-2.50). At lunch choices include 8-inch pizzas ($10-12) and sandwiches like smoked turkey and black forest ham ($5-9).

The Kealakekua Ranch Center on Hwy 11, about half a mile south of the Manago Hotel, has a **ChoiceMart** supermarket, Pasta Kitchen, a deli and a Chinese restaurant called Hong Kong Chop Suey.

Getting There & Away

Three Hele-On buses depart Captain Cook's Yano Hall weekdays (6am, 10:45am and 2:15pm) for points north, including Kainaliu/Honalo ($1.50, 10 minutes), Keauhou ($2.25, 30 minutes), and Kailua-Kona's Lanihau Center ($2.25, 40-45 minutes). Northbound buses continue on to Waimea, the Hamakua Coast and Hilo. Going in the other direction, the bus departs Yano Hall once daily at 5:20pm for Honaunau (75¢, 5 minutes).

KEALAKEKUA

Kealakekua means 'Path of the Gods,' a name commemorating the series of 40 heiau that once ran from Kealakekua Bay north to Kailua-Kona.

Though it's a teeny place, the town of Kealakekua is now the commercial center for Kona's hill towns. The Kona Coast's hospital is on the north side of town, a quarter mile inland from Hwy 11. The post office is on the corner of Hwy 11 and Haleki'i Rd; the town also has a few banks.

Kealakekua's library (☎ 323-7585) on Hwy 11 is open noon to 8pm on Monday, 10am to 5pm Tuesday to Friday and 10am to 1pm on Saturday; there is Internet access for those with a library card. Next door to the library is the coral mortar and lava-rock Kona Union Church, which dates back to 1854.

Kona Historical Society Museum

This stone and mortar building, built in 1875, is on the seaward side of Hwy 11, just north of the Kealakekua Grass Shack gift shop. Once a general merchandise store and post office, the structure now houses the society's office, archives and little museum (☎ 323-3222, Hwy 11; admission $2; open 9am-3pm Mon-Fri).

The museum holds some displays on the area's local history, illustrated with period photos, old bottles and other memorabilia. Visitors can make an appointment to peruse the society's impressive archive of historical photos (there are some 30,000) and research books.

The society is in the process of raising funds for a new **Living History Ranch** focusing on the 1890s through the 1920s to be built on a plot of land next door over the next few years. An historical ranch house, which will be reassembled onsite, has already been donated.

Greenwell Farms

Open for business since the 1850s, Greenwell Farms (☎ 323-2275, Hwy 11 between the 111- and 110-mile markers) grows its coffee on 150 acres, and also buys coffee cherry from other Kona farmers. Aided by the young volcanic soil of the Kona region, these handpicked coffee trees help yield the million pounds of Greenwell coffee sold last year. On the tour, which lasts 15-20 minutes, you'll find out various facts about coffee (for example, the bigger bean means a smoother taste); afterwards, put your knowledge to the test as you sample various Greenwell roasts.

Tours are offered 8am to 4:30pm Monday through Saturday; no appointment is necessary.

Amy B H Greenwell Ethnobotanical Garden

Amy Greenwell donated her gardens (☎ 323 3318, south of 110-mile-marker; suggested donation $4; open 8:30am-5pm Mon-Fri), full of landscaped walking paths and unusual plants, to Bishop Museums, the state museum of natural and cultural history. Named for the science that analyzes the traditions of a people and their plants, the gardens have informative placards explaining how Hawaiians took advantage of their limited resources while still emphasizing their respect for the land. Both plants and trees provided the raw goods for a variety of useful things, including food, medicine, canoes and dye.

Free guided tours happen on the second Saturday of each month at 10am. Call about other tours.

Kona Coffee Living History Farm

While this Kona Historical Society project (☎ 323-2006, near 110-mile marker; admission adult/child $30/15; tours 9am-1pm on the hour Mon-Fri, also by appointment) focuses on farm life from the early 1900s through 1945, the 7-acre farm is still in use, or 'living.' The tour includes an exploration of the property's small house, built in 1925, which authentically replicates the homestead of the early pioneers. The Japanese influence is evident, with interpreters in period costumes offering demonstrations and explanations of how Japanese immigrants lived. Outside, visitors experience the difficult, time-consuming work of a coffee picker by doing some actual picking, and witness various aspects of the arduous coffee-making process.

The costumed guides are low-key and informative, but the entry fee seems steep for what you get. However, tour guides provide ample insect repellant to combat the buggy farm.

Places to Stay

Areca Palms Bed & Breakfast (☎ 323-2276, 800-545-4390, fax 323-3749, Ⓦ www.konabedandbreakfast.com) Rooms $85-125, with full breakfast. Formerly Merryman's, Oregon natives Janice and Steve Glass now run this B&B located in a quiet residential area in Kealakekua, a quarter mile above Hwy 11. The house is like a cedar lodge: big and airy with a large deck, lots of natural wood, country furnishings and exposed-beam ceilings. All rooms have private bath, cable TV and big closets stocked with luxurious robes. The rose room ($125) has an ocean view. Guests have use of a spacious common living area, a guest phone, croquet and a Jacuzzi.

Banana Patch (☎ 322-8888, 800-988-2246, fax 322-7777, Ⓦ www.bananabanana.com) 1-bedroom cottage $85-125, 2-bedroom cottage $100/125/150 for 2/4/6 people. Formerly Reggie's Tropical Hideaway, these two cottages on a small coffee farm near central Kealakekua cater to a clothing-optional clientele. The two-bedroom cottage has high wooden ceilings, a full kitchen, a waterbed and a screened lanai. It also has a sundeck with a Jacuzzi surrounded by privacy screens. The funkier one-bedroom cottage has a full kitchen, king bed, futon, deck and Jacuzzi. This is a vacation rental, not a B&B, so breakfast isn't part of the deal. The economy room ($55) in Reggie's main house has a private entrance and bath, but only stay here if you're a dog-lover.

Places to Eat

Kona Mountain Café (☎ 323-2700, Hwy 11)
Open 6:30am-6pm Mon-Fri, 8am-5pm Sat,
and 8am-4pm Sun. This Kealakekua café
serves a volcano veggie sandwich ($6.50)
and a smoked turkey number with avocado,
cream cheese and red onion ($6.50), plus
the usual array of pastries and coffee drinks.
Eat on the lanai or enjoy the indoor coffee-
house atmosphere.

Philly Deli (☎ 322-6607, Hwy 11) Lunch
dishes $5-7.75. Open 7am-6pm Mon-Fri,
7am-2pm Sat & Sun. Formerly the Canaan
deli (and playfully referred to as Philly-
sophical Deli), this East Coast–style spot
resides in a warehouse and serves reasonably priced eggs, pancakes and other breakfasts items. The lunch menu features
sandwiches, burgers and daily specials like
eggplant Parmesan ($6).

For sweet treats in Kealakekua, stop by
Chris' Bakery (☎ 323-2444, Hwy 11), open
6am-1pm daily. Irresistible offerings include
cinnamon twists, brownies and doughnuts.

Getting There & Away

Three Hele-On buses depart Kealakekua's
Konawaena Elementary School weekdays
(6:05am, 10:50am and 2:20pm) for points
north, including Kainaliu/Honalo (75¢, 5
minutes), Keauhou ($1.50, 25 minutes), and
Kailua-Kona's Lanihau Center ($1.50, 40-45
minutes). Northbound buses continue on to
Waimea, the Hamakua Coast and Hilo. In
the other direction, the bus departs Konawaena four times daily at 10:25am, 1:55pm,
4:45pm, 5:15pm for Captain Cook ($1.50, 5
minutes).

KEALAKEKUA BAY

The north end of Kealakekua Bay has a
protected cove sheltering what is perhaps
the premier snorkeling spot on the Big Island. At the south end of the large bay – a
mile wide at its mouth – is Kealakekua Bay
State Historical Park, which encompasses
Hikiau Heiau and what was formerly
Napo'opo'o Beach.

Steep sea cliffs prevent land passage
between the two ends of the bay. The northern end is accessible only by sea or by a hike
along a dirt trail beginning inland near the
town of Captain Cook.

Kealakekua Bay is a state underwater
park and marine life conservation district.
Among the protected species here are
spinner dolphins that frequently swim into
the bay. Fishing is restricted, and the
removal of coral and rocks is prohibited.

An obelisk monument on the north side
of the bay marks the spot where Captain
Cook was killed at the water's edge.

The Final Days of Captain James Cook

Captain James Cook, the first known Westerner to visit Hawaii, sailed into Kealakekua Bay at dawn
on January 17, 1779. The beaches were lined with some 10,000 curious onlookers, and 1000
canoes sailed out to greet him.

On Cook's first evening ashore, the high priest performed a series of ceremonies recognizing
Cook as the incarnation of the god Lono. While these initial days with the Hawaiians were
friendly, Cook and his men were content to remain ignorant about the ceremonies and worship-
ful chanting, and they have since been criticized for making little effort to educate themselves
during this encounter.

Following an unexpected return to Kealakekua Bay, Cook and four of his seamen were killed by
the Hawaiians in a violent struggle at the north end of the bay on February 14. Cook's men abandoned him, and he was beaten to death in a mere 10 minutes; angry attackers continued to stab
the captain's lifeless corpse.

Ironically, the world's greatest navigator was such a poor swimmer that he apparently stumbled
into an angry crowd rather than swim a few yards out to a waiting boat.

Hale O Keawe heiau, Pu'uhonua O Hanaunau

Murals at St Benedict's, South Kona

Exploring at Kealekekua Bay

Standing guard at Pu'uhonua O Hanaunau

The unique travelers palm

Red bombax

Harlequin shrimp

Underwater forests

Snorkeling with butterfly fish

Kealakekua Bay State Historical Park

The 4-acre Kealakekua Bay State Historical Park is at the end of Napo'opo'o Rd, 4½ miles from Hwy 11.

This busy park's predominant feature is **Hikiau Heiau**, the large platform heiau above the beach. The park also has a boat landing, rest rooms, showers and a shack selling soft drinks and souvenirs. Alas, Napo'opo'o Beach no longer exists; in 1992 Hurricane Iniki swept away the sand, and now only rocks line the shore.

It's forbidden to launch kayaks near the heiau, but you can take off from another point: drive down Napo'opo'o Rd and head straight instead of veering right towards the heiau where there's an easy launch spot.

The real snorkeling prize in the area is the cove at the northern end of the bay. Some people snorkel over from the former Napo'opo'o Beach when it's calm, but it's a long haul and for strong swimmers only.

From the park, you can continue 4 miles south along a narrow paved road through scrub brush and lava to the Place of Refuge. The road is little more than one lane, but paved and passable. Be careful if you pull over, as grasses conceal some roadside trenches.

Captain Cook Monument Trail

Some may call this hike a hardy day of exercise, while others may find it masochistic. Even a triathlete would work up a sweat on this trail, which leads to the Captain Cook Monument and the cove at the north end of Kealakekua Bay. The reward? Excellent snorkeling, a natural bath once reserved for royalty and some historic sites.

It's not that the trail is particularly steep or uneven. The problem is that it's not consistently maintained, so it's best suited for hikers who enjoy challenging conditions. At times this can be a jungly path through tall elephant grasses, which scratch up exposed arms and legs. At other times people who use the trail for horseback rides to the monument keep it clear. Prepare for the worst and bring a pair of lightweight pants for protection.

To get to the trailhead, turn off Hwy 11 onto Napo'opo'o Rd and go down about 250 yards, where you'll find a dirt road immediately after the second telephone pole on the right.

Start walking down the dirt road and after 200 yards it will fork – stay to the left, which is essentially a continuation of the road you've been walking on. The route is fairly simple and in most places runs between two rock fences on an old jeep road. When in doubt, stay to the left.

Eventually the coast becomes visible and the trail veers to the left along a broad ledge. Go down the hill and then swing left to the beach. Once you're at the water, the **monument** marking Cook's place of death is just a few minutes' walk to the left.

Queen's Bath, a little lava pool with brackish spring-fed water, lies at the edge of the cove, a few minutes' walk from the Captain Cook Monument in the direction of the cliffs. The water is cool and refreshing, and this age-old equivalent of a beach shower is a great way to wash off the salt before hiking back – although the mosquitoes can get aggressive here.

A few minutes beyond Queen's Bath, the path ends at the cliffs called **Pali-kapu-o-Keoua,** the 'cliffs sacred to the chief Keoua.' The cliffs' numerous caves were the burial places of Hawaiian royalty, and it's speculated that some of Captain Cook's bones were placed here as well.

A few lower caves are accessible, but they don't contain anything other than beer cans. Fortunately, the ones higher up are not as easy to get to and probably still contain bones. All are sacred and should be left undisturbed.

The hike on Captain Cook Monument Trail takes about an hour down and 1½ hours up. It's hot and largely unshaded, and it's an uphill climb all the way back. There are no facilities at the bottom of the trail. Be sure to bring your own drinking water and snorkeling gear.

Manini Beach

This beach south of Napo'opo'o faces stunning cliffs; Captain Cook monument is in plain – albeit distant – sight. Don't come here for swimming or sunbathing: it's a rocky area with no sand, so you'll want to plunk down on your own chair or opt for an unshaded picnic table. However, turtles, tangs and other colorful fish make this an interesting (and easily accessible) snorkeling option. The best point of entry is to your right just after you enter the beach. Evenly spaced palm trees along the shore provide a haven for interesting birds, too. There's a portable bathroom, but no other amenities.

To get here, take Napo'opo'o Road to the end and turn left on the narrow road that connects Napo'opo'o and the Place of Refuge. Turn right on Manini Beach Road. There are a few improvised parking spaces.

Snorkeling

After working up a sweat on the Captain Cook Monument Trail, you can slip into the ocean from the rocks on the left side of the cement dock in front of the Captain Cook Monument. The water starts out about 5 feet deep and gradually deepens to about 30 feet. The cove is protected and usually very calm. Visibility is good, and coral, turtles and fish are abundant. Snorkeling here definitely lives up to the hype.

Snorkeling tour boats (see the Activities chapter and the activities section in Kailua-Kona) pull into the bay in the morning, but they generally don't come ashore, and most leave by lunchtime. Anyway, the cove is big enough so it doesn't feel crowded.

Kayaking

Although there are no longer kayak rental operations at the bay, you can rent kayaks a few miles away in the hillside towns. *Aloha Kayak Company* in Honalo (☎ 322-2868, *Hwy 11 opposite Teshima's restaurant*) rents single/double kayaks for $25/40 a day, including all equipment, life vests and a car rack. You can rent snorkel gear for an addi-

tional $5. The company also arranges four-hour guided kayak tours for $65 per person, with a minimum of three people.

The laid-back guys at *Kona Boy* (☎ 323-1234, Hwy 11, 1/2 mile north of Kealakekua) provide great info and rent single/double kayaks for $25/45. They hurry out at closing time to hit the water themselves, but if you're late returning your equipment, they'll work out a solution.

Diving

Several spots in the area draw divers, but aptly named **Long Lava Tube**, just north of Kealakekua Bay, is an intermediate dive site noted for having one of the longest lava tubes in Hawaii. Several skylights allow light to penetrate through the ceiling, but overall the tube is dark enough that you may see active nocturnal species even during the day. Crabs and other crustaceans, morays and even Spanish dancers make the tube their residence. Outside the tube you'll find countless other lava formations that shelter critters such as conger eels, Triton's trumpet shells and schooling squirrelfish. Bring your dive light!

KEEI BAY

Tanned surfers aren't ubiquitous on the Big Island, but they are at this popular surfing spot. Swimming is poor, but kayakers test out the waters alongside the surfers. It's also a spectacular, unobstructed place to watch the sunset. Behind the beach is a virtual forest of coconut trees offering tons of shade. No facilities here.

Take Napo'opo'o Road and turn left on the one-lane road towards the Place of Refuge. Pass Manini Beach Road and the first dirt road; turn right on the second dirt road. If you reach the Keei Transfer Station heading south, you've gone too far. As you drive into the beach, you'll pass lava coves that are too dangerous to explore. Continue on to the end and you'll reach the scenic 1/4- mile stretch of salt-and-pepper beach. If you don't want to navigate the bumpy road, it's only a 15-minute walk from the paved road to the beach.

KAINALIU

Kainaliu is a little town with positive energy. The focal point is the Aloha Angel Cafe and the adjoining *Aloha Theatre*, home of the Aloha Community Players. The bulletin board next to the theater has the current schedule, which can include everything from live music and dance to indie films.

The town is an interesting mix of old and new influences. Some shops selling traditional fabrics and dry goods have been here for generations, though they mingle with more contemporary stores selling island crafts and New Age clothing, and up-to-date used books.

Aloha Angel Cafe (☎ 322-3283, Hwy 11) Breakfast $6-9, lunch $6-13, dinner $14-22. Open 8am-3pm & 5pm-9pm. Under new management and recently expanded, this continues to be the best place to eat in town and even has a distant ocean view from its outside terrace. The menu includes vegetarian dishes, good salads and fresh fish specials. There are burritos or quesadillas with a side salad ($8) and more expensive dishes like filet mignon ($21). You can also get fruit smoothies, espresso and desserts. Bring a sweater if you come for dinner in the winter.

Evie's Natural Foods (☎ 322-0739) Breakfast/lunch $4-6. Open 8am-7pm weekdays, 9am-6pm Sat, 9am-5pm Sun. A little farther south on the seaward side of Hwy 11 is Evie's, selling organic produce, fruit juices, dairy products, salads, sandwiches and smoothies at reasonable prices. The café closes an hour before the store.

Seven Senses Restaurant (☎ 322-5083, Hwy 11) Open 11:30am-6pm Mon-Fri. This healthy gourmet newcomer emphasizes organic fare, with a Moroccan chicken wrap ($8), bison burger ($8) and various salads

($7-$10), plus a delicious, hard-to-believe-it's-lowfat chocolate mousse made with tofu and egg whites ($4). The restaurant has soothing music and funky chalkboards that do dual duty as art pieces.

Three Hele-On buses depart Kainaliu/Honalo weekdays (6:05am, 10:50am and 2:20pm) for points north, including Keauhou (15 minutes) and Kailua-Kona's Lanihau Center (25-35 minutes). Going in the other direction, the bus departs four times daily (10:15am, 1:45pm, 4:40pm, 5:05pm) for Kealakekua (5-10 minutes) and Captain Cook (10-15 minutes).

HONALO

Honalo, at the intersection of Hwys 11 and 180, barely qualifies as a village. See above for bus information.

Daifukuji Soto Mission, on the inland side of Hwy 11, is a big Buddhist temple with two altars, gold brocade, large drums and incense burners. Visitors are welcome to view the inside. As at all Buddhist temples, leave your shoes at the door.

Teshima's Restaurant (☎ 322-9140, Hwy 11) Restaurant open daily; lunch 6:30am-1:45pm, dinner 5pm-9pm. Singles/doubles $25/35. Family-run Teshima's is an unpretentious place serving fresh, authentic Japanese food to throngs of locals. The best deal is the lunch teishoku of miso soup, sashimi, sukiyaki, tsukemono and rice ($7.25). Oyako donburi with sashimi costs $9. The restaurant doesn't accept credit cards and doesn't have a liquor license.

In a building out back, Teshima's has 10 rooms that are mostly booked on a monthly basis ($300 per month). These small rooms are very basic, each with a double bed, a private bathroom and a cabinlike ambience.

SOUTH KONA

Glossary

a'a – rough lava

adobo – meat, usually chicken or pork, stewed in vinegar, garlic and soy sauce

ae – yes

ahi – yellowfin tuna

ahu – stone cairns used to mark a trail

ahupua'a – traditional land division, usually wedge-shaped and extending from the mountains to the sea

aikane – friend

'aina – land

akamai – smart, clever

aku – skipjack tuna

akua – god, spirit, idol

akule – bigeye mackerel

ali'i – chief, royalty

aloha – traditional greeting meaning love, welcome, goodbye

aloha' aina – love of the land

anaana – psycho-spiritual method of influencing or explaining events

ano ai – have a nice day

anuenue – rainbow

aole – no

'apapane – bright-red native Hawaiian honeycreeper

aumakua – ancestral spirit helper

awa – see *kava*

bento – Japanese word for a boxed lunch

crack seed – snack food, usually dried fruits or seeds; can be sour, salty or sweet

haku – lei garland worn on the head

hala – pandanus plant used for weaving

hale – house

hana – work; or bay, when used as a compound in place names

haole – Caucasian, literally 'without breath'

hapa – half; or person of mixed blood

hapa haole – half-white, used for a person, thing or idea

haupia – coconut pudding

Hauoli Makahiki Hou – Happy New Year

Hawaii nei – all the Hawaiian Islands, as distinguished from the Big Island

heiau – ancient Hawaiian temple

Hina – Polynesian goddess, wife of Ku and mother of Maui

holoholo – walk, drive, sail, travel or ramble around for pleasure

holoku – a long dress similar to the *muumuu*, but fitted and with a yoke and a train

holua – ancient Hawaiian sled or sled course

honu – turtle

ho'okipa – hospitality or the action of visiting

ho'okupu – an offering, usually wrapped in ti leaves

ho'olaulea – celebration, party

ho'oponopono – new beginning or a traditional reconciliation process

huhu – angry

hui – social group, club, organization

hula – traditional Hawaiian dance

hula halau – *hula* school or group

humuhumunukunukuapua'a – rectangular triggerfish

ice – a highly addictive, smokeable form of crystal methamphetamine

iliahi – Hawaiian sandalwood

imu – underground earthen oven used in traditional *luau* cooking

kahuna – wise person in any field; commonly a priest, healer or sorcerer

kahuna nui – high priest

kai – saltwater

kalo – see *taro*

kalua – traditional method of baking in an underground oven *(imu)*

kama'aina – native-born Hawaiian or a longtime resident; literally, 'child of the land'

kanaka – human being, man, person (usually of Hawaiian descent)

kane/Kane – man; also one of the four main Hawaiian gods

kapa – see *tapa*

kapu – taboo, part of strict ancient Hawaiian social system; today seen on signs, meaning 'Keep Out'

kaukau – food
kava kava – a mildly narcotic drink made from *Piper methysticum*, called *awa* in Hawaiian
keiki – child, children
kiawe – a relative of the mesquite tree; its branches are covered with thorns
ki'i – image, statue
kipuka – an area of land spared when lava flows around it; an oasis
ko – sugarcane
koa – native hardwood tree often used in woodworking
kohola – whale
kokua – help, cooperation; 'Please Kokua' on a trash can means, 'Don't litter'
kona – leeward; or a leeward wind
ko'olau – windward side
Ku – a Polynesian god of many manifestations, including war and fishing; husband of Hina
kukui – candlenut tree, Hawaii's official state tree; its oily nuts were once burned in lamps
kupuna – grandparent, respected elder

Laka – goddess of the hula
lanai – veranda, porch
lani – sky, heaven
lauhala – leaves of the *hala* plant used in weaving
laulau – wrapped package; bundles of pork or beef with salted fish steamed in ti leaves
lei – garland, usually of flowers, but also of leaves, shells, kukui nuts or feathers
lilikoi – passion fruit
limu – seaweed
lolo – stupid, crazy
lomi – to rub or soften; *lomi* salmon is raw, diced, marinated salmon
lomi lomi – traditional Hawaiian massage
Lono – god of harvest, agriculture, fertility and peace
luakini – a type of *heiau* dedicated to the war god Ku and used for human sacrifice
luau – traditional Hawaiian feast

mahalo – thank you
mahimahi – also called 'dolphin,' but actually a type of fish unrelated to that marine mammal

maile – native plant with fragrant leaves; often used for *lei*
makaainana – commoners; literally 'people that attend the land'
makai – toward the sea
makaku – creative, artistic *mana*
malasada – Portuguese fried dough; tasty, served warm and rolled in sugar
malihini – newcomer, visitor
mana – supernatural or spiritual power
manini – convict tang (a reef fish); or stingy
mano – shark
mauka – toward the mountains, inland
mauna – mountain
mele – song, chant
Menehune – the 'little people' who, according to legend, built many of Hawaii's fishponds and *heiau*
moana – ocean, open sea
moku – island
muumuu – long, loose-fitting dress introduced by the missionaries

nalu – wave
Neighbor Islands – refers to the main Hawaiian Islands, outside of Oahu
nene – a native goose; Hawaii's state bird
noni – Indian mulberry; a yellow, smelly fruit used medicinally

ohana – family, extended family
ohelo – low-growing native shrub with edible red berries, said to be sacred to the goddess Pele
ohi'a lehua – native Hawaiian tree with red tufted blossoms
okole – buttocks
olo – surfboards used by Hawaiian royalty
ono – delicious; also the name of the wahoo fish
opihi – toothsome limpet that tastes and chews like an oyster mushroom

pahoehoe – quick-flowing, smooth, ropy lava
pahu – wooden and sharkskin drum
pakalolo – marijuana; literally, 'crazy smoke'
pali – cliff
palila – rare native honeycreeper
paniolo – Hawaiian cowboy

pau – finished, no more
Pele – goddess of fire and volcanoes
piko – navel, umbilical cord
pili – a bunchgrass, commonly used for thatching houses
poha – gooseberry
pohaku – rock
poi – a gooey paste made from *taro* root, a staple of the Hawaiian diet
poke – bite-sized raw fish marinated in salt, seaweed, soy sauce and vinegar; anything chopped and marinated
Poliahu – goddess of snow
pono – righteous
pueo – Hawaiian short-eared owl
puka – any kind of hole or opening
pupu – snack food, hors d'oeuvres; shells
pu'u – hill, cinder cone
pu'uhonua –- place of refuge

saimin – the Hawaiian version of Japanese noodle soup *(ramen)*

tabi – Japanese split-toed shoes, used for reef-walking
tapa – cloth made from the beaten bark of the paper mulberry tree, used for early Hawaiian clothing *(kapa)*
taro – a plant with green heart-shaped leaves; cultivated in Hawaii for its root-stock, which is mashed to make *poi*
ti – common native plant; its long shiny leaves are used for wrapping food and making *hula* skirts *(ki in Hawaiian)*
tutu – aunt, respected older woman

ukulele – a stringed musical instrument derived from the Portuguese *braginha*
Uli – goddess of sorcery
ulu – breadfruit
ulu maika – ancient Hawaiian game
wa'a – canoe
wahine – woman
wai – freshwater
wikiwiki – hurry, quick

PIDGIN WORDS & EXPRESSIONS

aiyah! – Wow!
'ass right – You are correct
brah – brother, friend; also used for 'hey you'
broke da mouth – delicious
buggah – guy
chicken skin – goose bumps
coconut wireless – word of mouth
da kine – whatchamacallit; used whenever you can't think of the word you want but you know the listener knows what you mean
eat it – to fall down, take a digger
grinds – food, eats; 'ono grinds' is good food
haolefied – become like a haole (white man)
howzit? – hi, how's it going?
how you stay? – how are you?
humbug – a real hassle
junalunka – piece of junk, also pakajunk

keke – drunk, loaded
like beef? – wanna fight?
luna – boss
mo' bettah – much better, the best
no hum – no worry
powah surf – heavy surf, the kind of surfing you do in places with big swells
puka head – one not too bright; airhead
Puna butter – pakalolo from Puna; also 'Puna buds'
scoah – to get something really good
stick – surfboard
stink ear – when you only hear the bad stuff
stink eye – dirty look, evil eye
swipe – pineapple moonshine
talk story – any kind of conversation, gossip, tales
tanks – thanks; more commonly, 'tanks brah'

Online Resources

General Travel Information
Alternative Hawaii –
  W www.alternative-hawaii.com/taro
Big Island Visitors Bureau
  W www.bigisland.org
Gay Hawaii – W www.gayhawaii.com
Hawaii Webzine – W www.aloha-hawaii.com
Hawaii Visitors Bureau –
  W www.gohawaii.com
Kamuela Pages – W www.kamuela.com
Planet Hawaii – W www.planet-hawaii.com

Money & Banking
Western Union – W www.westernunion.com
Bank of Hawaii – W www.boh.com
First Hawaiian Bank – W www.fhb.com
Thomas Cook – W www.thomascook.com

Government & Politics
Environment Hawaii –
  W www.environment-hawaii.org
Hawaii County – W www.hawaii-county.com
Hawaii, Independent and Proud –
  W www.hawaii-nation.org
State of Hawaii – W www.state.hi.us

Books, Newspapers & Magazines
101 Things to Do on the Big Island –
  W www .hawaii101.com
Hawaii Tribune-Herald –
  W www.hilohawaiitribune.com
Pidgin Bible – www.pidginbible.org
This Week Big Island –
  W www.thisweek.com
West Hawaii Today –
  W www.westhawaiitoday.com

Festivals and Special Events
Hawaii International Film Festival –
  W www.hiff.org
Hawaii Races – W www.hawaiirace.com
Kona Coffee Festival –
  W www.konacoffeefest.com
Taro Festival –
  W www.alternative-hawaii.com/taro
International Film Festival – W www.hiff.org

Ironman Triathalon –
  W www.ironmanlive.com.
Kilauea Volcano Wilderness Runs –
  W www.volcanoartcenter.org,
Keauhou-Kona Triathlon –
  W www.keauhou triathlon.com
Kona Stampede & Parker Ranch Rodeo –
  W www.rodeohawaii.com

Activities
ATV Outfitters –
  W www.outfittershawaii.com
Big Island Race & Training Schedule –
  W www.bigislandraceschedule.com
Big Island Surf Reports –
  W www.hawaiisurfnews.com
Big Island Mountain Bike Association –
  W www.interpac.net/~mtbike/
County Aquatics Division –
  W www.hawaii-county.com/parks/
  aquatics_program_guide.htm.
E Mau Ma Ala Hele –
  W www.alakahakai.com
Fins & Fairways – W www.fishkona.com
Hawaii Cycling Club –
  W www.hawaiicyclingclub.com
Hiika's Healing Herb Garden –
  W www.hiiakas.com
Na Ala Hele Hawaii Trails And Access
  System – W www.hawaiitrails.org
Naui – W www.naui.org
Odyssey World Cycling Tours –
  W www.odyssey2000.com
PADI – W www.padi.com
Paradise Baloons –
  W www.paradiseballoons.com
People's Advocacy for Trails Hawaii –
  W www.hialoha.com/path/
Rodeo Hawaii – W www.rodeohawaii.com
Sierra Club Hawaii – W www.hi.sierraclub
  .org/Hawaii/mokuloa.html
Ski Hawaii – W www.skihawaii.com
UH at Hilo Vulcans –
  W http://vulcans.uhh.hawaii.edu.
Volcano Update – W http://wwwhvo.wr.usgs
  .gov/kilauea/update/

Volunteer Opportunities

Kalani Honua Oceanside Eco-Retreat –
  W www.kalani.com
Mauna Kea Observatories Support Services –
  W www.ifa.hawaii.edu/info/vis.
Volcanoes National Park – W www.ifa
  .hawaii.edu/info/vis/volunteers.html
Ironman Triathlon – W http://vnews
  .ironmanlive.com/vnews/volunteer

Travelers with Special Needs

Accessible Vans Hawaii –
  W www.accessiblevanshawaii.com/
Airline Directory –
  W www.everybody.co.uk/airindex.htm
Baby's Away – W www.babysaway.com
Pet Quarantine Regulations – W www
  .hawaiiag.org/hdoa/ai_aqs_info.htm
Society for the Advancement of Travel for
  the Handicapped – W www.sath.org

Places to Stay

All Islands Bed & Breakfast –
  W home.hawaii.rr.com/allislands/
Bed & Breakfast Hawaii –
  W www.bandb-hawaii.com
Hawaii's Best B&Bs – W www.bestbnb.com
Hawaii Island B&B Association –
  W www.stayhawaii.com/index.html
Ohana Net – W www.ohananet.com/travel/
  bednbrkfst.html

Getting There & Away

Air Brokers – W www.airbrokers.com
Air Canada – W www.aircanada.com
Air-Fare.com – W www.air-fare.com
Air Tech – W www.airtech.com
Air Treks – W www.airtreks.com
All America Auto Transport –
  W www.carmoving.com/aaat/
All Nippon Airways – W www.ana.co.jp
Aloha Airlines –
  W www.alohaairlines.com
American Trans Air – W www.ata.com
Boat Crew.Net – W www.boatcrew.net
Cheap Tickets –
  W www.cheaptickets.com
Council Travel –
  W www.counciltravel.com

Cut Rate Tickets –
  W www.cutratetickets.com
Expedia – W www.expedia.com
Hawaiian Airlines –
  W www.hawaiianair.com
Japan Air Lines – W www.jal.com
Kona Transportation – W www.konaweb
  .com/konaweb/transportation.html
King's Travel – W www.kingstravel.com
Latitutde 38 – W www.latitude38.com/
  crewlist/4-01.List/CruisingSkippers.html
Orbitz – W www.orbitz.com
Paragon Air – W www.paragonair.com
Pleasant Hawaiian Holidays –
  W www.2hawaii.com
Priceline – W www.priceline.com
SF Sailing.com – W http://63.67.53.238/cgi-bin/
  crewlist/crew_list.cfm?crewlist:skippers
Smarter Living –
  W www.smarterliving.com
Speedi Shuttle –
  W www.speedishuttle.com
STA Travel – W www.sta-travel.com
SunTrips – W www.suntrips.com
Trailfinders – W www.trailfinders.com
Travel CUTS/Voyages Campus –
  W www.travelcuts.com
Travelocity – W www.travelocity.com

Getting Around

Alamo – W www.alamo.com
Avis – W www.avis.com
Budget – W https://rent.drivebudget.com
DJs Rentals – W http://harleys.com
Dollar – W www.dollar.com
Hertz – W www.hertz.com
Kona Harley Davidson –
  W www.konaharleydavidson.com
Matson Navigation – W www.matson.com
MoveCars.com – W www.movecars.com
National – W www.nationalcar.com
Polynesian Adventures –
  W www.polyad.com
Roberts Hawaii –
  W www.roberts-hawaii.com
Transcar Auto Shippers –
  W www.transcar.org
Xtreme Rentals –
  W www.extreme-rentals.com

LONELY PLANET

You already know that Lonely Planet produces more than this one guidebook, but you might not be aware of the other products we have on this region. Here is a selection of titles which you may want to check out as well:

Diving & Snorkeling Hawaii
ISBN 1 86450 090 5
US$17.95 • UK£10.99

Oahu
ISBN 1 74059 201 8
US$16.99 • UK£9.99

Maui
ISBN 1 74059 271 9
US$14.99 • UK£8.99

Los Angeles
ISBN 1 74059 021 X
US$15.99 • UK£9.99

USA
ISBN 1 86450 308 4
US$24.99 • UK£14.99

South Pacific
ISBN 0 86442 717 4
US$24.95 • UK£15.99

Available wherever books are sold.

Lonely Planet Guides by Region

Lonely Planet is known worldwide for publishing practical, reliable and no-nonsense travel information in our guides and on our Web site. The Lonely Planet list covers just about every accessible part of the world. Currently there are 16 series: Travel guides, Shoestring guides, Condensed guides, Phrasebooks, Read This First, Healthy Travel, Walking guides, Cycling guides, Watching Wildlife guides, Pisces Diving & Snorkeling guides, City Maps, Road Atlases, Out to Eat, World Food, Journeys travel literature and Pictorials.

AFRICA Africa on a shoestring • Botswana • Cairo • Cairo City Map • Cape Town • Cape Town City Map • East Africa • Egypt • Egyptian Arabic phrasebook • Ethiopia, Eritrea & Djibouti • Ethiopian Amharic phrasebook • The Gambia & Senegal • Healthy Travel Africa • Kenya • Malawi • Morocco • Moroccan Arabic phrasebook • Mozambique • Namibia • Read This First: Africa • South Africa, Lesotho & Swaziland • Southern Africa • Southern Africa Road Atlas • Swahili phrasebook • Tanzania, Zanzibar & Pemba • Trekking in East Africa • Tunisia • Watching Wildlife East Africa • Watching Wildlife Southern Africa • West Africa • World Food Morocco • Zambia • Zimbabwe, Botswana & Namibia
Travel Literature: Mali Blues: Traveling to an African Beat • The Rainbird: A Central African Journey • Songs to an African Sunset: A Zimbabwean Story

AUSTRALIA & THE PACIFIC Aboriginal Australia & the Torres Strait Islands • Auckland • Australia • Australian phrasebook • Australia Road Atlas • Cycling Australia • Cycling New Zealand • Fiji • Fijian phrasebook • Healthy Travel Australia, NZ and the Pacific • Islands of Australia's Great Barrier Reef • Melbourne • Melbourne City Map • Micronesia • New Caledonia • New South Wales • New Zealand • Northern Territory • Outback Australia • Out to Eat – Melbourne • Out to Eat – Sydney • Papua New Guinea • Pidgin phrasebook • Queensland • Rarotonga & the Cook Islands • Samoa • Solomon Islands • South Australia • South Pacific • South Pacific phrasebook • Sydney • Sydney City Map • Sydney Condensed • Tahiti & French Polynesia • Tasmania • Tonga • Tramping in New Zealand • Vanuatu • Victoria • Walking in Australia • Watching Wildlife Australia • Western Australia
Travel Literature: Islands in the Clouds: Travel in the Highlands of New Guinea • Kiwi Tracks: A New Zealand Journey • Sean & David's Long Drive

CENTRAL AMERICA & THE CARIBBEAN Bahamas, Turks & Caicos • Baja California • Belize, Guatemala & Yucatán • Bermuda • Central America on a shoestring • Costa Rica • Costa Rica Spanish phrasebook • Cuba • Cycling Cuba • Dominican Republic & Haiti • Eastern Caribbean • Guatemala • Havana • Healthy Travel Central & South America • Jamaica • Mexico • Mexico City • Panama • Puerto Rico • Read This First: Central & South America • Virgin Islands • World Food Caribbean • World Food Mexico • Yucatán
Travel Literature: Green Dreams: Travels in Central America

EUROPE Amsterdam • Amsterdam City Map • Amsterdam Condensed • Andalucía • Athens • Austria • Baltic States phrasebook • Barcelona • Barcelona City Map • Belgium & Luxembourg • Berlin • Berlin City Map • Britain • British phrasebook • Brussels, Bruges & Antwerp • Brussels City Map • Budapest • Budapest City Map • Canary Islands • Catalunya & the Costa Brava • Central Europe • Central Europe phrasebook • Copenhagen • Corfu & the Ionians • Corsica • Crete • Crete Condensed • Croatia • Cycling Britain • Cycling France • Cyprus • Czech & Slovak Republics • Czech phrasebook • Denmark • Dublin • Dublin City Map • Dublin Condensed • Eastern Europe • Eastern Europe phrasebook • Edinburgh • Edinburgh City Map • England • Estonia, Latvia & Lithuania • Europe on a shoestring • Europe phrasebook • Finland • Florence • Florence City Map • France • Frankfurt City Map • Frankfurt Condensed • French phrasebook • Georgia, Armenia & Azerbaijan • Germany • German phrasebook • Greece • Greek Islands • Greek phrasebook • Hungary • Iceland, Greenland & the Faroe Islands • Ireland • Italian phrasebook • Italy • Kraków • Lisbon • The Loire • London • London City Map • London Condensed • Madrid • Madrid City Map • Malta • Mediterranean Europe • Milan, Turin & Genoa • Moscow • Munich • Netherlands • Normandy • Norway • Out to Eat – London • Out to Eat – Paris • Paris • Paris City Map • Paris Condensed • Poland • Polish phrasebook • Portugal • Portuguese phrasebook • Prague • Prague City Map • Provence & the Côte d'Azur • Read This First: Europe • Rhodes & the Dodecanese • Romania & Moldova • Rome • Rome City Map • Rome Condensed • Russia, Ukraine & Belarus • Russian phrasebook • Scandinavian & Baltic Europe • Scandinavian phrasebook • Scotland • Sicily • Slovenia • South-West France • Spain • Spanish phrasebook • Stockholm • St Petersburg • St Petersburg City Map • Sweden • Switzerland • Tuscany • Ukrainian phrasebook • Venice • Vienna • Wales • Walking in Britain • Walking in France • Walking in Ireland • Walking in Italy • Walking in Scotland • Walking in Spain • Walking in Switzerland • Western Europe • World Food France • World Food Greece • World Food Ireland • World Food Italy • World Food Spain **Travel Literature:** After Yugoslavia • Love and War in the Apennines • The Olive Grove: Travels in Greece • On the Shores of the Mediterranean • Round Ireland in Low Gear • A Small Place in Italy

Lonely Planet Mail Order

onely Planet products are distributed worldwide. They are also available by mail order from Lonely Planet, so if you have difficulty finding a title, please write to us. North and South American residents should write to 150 Linden St, Oakland, CA 94607, USA; European and African residents should write to 10a Spring Place, London NW5 3BH, UK; and residents of other countries to Locked Bag 1, Footscray, Victoria 3011, Australia.

INDIAN SUBCONTINENT & THE INDIAN OCEAN Bangladesh • Bengali phrasebook • Bhutan • Delhi • Goa • Healthy Travel Asia & India • Hindi & Urdu phrasebook • India • India & Bangladesh City Map • Indian Himalaya • Karakoram Highway • Kathmandu City Map • Kerala • Madagascar • Maldives • Mauritius, Réunion & Seychelles • Mumbai (Bombay) • Nepal • Nepali phrasebook • North India • Pakistan • Rajasthan • Read This First: Asia & India • South India • Sri Lanka • Sri Lanka phrasebook • Tibet • Tibetan phrasebook • Trekking in the Indian Himalaya • Trekking in the Karakoram & Hindukush • Trekking in the Nepal Himalaya • World Food India **Travel Literature:** The Age of Kali: Indian Travels and Encounters • Hello Goodnight: A Life of Goa • In Rajasthan • Maverick in Madagascar • A Season in Heaven: True Tales from the Road to Kathmandu • Shopping for Buddhas • A Short Walk in the Hindu Kush • Slowly Down the Ganges

MIDDLE EAST & CENTRAL ASIA Bahrain, Kuwait & Qatar • Central Asia • Central Asia phrasebook • Dubai • Farsi (Persian) phrasebook • Hebrew phrasebook • Iran • Israel & the Palestinian Territories • Istanbul • Istanbul City Map • Istanbul to Cairo • Istanbul to Kathmandu • Jerusalem • Jerusalem City Map • Jordan • Lebanon • Middle East • Oman & the United Arab Emirates • Syria • Turkey • Turkish phrasebook • World Food Turkey • Yemen **Travel Literature**: Black on Black: Iran Revisited • Breaking Ranks: Turbulent Travels in the Promised Land • The Gates of Damascus • Kingdom of the Film Stars: Journey into Jordan

NORTH AMERICA Alaska • Boston • Boston City Map • Boston Condensed • British Columbia • California & Nevada • California Condensed • Canada • Chicago • Chicago City Map • Chicago Condensed • Florida • Georgia & the Carolinas • Great Lakes • Hawaii • Hiking in Alaska • Hiking in the USA • Honolulu & Oahu City Map • Las Vegas • Los Angeles • Los Angeles City Map • Louisiana & the Deep South • Miami • Miami City Map • Montréal • New England • New Orleans • New Orleans City Map • New York City • New York City City Map • New York City Condensed • New York, New Jersey & Pennsylvania • Oahu • Out to Eat – San Francisco • Pacific Northwest • Rocky Mountains • San Diego & Tijuana • San Francisco • San Francisco City Map • Seattle • Seattle City Map • Southwest • Texas • Toronto • USA • USA phrasebook • Vancouver • Vancouver City Map • Virginia & the Capital Region • Washington, DC • Washington, DC City Map • World Food New Orleans **Travel Literature**: Caught Inside: A Surfer's Year on the California Coast • Drive Thru America

NORTH-EAST ASIA Beijing • Beijing City Map • Cantonese phrasebook • China • Hiking in Japan • Hong Kong & Macau • Hong Kong City Map • Hong Kong Condensed • Japan • Japanese phrasebook • Korea • Korean phrasebook • Kyoto • Mandarin phrasebook • Mongolia • Mongolian phrasebook • Seoul • Shanghai • South-West China • Taiwan • Tokyo • World Food Hong Kong • World Food Japan **Travel Literature**: In Xanadu: A Quest • Lost Japan

SOUTH AMERICA Argentina, Uruguay & Paraguay • Bolivia • Brazil • Brazilian phrasebook • Buenos Aires • Buenos Aires City Map • Chile & Easter Island • Colombia • Ecuador & the Galápagos Islands • Healthy Travel Central & South America • Latin American Spanish phrasebook • Peru • Quechua phrasebook • Read This First: Central & South America • Rio de Janeiro • Rio de Janeiro City Map • Santiago de Chile • South America on a shoestring • Trekking in the Patagonian Andes • Venezuela **Travel Literature**: Full Circle: A South American Journey

SOUTH-EAST ASIA Bali & Lombok • Bangkok • Bangkok City Map • Burmese phrasebook • Cambodia • Cycling Vietnam, Laos & Cambodia • East Timor phrasebook • Hanoi • Healthy Travel Asia & India • Hill Tribes phrasebook • Ho Chi Minh City (Saigon) • Indonesia • Indonesian phrasebook • Indonesia's Eastern Islands • Java • Lao phrasebook • Laos • Malay phrasebook • Malaysia, Singapore & Brunei • Myanmar (Burma) • Philippines • Pilipino (Tagalog) phrasebook • Read This First: Asia & India • Singapore • Singapore City Map • South-East Asia on a shoestring • South-East Asia phrasebook • Thailand • Thailand's Islands & Beaches • Thailand, Vietnam, Laos & Cambodia Road Atlas • Thai phrasebook • Vietnam • Vietnamese phrasebook • World Food Indonesia • World Food Thailand • World Food Vietnam

ALSO AVAILABLE: Antarctica • The Arctic • The Blue Man: Tales of Travel, Love and Coffee • Brief Encounters: Stories of Love, Sex & Travel • Buddhist Stupas in Asia: The Shape of Perfection • Chasing Rickshaws • The Last Grain Race • Lonely Planet…On the Edge: Adventurous Escapades from Around the World • Lonely Planet Unpacked • Lonely Planet Unpacked Again • Not the Only Planet: Science Fiction Travel Stories • Ports of Call: A Journey by Sea • Sacred India • Travel Photography: A Guide to Taking Better Pictures • Travel with Children • Tuvalu: Portrait of an Island Nation

Index

Bold indicates maps.

Places to Stay

Places to Eat

Boxed Text

MAP LEGEND

ROUTES

City   Regional

.........Freeway	.........Pedestrian Mall
.........Tollway	.........Steps
.........Primary Road	.........Tunnel
.........Secondary Road	.........Trail
.........Tertiary Road	.........Walking Tour
.........Dirt Road	.........Path

TRANSPORTATION

.........Train	.........Bus Route
.........Metro	.........Ferry

HYDROGRAPHY

.........River; Creek	.........Spring; Rapids
.........Canal	.........Waterfalls
.........Lake	.........Dry; Salt Lake

ROUTE SHIELDS

(80) Interstate Freeway   (101) US Highway   (95) State Highway   (G4) County Road

BOUNDARIES

.........International	.........County
.........State	.........Disputed

AREAS

.........Beach	.........Cemetery	.........Golf Course ... .Reservation
.........Building	.........Forest	.........Park ... .Sports Field
.........Campus	.........Garden; Zoo	.........Plaza ... .Swamp; Mangrove

POPULATION SYMBOLS

✪ NATIONAL CAPITAL ...National Capital	● **Large City** ....Large City	● Small City ....Small City
◉ STATE CAPITAL ....State Capital	● **Medium City** ....Medium City	● Town; Village ....Town; Village

MAP SYMBOLS

■ ....Place to Stay   ▼ ....Place to Eat   ● ....Point of Interest

.........Airfield	.........Church	.........Museum	.........Snorkel Site
.........Airport	.........Cinema	.........Observatory	.........Stately Home
.........Archeological Site; Ruin	.........Dive Site	.........Park	.........Surfing
.........Bank	.........Dolphin Watching	.........Parking Area	.........Synagogue
.........Baseball Diamond	.........Footbridge	.........Pass	.........Tao Temple
.........Battlefield	.........Gas Station	.........Picnic Area	.........Taxi
.........Bike Trail	.........Hospital	.........Police Station	.........Telephone
.........Border Crossing	.........Information	.........Pool	.........Theater
.........Buddhist Temple	.........Internet Access	.........Post Office	.........Toilet - Public
.........Bus Station; Terminal	.........Lighthouse	.........Pub; Bar	.........Trailhead
.........Cable Car; Chairlift	.........Lookout	.........RV Park	.........Tram Stop
.........Campground	.........Mile Marker	.........Shelter	.........Transportation
.........Cathedral	.........Mission	.........Shopping Mall	.........Volcano
.........Cave	.........Monument	.........Skiing - Cross Country	.........Whale Watching
.........Chalet	.........Mountain	.........Skiing - Downhill	.........Winery

LONELY PLANET OFFICES

Australia
Locked Bag 1, Footscray, Victoria 3011
☎ 03 8379 8000 fax 03 8379 8111
email talk2us@lonelyplanet.com.au

USA
150 Linden Street, Oakland, CA 94607
☎ 510 893 8555, TOLL FREE 800 275 8555
fax 510 893 8572
email info@lonelyplanet.com

UK
10a Spring Place, London NW5 3BH
☎ 020 7428 4800 fax 020 7428 4828
email go@lonelyplanet.co.uk

France
1 rue du Dahomey, 75011 Paris
☎ 01 55 25 33 00 fax 01 55 25 33 01
email bip@lonelyplanet.fr
www.lonelyplanet.fr

World Wide Web: www.lonelyplanet.com *or* AOL keyword: lp
Lonely Planet Images: lpi@lonelyplanet.com.au